FIND IT FAST . . . FIND IT EASILY

If you write, dictate, type, or check the writing of others, this compact, handy guide is simpler and much faster to use than a regular dictionary. Pocket-size to carry with you or to fit in a top desk drawer, this spelling guide saves you valuable time when you need quick answers.

Plus all the outstanding features that make the INSTANT SPELLING DICTIONARY better than the rest:

- CROSS REFERENCING OF HOMONYMS AND EASILY CONFUSED WORDS
- ALTERNATIVE SPELLINGS LISTED
- CLEAR DIVISION OF SYLLABLES
- FAMOUS NAMES, PROPER NOUNS, TECHNICAL WORDS
- COMPREHENSIVE RULES FOR SPELLING, WORD DIVISION, PUNCTUATION, CAPITALIZATION, AND MORE

QUANTITY SALES

Most Dell books are available at special quantity discounts when purchased in bulk by corporations, organizations, and special-interest groups. Custom imprinting or excerpting can also be done to fit special needs. For details write: Dell Publishing, 666 Fifth Avenue, New York, NY 10103. Attn.: Special Sales Department.

INDIVIDUAL SALES

Are there any Dell books you want but cannot find in your local stores? If so, you can order them directly from us. You can get any Dell book in print. Simply include the book's title, author, and ISBN number if you have it, along with a check or money order (no cash can be accepted) for the full retail price plus $2.00 to cover shipping and handling. Mail to: Dell Readers Service, P.O. Box 5057, Des Plaines, IL 60017.

Instant Spelling Dictionary

NEW THIRD EDITION

Prepared by

Margaret M. Dougherty

Julia H. Fitzgerald

Donald O. Bolander, B.S., M.A.

Director of Education, Career Institute

25,000 WORDS
SPELLED—DIVIDED—ACCENTED
INCLUDING COMPLETE RULES FOR SPELLING, WORD DIVISION, PUNCTUATION, CAPITALIZATION, ABBREVIATING, WORD COMPOUNDING, FORMS OF ADDRESS, AND PROOFREADER'S MARKS

A LAUREL BOOK
Published by
Dell Publishing
a division of
Bantam Doubleday Dell Publishing Group, Inc.
666 Fifth Avenue
New York, New York 10103

ISBN: 0-440-20533-6

Reprinted by arrangement with Career Publishing, Inc.

Printed in the United States of America

Published simultaneously in Canada

August 1990

10 9 8 7 6 5 4 3 2 1

RAD

PURPOSE OF THIS BOOK

The main purpose of the *Instant Spelling Dictionary* is to provide a quick, easy way to determine the *correct spelling,* the *correct division,* and the *correct accent* of 25,000 English words. The use of this spelling dictionary will reduce, by at least two-thirds, the time normally taken to find a word in a regular dictionary. Both for the individual and a business office, this book can bring great savings in time and money.

All persons who write, dictate, transcribe, or check the writing of others will find daily use for this book. In particular, students, authors, proofreaders, typists, and secretaries will find that this dictionary is an accurate, rapid guide that will both ease and speed up their work. In offices, instead of having one or two regular dictionaries available for several people, separate copies of the *Instant Spelling Dictionary* can be furnished to all stenographers, typists, writers, and executives at low cost.

In addition to the 25,000-word list, the dictionary contains special sections (with rules) on: (1) Spelling, (2) Word Division, (3) Punctuation, (4) Capitalization, (5) Abbreviation, (6) Compounding of Words, (7) Forms of Address, and (8) Proofreader's Marks.

SPECIAL FEATURES

25,000 Most Useful English Words
The 25,000 words included in this dictionary are the most important and useful words in the English language. Many short words of one or two syllables have been omitted except where they may contain a difficulty or can be confused with other words. A large number of technical words are included.

Word Division and Accents
The syllables into which a word may be divided are shown by an accent mark or a centered period. The main accented syllable is shown by use of a heavy accent mark (a·bil′i·ties). If a word contains two accents, the syllable that is given less emphasis is indicated by a light accent mark (ab′o·li′tion).

Homonyms and Other Words Often Confused
The definition of homonyms and other words that are often confused because of spelling or pronunciation is given in small type below the word. Each such word is cross-referenced to avoid use of the wrong word.

Usage Rules
Comprehensive rules for correct spelling, word division, punctuation, capitalization, abbreviating, word compounding, and forms of address are included in the special sections at the back of this book.

CONTENTS

A

aard′vark′
Aar′on
ab′a·cus
ab′a·lo′ne
a·ban′don
a·ban′don·ment
a·based′
a·base′ment
a·bash′ment
a·bas′ing
a·bate′ment
a·bat′ing
ab′at·toir
ab′ba·cy
ab′be
ab′bess
ab′bey
ab′bot
ab·bre′vi·ate
ab·bre′vi·at·ed
ab·bre′vi·a′tion
ab′di·cate
ab′di·ca′tion
ab′do·men
ab·dom′i·nal
ab·duct′
ab·duc′tion
ab·duc′tor
ab·er′rance
ab·er′rant
ab′er·ra′tion
a·bet′ted
a·bey′ance
a·bey′ant
ab·hor′
ab·horred′
ab·hor′rence
ab·hor′rent
ab·hor′ring
a·bide′
a·bid′ing
a·bil′i·ty
ab′ject
ab·jec′tion
ab·ject′ly
ab·jure′
ab·jur′ing
ab′la·tive
a·blaze′
a′ble-bod′ied
a·bloom′
ab·lu′tion
a′bly
ab′ne·gate
ab′ne·ga′tion
ab·nor′mal
ab′nor·mal′i·ty
ab·nor′mal·ly
a·board′
a·bode′
a·bol′ish
ab′o·li′tion
ab′o·li′tion·ist
A′-bomb′
a·bom′i·na·ble
a·bom′i·na·bly
a·bom′i·nat·ed
a·bom′i·na′tion
ab′o·rig′i·nal
ab′o·rig′i·nes
a·bort′
a·bor′tion·ist
a·bor′tive
a·bound′ing
a·bout′-face′
a·bove′board′
ab′ra·ca·dab′ra
a·brade′
a·brad′ed
A′bra·ham
a·bra′sion
a·bra′sive
a·breast′
a·bridge′
a·bridg′ing
a·bridg′ment
a·broad′
ab′ro·gate
ab′ro·gat′ed
ab′ro·gat′ing
ab′ro·ga′tion
ab′ro·ga′tor
a·brupt′
a·brupt′ly
ab′scess
ab′scessed
ab·scond′ed
ab′sence
ab′sent, *adj.*
ab′sen·tee′
ab′sen·tee′ism
ab′sent-mind′ed
ab′sinthe
ab′so·lute′ly
ab′so·lu′tion

ab′so·lut·ism′
ab′so·lut·is′tic
ab·solve′
ab·solved′
ab·sol′vent
ab′sorb′a·bil′i·ty
ab·sorbed′
ab·sorb′ed·ly
ab·sorb′ent
ab·sorb′ing
ab·sorp′tion
ab·sorp′tive
ab·stained′
ab·stain′er
ab·ste′mi·ous
ab·sten′tion
ab·sten′tious
ab′sti·nence
ab′sti·nent
ab′stract, *adj.* and *n.*
ab·stract′, *v.*
ab·stract′ed
ab·strac′tion
ab′stract·ly
ab·struse′
ab·struse′ly
ab·surd′i·ty
ab·surd′ly
a·bun′dance
a·bun′dant
a·bused′
a·bus′ing
a·bu′sive·ness
a·but′ment
a·but′ted
a·but′ting
a·bysm′
a·bys′mal
a·byss′
Ab′ys·sin′i·a
a·ca′cia
ac′a·dem′ic
ac′a·dem′i·cal·ly
a·cad′e·mi′cian
a·cad′e·my
A·ca′di·a
a·can′thus
a′ cap·pel′la
ac·cede′
consent (*see:* exceed)

ac·ced′ence
ac·cel′er·ate
ac·cel′er·a′tion
ac·cel′er·a′tor
ac′cent
ac·cen′tu·ate
ac·cen′tu·a′tion
ac·cept′
to receive (*see:* except)

ac·cept′a·bil′i·ty
ac·cept′a·ble
ac·cept′ance
ac′cep·ta′tion
ac′cess
right to use (*see:* excess)

ac·ces′sa·ry
law (*see:* accessory)

ac·ces′si·bil′i·ty
ac·ces′si·ble
ac·ces′sion
ac·ces′so·ry
extra thing (*see:* accessary)

ac′ci·dence
ac′ci·dent
ac′ci·den′tal·ly
ac·claim′ing
ac′cla·ma′tion
ac·cli′mate
ac·cli·ma′tion
ac·cli′ma·ti·za′tion
ac·cli′ma·tize
ac·cliv′i·ty
ac′co·lade′
ac·com′mo·date
ac·com′mo·dat′ing
ac·com′mo·da′tion
ac·com′mo·da′tive
ac·com′pa·nied
ac·com′pa·ni·ment
ac·com′pa·nist
ac·com′pa·ny·ing
ac·com′plice
ac·com′plish
ac·com′plish·ment
ac·cord′a·ble
ac·cord′ance
ac·cord′ed
ac·cord′ing·ly
ac·cor′di·on
ac·cor′di·on·ist
ac·cost′ed
ac·couche′ment

ac·count'a·bil'i·ty
ac·count'a·ble
ac·count'an·cy
ac·count'ant
ac·count'ing
ac·cou'ter·ment
ac·cred'it
ac·cre'tion
ac·cru'al
ac·crue'
ac·crue'ment
ac·cu'mu·late
ac·cu'mu·lat'ing
ac·cu'mu·la'tion
ac'cu·ra·cy
ac'cu·rate·ly
ac·curs'ed
ac'cu·sa'tion
ac·cu'sa·tive
ac·cu'sa·to'ry
ac·cuse'
ac·cused'
ac·cus'ing·ly
ac·cus'tom
ac·cus'tomed
a·cer'bi·ty
ac'e·tate
a·ce'tic
ac'e·tone
a·cet'y·lene
ac'e·tyl·sal'i·cyl'ic
ached
a·chiev'a·ble
a·chieve'
a·chieved'
a·chieve'ment
a·chiev'ing
A·chil'les
ach'ing·ly
ach'ro·mat'ic
a·cid'ic
a·cid'i·fi·ca'tion
a·cid'i·fy
a·cid'i·ty
ac'i·do'sis
a·cid'u·late
a·cid'u·la'tion
ac·knowl'edge
ac·knowl'edg·ing
ac·knowl'edg·ment
ac'o·lyte
ac'o·nite
a·cous'tic
a·cous'ti·cal·ly
a·cous'tics
ac·quaint'ance
ac'qui·esce'
ac'qui·es'cence
ac'qui·es'cent
ac'qui·esc'ing
ac·quire'ment
ac·quir'er
ac'qui·si'tion
ac·quis'i·tive
ac·quit'
ac·quit'tal
ac·quit'tance
ac·quit'ted
a'cre·age
ac'rid
a·crid'i·ty
ac'rid·ly
ac'ri·mo'ni·ous
ac'ri·mo'ny
ac'ro·bat
ac'ro·bat'ics
ac'ro·nym
a·cross'
act'ing
ac·tin'ic
ac·tin'i·um
ac'tion·a·ble
ac'ti·vate
ac'ti·va'tion
ac'tive·ly
ac·tiv'i·ty
ac'tor
ac'tress
ac'tu·al
ac'tu·al'i·ty
ac'tu·al·ly
ac'tu·ar'i·al
ac'tu·ar'y
ac'tu·ate
ac'tu·a'tion
ac'tu·a'tor
a·cu'i·ty
a·cu'men
a·cute'ly
ad'age
a·da'gio
ad'a·mant
ad'a·man'tine
a·dapt'
adjust *(see:* adept, adopt)
a·dapt'a·bil'i·ty
a·dapt'a·ble
ad'ap·ta'tion
a·dap'tive

ad·den′dum
(*plural:* -da)

ad′der
ad′dict, *n.*
ad·dict′, *v.*
ad·dict′ed
ad·dic′tion
ad·di′tion·al
ad′di·tive
ad′dled
ad·dress′
ad·dress·ee′
ad·dress′ing
ad·duce′
ad·duce′a·ble
ad·duc′ing
ad·duct′
ad·duc′tion
ad′e·noid
ad′e·noi′dal
a·dept′
skillful (*see:* adapt; adopt)

a·dept′ness
ad′e·qua·cy
ad′e·quate
ad′e·quate·ly
ad·here′
ad·her′ence
ad·her′ent
ad·her′ing
ad·he′sion
ad·he′sive
a·dieu′
ad in′fi·ni′tum
ad′i·pose
Ad′i·ron′dacks
ad·ja′cen·cy
ad·ja′cent
ad′jec·tive
ad·joined′
ad·join′ing
ad·journed′
ad·journ′ment
ad·judge′
ad·judg′ing
ad·ju′di·cate
ad·ju′di·ca′tion
ad·ju′di·ca′tive
ad·ju′di·ca′tor
ad′junct
ad·junc′tive
ad·jure′
ad′ju·ra′tion
ad·just′
ad·just′a·ble
ad·just′er
ad·just′ment
ad′ju·tant
ad·lib′
ad·min′is·ter
ad·min′is·trate
ad·min′is·tra′tion
ad·min′is·tra′tive
ad·min′is·tra′tor
ad′mi·ra·ble
ad′mi·ral
ad′mi·ral·ty
ad′mi·ra′tion
ad·mired′
ad·mir′er
ad·mir′ing
ad·mis′si·bil′i·ty
ad·mis′si·ble
ad·mis′sion
ad·mis′sive
ad·mit′tance
ad·mit′ted
ad·mix′ture
ad·mon′ish
ad·mon′ish·ment
ad′mo·ni′tion
ad·mon′i·to′ry
a·do′be
ad′o·les′cence
ad′o·les′cent
a·dopt′
take for one's own (*see:* adapt; adept)

a·dop′tion
a·dop′tive
a·dor′a·ble
ad′o·ra′tion
a·dored′
a·dor′ing
a·dorned′
a·dorn′ing
a·dorn′ment
ad·re′nal
ad·ren′a·lin
a·drift′
a·droit′
a·droit′ly
ad·sorb′
ad·sorb′ent
ad·sorp′tion
ad′u·late
ad′u·la′tion
ad′u·la·to′ry

a·dul′ter·ant
a·dul′ter·ate
a·dul′ter·a′tion
a·dul′ter·a′tor
a·dul′ter·er
a·dul′ter·ess
a·dul′ter·ous
a·dul′ter·y
a·dult′hood
ad·um′brate
ad va·lo′rem
ad·vance′
ad·vanced′
ad·vance′ment
ad·vanc′ing
ad·van′tage
ad′van·ta′geous
ad′vent
ad′ven·ti′tious
ad·ven′tive
ad·ven′ture
ad·ven′tur·er
ad·ven′ture·some
ad·ven′tur·ous
ad·ver′bi·al
ad′ver·sar′y
ad·verse′
ad·ver′si·ty
ad·vert′ent
ad′ver·tise
ad′ver·tise′ment
ad′ver·ti′ser
ad′ver·tis′ing
ad·vice′, *n.*
ad·vis′a·bil′i·ty
ad·vis′a·ble
ad·vise′, *v.*
ad·vised′
ad·vis′ed·ly
ad·vis′er (·or)
ad·vi′so·ry
ad′vo·cate
ad′vo·ca′tor
aer′ate
aer·a′tion
aer′a·tor
aer′i·al
aer′i·al·ist
aer′o·dy·nam′ics
aer′o·naut
aer′o·nau′tics
aer′o·plane
a′er·o·sol′
Ae′sop
aes′thete
aes·thet′ic
af′fa·bil′i·ty
af′fa·ble
af·fair′
af·fect′
to influence *(see: effect)*
af′fec·ta′tion
af·fect′ed
af·fec′tion
af·fec′tion·ate
af·fec′tive
af·fi′ance
af′fi·da′vit
af·fil′i·ate
af·fil′i·a′tion
af·fin′i·ty
af·firm′
af′fir·ma′tion
af·firm′a·tive
af·firm′a·to·ry
af·fix′
af·flict′
af·flic′tion
af′flu·ence
af′flu·ent
wealthy *(see: effluent)*
af·ford′
af·fray′
af·front′
af′ghan
Af·ghan′i·stan
a·flame′
a·float′
a·flut′ter
a·fore′said
a·fore′thought′
a·fraid′
a·fresh′
Af′ri·ca
Af′ri·can
af′ter·birth′
af′ter·ef·fect′
af′ter·glow′
af′ter·math
af′ter·noon′
af′ter·thought′
af′ter·ward
a·gainst′
a·gape′
ag′ate
a′ged
age′less

a′gen·cy
a·gen′da
(*singular:* -dum)

ag·glu′ti·nate
ag·glu′ti·na′tion
ag·gran′dize·ment
ag′gra·vate
ag′gra·vat′ing
ag′gra·va′tion
ag′gra·va′tor
ag′gre·gate
ag′gre·gate·ly
ag′gre·ga′tion
ag′gre·ga′tive
ag·gres′sion
ag·gres′sive
ag·gres′sor
ag·grieve′
ag·grieved′
a·ghast′
ag′ile·ly
a·gil′i·ty
ag′ing
ag′i·tate
ag′i·tat·ed
ag′i·ta′tion
ag′i·ta′tor
ag·nos′tic
ag·nos′ti·cal·ly
ag·nos′ti·cism
ag′o·nize
ag′o·niz′ing
ag′o·ny
ag′o·ra·pho′bi·a
a·grar′i·an
a·gree′a·bil′i·ty
a·gree′a·ble
a·greed′
a·gree′ment
ag′ri·cul′tur·al
ag′ri·cul′ture
ag′ro·nom′ics
a·gron′o·my
a·ground′
a′gue
aid
help

aide
military assistant

aide′-de-camp
ai′ler·on
ail′ment
aim′less
air base
air′-borne′
air brake
air coach
air′-con·di′tion
air′-cool′
air′craft
Aire′dale
air field
air force
air′i·ly
air′i·ness
air lift
air line
air mail
air′mind′ed
air′plane′
air pocket
air′port′
air pressure
air pump
air raid
air rifle
air′ship′
air′sick·ness
air speed
air′strip′
air′tight′
air′way′
air′wor′thy
aisle
passageway (*see:* isle)

Al′a·bam′a
al′a·bas′ter
a′ la carte′
a·lac′ri·ty
a′ la king′
a′ la mode′
a·larm′ing
a·larm′ist
A·las′ka
Al·ba′ni·a
Al′ba·ny
al′ba·tross
al·be′it
al·bi′no
al′bum
al·bu′men
egg white

al·bu′min
class of protein

Al′bu·quer′que
Al′ca·traz

al′che•mist
al′che•my
al′co•hol
al′co•hol′ic
al′co•hol•ism′
al′cove
al′der•man
al′der•man′ic
a•lert′ly
A•leu′tians
al•fal′fa
al′ga
(*plural:* algae)

al′ge•bra
al′ge•bra′ic
al′ge•bra′i•cal•ly
al•go•rith′mic
a′li•as
al′i•bi
al′i•bi•ing
al′ien
al′ien•a•ble
al′ien•ate
al′ien•a′tion
a•lign′
(same as aline)

a•lign′ment
al′i•ment
al′i•men′ta•ry
al′i•men•ta′tion
al′i•mo′ny
a•line′
(same as align)

al′i•quot
al′ka•li
al′ka•line
al′ka•lin′i•ty
al′ka•lize
al′ka•loid
all′-a•round′
al•lay′
al′le•ga′tion
al•lege′
al•lege′a•ble
al•leg′ed•ly
al•leg′ing
Al′le•ghe′nies
al•le′giance
al′le•gor′ic
al′le•gor′i•cal
al′le•go′rist
al′le•go•rize
al′le•go•ry
al•le′gro
al′le•lu′ia
al•ler′gic
al′ler•gy
al•le′vi•ate
al•le′vi•a′ting
al′ley
backstreet

al•li′ance
al•lied′
al•lies′
friends

al′li•ga′tor
al•lit′er•ate
al•lit′er•a′tion
al•lit′er•a′tive
al′lo•cate
al′lo•ca′tion
al′lo•path′ic
al•lot′ment
al•lot′ted
al•low′a•ble
al•low′ance
al•lowed′
al′loy
all right
all′spice′
al•lude′
refer to (*see:* elude)

al•lure′
al•lure′ment
al•lur′ing
al•lu′sion
indirect reference
(*see:* illusion)

al•lu′sive
al•lu′vi•al
al•lu′vi•um
al•ly′
friend

al′ma ma′ter
al′ma•nac
al•might′y
al′mond
al′most
a•lo′ha
a•loof′ness
a•loud′
al•pac′a
al′pha•bet′i•cal
al′pha•bet•ize
al′pha•nu•mer′ic
al•read′y

al·right′
(incorrect form of *all right*)

al′tar
part of church

al′ter
to make different

al′ter·a·bil′i·ty
al′ter·a·ble
al′ter·a′tion
al′ter·cate
al′ter·ca′tion
al′ter e′go
al′ter·nat·ed
al′ter·nat·ing
al′ter·na′tion
al·ter′na·tive
al·though′
al·tim′e·ter
al′ti·tude
al′to·geth′er
al′tru·ism
al′tru·is′ti·cal·ly
al′um
a·lu′mi·num
a·lum′na
fem. sing. (plural: alumnae)

a·lum′nus
masc. sing. (plural: alumni)

al′ways
a·mal′gam
a·mal′gam·ate
a·mal′gam·a′tion
a·man′u·en′sis
a·mass′ment
am′a·teur
am′a·teur′ish
am′a·to′ry
a·mazed′
a·maze′ment
a·maz′ing
Am′azon
am·bas′sa·dor
am·bas′sa·do′ri·al
am·bas′sa·dress
am′ber
am′ber·gris
am′bi·dex·ter′i·ty
am′bi·dex′trous
am′bi·ent
am′bi·gu′i·ty
am·big′u·ous
am·bi′tion
am·bi′tious
am·biv′a·lent
am′bled
am′bling·ly
am·bro′sia
am·bro′sian
am′bu·lance
am′bu·lant
am′bu·late
am′bu·la′tion
am′bu·la·to′ry
am′bushed
am′bush·er
am′bush·ment
a·me′ba
a·me′bic
a·me′boid
a·mel′io·ra·ble
a·mel′io·rate
a·mel′io·ra′tion
a·mel′io·ra′tive
a·me′na·bil′i·ty
a·me′na·ble
a·mend′ed
a·mend′a·ble
a·mend′ment
a·men′i·ty
A·mer′i·ca
A·mer′i·can
A·mer′i·ca′na
A·mer′i·can·ism′
A·mer′i·can·i·za′tion
A·mer′i·can·ize
am′e·thyst
a′mi·abil′i·ty
a′mi·a·ble
a′mi·a·bly
am′i·ca·bil′i·ty
am′i·ca·ble
am′i·ca·bly
am′ice
a·mid′ships
a·mi′go
a·min′o
Am′ish
am′i·ty
am′me′ter
am·mo′nia
am′mu·ni′tion
am·ne′sia
am′nes·ty
a·moe′ba
(see: ameba)

a·mor′al
a′mo·ral′i·ty
a·mor′al·ly
am′o·rous
a·mor′phism
a·mor′phous
am′or·ti·za′tion
am′or·tize
am′or·tiz·ing
a·mount′
a·mour′
am′per·age
am′pere
am′per·sand
am·phib′i·an
am·phib′i·ous
am′phi·the′a·ter
am′ple
am′pli·fi·ca′tion
am′pli·fied
am′pli·fi′er
am′pli·fy′ing
am′pli·tude
am′ply
am′poule
(or: ampule)
am′pu·tate
am′pu·ta′tion
am′pu·tee′
am′u·let
a·mused′
a·muse′ment
a·mus′ing
Am′vets
a·nab′o·lism
a·nach′ro·nism
a·nach′ro·nis′tic
an′a·con′da
an′a·gram
a′nal
an′al·ge′sic
an′a·log′ic
a·nal′o·gize
a·nal′o·gous
an′a·logue
a·nal′o·gy
(plural: -gies)
a·nal′y·sis
(plural: -ses)
an′a·lyst
an′a·lyt′ic
an′a·lyt′i·cal
an′a·lyze
an′a·lyz·ing
an′a·pest
an·ar′chic
an′ar·chism
an′ar·chist
an′ar·chy
a·nath′e·ma
a·nath′e·ma·tize
an′a·tom′i·cal
a·nat′o·mist
a·nat′o·my
an′ces·tor
an·ces′tral
an′ces·try
an′chor·age
an′cho·rite
an′cho·vy
an′cient·ly
an′cil·lar′y
an′con
an·dan′te
and′i·ron
an′dro·gen
an′ec·dote
a·ne′mi·a
a·ne′mic
an′e·mom′e·ter
a·nem′o·ne
a·nent′
an′er·oid
an′es·the′sia
an′es·thet′ic
an·es′the·tist
an·es′the·tize
an′eu·rysm
an·gel′ic
an·gel′i·cal·ly
An′ge·lus
an·gi′na pec′to·ris
an′gle
an′gle·worm
An′gli·can
An′gli·cism
An′gli·ci·za′tion
An′gli·cize
an′gling
An′glo-A·mer′
i·can
An′glo·phile
An′glo-Sax′on
An·go′ra
an′gri·ly
an′gry
an′guish
an′guished
an′gu·lar

an′gu·lar′i·ty
an·hy′drous
an′ile
an′i·line
a·nil′i·ty
an′i·mad·ver′sion
an′i·mad·vert′
an′i·mal′cu·lar
an′i·mal′cule
an′i·mal·ism
an′i·mal′i·ty
an′i·mate
an′i·mat′ed·ly
an′i·mat′ing
an′i·ma′tion
an′i·mos′i·ty
an′i·mus
an′ise
an′i·seed
an′kle
an′klet
an′nal·ist
an′nal·is′tic
an′nals
An·nap′o·lis
an·neal′
an′ne·lid
an·nex′, *v.*
an′nex, *n.*
an·nex′a·ble
an′nex·a′tion
an·ni′hi·late
an·ni′hi·la′tion
an·ni′hi·la′tor
an′ni·ver′sa·ry
an′no Dom′i·ni
an′no·tate
an′no·ta′tion
an·nounce′
an·nounce′ment
an·nounc′er
an·nounc′ing
an·noy′ance
an·noyed′
an·noy′ing
an′nu·al
an′nu·al·ly
an·nu′i·tant
an·nu′i·ty
an·nul′
an′nu·lar
an′nu·let
an·nulled′
an·nul′ling
an·nul′ment
an′num
an·nun′ci·ate
an·nun′ci·a′tion
an·nun′ci·a′tor
an′ode
an′o·dyne
a·noint′
a·noint′ment
a·nom′a·lism
a·nom′a·lous
a·nom′a·ly
an′o·nym′i·ty
a·non′y·mous
a·non′y·mous·ly
a·noph′e·les
an·oth′er
an′swer
an′swer·a·ble
ant·ac′id
an·tag′o·nism
an·tag′o·nist
an·tag′o·nis′tic
an·tag′o·nize
ant·arc′tic
Ant·arc′ti·ca
an′te
stake (*see:* anti)

ant′eat′er
an′te bel′lum
an′te·ced′ence
an′te·ced′ent
an′te·date
an′te·di·lu′vi·an
an′te·lope
an′te me·rid′i·em
an·ten′na
an′te·pe′nult
an·te′ri·or
an′te·room
an′them
an′ther
an′tho·log′i·cal
an·thol′o·gist
an·thol′o·gy
an′thra·cite
an′thrax
(*plural:* -thraces)

an′thro·poid
an′thro·po·log′
i·cal
an′thro·pol′o·gist
an′thro·pol′o·gy
an′thro·po·mor′
phic

an′ti
against *(see:* ante)

an′ti·bi·ot′ic
an′ti·bod′y
an′tic
An′ti·christ′
an·tic′i·pate
an·tic′i·pat·ing
an·tic′i·pa′tion
an·tic′i·pa′tive
an·tic′i·pa·to′ry
an′ti·cler′i·cal
an′ti·cli′max
an′ti·dote
an′ti·freeze′
an′ti·gen
an′ti·his′ta·mine
an′ti·ma·cas′sar
an′ti·mo′ny
an′ti·pas′to
an·tip′a·thet′ic
an·tip′a·thy
an′ti·phon
an·tiph′o·nal
an·tip′o·dal
an′ti·pode
an·tip′o·des
an′ti·quar′i·an
an′ti·quar′y
an′ti·quate
an′ti·quat′ed
an′ti·quat·ing
an·tique′
an·tiq′ui·ty
an′ti-Sem′i·tism
an′ti·sep′sis
an′ti·sep′tic
an′ti·so′cial
an·tith′e·sis
an′ti·thet′ic
an′ti·thet′i·cal·ly
an′ti·tox′ic
an′ti·tox′in
an′ti·trust′
ant′ler
an′to·nym
a′nus
an′vil
anx·i′e·ty
anx′ious·ly
an′y·bod′y
an′y·how
an′y·one
an′y·place
an′y·thing
an′y·way
an′y·where
a·or′ta
a·or′tic
a·pace′
A·pach′e
a·part′
a·part′heid
a·part′ment
ap′a·thet′ic
ap′a·thet′i·cal·ly
ap′a·thy
a·pe′ri·ent
a·pe′ri·tif′
ap′er·ture
a′pex
a·pha′sia
a·pha′si·ac
a·pha′sic
a·phe′li·on
a′phid
aph′o·rism
aph′o·ris′tic
aph′ro·dis′i·ac
Aph′ro·di′te
a′pi·a·rist
a′pi·ar′y
ap′i·cal
a′pi·cul′tur·al
a′pi·cul′ture
a·piece′
ap′ish
ap′ish·ly
a·plen′ty
a·plomb′
a·poc′a·lypse
a·poc′a·lyp′tic
A·poc′ry·pha
a·poc′ry·phal
ap′o·ge′al
ap′o·ge′an
ap′o·gee
A·pol′lo
a·pol′o·get′ic
a·pol′o·get′ics
a·pol′o·gize
a·pol′o·giz′ing
ap′o·logue
a·pol′o·gy
ap′o·plec′tic
ap′o·plex′y
a·pos′ta·sy
a·pos′tate
a·pos′ta·tize
a pos·te′ri·o′ri

a·pos′tle
a·pos′tle·ship
ap′os·tol′ic
ap′os·tol′i·cism
a·pos′tro·phe
ap·os·troph′ic
a·pos′tro·phize
a·poth′e·car′y
ap′o·thegm
ap′o·theg·mat′ic
a·poth′e·o′sis
a·poth′e·o·size
Ap′pa·la′chi·ans
ap·pall′
ap·palled′
ap·pall′ing
ap′pa·nage
ap′pa·ra′tus
ap·par′el
ap·par′ent
ap·par′ent·ly
ap′pa·ri′tion
ap·pealed′
ap·peal′a·ble
ap·peal′er
ap·peal′ing
ap·pear′ance
ap·peared′
ap·peas′a·ble
ap·pease′
ap·pease′ment
ap·peas′er
ap·peas′ing·ly
ap·pel′lant
ap·pel′late
ap′pel·la′tion
ap·pel′la·tive

ap·pend′age
ap·pend′aged
ap·pend′ant
ap′pen·dec′to·my
ap·pend′ed
ap·pen′di·ci′tis
ap·pen′dix
ap′per·cep′tion
ap′per·cep′tive
ap′per·tain′
ap′pe·tite
ap′pe·tiz′er
ap′pe·tiz′ing
ap·plaud′
ap·plaud′er
ap·plause′
ap′ple·sauce′
ap·pli′ance
ap′pli·ca·bil′i·ty
ap′pli·ca·ble
ap′pli·cant
ap′pli·ca′tion
ap′pli·ca′tive
ap′pli·ca·to′ry
ap′pli·que′
ap·ply′
ap·point′a·ble
ap·point·ee′
ap·point′er
ap·poin′tive
ap·point′ment
Ap′po·mat′tox
ap·por′tion
ap·por′tion·er
ap·por′tion·ment
ap·pos′a·ble
ap·pose′

ap′po·site
appropriate *(see:* opposite)

ap′po·si′tion
ap·pos′i·tive
ap·prais′a·ble
ap·prais′al
ap·praise′
ap·praise′ment
ap·prais′er
ap·prais′ing·ly
ap·pre′ci·a·ble
ap·pre′ci·ate
ap·pre′ci·a·to′ry
ap·pre′ci·a′tion
ap·pre′ci·a′tive
ap·pre′ci·a′tive·ly
ap′pre·hend′
ap′pre·hen′si·bil′i·ty
ap′pre·hen′si·ble
ap′pre·hen′sion
ap′pre·hen′sive
ap·pren′tice
ap·pren′ticed
ap·pren′tice·ship
ap·prise′
ap·pris′ing
ap·proach′
ap·proach′a·bil′i·ty
ap·proach′a·ble
ap′pro·ba′tion
ap·pro′pri·ate
ap·pro′pri·ate·ly
ap·pro′pri·at·ing

ap·pro′pri·a′tion
ap·pro′pri·a′tive
ap·prov′a·ble
ap·prov′al
ap·proved′
ap·prov′ing·ly
ap·prox′i·mate·ly
ap·prox′i·mat·ing
ap·prox′i·ma′tion
ap·pur′te·nance
ap·pur′te·nant
a′pri·cot
A′pril
a pri·o′ri
a′pron
ap′ro·pos′
apse
ap′ti·tude
apt′ly
aq′ua·lung′
aq′ua·ma·rine′
aq′ua·plane′
a·quar′i·um
a·quat′ic
a·quat′i·cal·ly
aq′ua·tint′
aq′ue·duct
a′que·ous
aq′ui·line
ar′a·besque′
A·ra′bi·a
Ar′a·bic
ar′a·ble
a·rach′nid
ar′bi·ter
ar′bi·tra·ble
ar·bit′ra·ment
ar′bi·trar′i·ly
ar′bi·trar′y
ar′bi·trate
ar′bi·trat′ing
ar′bi·tra′tion
ar′bi·tra′tive
ar′bi·tra′tor
ar′bor
ar·bo′re·al
ar′bo·res′cent
ar′bo·re′tum
ar′bor vi′tae
ar′bu·tate
ar·bu′tus
ar·cade′
ar′chae·ol′o·gy
(also: archeology)
ar·cha′ic
ar·cha′i·cal·ly
ar′cha·ism
ar′cha·ist
ar′cha·is′tic
arch′an′gel
arch′bish′op
arch′dea′con
arch′di′o·cese
arch′du′cal
arch′duch′ess
arch′duke′
ar′che·o·log′ic
ar′che·ol′o·gist
ar′che·ol′o·gy
(also: archaeology)
arch′er·y
ar′che·type
ar′chi·pel′a·go
ar′chi·tect
ar′chi·tec·ton′ic
ar′chi·tec′tur·al
ar′chi·tec′ture
ar·chi′val
ar′chives
ar′chi·vist
Arc′tic Cir′cle
arch′way
arc′tic
Arc·tu′rus
ar′den·cy
ar′dent·ly
ar′dor
ar′du·ous
ar′du·ous·ly
ar′e·a
ar′e·a·way′
a·re′na
Ar′gen·ti′na
ar′gon
Ar′go·naut
Ar′gonne
ar′go·sy
ar′gu·a·ble
ar′gued
ar′gu·ing
ar′gu·ment
ar′gu·men·ta′tion
ar′gu·men′ta·tive
a′ri·a
a·rid′i·ty
ar′id·ness
Ar′ies
a·ris′en
a·ris′ing
ar′is·toc′ra·cy

a·ris′to·crat
a·ris′to·crat′ic
a·ris′to·crat′i·cal·ly
Ar′is·to·te′lian
Ar′is·tot′le
a·rith′me·tic
ar′ith·met′i·cal
a·rith′me·ti′cian
Ar′i·zo′na
Ar′kan·sas
Ar′ling·ton
ar·ma′da
ar′ma·dil′lo
ar′ma·ment
ar′ma·ture
arm′chair′
Ar·me′ni·a
arm′ful
ar′mi·stice
arm′let
ar′mor
(or: armour)
ar′mored
ar′mor-plat′ed
ar′mor·y
arm′pit′
ar′my
ar′ni·ca
a·ro′ma
ar′o·mat′ic
ar′o·mat′i·cal·ly
a·rose′
a·round′
a·rous′al
a·rouse′
a·rous′ing
ar·peg′gi·o
ar·raign′
ar·raign′er
ar·raign′ment
ar·range′
ar·range′a·ble
ar·range′ment
ar·rang′ing
ar′rant
ar·ray′
ar·ray′al
ar·rayed′
ar·ray′ing
ar·rear′
ar·rear′age
ar·rest′
ar·rest′ing
ar·riv′al
ar·rive′
ar·riv′ing
ar′ro·gance
ar′ro·gant
ar′ro·gate
ar′ro·gat·ing
ar′ro·ga′tion
ar′row·head′
ar′row·root′
ar·roy′o
ar′se·nal
ar′se·nate
ar′se·nic
ar′son
ar·te′ri·al
ar·te′ri·o·scle′ro·sis
ar′ter·y
ar·te′sian
art′ful
art′ful·ly
ar·thrit′ic
ar·thri′tis
ar′thro·pod
ar′ti·choke
ar′ti·cle
ar·tic′u·lar
ar·tic′u·late
ar·tic′u·lat·ed
ar·tic′u·la′tive
ar·tic′u·la′tor
art′i·er
ar′ti·fact
ar′ti·fice
ar′ti·fi′cial
ar′ti·fi′ci·al′i·ty
ar·til′ler·y
ar·til′ler·y·man
ar′ti·san
art′ist
ar·tiste′
ar·tis′tic
ar·tis′ti·cal·ly
art′ist·ry
art′less
art′y
Ar′y·an
as·bes′tos
as·cend′
as·cend′an·cy
as·cend′ant
as·cen′sion
as·cent′
as′cer·tain′
as′cer·tain′a·ble

as'cer·tain'ment
as·cet'ic
as·cet'i·cal·ly
as·cet'i·cism
a·scor'bic
as·crib'a·ble
as·cribe'
as·crip'tion
a·sep'sis
a·sep'tic
a·sep'ti·cal·ly
a·sex'u·al
a·sex'u·al'i·ty
a·shamed'
a·sham'ed·ly
ash'en
ash'y
A'si·at'ic
as'i·nine
as'i·nin'i·ty
a·skance'
a·skew'
a·sleep'
as·par'a·gus
as'pect
as'pen
as·per'i·ty
as·perse'
as·pers'er
as·per'sion
as'phalt
as·phal'tic
as·phyx'i·a
as·phyx'i·ate
as·phyx'i·a'tion
as·phyx'i·at'ing
as·phyx'i·a'tor
as'pic
as·pir'ant
as'pi·rate
as'pi·ra'tion
as'pi·ra'tor
as·pire'
as'pi·rin
as·pir'ing·ly
as·sail
as·sail'ant
as·sail'ment
as·sas'sin
as·sas'si·nate
as·sas'si·na'tion
as·sas'si·na'tor
as·sault'
as·sault'a·ble
as·sault'er
as·say'
as·say'a·ble
as·sayed'
as·say'er
as·say'ing
as·sem'blage
as·sem'ble
as·sem'bling
as·sem'bly
as·sem'bly·man
as·sent'
as·sent'er
as·sent'ing·ly
as·sert'
as·sert'er
as·ser'tion
as·ser'tive
as·sess'
as·sess'a·ble
as·sess'ment
as·ses'sor
as'set
as·sev'er·ate
as·sev'er·a'tion
as'si·du'i·ty
as·sid'u·ous
as·sign'a·bil'i·ty
as·sign'a·ble
as'sig·na'tion
as·sign·ee'
as·sign'ment
as·sign·or'
as·sim'i·la·bil'i·ty
as·sim'i·la·ble
as·sim'i·late
as·sim'i·la'tion
as·sim'i·la'tive
as·sim'i·la'tor
as·sist'ance
as·sist'ant
as·sist'er
as·sist'or, *law*
as·size'
as·so'ci·ate
as·so'ci·at'ing
as·so'ci·a'tion
as·so'ci·a'tive
as'so·nance
as'so·nant
as·sort'ed
as·sort'ment
as·suage'
as·suage'ment
as·suag'ing
as·sum'a·ble
as·sum'a·bly

as·sume′
as·sum′ed·ly
as·sum′er
as·sum′ing
as·sump′tion
as·sur′a·ble
as·sur′ance
as·sure′
as·sur′ed·ly
as·sur′ing
as′ter·isk
as′ter·oid
asth′ma
asth·mat′ic
asth·mat′i·cal·ly
as′tig·mat′ic
as′tig·mat′i·cal·ly
a·stig′ma·tism
a·stir′
as·ton′ished
as·ton′ish·ing
as·ton′ish·ment
as·tound′ed
as·tound′ing
a·strad′dle
as′tra·khan
as′tral
a·stray′
a·stride′
as·trin′gen·cy
as·trin′gent
as·trol′o·ger
as′tro·log′i·cal
as·trol′o·gy
as′tro·naut
as·tron′o·mer
as′tro·nom′ic
as·tron′o·my
as′tro·phys′i·cal
as′tro·phys′ics
as·tute′
as·tute′ly
a·sun′der
a·sy′lum
a′sym·met′ric
a′sym·met′ri·cal·ly
a·sym′me·try
a·syn′chro·nous
at′a·vist
at′a·vis′ti·cal·ly
a·tax′i·a
a·tax′ic
at′el·ier
a′the·ism
a′the·ist
a′the·is′tic
a′the·is′ti·cal·ly
Ath′ens
ath′lete
ath·let′ic
ath·let′i·cal·ly
a·thwart′
a·tin′gle
At·lan′tic
at′las
at′mo·sphere
at′mo·spher′ic
at′mo·spher′i·cal·ly
at′oll
at′om
a·tom′ic
at′om·i·za′tion
at′om·ize
at′om·iz′er
a·ton′al·ism
a·ton′al·is′tic
a′to·nal′i·ty
a·tone′ment
a·ton′ing
a′tri·um
a·tro′cious
a·troc′i·ty
a·troph′ic
at′ro·phied
at′ro·phy
at·tach′a·ble
at′ta·ché′
at·tached′
at·tach′ment
at·tack′
at·tack′er
at·tain′
at·tain′a·bil′i·ty
at·tain′a·ble
at·tain′er
at·tain′ment
at·taint′
at′tar
at·tempt′
at·tempt′er
at·tend′
at·tend′ance
at·tend′ant
at·ten′tion
at·ten′tive
at·ten′u·ate
at·ten′u·a′tion
at·test′
at′tes·ta′tion

at·test′er
at′tic
at·tire′
at·tire′ment
at·tir′ing
at′ti·tude
at′ti·tu′di·nize
at·tor′ney
at·tor′ney at law
at·tor′ney general
at·tract′
at·tract′a·bil′i·ty
at·tract′a·ble
at·trac′tion
at·trac′tive
at·trac′tor
at·trib′ut·a·ble
at·trib′ute, *v.*
at′tri·bute, *n.*
at′tri·bu′tion
at·trib′u·tive
at·tri′tion
at·tune′ment
at·tun′ing
au′burn
auc′tion
auc′tion·eer′
au·da′cious
au·dac′i·ty
au′di·bil′i·ty
au′di·ble
au′di·bly
au′di·ence
au′di·o
au′dit
au·di′tion
au′di·tor
au′di·to′ri·um
au′di·to′ry
Au′du·bon
au′ger
tool *(see:* augur)

aught
zero *(see:* ought)

aug·ment′
aug·ment′a·ble
aug′men·ta′tion
aug·ment′a·tive
au grat′in
au′gur
predict *(see:* auger)

Au′gust
auld lang syne
au′ra
au′ral
au′re·ate
au′re·ole
au′re·o·my′cin
au re·voir′
au′ri·cle
au·ric′u·lar
au·rif′er·ous
au·ro′ra bo′re·a′lis
aus′pice
aus·pi′cious
aus·tere′
aus·tere′ly
aus·ter′i·ty
Aus·tral′ia
Aus′tri·a
au′tar·chy
au·then′tic
au·then′ti·cal·ly
au·then′ti·cate
au·then′ti·ca′tion
au′then·tic′i·ty
au′thor·ess
au·thor′i·tar′i·an
au·thor′i·ta′tive
au·thor′i·ty
au′thor·i·za′tion
au′thor·ize
au′thor·ized
au′thor·iz·ing
au′thor·ship
au′to·bi·og′
ra·pher
au′to·bi′o·graph′ic
au′to·bi·og′ra·phy
au·toc′ra·cy
au·to·crat′ic
au′to·crat′i·cal·ly
au′to·graph
au′to·mat′ic
au′to·mat′i·cal·ly
au′to·ma′tion
au·tom′a·tism
au·tom′a·ton
au′to·mo·bile
au′to·mo′tive
au·to·nom′ic
au·ton′o·mist
au·ton′o·mous
au·ton′o·my
au′top·sy
au′to·sug·ges′tion
au′tumn
au·tum′nal
aux·il′ia·ry

a·vail'a·bil'i·ty
a·vail'a·ble
a·vailed'
av'a·lanche
a·vant-garde'
av'a·rice
av'a·ri'cious
A've Ma·ri'a
a·venged'
a·veng'er
a·veng'ing
av'e·nue
av'er·age
a·verred'
a·ver'ring
a·verse'
a·ver'sion
a·vert'ed
a·vert'i·ble
a'vi·a·rist
a'vi·ar'y
a'vi·a'tion
a'vi·a'tor
a'vi·a'trix
a·vid'i·ty
av'id·ly
av'o·ca'do
av'o·ca'tion
a·void'a·ble
a·void'a·bly
a·void'ance
a·void'ed
av'oir·du·pois'
a·vow'al
a·vowed'
a·vow'ed·ly
a·vun'cu·lar
a·wait'
a·wake'
a·waked'
(*or:* awoke)

a·wak'en
a·wak'en·ing
a·wak'ing
a·ward'ed
a·ware'ness
a·way'
distance
a·weigh'
nautical term

awe'some
awe'-strick'en
aw'ful·ly
awk'ward·ly
awn'ing
a·wry'
ax'i·al
ax'i·al·ly
ax·il'la
ax'il·lar'y
ax'i·om
ax'i·o·mat'ic
ax'is
(*plural:* axes)

a·zal'ea
az'i·muth
A·zores'
Az'tec
az'ure

B

bab'bitt
bab'ble
bab'bler
bab'bling
ba'bied
ba'bies
ba·boon'
ba·bush'ka
ba'by·hood
ba'by·ing
ba'by·ish
Bab'y·lon
Bab'y·lo'ni·an
ba'by-sit'ter
bac'ca·lau're·ate
bac'ca·rat
bac'cha·nal
Bac'cha·na'li·a
bac'chant
bac·chan'te
Bac'chus
bach'e·lor
bach'e·lor·hood'

ba·cil′lus
(*plural:* -cilli)

back′bite′
back′bit′ing
back′bone′
back′door′
back′drop′
back′er
back′field′
back′fire′
back′gam′mon
back′ground′
back′hand′
back′hand′ed
back′ing
back′lash′
back′log′
back′side′
back′slide′
back′slid′ing
back′stage′
back′stop′
back′stroke′
back talk
back′track′
back′ward
back′wa′ter
back′woods′man
ba′con
bac·te′ri·a, *plural*
bac·te′ri·al
bac·te′ri·cid′al
bac·te′ri·cide
bac·te′ri·o·log′i·cal
bac·te′ri·ol′o·gist
bac·te′ri·ol′o·gy
bac·te′ri·o·phage
bac·te′ri·um, *sing.*
badge
badg′er
bad′i·nage′
bad′ly
bad′min·ton
bad′-tem′pered
baf′fle
baf′fle·ment
baf′fler
baf′fling
bag′a·telle′
bag′gage
bagged
bag′gi·ly
bag′ging
bag′gy
bagn′io
bag′pipe′
bag′pip′er
ba·guette′
bailed
set free (*see:* baled)

bail′iff
bail′i·wick
bails′man
bait
attraction (*see:* bate)

baize
Ba′ke·lite
bak′er
bak′er·y
bak′ing
bal′a·lai′ka
bal′ance
bal′anc·ing
bal·brig′gan
bal′co·nies
bal′co·ny
bald′ness
bal′der·dash
bald′pate′
baled
packaged (*see:* bailed)

bale′ful
bal′er
Ba′li
Ba′li·nese′
bal′ing
Bal′kan
balk′i·er
balk′ing
balk′y
bal′lad
bal′last
ball bear′ing
bal′le·ri′na
bal′let
bal·lis′tics
bal′lis·ti′cian
bal·loon′
bal·loon′ist
bal′lot
bal′lot box
ball′play′er
ball′room′
bal′ly·hoo
balm′i·ness
balm′y

bal′sa
bal′sam
Bal′tic
Bal′ti·more
bal′us·trade′
bam·bi′no
bam·boo′
bam·boo′zle
bam·boo′zler
ban
forbid *(see:* banns)

ba′nal
ba·nal′i·ty
ba·nan′a
band′age
band′ag·ing
ban·dan′na
band′box′
ban·deau′
(plural: -eaux)

ban′died
ban′dit
ban′dit·ry
band′mas′ter
ban′do·leer′
bands′man
band′stand
band′wag′on
ban′dy
ban′dy·ing
bane′ful
ban′gle
ban′ish
ban′ish·ment
ban′is·ter
ban′jo
bank account
bank′book′
bank′er
bank′ing
bank note
bank′rupt
bank′rupt·cy
banned
ban′ner
ban′ning
banns
notice of marriage
(see: ban)

ban′quet
ban′shee
ban′tam·weight′
ban′ter
ban′yan
ban′zai′
bap′tism
bap·tis′mal
Bap′tist
bap′tis·ter·y
bap·tize′
bap·tized′
bap·tiz′ing
bar·bar′i·an
bar·bar′i·an·ism
bar·bar′ic
bar·bar′i·cal·ly
bar′ba·rism
bar·bar′i·ty
bar′ba·rize
bar′ba·rous
Bar′ba·ry
bar′be·cue
barbed wire
also: barb wire

bar′ber′ry
bar′ber·shop′
bar′bi·tal
bar·bi′tu·rate
barb′less
bar′ca·role
Bar′ce·lo′na
bare
naked *(see:* bear)

bare′back′
bare′boat
bared
bare′faced
bare′foot′ed
bare′hand′ed
bare′head′ed
bare′ness
bar′er
bare′leg·ged
bare′ly
bar′gain
bar′gain·er
barge
bar′ic
bar′ing
bar′ite
bar′i·tone
bar′i·um
bark′er
bark′ing
bar′ley
bar′maid′
bar′na·cle
barn dance

barn′storm′ing
barn′yard′
bar′o·graph
ba·rom′e·ter
bar′o·met′ric
bar′on
nobleman *(see:* barren)

bar′on·ess
bar′on·et
ba·ro′ni·al
bar′o·ny
ba·roque′
bar′o·scope
bar′o·scop′ic
ba·rouche′
bar′racks
bar′ra·cu′da
bar·rage′
bar′ra·trous
barred
bar′rel
bar′ren
unproductive *(see:* baron)

bar·rette′
bar′ri·cade′
bar′ri·cad′ing
bar′ri·er
bar′ring
bar′ris·ter
bar′room′
bar′row
bar′tender
bar′ter
bas′al
bas′al·ly
bas′al me·tab′o·lism
ba·salt′
bas′cule
base′ly
bas′ing
base′ball′
base′board′
base′born
base hit
base′less
base line
base′ment
bash′ful
bas′ic
bas′i·cal·ly
bas′i·lar
ba·sil′i·ca
bas′i·lisk
ba′sin
ba′sis
(plural: bases)

bask
bas′ket
bas′ket·ball
bas′ket·work′
Basque
bas′-re·lief′
bas′set
bas′si·net′
bas′so
bas·soon′
bas·soon′ist
bass viol
bass′wood′
bas′tard
bas′tar·dy
baste
bast′er
Bas·tille′
bast′ing
bas′tion
bate
lessen *(see:* bait)

ba·teau′
(plural: -teaux)

bath, *n.*
bathe, *v.*
bath′er
ba·thet′ic
bath′house′
bath′ing
ba′thos
bath′robe′
bath′room′
bath′tub′
bath′y·sphere
ba·tik′
ba·tiste′
ba·ton′
Bat′on Rouge′
bat·tal′ion
bat′ten
bat′ter
bat′ter·ing
bat′ter·y
bat′tle
bat′tle cruiser
bat′tle cry
bat′tle fatigue
bat′tle·field

bat′tle·ground
bat′tle·ment
bat′tle·ship′
bau′ble
baux′ite
Ba·var′i·a
bawd′i·ly
bawd′y
bawl
bay′ber′ry
bay′o·net
Ba′yonne′
bay′ou
ba·zaar′
fair (*see:* bizarre)

ba·zoo′ka
beach
shore (*see:* beech)

beach′comb′er
beach′head
bea′con
bead′ed
bead′ing
bea′dle
bead′y
bea′gle
beak′er
beak′less
beam′ing
beam′less
bear
animal (*see:* bare)

bear′a·ble
beard′ed
beard′less
bear′er
bear′ing
bear′ish
bear′skin′
beast′li·ness
beast′ly
beat
defeat (*see:* beet)

beat′en
be′a·tif′ic
be·at′i·fi·ca′tion
be·at′i·fied
be·at′i·fy
beat′ing
be·at′i·tude
beau geste′
beau′te·ous
beau′ti·cian
beau′ti·ful
beau′ti·fi′er
beau′ti·fy
beau′ty shop
beaux-arts′
bea′ver
be·calm′
be·came′
be·cause′
beck′on
beck′on·ing
be·cloud′
be·come′
be·com′ing
be·daze′
be·daz′zle
be·daz′zling
bed′bug
bed′cham′ber
bed′clothes′
bed′ded
bed′ding
be·deck′
be·dev′il
be·dev′il·ment
bed′fast
bed′fel′low
be·dim′
be·di′zen
bed′lam
Bed′ou·in
bed′pan′
be·drag′gle
bed′rid′den
bed′rock′
bed′room′
bed′side′
bed′spread′
bed′stead
bed·time′
beech
tree (*see:* beach)

beech′nut
beef
(*plural:* beeves)

beef′i·ness
beef′steak′
beef′y
bee′hive′
bee′line′
Be·el′ze·bub
beer
beverage (*see:* bier)

beer′y
bees′wax′
beet
(*see:* beat)

Bee′tho·ven
bee′tle·browed′
be·fall′
be·fall′en
be·fell′
be·fit′
be·fit′ting·ly
be·fog′
be·fogged′
be·fog′ging
be·fore′
be·fore′hand′
be·foul′
be·friend′
be·fud′dle
be·gan′
be·get′
beg′gar
beg′gar·li·ness
beg′gar·ly
beg′ging
be·gin′
be·gin′ner
be·gin′ning
be·gone′
be·go′ni·a
be·got′ten
be·grime′
be·grudge′
be·guile′
be·guil′er
be·guil′ing·ly

be·gun′
be·half′
be·haved′
be·hav′ing
be·hav′ior·ism
be·hav′ior·is′tic
be·head′ed
be·held′
be·he′moth
be·hest′
be·hind′
be·hold′er
be·hold′ing
be·hoove′
beige
be′ing
Bei′rut
be·jew′el
be·jew′eled
be·la′bor
be·lat′ed
be·lay′
be·lea′guer
be·lea′guered
be·lea′guer·ment
bel′fry
Bel′gian
Bel′gium
be·lie′
be·lief′
be·liev′a·ble
be·lieve′
be·liev′er
be·liev′ing·ly
be·lit′tle
be·lit′tling
bel′la·don′na

bell′boy′
belles′-let′tres
bell′hop′
bel′li·cose
bel′li·cos′i·ty
bel·lig′er·ence
bel·lig′er·ent
bel′lows
bell′weth′er
bel′ly
be·longed′
be·long′ing
be·lov′ed
be·low′
belt′ed
belt′ing
be·ly′ing
be·mire′
be·mir′ing
be·moaned′
be·moan′ing
be·mused′
be·mus′ing
bend′er
bend′ing
be·neath′
ben′e·dict
ben′e·dic′tion
ben′e·dic′to·ry
ben′e·fac′tion
ben′e·fac′tor
ben′e·fac′tress
ben′e·fice
be·nef′i·cence
be·nef′i·cent
ben′e·fi′cial
ben′e·fi′ci·a·ry

ben′e·fit′ed
ben′e·fit′ing
be·nev′o·lence
be·nev′o·lent
Ben′gal
be·night′ed
be·nign′
be·nig′nan·cy
be·nig′nant
be·nig′ni·ty
ben′i·son
ben′zene
ben′zine
ben′zo·ate
ben′zol
be·queath′
be·queath′al
be·quest′
be·rat′ed
be·rat′ing
be·reaved
be·reave′ment
be·reav′ing
be·ret′
ber′i·ber′i
Berk′shires
Ber·mu′da
ber′ry
ber′serk
berth
bed *(see:* birth)
ber′yl
be·ryl′li·um
be·seeched′
be·seech′ing
be·seem′
be·set′
be·set′ting
be·sides′
be·siege′
be·sieg′er
be·smear′
be·smirch′
be·smirch′er
be·sot′
be·spec′ta·cled
Bes′se·mer
bes′tial
bes′ti·al′i·ty
be·stir′
best-known
be·stow′
be·stow′a·ble
be·stow′al
best sel′ler
be′ta
be′ta·tron
be′tel
beth′el
Beth′le·hem
be·tide′
be·times′
be·to′ken
be·tray′
be·tray′al
be·tray′er
be·troth′
be·troth′al
be·trothed′
be·troth′ment
bet′ter
bet′ting
be·tween′
be·twixt′
bev′a·tron
bev′el
bev′eled
bev′el·ing
bev′er·age
bev′y
be·wail′
be·wail′ing
be·ware′
be·wil′der
be·wil′dered
be·wil′dered·ly
be·wil′der·ing
be·wil′der·ment
be·witch′
be·witch′ing
be·witch′ment
be·yond′
be·zique′
bi·an′nu·al
bi·an′nu·al·ly
bi′as
bi′ased
bi′as·ing
bi·ax′i·al
bi′be·lot
Bi′ble
Bib′li·cal
bib′li·og′ra·pher
bib′li·o·graph′ic
bib′li·og′ra·phy
bib′li·o·ma′ni·a
bib′li·o·phile
bib′u·lous
bi·cam′er·al
bi·car′bo·nate

bi·cen′te·nar′y
bi′cen·ten′ni·al
bi′ceps
bi·chlo′ride
bick′er
bi·cus′pid
bi·cus′pi·date
bi′cy·cle
bi′cy·cler
bi′cy·clist
bid′da·ble
bid′der
bid′ding
bid′dy
bide
bid′ing
bi·en′ni·al
bi·en′ni·al·ly
bier
 coffin stand (*see:* beer)

bi·fo′cal
bi′fur·cate
bi′fur·ca′tion
big′a·mist
big′a·mous
big′a·my
big′ger
bight
 loop (*see:* bite)

big′ot·ed
big′ot·ry
bi′jou
Bi·ki′ni
bi·la′bi·al
bi·lat′er·al
bi·lat′er·al·ly
bilge
bil′i·ar′y
bi·lin′gual
bi·lin′gual·ly
bil′ious
bil′ious·ly
bill′a·ble
bill′board′
bill′er
bil′let
bil′let-doux
bill′fold′
bil′liard·ist
bil′liards
bil′lings·gate′
bil′lion
bil′lion·aire
bil′lionth
bil′low
bil′low·y
bil′ly
bi′me·tal′lic
be′me·tal·lism
bi·month′ly
bi′na·ry
bi′nate
bind′er
bind′er·y
bind′ing
bin′go
bin′na·cle
bi·noc′u·lar
bi·no′mi·al
bi·no′mi·al·ly
bi′o·chem′ist
bi′o·chem′is·try
bi′o·gen′e·sis
bi·og′ra·pher
bi′o·graph′ic
bi′o·graph′i·cal
bi·og′ra·phy
bi′o·log′i·cal
bi·ol′o·gist
bi·ol′o·gy
bi′o·met′ric
bi·om′e·try
bi·par′ti·san
bi·par′tite
bi′par·ti′tion
bi′ped
bi′plane′
birch′bark′
bird′s′-eye′
bi·ret′ta
birth
 being born (*see:* berth)

birth′day′
birth′mark′
birth′place′
birth′ rate
birth′right
birth′stone
bis′cuit
bi·sect′
bi·sec′tion
bi·sec′tion·al·ly
bi·sec′tor
bish′op
bish′op·ric
bis′muth
bi′son

bisque
bis·sex′tile
bis′ter
bite
cut into *(see:* bight)

bit′ing
bit′ter
bit′ter·ly
bit′tern
bit′ter·root′
bit′ters
bit′ter·sweet′
bi·tu′men
bi·tu′mi·noid
bi·tu′mi·nous
bi·va′lence
bi·va′lent
bi′valve′
bi·val′vu·lar
biv′ou·ac
biv′ou·acked
biv′ou·ack·ing
bi·week′ly
bi·zarre′
queer *(see:* bazaar)

blab
blab′ber
black′a·moor
black′ball′
black′ber′ry
black′bird′
black′board′
black′en
black′en·er
black′er
black′face′
Black′foot′
black′guard
black′head′
Black Hills
black′ing
black′ish
black′jack′
black′ly
black′mail′
black′out′
black′ sheep
black′smith′
blad′der
blade
blade′less
blam′a·ble
blame′ful
blame′less
blame′wor′thy
blam′ing
blanch
blanc·mange′
bland
blan′dish
blan′dish·ment
bland′ly
blan′ket
blank′ly
blare
blar′ney
bla·se′
blas·pheme′
blas·phem′er
blas′phe·mous
blas′phe·my
blast′ed
blast′er
blas′tu·la
bla′tan·cy
bla′tant
bla′tant·ly
blaze
blazed′
blaz′ing
bla′zon
bla′zon·ry
bleach′er
bleak
bleak′ly
blear′i·ness
blear′y
bleat′ing
bleed′ing
blem′ish
blend′er
blend′ing
bless, *v.*
bless′ed
bless′ing
blight
blind′er
blind′fold′
blind′ing
blind′ly
blind′ness
blink′er
blink′ing
bliss′ful
blis′ter
blithe′ly
blitz′krieg′
bliz′zard
bloat

bloc
group

block
cube

block·ade′
block·ad′ed
block·ad′ing
block′bus′ter
block′head′
block′house′
block′i·er
block′y
blond′ness
blood bank
blood′cur′dling
blood′hound′
blood′i·ly
blood′less
blood′let′ting
blood poi′son·ing
blood pres′sure
blood′root′
blood′shed′
blood′shot
blood′stained′
blood′stone′
blood′suck′er
blood′thirst′i·ly
blood′thirst′y
blood ves′sel
blood′y
bloom′ers
bloom′ing·ly
blos′som
blotch
blotch′y
blot′less
blot′ter
blot′ting
blouse
blow′er
blow′fly′
blow′i·ness
blown
blow′out′
blow′pipe′
blow′torch′
blow′up′
blow′y
blowz′y
blub′ber
blub′ber·y
bludg′eon
blue
color *(see:* blew)

Blue′beard′
blue′bell′
blue′ber′ry
blue′bird′
blue′jack′et
blue′jay′
blue′-pen′cil
blue′print′
blue′stock′ing
bluff′er
blu′ing
blu′ish
blun′der
blun′der·buss
blun′der·er
blun′der·ing
blunt′ly
blur
blurred
blur′ring
blur′ry
blurt′ed
blushed
blush′ing
blus′ter
blus′ter·ing
blus′ter·ous
blus′ter·y
bo′a
boar
male pig *(see:* bore)

board′er
board′ing
boarding house
boarding school
board′walk′
boast′er
boast′ful
boast′ing·ly
boat′house′
boat′ing
boat′load
boat′swain
bobbed
bob′bin
bob′bing
bob′by·sox′er
bob′cat′
bob′o·link
bob′sled′
bob′tail′
bob′white′
Boc·cac′ci·o

bod′ice
bod′i·ly
bod′kin
bod′y
bod′y·guard′
Bo′er
bo′gey
one over par

bog′gi·ness
bog′gish
bog′gy
swampy

bo′gus
bo′gy
goblin

Bo·he′mi·a
boil′er
boil′ing
Boi′se
bois′ter·ous
bold′face′
bold′ly
bole
tree trunk *(see:* boll; bowl)

bo·le′ro
Bo·liv′i·a
boll
seed pod *(see:* bole; bowl)

bo·lo′gna
Bol′she·vik
bol′ster
bolt′less
bomb
bom·bard′
bom′bar·dier′
bom·bard′ment
bom′bast
bom·bas′tic
Bom·bay′
bomb′er
bomb′proof′
bomb′sight′
bo′na fide
bo·nan′za
Bo′na·parte
bon′bon′
bond′age
bond′ed
bond′hold′er
bonds′man
bone′-dry′
bone′less
bon′er
bon′fire′
bon′i·er
bon′ing
bo·ni′to
bon jour′
bon mot′
bon′net
bon′ni·ly
bon′ny
bo′nus
bon vo·yage′
bon′y
boo′by
boo′dle
boog′ie-woog′ie
book′bind′er
book′bind′er·y
book′case′
book club
book end
book′ie
book′ish
book′keep′ing
book′let
book′lore′
book′mak′er
book′mark′
book′plate′
book′rack′
book′sell′er
book′shop′
book′store′
book′worm′
boom′er·ang
boon′dog′gle
boor′ish
boost′er
boot′black
boot·ee′
booth
boot′jack′
boot′leg′
boot′leg′ging
boot′less
boo′ty
booze
bo′rate
bo′rax
Bor·deaux′
bor′der
bor′der·land′
bor′der·line′
bore
pierce *(see:* boar)

bo′re·al
Bo′re·as
bore′dom
bo′ric
bor′ing
born, *adj.*
borne, *v.*
bo′ron
bor′ough
bor′row
borsch
bos′om
Bos′po·rus
boss′y
Bos′ton
Bos·to′ni·an
bo′sun
bo·tan′i·cal
bot′a·nist
bot′a·ny
botch
botch′y
bot′fly′
both′er
both′er·some
bot′tle
bot′tle-fed
bot′tle·neck′
bot′tling
bot′tom
bot′u·lism
bou·cle′
bou′doir
bought
bouil′lon
soup *(see:* bullion)

boul′der
boul′e·vard
bounce
bounc′er
bounc′ing
bound′a·ry
bound′en
bound′er
bound′less
boun′te·ous
boun′ti·ful
boun′ty
bou·quet′
bour′bon
bour·geois′
bour′geoi·sie′
bou′ton·niere′
bo′vine
bowd′ler·ize
bow′el
bow′er
bow′er·y
bow′ie
bow′knot′
bowl
deep dish *(see:* bole; boll)

bow′leg′
bow′leg′ged
bow′line
bowl′ing
bow′man
bow′string′
box′car
box′er
box′ing

boy
young male *(see:* buoy)

boy′cott
boy′cott·er
boy′hood
boy′ish
boy′sen·ber′ry
brace′let
brac′er
brac′ing
brack′et
brack′ish
brag′ga·do′ci·o
brag′gart
brag′gart·ism
brag′ger
brag′ging
Brah′ma
Braille
brain′i·er
brain′less
brain′pan′
brain′wash′ing
brain′y
braise
cook *(see:* braze)

braised
brais′ing
brake
slow: stop *(see:* break)

brake′man
bram′ble
bram′bly

bran′died
bran′dish
brand′-new′
bran′dy
bra′sier
also: brazier

bras′sard
brass′ie
bras·siere′
brass′i·ness
brass′y
bra·va′do
brave′ly
brav′ery
bra′vo
brawn′i·er
brawn′y
braze
solder *(see:* braise)

bra′zen
bra′zier
also: brasier

Bra·zil′
Bra·zil′ian
braz′ing
breach
breaking *(see:* breech)

bread
food *(see:* bred)

breadth
size *(see:* breath)

bread′win′ner

break
shatter *(see:* brake)

break′a·ble
break′age
break′down′
break′er
break′fast
break′neck′
break′through′
break′up′
break′wa′ter
breast
breast′bone′
breast′pin′
breast′plate′
breast′work′
breath, *n.*
air *(see:* breadth)

breathe, *v.*
breath′er
breath′ing
breath′less·ly
breath′tak′ing
bred
p.t. of breed *(see:* bread)

breech
lower part *(see:* breach)

breech′cloth′
breech′es
breed
breed′ing
breeze
breez′i·ly

breez′y
breth′ren
bre·vet′
bre′vi·ar′y
brev′i·ty
brew′er·y
brew′ing
bri′ar·y
bribed
brib′er·y
brib′ing
bric′-a-brac′
brick′bat′
brick′lay′er
brick′work′
brid′al
wedding *(see:* bridle)

bride′groom′
brides′maid′
bride′well
bridge′a·ble
bridge′head
bridge′work′
bridg′ing
bri′dle
harness *(see:* bridal)

brief′case′
brief′ing
brief′ly
bri·gade′
brig′a·dier′
brig′and
brig′an·tine
bright′en
bright′ly
bril′liance

bril′lian•cy
bril′liant
bril′lian•tine
brim′ful′
brim′less
brimmed
brim′ming
brim′stone′
brin′dle
brine
bring′ing
bring′ing-up′
brin′i•ness
brink
brin′y
bri•quette′
bris′ket
brisk′ly
bris′tle
bris′tli•ness
bris′tling
brist′ly
Brit′ain
Bri•tan′ni•a
Bri•tan′nic
Brit′ish
Brit′on
Brit′ta•ny
brit′tle
broach
open *(see:* brooch)

broad′ax′
broad′cast′
broad′cloth′
broad′en
broad′loom′
broad′ly
broad′-mind′ed
broad′side′
broad′sword′
bro•cade′
bro•cad′ed
broc′co•li
bro•chure′
bro′gan
brogue
broil′er
broke
bro′ken
bro′ken-heart′ed
bro′ker
bro′ker•age
bro′mide
bro′mine
bron′chi•al
bron•chi′tis
bron′co
bronze
bronz′ing
brooch
pin *(see:* broach)

brood′er
brood′ing•ly
brood′y
brook′let
Brook′lyn
broom′stick′
broth
broth′el
broth′er
broth′er•hood
broth′er-in-law′
broth′er•li•ness
broth′er•ly
brougham
brow′beat′
brow′beat′ing
brown′ie
brown′ish
brown′ness
brown′stone′
browse
brows′ing
bru′in
bruise
bruis′er
bruis′ing
bruit
spread report *(see:* brute)

bru•nette′
brunt
brush′y
brush′wood′
brusque
Brus′sels
bru′tal
bru•tal′i•ty
brute
animal-like *(see:* bruit)

brut′ish•ly
bub′ble
bub′bling•ly
bub′bly
bu•bon′ic
buc′ca•neer′
Bu•chan′an

buck′a·roo
buck′board′
buck′et
buck′et·ful
buck′eye′
buck′le
buck′ler
buck′ram
buck′shot′
buck′skin′
buck′tooth′
buck′wheat′
bu·col′ic
bu·col′i·cal·ly
Bu′da·pest
bud′less
Bud′dha
Bud′dhism
Bud′dhist
bud′dy
budge
budg′et
budg′et·ar·y
budg′et·ing
Bue′nos Ai′res
buf′fa·lo
buff′er
buf′fet, *v.*
buf·fet′, *n.*
buf·foon′
buf·foon′er·y
bug′a·boo
bug′gy
bu′gle
bu′gler
build′er
build′ing
build′-up′
built′-in′
bulb′ar
bulb′ous
bulge
bulg′ing
bulk′head′
bulk′i·er
bulk′i·ness
bulk′y
bull′dog′
bull′doz′er
bul′let
bul′le·tin
bul′let·proof′
bull′fight′
bull′fight′er
bull′finch′
bull′frog′
bull′head′
bull′head′ed
bul′lied
bul′lion
gold *(see:* bouillon)
bull′ock
bull's′-eye′
bull′whip′
bul′ly
bul′rush′
bul′wark
bum′ble·bee′
bum′bling
bump′er
bump′kin
bump′tious
bump′i·er
bump′y
bunch′i·er
bunch′y
bun′co
bun′combe
bun′dle
bun′dling
bun′ga·low
bung′hole′
bun′gle
bun′gler
bun′gling·ly
bun′ion
bunk′er
bunk′house′
bun′ny
Bun′sen
bunt′ing
buoy
marker *(see:* boy)
buoy′an·cy
buoy′ant
bur′den
bur′den·some
bur′dock′
bu′reau
bu·reauc′ra·cy
bu′reau·crat
bu′reau·crat′ic
bur′geon
bur′gess
burgh′er
bur′glar
bur·glar′i·ous
bur′glar·ize
bur′glar·proof′

bur'glar·y
bur'go·mas'ter
bur'i·al
bur'ied
bur'lap
bur·lesque'
bur'ley
tobacco
bur'li·ness
bur'ly
strong
Bur'ma
Bur·mese'
burned
burn'er
burn'ing
bur'nish
bur·noose'
burnt
bur'ring
bur'ro
donkey
bur'row
animal shelter
bur'sa
bur'sar

bur·si'tis
burst
burst'ing
bur'y
bur'y·ing
bush'el
bush'i·er
bush'ing
bush'man
bush'mas'ter
bush'y
bus'i·er
bus'i·ly
busi'ness
business college
busi'ness·man
bus'kin
bus'ses
bus'tard
bus'tle
bus'tler
bus'tling·ly
bus'y
bus'y·bod'y
bus'y·ness
bu'tane
butch'er

butch'er·y
but'ler
butte
but'ter
but'ter·cup'
but'ter·fat'
but'ter·fin'gers
but'ter·fly'
but'ter·milk'
but'ter·scotch'
but'ter·y
but'tocks
but'ton·hole'
but'tress
bux'om·ness
buy'ing
buzz'ard
buzz'er
by'gone'
by'law'
by'line'
by'pass'
by'-prod'uct
by'stand'er
by'word'
Byz'an·tine

C

ca·bal'
cab'a·lis'tic
cab'al·le'ro
ca·ba'na
cab'a·ret'

cab'bage
cab'by
cab'in
cab'i·net
cab'i·net·mak'er

ca'ble·gram
ca'bling
ca·boose'
cab'ri·o·let'
ca·ca'o

cache
cached
ca·chet′
cach′in·nate
cack′le
ca·coph′o·nous
ca·coph′o·ny
cac′tus
ca·dav′er
ca·dav′er·ous
cad′die
cad′dish
ca′dence
ca′den·cy
ca·den′za
ca·det′
ca·det′cy
cad′mi·um
ca′dre
ca·du′ce·us
Cae′sar
Cae·sar′e·an
ca·fe′
caf′e·te′ri·a
caf′feine
caf′tan
cage′ling
cage′y
cag′i·er
cag′i·ly
cairn
Cai′ro
cais′son
cai′tiff
ca·jole′
ca·jol′er·y
cake′walk′

cal′a·bash
cal′a·boose
cal′a·mine
ca·lam′i·tous
ca·lam′i·ty
cal·car′e·ous
cal·cif′er·ous
cal′ci·fi·ca′tion
cal′ci·fy
cal′ci·mine
cal′ci·na′tion
cal′cine
cal′cite
cal′ci·um
cal′cu·la·ble
cal′cu·late
cal′cu·lat′ing
cal′cu·la′tion
cal′cu·lus
cal′dron
cal′en·dar
table of year
cal′en·der
machine
ca·len′du·la
calf
(*plural:* calves)
cal′i·ber
cal′i·brate
cal′i·bra′tion
cal′i·bra′tor
cal′i·co
Cal′i·for′nia
cal′i·per
ca′liph

cal′is·then′ics
calked
calk′er
cal′la
cal·lig′ra·pher
cal·lig′ra·phy
call′ing
cal·li′o·pe
cal·los′i·ty
cal′lous, *adj.*
cal′low
cal′lus, *n.*
calm′ly
cal′o·mel
ca·lor′ic
cal′o·rie
cal′o·rif′ic
cal′o·rim′e·ter
ca·lum′ni·ate
ca·lum′ni·a′tion
ca·lum′ni·a′tor
ca·lum′ni·ous
cal′um·ny
Cal′va·ry
Cal′vin·ist
Cal′vin·is′tic
Ca·lyp′so
ca′lyx
ca′ma·ra′de·rie
cam′a·ril′la
cam′ber
cam′bi·um
cam′bric
cam′el
ca·mel′lia
Cam′e·lot
Cam′em·bert

cam′e·o
cam′er·a
cam′er·a·man
cam′i·sole
cam′o·mile
cam′ou·flage
cam·paign′
cam′pa·ni′le
camp′er
camp′fire′
cam′phor
cam′phor·at′ed
cam·phor′ic
cam′pus
Can′a·da
Ca·na′di·an
ca·naille′
ca·nal′
can′a·pe
appetizer *(see:* canopy)

ca·nard′
ca·nar′y
ca·nas′ta
can′can
can′cel
can′celed
can′cel·er
can′cel·ing
can′cel·la′tion
can′cer
can′cer·ous
can′de·la′bra
can·des′cence
can·des′cent
can′did
can′di·da·cy
can′di·date
can′di·da·ture
can′did·ly
can′died
can′dle
can′dle·light′
Can′dle·mas
can′dle·pow′er
can′dler
can′dle·stick
can′dor
can′dy
ca′nine
can′is·ter
can′ker
can′ker·ous
can′na
canned
can′ner
can′ner·y
can′ni·bal
can′ni·bal·ism′
can′ni·ly
can′ni·ness
can′ning
can′non
(see: canon)

can′non·ade′
can′not
can′ny
ca·noe′
ca·noe′ing
can′on
church law *(see:* cannon)

ca·non′i·cal
can′on·ize
can′o·py
covering *(see:* canape)

can·ta′bi·le
can′ta·loupe
can·tan′ker·ous
can·ta′ta
can·teen′
can′ter
gallop *(see:* cantor)

can′ti·cle
can′ti·lev′er
can′to
can′ton
Can′ton·ese′
can′tor
chanter *(see:* canter)

can′vas
cloth

can′vass
examine

can′yon
ca′pa·bil′i·ty
ca′pa·ble
ca·pa′cious
ca·pac′i·ty
ca·par′i·son
ca′per
cap′ful
cap′il·lar′y
cap′i·tal
city, property *(see:* capitol)

cap′i·tal·ism′
cap′i·tal·ist
cap′i·tal·is′tic
cap′i·tal·i·za′tion
cap′i·tal·ize
cap′i·ta′tion
cap′i·tol
building *(see:* capital)

ca·pit′u·late
ca·pit′u·la′tion
ca′pon
ca·price′
ca·pri′cious
cap′ri·ole
Cap′ri·corn
cap·size′
cap·siz′ing
cap′su·lar
cap′sule
cap′tain
cap′tain·cy
cap′tion
cap′tious
cap′ti·vate
cap′ti·vat′ing
cap′ti·va′tion
cap′ti·va′tor
cap′tive
cap·tiv′i·ty
cap′tor
cap′ture
cap′tur·ing
cap′u·chin
Ca·rac′as
car′a·cul

ca·rafe′
car′a·mel
car′at
weight *(see:* caret; carrot)

car′a·van
car′a·vel
car′a·way
car′bide
car′bine
car′bo·hy′drate
car·bol′ic
car′bon
car′bo·na′ceous
car′bon·ate
car′bon·a′tion
car′bon dioxide
car′bon·if′er·ous
car′bon·ize
car′bo·run′dum
car′bun·cle
car′bu·re′tor
car′cass
car′ci·no′ma
car·cin′o·gen
card′board′
car′di·ac
car′di·gan
car′di·nal
car′di·nal·ate
card′ing
car′di·o·graph′
car′di·og′ra·phy
ca·reen′
ca·reer′
care′free′

care′ful
care′ful·ly
care′less
care′less·ly
ca·ress′
ca·ress′ing·ly
car′et
symbol *(see:* carat; carrot)

care′tak′er
care′worn
car′fare′
car′go
Car′ib·be′an
car′i·bou
car′i·ca·ture
car′i·ca·tur′ist
car′ies
car′il·lon
car′i·ous
car′load′
Car′mel·ite
car·min′a·tive
car′mine
car′nage
car′nal
car·nal′i·ty
car′nal·ly
car·na′tion
car·nel′ian
car′ni·val
car·niv′o·ral
car′ni·vore
car·niv′o·rous
car′ol
car′ol·er

Car′o·li′na
car′om
ca·rot′id
ca·rous′al
ca·rouse′
ca·rous′ing
car′pen·ter
car′pen·try
car′pet
car′pet·bag′ger
car′pet·ing
car′pus
car′riage
car′ri·er
car′ri·on
car′rot
vegetable *(see:* carat; caret)

car′rou·sel′
car′ry
car′ry·back
car′ry-o′ver
cart′age
carte′ blanche′
car·tel′
car′ti·lage
car′ti·lag′i·nous
car·tog′ra·pher
car′to·graph′ic
car·tog′ra·phy
car′ton
box

car·toon′
drawing

car·toon′ist
car′tridge
carv′ing
car′y·at′id
cas·cade′
cas·car′a
case′hard′en
ca′se·in
case′mate
case′ment
ca′se·ous
cash′ew
cash·ier′
cash′mere
cas′ing
ca·si′no
cas′ket
Cas′pi·an
cas′se·role
cas′sock
cast
throw off *(see:* caste)

cas′ta·net′
cast′a·way′
caste
social system *(see:* cast)

cas′tel·lat·ed
cas′ter
swivel wheel, or one who casts *(see:* castor)

cas′ti·gate
cas′ti·ga′tion
Cas′til′ian
cast′ing
cas′tle
cast′off′
cas′tor
swivel wheel, or medicinal oil *(see:* caster)

cas′trate
cas·tra′tion
cas′u·al·ly
cas′u·al·ty
cas′u·is′tic
ca·tab′o·lism
cat′a·clysm
cat′a·clys′mic
cat′a·comb
cat′a·falque
cat′a·lep′sis
cat′a·lep′sy
cat′a·lep′tic
cat′a·logue
(or: catalog)

ca·tal′pa
ca·tal′y·sis
cat′a·lyt′ic
cat′a·lyst
cat′a·lyze
cat′a·ma·ran′
cat′a·mount′
cat′a·pult
cat′a·ract
ca·tarrh′
ca·tas′tro·phe
cat′a·stroph′ic
catch′all′
catch′er
catch′i·er
catch′y

cat′e·chism
cat′e·chis′mal
cat′e·chist
cat′e·chi·za′tion
cat′e·chize
cat′e·chu′men
cat′e·chu′me·nal
cat′e·gor′i·cal
cat′e·go′ry
cat′e·nate
ca′ter
cat′er-cor′nered
ca′ter·er
cat′er·pil′lar
cat′er·waul′ing
cat′fish′
ca·thar′sis
ca·thar′tic
ca·the′dral
cath′e·ter
cath′ode
Cath′o·lic
Ca·thol′i·cism
cath′o·lic′i·ty
ca·thol′i·cize
cat′kin
cat′nap′
cat′nip
cat′-o'nine′-tails′
cat's′-paw′
cat′sup
cat′tle
cat′ty
cat′walk′
Cau·ca′sian
cau′cus
cau′dal
caught
caul′dron
cau′li·flow′er
caus′al
cau·sal′i·ty
cau·sa′tion
caus′a·tive
cause′less
cause′way′
caus′tic
caus′ti·cal·ly
cau′ter·i·za′tion
cau′ter·ize
cau′ter·y
cau′tion
cau′tion·ar′y
cau′tious
cav′al·cade′
cav′a·lier′
cav′al·ry
cav′ern
cav′ern·ous
cav′i·ar
cav′il
cav′i·ty
ca·vort′
ca·vort′ing
cay·enne′
cay′man
Ca·yu′ga
cay·use′
ceased
cease′less
ceas′ing
ce′dar
ced′ed
ce·dil′la
ced′ing
ceil′ing
Cel′a·nese′
cel′e·brant
cel′e·brate
cel′e·bra′tion
ce·leb′ri·ty
ce·ler′i·ty
cel′er·y
ce·les′tial
cel′i·ba·cy
cel′i·bate
cel′lar
cel′list
cel′lo
cel′lo·phane
cel′lu·lar
cel′lu·loid
cel′lu·lose
Celt′ic
ce·ment′
cem′e·ter′y
ce′no·bite
ce′no·bit′ic
cen′o·taph
cen′ser
incense container
cen′sor
person who judges
cen·so′ri·al
cen·so′ri·ous
cen′sor·ship
cen′sur·a·bil′i·ty
cen′sur·a·ble
cen′sured
cen′sur·ing

cen′sus
cen′taur
cen·ta′vo
cen′te·nar′i·an
cen′te·nar′y
cen·ten′ni·al
cen′ter·piece′
cen′ti·grade
cen′ti·me′ter
cen′ti·pede
cen′tral
cen′tral·i·za′tion
cen′tral·ize
cen·trif′u·gal
cen′tri·fuge
cen·trip′e·tal
cen′tu·ple
cen·tu′ri·on
cen′tu·ry
ce·phal′ic
ce·ram′ic
cer′a·mist
ce′re·al
cer′e·bel′lum
cer′e·bel′lar
cer′e·bral
cer′e·brum
cer′e·mo′ni·al
cer′e·mo′ni·ous
cer′e·mo′ny
ce·rise′
ce′ri·um
cer′tain
cer′tain·ly
cer′tain·ty
cer·tif′i·cate
cer′ti·fi·ca′tion
cer′ti·fied
cer′ti·fy
cer′ti·fy′ing
cer′ti·o·ra′ri
cer′ti·tude
ce·ru′le·an
cer′vi·cal
cer′vix
ces·sa′tion
ces′sion
giving up *(see: session)*
cess′pool′
Cey·lon′
chafed
chaff′er
chaf′ing
cha·grin′
chain gang
chain reaction
chain′-smoke′
chain store
chair′man
chaise′ longue′
chal·ced′o·ny
cha·let′
chal′ice
chalk′i·ness
chalk′y
chal′lenge
chal′leng·er
chal′lis
cham′ber
cham′ber·lain
cham′ber·maid′
cham′bray
cha·me′le·on
cham′ois
cham·pagne′
cham′pi·on
chan′cel
chan′cel·ler·y
chan′cel·lor
chan′cer·y
chan′de·lier′
change′a·bil′i·ty
change′a·ble
changed
change′ling
chan′neled
chan′nel·ing
chant′ey
chan′ti·cleer
cha′os
cha·ot′ic
chap′el
chap′er·on
chap′lain
chap′let
chap′ter
char′ac·ter
char′ac·ter·is′tic
char′ac·ter·i·za′tion
char′ac·ter·ize
cha·rade′
char′coal′
charge′a·ble
char·ge′ d'af·faires′
charged
charg′ing
char′i·ot

char′i·ot·eer′
char′i·ta·ble
char′i·ty
char′la·tan
charm′ing
char′nel
char′ter
char·treuse′
chart′room
char′wo′man
chased
chas′ing
chasm
chas′sis
chaste
chas′ten
chas·tise′
chas·tis′er
chas′ti·ty
chas′u·ble
cha·teau′
chat′e·laine
Chat′ta·noo′ga
chat′tel
chat′ter
chat′ti·ly
chat′ty
chauf′feur
chau·tau′qua
chau′vin·ism
cheap′en
cheap′ened
cheat′er
check′book′
check′er
check′er·board′
check′ered
check′room
check′up′
cheek′y
cheer′ful
cheer′i·ly
cheer′y
cheese′cloth′
chees′y
chee′tah
chem′i·cal
che·mise′
chem′ist
chem′is·try
chem′ur·gy
che·nille′
cher′ish
Cher′o·kee
che·root′
cher′ry
cher′ub
Ches′a·peake
chess′board′
chest′nut
chest′y
chev′a·lier′
chev′i·ot
chev′ron
chew′ing
Chey·enne′
Chi·ca′go
chi·can′er·y
chick′a·dee
chick′en
chick′en pox
chic′le
chic′o·ry
chide
chid′ing
chief′tain
chif·fon′
chif′fo·nier′
chig′ger
chi′gnon
Chi·hua′hua
chil′blain
child′bear′ing
child′birth′
child′hood
child′ish
chil′dren
Chil′e
chil′i
chill′i·ness
chill′y
chimed
chim′ing
chim′ney
chim′pan·zee′
Chi′na·town′
chin·chil′la
Chi·nese′
chinned
chin′ning
Chi·nook′
chintz
chip′munk
chipped
chip′per
chip′ping
chi′ro·graph′i·cal
chi·rog′ra·phy
chi·rop′o·dist
chi·rop′o·dy
chi′ro·prac′tic

chi′ro·prac′tor
chir′ruped
chir′rup·ing
chis′el
chis′el·er
chit′-chat′
chiv′al·rous
chiv′al·ry
chlo′rate
chlo′ric
chlo′ride
chlo′rin·a′tion
chlo′rine
chlo′ro·form
chlo′ro·my′ce·tin
chlo′ro·phyll
choc′o·late
choice′ly
choic′est
choir
choked
chok′ing
chol′er
chol′e·ra
chol′er·ic
cho·les′ter·ol
choose
chop′per
chop′ping
chop′py
chop′stick′
chop′ su′ey
cho′ral
chord
music (*see:* cord)
cho′re·a
cho′re·og′ra·pher
cho′re·og′ra·phy
chor′is·ter
chor′tle
chor′tling
cho′rus
cho′sen
chow′der
chris′ten
Chris′ten·dom
chris′ten·ing
Chris′tian
Chris′ti·an′i·ty
Christ′like′
Christ′mas
chro′mate
chro·mat′ic
chro·mat′i·cal·ly
chro′mi·um
chro′mo·some
chron′ic
chron′i·cal·ly
chron′i·cle
chron′i·cler
chron′i·cling
chron′o·log′
i·cal·ly
chro·nol′o·gist
chro·nol′o·gy
chro·nom′e·ter
chrys′a·lid
chrys′a·lis
chry·san′the·mum
chrys′o·lite
chub′bi·ness
chub′by
chuck′le
chuck′ling
chum′mi·ly
chum′my
chunk′y
church′go′er
church′ly
church′man
church′yard′
churl′ish
churn′er
chute
chut′ney
chyle
chyme
ci·bo′ri·um
ci·ca′da
cic′a·trix
Cic′e·ro
ci′der
ci·gar′
cig′a·rette′
cil′ia
cil′i·ar′y
cin·cho′na
Cin′cin·nat′i
cinc′ture
cin′der
Cin′der·el′la
cin′e·ma
cin′na·bar
cin′na·mon
ci′pher
cir′ca
cir′cled
cir′clet
cir′cling
cir′cuit

cir·cu′i·tous
cir′cu·lar
cir′cu·lar·i·za′tion
cir′cu·lar·ize
cir′cu·late
cir′cu·la′tion
cir′cu·la·to′ry
cir′cum·cise
cir′cum·ci′sion
cir·cum′fer·ence
cir′cum·flex
cir′cum·lo·cu′tion
cir′cum·nav′i·gate
cir′cum·scribe′
cir′cum·scrip′tion
cir′cum·spect
cir′cum·spec′tion
cir′cum·stance
cir′cum·stan′tial
cir′cum·stan′ti·ate
cir′cum′vent
cir′cum·ven′tion
cir′cus
cir·rho′sis
cir·rhot′ic
cir′rus
cis′tern
cit′a·del
ci·ta′tion
cit′ies
cit′ing
cit′i·zen
cit′i·zen·ship
cit′rate
cit′ric
cit′ron
cit′ron·el′la
cit′rous, *adj.*
cit′rus, *n.*
cit′y
(*plural:* cities)

cit′y-state′
civ′et
civ′ic
ci·vil′ian
ci·vil′i·ty
civ′i·li·za′tion
civ′i·lize
civ′i·liz·ing
civ′il·ly
clab′ber
claim′ant
claim′er
clair·voy′ance
clair·voy′ant
clam′ber
clam′mi·ness
clam′my
clam′or
clam′or·ous
clan·des′tine
clan′gor
clan′gor·ous
clan′nish
clans′man
clap′board
clapped
clap′per
clap′ping
clap′trap′
clar′et
clar′i·fi·ca′tion
clar′i·fied
clar′i·fy
clar′i·fy·ing
clar′i·net′
clar′i·on
clar′i·ty
clas′sic
clas′si·cal
clas′si·cal·ly
clas′si·cism
clas′si·cist
clas′si·fi·ca′tion
clas′si·fied
clas′si·fy
clas′si·fy′ing
class′room′
clat′ter
clause
claus′tro·pho′bi·a
clav′i·chord
clav′i·cle
cla·vier′
clay′ey
clean′er
clean′li·ness
cleansed
cleans′ing
clear′ance
clear′-cut′
clear′ing·house′
cleav′age
cleaved
cleav′er
cleav′ing
Clem′en·ceau′
clem′en·cy
clem′ent
Cle′o·pat′ra

cler′gy·man
cler′ic
cler′i·cal
clerk′ship
clev′er·ly
cli·che′
click
sound *(see:* clique)

cli′ent
cli·en′tal
cli′en·tele′
cli·mac′ter·ic
cli·mac′tic
cli′mate
cli′ma·to·log′i·cal
cli′ma·tol′o·gy
cli′max
climbed
climb′ing
clinch′er
cling′ing
clin′ic
clin′i·cal
cli·ni′cian
clink′er
cli·nom′e·ter
clipped
clip′per
clip′ping
clique
group *(see:* click)

cli′to·ris
cloak′room′
clob′ber
cloche
clock′wise′
clock′work′
clog′ging
clois′ter
closed
close′ly
close′-mouthed′
clos′est
clos′et·ed
close′-up′
clos′ure
cloth, *n.*
clothes, *n.*
cloth′ier
cloth′ing
cloud′burst′
cloud′i·ness
cloud′y
clo′ven
clo′ver
clown′ish
cloy′ing·ly
clubbed
club′bing
club′foot′
clum′si·ly
clum′sy
clus′ter
clut′ter
coach′man
co·ag′u·late
co·ag′u·la′tion
co·ag′u·la·tor
co′a·lesce′
co′a·les′cence
co′a·les′cent
co′a·lesc′ing
co′a·li′tion
coarse
rough *(see:* course)

coars′en
coast′al
coast′er
coast guard
coast′line′
coat′ing
coat′room′
coax
co·ax′i·al
coax′ing·ly
co′balt
cob′bler
cob′ble-stone′
co′bra
cob′web′
co·caine′
coc′cus
coc′cyx
coch′i·neal′
cock·ade′
cock′a·too′
cock′crow′
cock′er·el
cock′eyed′
cock′le
cock′le·shell′
cock′ney
cock′pit′
cock′roach′
cock′sure′
cock′tail′
cock′y
co′coa
co′co·nut′

co·coon′
cod′dle
cod′ed
co′deine
co′dex
cod′fish′
codg′er
cod′i·cil
cod′i·fi·ca′tion
cod′i·fied
cod′i·fy
co′ed·u·ca′tion
co′ef·fi′cient
co·e′qual
co·erce′
co·erc′ing
co·er′cion
co·er′cive
co′ex·ec′u·tor
co′ex·ist′ence
cof′fee·pot′
cof′fer·dam′
cof′fin
co′gen·cy
co′gent
cog′i·tate
cog′i·tat·ing
cog′i·ta′tion
co′gnac
cog′nate
cog·ni′tion
cog′ni·zance
cog′ni·zant
cog·no′men
cog′wheel′
co·hab′it
co·hab′i·tant
co·here′
co·her′ence
co·her′ent
co·her′ing
co·he′sion
co·he′sive·ness
co′hort
coif·fure′
coin′age
co′in·cide′
co·in′ci·dence
co·in′ci·den′tal
co′in·cid′ing
co′i·tus
coked
cok′ing
col′an·der
cold′-blood′ed
cold′-heart′ed
cole′slaw′
col′ic
col′ick·y
col′i·se′um
co·li′tis
col·lab′o·rate
col·lab′o·rat·ing
col·lab′o·ra′tion
col·lab′o·ra′tor
col·lapse′
col·lapsed′
col·laps′i·ble
col·laps′ing
col′lar·bone′
col·late′
col·lat′er·al
col·la′tion
col·la′tor
col′league
col·lec′tible
col·lec′tion
col·lec′tive·ly
col·lec′tor
col′leen
col′lege
col·le′giate
col·lide′
col·lid′ing
col′lie
col′lier
col′lier·y
col·li′sion
col′lo·cate
col′lo·ca′tion
col·lo′di·on
col′loid
col′lop
col·lo′qui·al
col·lo′qui·al·ism′
col′lo·quy
col·lude′
col·lud′ing
col·lu′sion
col·lu′sive·ly
co·logne′
Co·lom′bi·a
S. Am. country *(see:* Columbia)
co′lon
colo′nel
co·lo′ni·al
co·lon′ic
col′o·nies
col′o·nist

col'o·ni·za'tion
col'o·nize
col'on·nade'
col'o·ny
Col'o·rad'o
col'or·a'tion
col'o·ra·tu'ra
col'or·cast'
col'ored
col'or·ful
co·los'sal
Col'os·se'um
co·los'sus
colt'ish
Co·lum'bi·a
name for U.S.A.
(see: Colombia)
col'um·bine
co·lum'bi·um
Co·lum'bus
col'umn
co·lum'nar
col'um·nist
co'ma
com'a·tose
com'bat
com·bat'ant
com·bat'ive
com'bi·na'tion
com·bine'
com·bus'ti·ble
com·bus'tion
come'back'
co·me'di·an
co·me'di·enne'
com'e·dy
come'li·ness
come'ly
com'et
com'fort
com'fort·a·ble
com'fort·er
com'ic
com'i·cal
Com'in·form
com'ing
com'ma
com·mand'
com'man·dant'
com'man·deer'
com·mand'er
com·mand'ing
com·mand'ment
com·man'do
com·mem'o·rate
com·mem'
o·rat·ing
com·mem'o·ra'
tion
com·mence'
com·mence'ment
com·menc'ing
com·mend'
com·mend'a·ble
com'men·da'tion
com·mend'a·to'ry
com·men'su·ra·ble
com·men'su·rate
com·men'su·ra'
tion
com'ment
com'men·tar'y
com'men·ta'tor
com'merce
com·mer'cial
com·mer'cial·ize
com·min'gle
com·min'gling
com'mi·nute
com'mi·nu'tion
com·mis'er·ate
com·mis'er·a'tion
com'mis·sar
com'mis·sar'i·at
com'mis·sar'y
com·mis'sion
com·mis'sion·er
com·mit'
com·mit'ment
com·mit'tal
com·mit'ted
com·mit'tee
com·mode'
com·mo'di·ous
com·mod'i·ty
com'mo·dore
com'mon·er
com'mon·place'
com'mon·weal'
com'mon·wealth'
com·mo'tion
com'mu·nal
com·mune', *v.*
com'mune, *n.*
com·mu'ni·ca·ble
com·mu'ni·cant
com·mu'ni·cate
com·mu'ni·cat·ing
com·mu'ni·ca'tion
com·mun'ion

com·mu′ni·que′
com′mu·nism
com′mu·nist
com′mu·nis′tic
com·mu′ni·ty
com′mu·tate
com′mu·ta′tion
com·mute′
com·mut′er
com·mut′ing
com·pact′
com·pan′ion
com·pan′ion·ate
com·pan′ion·ship
com·pan′ion·way′
com′pa·ny
(plural: -nies)

com′pa·ra·ble
com·par′a·tive
com·pare′
com·par′ing
com·par′i·son
com·part′ment
com′pass
com·pas′sion
com·pas′sion·ate
com·pat′i·bil′i·ty
com·pat′i·ble
com·pa′tri·ot
com·pel′
com·pelled′
com·pel′ling
com·pen′di·ous
com·pen′di·um
com′pen·sate
com′pen·sat′ing
com′pen·sa′tion
com·pen′sa·to′ry
com·pete′
com′pe·tence
com′pe·tent
com′pe·ti′tion
com·pet′i·tive·ly
com·pet′i·tor
com′pi·la′tion
com·pile′
com·pil′ing
com·pla′cen·cy
com·pla′cent
com·plain′
com·plain′ant
com·plaint′
com·plai′sance
com′ple·ment
that which completes *(see:* compliment)

com′ple·men′ta·ry
com·plete′
com·ple′tion
com·plex′, *adj.*
com′plex, *n.*
com·plex′ion
com·plex′i·ty
com·pli′ance
com·pli′ant
com′pli·cate
com′pli·cat′ed
com′pli·ca′tion
com·plic′i·ty
com·plied′
com′pli·ment
praise *(see:* complement)

com′pli·men′ta·ry
com·ply′
com·ply′ing
com·po′nent
com·port′
com·pose′
com·posed′
com·pos′ed·ly
com·pos′er
com·pos′ite
com′po·si′tion
com·pos′i·tor
com′post
com·po′sure
com′pote
com′pound, *adj., n.*
com·pound′, *v.*
com′pre·hend′
com′pre·hen′si·ble
com′pre·hen′sion
com′pre·hen′sive
com·press′, *v.*
com′press, *n.*
com·press′i·ble
com·pres′sion
com·pres′sor
com·prise′
com·pris′ing
com′pro·mise
comp·trol′ler
(also: controller)

com·pul′sion
com·pul′so·ri·ly

com·pul′so·ry
com·punc′tion
com·put′a·ble
com′pu·ta′tion
com·pute′
com·put′er
com·put′ing
com′rade
con′cat·e·na′tion
con·cave′
con·cav′i·ty
con·ceal′
con·ceal′ment
con·cede′
con·ced′ed
con·ced′ing
con·ceit′
con·ceit′ed·ly
con·ceiv′a·bil′i·ty
con·ceiv′a·ble
con·ceive′
con·ceiv′ing
con′cen·trate
con′cen·trat′ing
con′cen·tra′tion
con·cen′tric
con′cen·tric′i·ty
con′cept
con·cep′tion
con·cep′tu·al
con·cern′
con·cern′ing
con′cert
con·cert′ed
con′cer·ti′na
con·cer′to
con·ces′sion
conch
con′ci·erge′
con·cil′i·ate
con·cil′i·at·ing
con·cil′i·a′tion
con·cil′i·a′tor
con·cil′i·a·to′ry
con·cise′ly
con′clave
con·clude′
con·clud′ing
con·clu′sion
con·clu′sive
con·coct′
con·coc′tion
con·com′i·tant
con′cord
con·cord′ance
con·cor′dat
con′course
con′crete
con′cu·bine
con·cu′pis·cence
con·cu′pis·cent
con·cur′
con·curred′
con·cur′rence
con·cur′rent
con·cur′ring
con·cus′sion
con·demn′
con′dem·na′tion
con·demned′
con·demn′ing
con′den·sa′tion
con·dense′
con·dens′er
con′de·scend′
con′de·scen′sion
con′di·ment
con·di′tion
con·di′tion·al·ly
con·dole′
con·do′lence
con·dol′ing
con′do·min′i·um
con·done′
con·duce′
con·du′cive
con′duct, *n.*
con·duct′, *v.*
con·duct′ance
con·duc′tion
con·duc′tive
con′duc·tiv′i·ty
con·duc′tor
con′duit
Con′el·rad
co′ney
con·fec′tion
con·fec′tion·er′y
con·fed′er·a·cy
con·fed′er·ate
con·fed′er·a′tion
con·fer′
con′fer·ee′
con′fer·ence
con·ferred′
con·fer′ring
con·fessed′
con·fess′ed·ly
con·fes′sion
con·fes′sion·al
con·fes′sor

con·fet′ti
con′fi·dant′
con·fide′
con·fid′ed
con′fi·dence
con′fi·dent
con′fi·den′tial
con·fid′ing
con·fig′u·ra′tion
con·fine′, *v.*
con′fine, *n.*
con·fine′ment
con·fin′ing
con·firm′
con′fir·ma′tion
con·firm′a·to′ry
con·firmed′
con′fis·cate
con′fis·cat′ing
con′fis·ca′tion
con·fis′ca·to′ry
con′fla·gra′tion
con·flict′, *v.*
con′flict, *n.*
con·flic′tion
con′flu·ence
con·form′
con·form′ance
con′for·ma′tion
con·form′ist
con·form′i·ty
con·found′
con·front′
con′fron·ta′tion
Con·fu′cian·ism
Con·fu′cius
con·fuse′
con·fused′
con·fus′ing
con·fu′sion
con′fu·ta′tion
con·fute′
con′ga
con·geal′
con·gen′ial
con·ge′ni·al′i·ty
con·gen′i·tal
con·gest′
con·ges′tion
con·glom′er·ate
con·glom′er·a′tion
con·grat′u·late
con·grat′u·lat′ing
con·grat′u·la′tion
con·grat′u·la·to′ry
con′gre·gate
con′gre·ga′tion
con′gre·ga′tion·al
con′gress
con·gres′sion·al
con′gress·man
con′gru·ence
con′gru·ent
con·gru′i·ty
con′gru·ous
con′ic
con′i·cal·ly
co′ni·fer
co·nif′er·ous
con·jec′tur·al
con·jec′ture
con·join′
con′ju·gal
con′ju·gate
con′ju·ga′tion
con·junc′tion
con′junc·ti′va
con·junc′tive
con·junc′ti·vi′tis
con′ju·ra′tion
con′jure
con·nect′
Con·nect′i·cut
con·nec′tion
con·nec′tive
con′nec·tiv′i·ty
conn′ing (tower)
con·niv′ance
con·nive′
con′nois·seur′
con′no·ta′tion
con′no·ta′tive
con·note′
con·not′ing
con·nu′bi·al
con′quered
con′quer·ing
con′quer·or
con′quest
con·quis′ta·dor
con′san·guin′e·ous
con′san·guin′i·ty
con′science
con′sci·en′tious
con′scion·a·ble
con′scious
con·script′, *v.*
con′script, *n., adj.*
con·scrip′tion
con′se·crate
con′se·crat·ing

con′se·cra′tion
con·sec′u·tive
con·sen′sus
con·sent′
con′se·quence
con′se·quen′tial
con′se·quent′ly
con′ser·va′tion
con·serv′a·tism
con·serv′a·tive
con·serv′a·to′ry
conserve′, *v.*
con′serve, *n.*
con·serv′ing
con·sid′er
con·sid′er·a·ble
con·sid′er·ate
con·sid′er·a′tion
con·sign′
con′sign·ee′
con·sign′ment
con·sist′
con·sist′en·cy
con·sist′ent
con·sis′to·ry
con′so·la′tion
con·sol′a·to′ry
con·sole′, *v.*
con′sole, *n.*
con·sol′i·date
con·sol′i·dat·ing
con·sol′i·da′tion
con·sol′ing
con′som·me′
con′so·nant
con′sort, *n.*
con·sort′, *v.*
con·spic′u·ous
con·spir′a·cy
con·spir′a·tor
con·spir′a·to′ri·al
con·spire′
con·spir′ing
con′sta·ble
con·stab′u·lar′y
con′stan·cy
con′stant
Con′stan·ti·no′ple
con′stel·la′tion
con′ster·na′tion
con·sti·pate
con′sti·pa′tion
con·stit′u·en·cy
con·stit′u·ent
con′sti·tute
con′sti·tu′tion
con′sti·tu′tion·al
con′sti·tu′tion·al′
  i·ty
con·strained′
con·strain′ing
con·straint′
con·strict′
con·stric′tion
con·struct′
con·struc′tion
con·struc′tive·ly
con·strue′
con·strued′
con·stru′ing
con′sul
  diplomat (*see:* council; counsel)
con′su·lar
con′su·late
con·sult′
con·sult′ant
con′sul·ta′tion
con·sume′
con·sum′er
con·sum′ing
con′sum·mate, *v.*
con′sum·ma′tion
con·sump′tion
con·sump′tive
con′tact
con·ta′gion
con·ta′gious
con·tain′er
con·tain′ing
con·tain′ment
con·tam′i·nate
con·tam′i·nat·ing
con·tam′i·na′tion
con′tem·plate
con′tem·plat·ing
con′tem·pla′tion
con′tem·pla′tive
con·tem′po·ra′
  ne·ous
con·tem′po·ra′ry
con·tempt′
con·tempt′i·ble
con·temp′tu·ous
con·tend′
con′tent, *n.*
con·tent′, *v.*
con·ten′tion
con·ten′tious
con·tent′ment

con·ter′mi·nous
con′test, *n.*
con·test′, *v.*
con·test′ant
con′text
con·tex′tu·al
con′ti·gu′i·ty
con·tig′u·ous
con′ti·nence
con′ti·nent
con′ti·nen′tal
con·tin′gen·cy
con·tin′gent
con·tin′u·al·ly
con·tin′u·ance
contin′u·a′tion
con·tin′ue
con·tin′u·ing
con′ti·nu′i·ty
con·tin′u·ous
con·tin′u·um
con·tort′
con·tor′tion
con′tour
con′tra·band
con′tra·bass′
con′tra·cep′tion
con′tra·cep′tive
con·tract′, *v.*
con′tract, *n.*
con·trac′tile′
con·trac′tion
con·trac′tor
con·trac′tu·al
con′tra·dict′
con′tra·dic′tion
con′tra·dic′to·ry

con·tral′to
con·trap′tion
con′tra·pun′tal
con′tra·ri·ness
con′tra·ry
con′trast, *n.*
con·trast′, *v.*
con′tra·vene′
con′tra·ven′tion
con·trib′ute
con·trib′ut·ing
con′tri·bu′tion
con·trib′u·to′ry
con·trite′ly
con·tri′tion
con·triv′ance
con·trive′
con·triv′ing
con·trol′
con·trol′la·ble
con·trolled′
con·trol′ler
(*also:* comptroller)
con·trol′ling
con′tro·ver′sial
con′tro·ver′sy
con′tro·vert
con′tu·ma′cious
con′tu·ma·cy
con′tu·me·ly
con·tu′sion
co·nun′drum
con′va·lesce′
con′va·les′cence
con′va·les′cent
con′va·lesc′ing

con·vec′tion
con·vene′
con·ven′ience
con·ven′ient
con·ven′ing
con′vent
con·ven′tion
con·ven′tion·al
con·ven′tion·al′i·ty
con·verge′
con·ver′gence
con·verg′ing
con·ver′sant
con′ver·sa′tion
con′ver·sa′tion·al
con·verse′, *v.*
con′verse, *n.*
con·vers′ing
con·ver′sion
con·vert′, *v.*
con′vert, *n.*
con·vert′er
(*or:* -tor)
con·vert′i·ble
con′vex
con·vex′i·ty
con·vey′
con·vey′ance
con·vict′, *v.*
con′vict, *n.*
con·vic′tion
con·vince′
con·vinc′ing·ly
con·viv′i·al
con·viv′i·al′i·ty

con′vo·ca′tion
con·voke′
con·vok′ing
con′vo·lute
con′vo·lu′tion
con′voy
con·vulse′
con·vul′sion
coo′ing
cook′book′
cook′y
cool′er
cool′ie
Chinese laborer *(see:* coolly; coulee)

cool′ly
in cool manner *(see:* coolie; coulee)

co-op′
store, society

coop
cage

coop′er
co·op′er·ate
(or: co-operate)

co·op′era′tion
co·op′er·a·tive
co·or′di·nate
(or: co-ordinate)

co·or′di·na′tion
co·or′di·na′tor
Co′pen·ha′gen
Co·per′ni·cus
co′pi′lot
cop′ing
co′pi·ous
cop′per·plate′
cop′u·late
cop′u·la′tion
cop′y·hold′er
cop′y·ing
cop′y·right′
co·quet′, *v.*
co·quette′, *n.*
co·quet′tish
cor′al
cord
string *(see:* chord)

cord′age
cor·dial′i·ty
cor′dial·ly
cord′ite
cor′don
cor′do·van
cor′du·roy
co′re·spond′ent
legal *(see:* correspondent)

Co·rin′thi·an
cork′screw′
cor′mo·rant
cor′ne·a
cor′ne·al
cor′ner·stone′
cor·net′
corn′flow′er
cor′nice
corn′starch′
cor′nu·co′pi·a
Corn·wal′lis
cor′ol·lar′y
co·ro′na
cor′o·nar′y
cor′o·na′tion
cor′o·ner
cor′o·net
cor′po·ral
cor′po·rate
cor′po·ra′tion
cor·po′re·al
corps
military unit

corpse
dead body

cor′pu·lence
cor′pu·lent
cor′pus·cle
cor′pus de·lic′ti
cor·ral′
cor·rect′
cor·rec′tion
cor′re·late
cor′re·la′tion
cor·rel′a·tive
cor′re·spond′ence
cor′re·spond′ent
writer *(see:* corespondent)

cor′re·spond′ing
cor′ri·dor
cor′ri·gi·ble
cor·rob′o·rate
cor·rob′o·ra′tion
cor·rob′o·ra′tor
cor·rob′o·ra·to′ry

cor·rode′
cor·rod′ing
cor·ro′sion
cor·ro′sive
cor′ru·gate
cor′ru·ga′tion
cor·rupt′
cor·rupt′i·ble
cor·rup′tion
cor·sage′
cor′sair
cor′set
Cor′si·ca
cor·tege′
cor′tex
cor′ti·sone
co·run′dum
cor′us·cate
cor·vette′
co·se′cant
co′sine
cos·met′ic
cos′mic
cos·mog′o·ny
cos·mog′ra·phy
cos·mol′o·gy
cos′mo·pol′i·tan
cos·mop′o·lite
cos′mos
cost′li·ness
cost′ly
cos′tume
co·tan′gent
co′tan·gen′tial
co′te·rie
co·til′lion
cot′tage

cot′ton·seed′
cot′ton·tail
cot′ton·wood′
couch′ant
cou′gar
cou′lee
ravine *(see:* coolie; coolly)

coun′cil
assembly *(see:* counsel; consul)

coun′ci·lor
coun′sel
advice *(see:* council; consul)

coun′se·lor
coun′te·nance
coun′ter
coun′ter·act′
coun′ter·at·tack′
coun′ter·clock′wise′
coun′ter·es′pi·o·nage
coun′ter·feit
coun′ter·mand′
coun′ter·part′
coun′ter·point′
coun′ter·sign
count′ess
count′less
coun′try
(plural: -tries)

coun′try·side′
coun′ty

cou′plet
cou′pling
cou′pon
cour′age
cou·ra′geous
cour′i·er
course
direction *(see:* coarse)

cours′er
cour′te·ous
cour′te·san
cour′te·sy
court′house′
cour′ti·er
court′-mar′tial
court′room′
court′ship
cous′in
cou·tu′ri·er
cov′e·nant
Cov′en·try
cov′er·age
cov′ered
cov′er·let
cov′ert·ly
cov′et·ous
cov′ey
cow′ard·ice
cow′boy′
cow′catch′er
cow′er
cow′hide′
cow′lick′
cowl′ing
co-work′er

cow′pox′
cow′punch′er
cow′rie
cox′comb′
cox′swain
coy·o′te
co′zi·ly
crab′bing
crab′by
crack′down′
crack′er
crack′ing
crack′le
cra′dle
craft′i·ly
crafts′man
craft′y
crammed
cram′ming
cramped
cran′ber′ry
craned
cran′ing
cra′ni·ol′o·gy
cra′ni·um
crank′case′
crank′y
cran′nied
cran′ny
crap′pie
crashed
crass′ly
cra′ter
crat′ing
cra·vat′
craved
cra′ven
crav′ing
craw′fish′
crawl′ing
cray′on
crazed
cra′zi·ly
cra′zy
creak
creak′y
cream′er·y
creased
creas′ing
cre·ate′
cre·a′tion
cre·a′tive·ly
cre·a′tor
crea′ture
cre′dence
cre·den′tial
cred′i·bil′i·ty
cred′i·ble
cred′it
cred′it·a·ble
cred′i·tor
cre′do
cre·du′li·ty
cred′u·lous
creek
creep′ing
cre′mate
cre·ma′tion
cre′ma·to′ry
cren′el·ate
Cre′ole
cre′o·sote
crep′i·tate
cre·pus′cu·lar
cre·scen′do
cres′cent
crest′ed
crest′fall′en
cre·ta′ceous
cre′tin
cre·tonne′
cre·vasse′
crack in ice
crev′ice
narrow crack
crib′bage
crib′bing
crick′et
cried
cri′er
Cri·me′a
crim′i·nal
crim′i·nal′i·ty
crim′i·nal·ly
crim′i·nol′o·gist
crim′i·nol′o·gy
crim′son
cringed
cring′ing
crin′kle
crin′o·line
crip′pled
crip′pling
cri′sis
crisp′ly
criss′cross′
cri·te′ri·on
crit′ic
crit′i·cal
crit′i·cism

crit′i·cize
crit′i·ciz·ing
cri·tique′
cro·cheted′
cro·chet′ing
crock′er·y
croc′o·dile
croc′o·dil′i·an
cro′cus
Croe′sus
croix′ de guerre′
Cro-Mag′non
crook′ed
croon′er
crop′ping
cro·quet′
game

cro·quette′
ball of meat

cro′sier
cross′breed′
cross′cut
cross′-ex·am′i·na′
tion
cross′ ref′er·ence
cross′road′
cross′ sec′tion
crotch′et·y
cro′ton
tree or oil

crou′pi·er
crou′ton
toast

crow′bar′
crowd′ed
crow′ing
crowned
cru′cial
cru′ci·ble
cru′ci·fied
cru′ci·fix
cru′ci·fix′ion
cru′ci·form
cru′ci·fy
crude′ly
cru′di·ty
cru′el·ly
cru′el·ty
cru′et
cruised
cruis′er
cruis′ing
crul′ler
crum′ble
crum′pet
crum′ple
crum′pling
cru·sade′
cru·sad′ing
crus·ta′cean
cry′ing
cryp′tic
cryp′to·gram
cryp·tog′ra·phy
crys′tal
crys′tal·line
crys′tal·li·za′tion
crys′tal·lize
cubed
cu′bic
cu′bi·cal
cube-shaped

cu′bi·cle
compartment

cub′ism
cuck′old
cuck′oo
cu′cum·ber
cud′dled
cud′dling
cudg′el
cui·sine′
cul′-de-sac′
cu′li·nar′y
cul′mi·nate
cul′mi·na′tion
cul′pa·bil′i·ty
cul′pa·ble
cul′prit
cul′ti·pack′er
cul′ti·vate
cul′ti·va′tion
cul′tur·al
cul′tured
cul′vert
cum′ber·some
cum′brous
cum lau′de
cu′mu·late
cu′mu·la′tion
cu′mu·la′tive
cu′mu·lus
cu·ne′i·form
cun′ning·ly
cup′board
cup′ful
cu·pid′i·ty
cu′po·la

cup′ping
cur′a·bil′i·ty
cur′a·ble
cu·ra′re
cu′rate
cur′a·tive
cu·ra′tor
curb′stone′
cur′dle
cur′dling
cure′-all′
cur′few
cur′ing
cu′ri·o
cu′ri·os′i·ty
cu′ri·ous
cu′ri·um
cur′lew
curl′i·cue
curl′ing
curl′y
cur′rant
berry

cur′ren·cy
cur′rent
flow

cur·ric′u·lar
cur·ric′u·lum
(plural: -lums; -la)

cur′ried
cur′ry·comb′
cur′ry·ing
cursed
curs′ing
cur′sive
cur′so·ry
cur·tail′
cur′tain
curt′ly
curt′sy
cur·va′ceous
cur′va·ture
curved
cur′vi·lin′e·ar
curv′ing
cush′ion
cus′pid
cus′pi·dor
cus′tard
cus·to′di·al
cus·to′di·an
cus′to·dy
cus′tom
cus′tom·ar′y
cus′tom·er
cus′tom·house′
cus′tom-made′
cu·ta′ne·ous
cut′a·way′
cu′ti·cle
cut′lass
cut′ler·y
cut′let
cut rate
cut′throat′
cut′ting
cut′tle·fish′
cy·an′ic
cy′a·nide
cy·an′o·gen
cy′a·no′sis
cy′a·not′ic
cy′ber·net′ics
cyc′la·men
cy′cle
cy′clic
cy′cli·cal
cy′cling
cy′clist
cy·clom′e·ter
cy′clone
cy′clo·pe′di·a
cy′clo·ram′a
cy′clo·tron
cyg′net
young swan *(see:* signet)

cyl′in·der
cy·lin′dri·cal
cym′bal
brass plate *(see:* symbol)

cyn′ic
cyn′i·cal·ly
cyn′i·cism
cy′no·sure
cy′press
cyst′ic
cy·tol′o·gy
cy′to·plasm
czar′ism
Czech′o·slo·va′ki·a

D

dab′bing
dab′ble
dab′bling
dachs′hund′
Da′cron
dac′tyl
dad′dy
da′do
daf′fo·dil
dag′ger
da·guerre′o·type
dahl′ia
dai′ly
dain′ti·ly
dain′ty
dai′qui·ri
dair′y
da′is
Dal′las
dal′li·ance
dal′lied
dal′ly
Dal·ma′tian
dam′age
dam′ag·ing·ly
dam′a·scene
Da·mas′cus
dam′ask
dammed
blocked *(see:* damned)

dam′ming
dam′na·ble
dam·na′tion
damned
condemned *(see:* dammed)

damn′ing
Dam′o·cles
damp′en
dam′sel
danced
danc′er
danc′ing
dan′de·li′on
dan′di·fied
dan′dle
dan′druff
dan′dy
dan′ger·ous
dan′gle
dan′gled
dan′gling
Dan′ish
dank′ness
dan·seuse′
Dan′te
Dan′ube
dap′per
Dar′da·nelles′
dare′dev′il
dar′ing
dark horse
dark′room′
dar′ling
Dar′win
dash′board′
dashed
dash′ing
das′tard·ly
data
(sing.: datum)

dat′ed
date′less
da′tive
da′tum, *sing.*
daugh′ter
daugh′ter-in-law′
daunt′less
dau′phin
dav′en·port
dav′it
daw′dle
daw′dling
day′break′
day coach
day′dream′
day′light′
day′time′
dazed
daz′ed·ly
daz′ing
daz′zle
daz′zling·ly
dea′con
dea′con·ess
dead′li·er
dead′line′
dead′ly
dead′wood′
deaf′en·ing·ly
deaf′-mute′

deaf′ness
deal′ing
dearth
death′bed′
death′ly
death′ rate
death′watch′
de•ba′cle
de′bar•ka′tion
de•bar′ment
de•bar′ring
de•based
de•bas′ing
de•bat′a•ble
de•bate′
de•bat′ing
de•bauch′
de•bauch′er•y
de•ben′ture
de•bil′i•tate
de•bil′i•ta′tion
de•bil′i•ty
deb′it
deb′o•nair′
de•bris′
debt′or
De•bus′sy
de′but
deb′u•tante
dec′ade
de•ca′dence
de•ca′dent
dec′a•gon
dec′a•he′dron
de•cal′co•ma′ni•a
Dec′a•logue
dec′a•me′ter
de•camp′ment
de′can•ta′tion
de•cant′er
de•cap′i•tate
de•cap′i•ta′tion
de•cath′lon
de•cayed′
de•cay′ing
de•ceased′
de•ce′dent
de•ceit′ful
de•ceive′
de•ceiv′ing•ly
de•cel′er•ate
de•cel′er•a′tion
De•cem′ber
de′cen•cy
de•cen′ni•al
de′cent•ly
de•cen′tral•ize
de•cep′tion
de•cep′tive
dec′i•bel
de•cide′
de•cid′ed•ly
de•cid′u•ous
dec′i•mal
dec′i•mate
dec′i•ma′tion
de•ci′pher
de•ci′pher•a•ble
de•ci′sion
de•ci′sive
de•claim′
dec′la•ma′tion
de•clam′a•to′ry
dec′la•ra′tion
de•clar′a•tive
de•clar′a•to′ry
de•clare′
de•clas′si•fy
de•clen′sion
dec′li•na′tion
de•clined′
de•clin′ing
de•cliv′i•ty
de•coc′tion
de•code′
de•cod′ing
de′colle•te′
de′com•pose′
de′com•po•si′tion
de′con•tam′i•nate
de′con•tam′i•na′tion
de•cor′
dec′o•rate
dec′o•ra′tion
de•co′rum
de•coyed′
de•coy′ing
de•crease′, *v.*
de•creed′
de•cree′ing
de•crep′it
de•crep′i•tude
de′cre•scen′do
de•cried′
de•cry′
de•cum′bent
ded′i•cate
ded′i•ca′tion
ded′i•ca•to′ry
de•duced′

de·duc′i·ble
de·duc′ing
de·duct′i·ble
de·duc′tion
de·duc′tive·ly
deep′-seat′ed
deer′skin′
de·faced′
de·fac′ing
de fac′to
de·fal′cate
de′fal·ca′tion
def′a·ma′tion
de·fam′a·to′ry
de·famed′
de·fault′
de·feat′ed
de·feat′ist
def′e·cate
def′e·ca′tion
de·fect′ed
de·fec′tion
de·fend′
de·fend′ant
de·fend′er
de·fense′less
de·fen′si·bil′i·ty
de·fen′si·ble
de·fen′sive
def′er·ence
def′er·en′tial
respectful *(see: differential)*
de·ferred′
de·fer′ring
de·fi′ance
de·fi′ant·ly
de·fi′cien·cy
de·fi′cient
def′i·cit
de·fied′
de·filed′
de·file′ment
de·fil′ing
de·fin′a·ble
de·fined′
de·fin′ing
def′i·nite·ly
def′i·ni′tion
de·fin′i·tive
de·flat′ed
de·fla′tion
de·fla′tion·ar′y
de·flect′ed
de·flec′tion
de·for′est·a′tion
de′for·ma′tion
de·formed′
de·form′i·ty
de·fraud′ed
de·frayed′
de·fray′ing
de·frost′er
de·funct′
de·fy′ing
de·gen′er·a·cy
de·gen′er·ate
de·gen′er·a′tion
deg′ra·da′tion
de·grad′ed
de·grad′ing
de·gree′
de·hy′drate
de′hy·dra′tion
de·ic′er
de′i·fi·ca′tion
de′i·fied
de′i·fy
deign
de′i·ty
de·ject′ed
de·jec′tion
Del′a·ware
de·layed′
de·lay′ing
de·lec′ta·ble
de′lec·ta′tion
del′e·gate
del′e·ga′tion
de·let′ed
del′e·te′ri·ous
de·le′tion
Del′hi
de·lib′er·ate
de·lib′er·a′tion
de·lib′er·a′tive
del′i·ca·cy
del′i·cate·ly
del′i·ca·tes′sen
de·li′cious
de·light′ed
de·light′ful
de·lim′i·ta′tion
de·lin′e·ate
de·lin′e·a′tion
de·lin′quen·cy
de·lin′quent
del′i·quesce′
del′i·ques′cence
de·lir′i·ous

de·lir′i·um
de·liv′er·ance
de·liv′er·y
Del′phic
del·phin′i·um
de·lud′ed
de·lud′ing
del′uged
de·lu′sion
de·lu′so·ry
de luxe′
delved
delv′ing
de·mag′net·ize
dem'a·gog′ic
dem′a·gogue
dem′a·gogu'er·y
dem′a·go'gy
de·mand′ed
de'mar·ca′tion
de·mean′
de·mean′or
de·ment′ed
de·men′tia
de·mer′it
de·mesne′
dem′i·god'
dem′i·john
de·mil'i·ta·ri·za′tion
de·mil′i·tar·ize
dem′i·monde
de·mise′
dem′i·tasse'
de·mo'bi·li·za′tion
de·mo′bil·ize
de·moc′ra·cy
dem′o·crat
dem'o·crat′ic
de·mol′ish
dem'o·li′tion
de′mon
de·mon'e·ti·za′tion
de·mon′e·tize
de·mo′ni·ac
de·mon′ic
de·mon′stra·ble
dem′on·strate
dem′on·strat·ing
dem'on·stra′tion
de·mon′stra·tive
de·mor′al·ize
de·mor′al·iz·ing
De·mos′the·nes
de·mot′ed
de·mo′tion
de·mul′cent
de·mur′, *v.* object
de·mure′ coy
de·mur′rage
de·murred′
de·mur′ring
de·na′tion·al·ize
de·nat′u·ral·ize
de·na′tured
de·ni′al
de·nied′
den′im
den′i·zen
Den′mark
de·nom'i·na′tion
de·nom′i·na'tor
de'no·ta′tion
de·note′
de·not′ing
de'noue·ment′
de·nounced′
de·nounc′ing
dense′ly
den′si·ty
den′tal
den′ti·frice
den′tist
den′tist·ry
den·ti′tion
den′ture
de·nude′
de·nun'ci·a′tion
de·nun′ci·a·to'ry
Den′ver
de·ny′ing
de·o′dor·ant
de·o′dor·ize
de·part′ed
de·part′ment
de'part·men′tal
de·par′ture
de·pend'a·bil′i·ty
de·pend′a·ble
de·pend′ence
de·pend′en·cy
de·pend′ent
de·pict′
de·pic′tion
de·pil′a·to'ry
de·plet′ed
de·ple′tion

de·plor'a·ble
de·plored'
de·plor'ing
de·ploy'ment
de·pop'u·late
de·port'ed
de'por·ta'tion
de·port'ment
de·posed'
de·pos'ing
de·pos'it
de·pos'i·tar'y
trustee

dep'o·si'tion
de·pos'i·tor
de·pos'i·tor'y
storehouse

dep'ra·va'tion
de·praved'
de·prav'i·ty
dep're·cate
dep're·cat'ing
dep're·ca'tion
dep're·ca·to'ry
de·pre'ci·ate
de·pre'ci·a'tion
dep're·da'tion
de·pres'sant
de·pressed'
de·press'ing
de·pres'sion
dep'ri·va'tion
de·prived'
de·priv'ing
depth
dep'u·ta'tion
de·pute'
dep'u·tize
dep'u·ty
de·rail'ment
de·range'ment
de·rang'ing
der'e·lict
der'e·lic'tion
de·rid'ing
de ri·gueur'
de·ri'sion
de·ri'sive
der'i·va'tion
de·riv'a·tive
de·rived'
de·riv'ing
der'ma·tol'o·gist
der'ma·tol'o·gy
der'o·ga'tion
de·rog'a·to'ri·ly
de·rog'a·to'ry
der'rick
der'rin·ger
der'vish
des'cant
de·scend'ant
de·scend'ed
de·scent'
de·scribed'
de·scrip'tion
de·scrip'tive
de·scry'ing
des'e·crate
des'e·cra'tion
de·seg're·ga'tion
de·sen'si·tize
des'ert, *n.*
arid land

de·sert', *v.*
abandon *(see:* des-sert)

de·sert'er
de·ser'tion
de·served'
de·serv'ed·ly
de·serv'ing
des'ic·cate
des'ic·ca'tion
de·sign'
des'ig·nate
des'ig·na'tion
de·sign'er
de·sign'ing
de·sir'a·ble
de·sir'ous
de·sist'
des'o·late
des'o·la'tion
de·spaired'
de·spair'ing
des'per·a'do
des'per·ate
des'per·a'tion
des'pi·ca·ble
de·spised'
de·spis'ing
de·spite'
de·spoil'ing
de·spond'en·cy
de·spond'ent
des'pot
des·pot'ic

des·sert′
last course *(see:* des-ert)

des′ti·na′tion
des′tine
des′ti·ny
des′ti·tute
des′ti·tu′tion
de·stroyed′
de·stroy′er
de·struct′i·ble
de·struc′tion
de·struc′tive
des′ue·tude
des′ul·to′ry
de·tached′
de·tach′ment
de·tail′
de·tain′
de·tect′
de·tec′tion
de·tec′tive
de·ten′tion
de·ter′
de·ter′gent
de·te′ri·o·rate
de·te′ri·o·ra′tion
de·ter′mi·na·ble
de·ter′mi·nant
de·ter′mi·nate
de·ter′mi·na′tion
de·ter′mine
de·ter′min·ism
de·terred′
de·ter′rent
de·ter′ring
de·test′a·ble
de′tes·ta′tion
de·throne′
det′o·nate
det′o·na′tion
de′tour
de·tract′
de·trac′tion
det′ri·ment
det′ri·men′tal
De·troit′
deu·te′ri·um
deu′ter·on
Deu′ter·on′o·my
de·val′u·ate
de·val′u·a′tion
dev′as·tate
dev′as·tat′ing
dev′as·ta′tion
de·vel′op(e)
de·vel′op·ment
de·vel′op·men′tal
de′vi·ate
de′vi·a′tion
de·vice′, *n.*
dev′il·ish
de′vi·ous
de·vis′a·ble
de·vise′, *v.*
de·vis′ee
de·vi′tal·ize
de·void′
de·volve′ment
de·vot′ed
dev′o·tee′
de·vo′tion
de·vo′tion·al
de·vour′
de·vout′
Dew′ey
dew′y
dex·ter′i·ty
dex′ter·ous
dex′tral
dex′trin
dex′trose
dex′trous
di′a·be′tes
di′a·bet′ic
di′a·bol′ic
di′a·crit′i·cal
di′a·dem
di′ag·nose′
di′ag·no′sis
di′ag·nos′tic
di′ag·nos·ti′cian
di·ag′o·nal
di′a·gram
di′a·gram·mat′ic
di′a·lect
di′a·lec′tic
di′al·ing
di′a·logue
di·al′y·sis
di′a·lyt′ic
di·am′e·ter
di′a·met′ric
dia′mond
di′a·net′ics
di′a·per
di·aph′a·nous
di′a·phragm
di′ar·rhe′a
di′a·ry

di′a•stase
di′a•stat′ic
di•as′to•le
di′as•tol′ic
di′a•ther′mic
di′a•ther′my
di′a•ton′ic
di′a•tribe
di•chot′o•mous
di•chot′o•my
di′chro•mat′ic
dick′er
dick′ey
dic′tate
dic′tat•ing
dic•ta′tion
dic′ta•tor
dic′ta•to′ri•al
dic′tion
dic′tion•ar′y
dic′tum
(*plural:* -tums; -ta)
di•dac′tic
di•dac′ti•cism
died
perished (*see:* dyed)
di′e•lec′tric
Die′sel
di′e•tar′y
di′e•tet′ic
di′e•ti′tian
dif′fer•ence
dif′fer•ent
dif′fer•en′tial
distinctive (*see:* def-erential)
dif′fer•en′ti•ate
dif′fi•cult
dif′fi•cul′ty
dif′fi•dence
dif′fi•dent
dif•frac′tion
dif•fuse′
dif•fu′sion
dif•fu′sive
di•gest′, *v.*
di′gest, *n.*
di•gest′i•ble
di•ges′tion
dig′ging
dig′it•al
dig′i•tal′is
dig′ni•fied
dig′ni•fy
dig′ni•fy•ing
dig′ni•tar′y
dig′ni•ty
di•gress′
di•gres′sion
di•he′dral
di•lap′i•dat′ed
di•lap′i•da′tion
dil′a•ta′tion
di•late′
di•lat′ing
di•la′tion
dil′a•to′ry
di•lem′ma
dil′et•tan′te
dil′i•gence
dil′i•gent
di•lut′ing
di•lu′tion
di•lu′vi•al
di•men′sion
di•min′ish
di•min′eu•en′do
dim′i•nu′tion
di•min′u•tive
dim′i•ty
dim′ming
dim′ness
dim′ple
dined
din′er
di•nette′
din′ghy
boat
din′gi•ly
din′gy
dull or dirty
din′ing
din′ner
di′no•saur
di•oc′e•san
di′o•cese
Di•og′e•nes
di′o•ram′a
di•ox′ide
diph•the′ri•a
diph′thong
di•plo′ma
di•plo′ma•cy
dip′lo•mat
dip′lo•mat′ic
dip′lo•mat′i•cal•ly
dipped
dip′per
dip′so•ma′ni•a

dip′ter·ous
di·rect′
di·rec′tion
di·rec′tor
di·rec′tor·ate
di·rec′to·ry
dire′ly
dirge
dir′i·gi·ble
dirn′dl
dirt′i·er
dirt′y
dis′a·bil′i·ty
dis·a′bled
dis·a′bling
dis′a·buse′
dis·ad′van′tage
dis·ad′van·ta′geous
dis′af·fect′ed
dis′a·gree′a·ble
dis′a·gree′ment
dis′al·low′ance
dis′ap·pear′ance
dis′ap·point′ment
dis′ap·prov′al
dis′ap·prove′
dis′ap·prov′ing
dis·arm′
dis·ar′ma·ment
dis′ar·range′
dis′ar·ray′
dis·as′ter
dis·as′trous
dis′a·vow′
dis·band′
dis·bar′
dis·bar′ment
dis·bar′ring
dis′be·lief′
dis′be·lieve′
dis·burse′
dis·burse′ment
disc
(*also:* disk)

dis·card′, *v.*
dis·cern′
dis·cern′i·ble
dis·cern′ing
dis·charge′
dis·ci′ple
dis′ci·pli·nar′y
dis′ci·pline
dis·claim′
dis·claim′er
dis·close′
dis·clo′sure
dis′coid
dis·col′or
dis′col·or·a′tion
dis·com′fi·ture
dis·com′fort
dis′com·mode′
dis′con·cert′
dis′con·nect′
dis·con′so·late
dis′con·tent′
dis′con·tin′u·a′tion
dis′con·tin′ue
dis′cord
dis·cord′ant
dis′count
dis·coun′te·nance
dis·cour′age
dis·cour′age·ment
dis·cour′ag·ing
dis·course′
dis·cour′te·ous
dis·cour′te·sy
dis·cov′er
dis·cov′er·y
dis·cred′it
dis·cred′it·a·ble
dis·creet′
prudent (*see:* discrete)

dis·crep′an·cy
dis·crete′
separate (*see:* discreet)

dis·cre′tion
dis·cre′tion·ar′y
dis·crim′i·nate
dis·crim′i·nat′ing
dis·crim′i·na′tion
dis·crim′i·na·to′ry
dis·cur′sive
dis′cus
athletic device

dis·cuss′
talk

dis·cus′sion
dis·dain′
dis·ease′
dis·eased′
dis′em·bark′
dis′em·bar·ka′tion
dis′em·bod′i·ment

dis'em·bod'y
dis'en·chant'
dis'en·gage'
dis·fa'vor
dis·fig'ure
dis·fig'ur·ing
dis·fran'chise
dis·gorge'
dis·grace'
dis·grace'ful
dis·grun'tled
dis·guise'
dis·gust'
dis·gust'ing·ly
dis'ha·bille'
dis·har'mo·ny
dish'cloth'
dis·heart'en
di·shev'eled
dis·hon'est
dis·hon'es·ty
dis·hon'or·a·ble
dish'pan'
dish tow'el
dis'il·lu'sion
dis·in'cli·na'tion
dis'in·fect'
dis'in·fect'ant
dis'in·fec'tion
dis'in·her'it
dis·in'te·grate
dis·in·te·gra'tion
dis'in·ter'
dis·in'ter·est·ed
dis·joint'ed
dis·junc'tion
disk
(*also:* disc)
dis·like'
dis'lo·cate
dis'lo·ca'tion
dis·lodge'
dis·loy'al
dis·loy'al·ty
dis'mal
dis·man'tle
dis·may'
dis·mem'ber
dis·miss'
dis·miss'al
dis·mount'
dis'o·be'di·ence
dis'o·be'di·ent
dis'o·bey'
dis'o·beyed'
dis·or'dered
dis·or'der·li·ness
dis·or'der·ly
dis·or'gan·i·za'
tion
dis·or'gan·ize
dis·own'
dis·par'age
dis·par'ag·ing·ly
dis'pa·rate
dis·par'i·ty
dis·pas'sion·ate
dis·patch'
dis·pel'
dis·pelled'
dis·pel'ling
dis·pen'sa·bil'i·ty
dis·pen'sa·ble
dis·pen'sa·ry
dis·pen·sa'tion
dis·pen'sa·to'ry
dis·pense'
dis·per'sal
dis·perse'
dis·per'sion
dis·pir'it·ed
dis·place'ment
dis·play'
dis·please'
dis·pleas'ing
dis·pleas'ure
dis·port'
dis·pos'a·ble
dis·pos'al
dis·pose'
dis'po·si'tion
dis'pos·sess'
dis'pro·por'tion
dis·prove'
dis·put'a·bil'i·ty
dis·put'a·ble
dis'pu·tant
dis'pu·ta'tion
dis·pute'
dis'qual·i·fi·ca'
tion
dis·qual'i·fied
dis·qual'i·fy
Dis·rae'li
dis're·gard'
dis·rep'u·ta·ble
dis're·pute'
dis're·spect'
dis·robe'

dis·rupt′
dis·rup′tion
dis′sat·is·fac′tion
dis·sat′is·fied
dis·sect′
dis·sec′tion
dis·sem′ble
dis·sem′i·nate
dis·sem′i·na′tion
dis·sen′sion
dis·sent′
dis′ser·ta′tion
dis·serv′ice
dis′si·dence
dis′si·dent
dis·sim′i·lar
dis·sim′i·lar′i·ty
dis′si·mil′i·tude
dis·sim′u·late
dis·sim′u·la′tion
dis′si·pate
dis′si·pat′ed
dis′si·pa′tion
dis·so′ci·ate
dis·so′ci·a′tion
dis·sol′u·bil′i·ty
dis·sol′u·ble
dis′so·lute
dis′so·lu′tion
dis·solve′
dis·solv′ing
dis′so·nance
dis′so·nant
dis·suade′
dis·sua′sion
dis′taff
dis′tance
dis′tant
dis·taste′ful
dis·tem′per
dis·tend′
dis·ten′si·ble
dis·ten′tion
dis·till′
dis′til·late
dis′til·la′tion
dis·till′er
dis·till′er·y
dis·tinct′
dis·tinc′tion
dis·tinc′tive
dis′tin·gue′
dis·tin′guish
dis·tin′guish·a·ble
dis·tin′guished
dis·tort′
dis·tor′tion
dis·tract′
dis·trac′tion
dis·traught′
dis·tress′ing
dis·trib′ute
dis′tri·bu′tion
dis·trib′u·tive
dis·trib′u·tor
dis′trict
dis·trust′
dis·turb′
dis·turb′ance
di·sul′fide
dis·un′ion
dis′u·nite′
dis·use′
dith′er
dith′y·ram′bic
dit′to
dit′ty
di′u·ret′ic
di·ur′nal
di′va
di·va′lent
di′van
div′er
di·verge′
di·ver′gence
di·ver′gent·ly
di′verse
di·ver′si·fi·ca′tion
di·ver′si·fy
di·ver′sion
di·ver′si·ty
di·vert′
di·ver·tisse·ment′
di·vest′
di·vide′
div′i·dend
di·vid′er
div′i·na′tion
di·vin′a·to′ry
di·vine′
di·vin′er
div′ing
di·vin′i·ty
di·vis′i·bil′i·ty
di·vi′sion
di·vi′sor
di·vorce′
di·vor′cee′
div′ot
di·vulge′
di·vulg′ing

Dix′ie
diz′zi·ness
diz′zy
doc′ile
do·cil′i·ty
dock′et
dock′mas′ter
dock′yard′
doc′tor
doc′tor·ate
doc′tri·naire′
doc′trine
doc′u·ment
doc′u·men′ta·ry
doc′u·men·ta′tion
dod′der
dodg′ing
dog′catch′er
dog′-eared′
dog′ged
dog′ger·el
dog′gy
dog′house′
do′gie
dog′ma
dog·mat′ic
dog′ma·tism
dog′trot′
doi′ly
dol′drum
dole′ful
dole′ful·ly
dol′ing
dol′lar
dol′man
dol′o·mite
dol′or·ous
dol′phin
dolt′ish
do·main′
do·mes′tic
do·mes′ti·cate
do·mes′ti·ca′tion
do′mes·tic′i·ty
dom′i·cile
dom′i·nance
dom′i·nant
dom′i·nate
dom′i·na′tion
dom′i·neer′
dom′i·neer′ing
Do·min′i·can
dom′i·nie
do·min′ion
dom′i·no
do′nate
do′nat·ing
do·na′tion
don′key
don′na
do′nor
Don Qui·xo′te
doo′dle
doo′dling
dooms′day′
door′bell′
door′man′
door′way′
doped
dop′ing
Dor′ic
dor′man·cy
dor′mant
dor′mer
dor′mi·to′ry
dor′mouse′
dor′sal
do′ry
dos′age
dosed
dos′ing
dos′si·er
Dos′to·ev′ski
dot′age
do′tard
dot′ed
fond of
dot′ing
dot′ted
to dot
dou′ble
dou′ble-cross′
dou·ble-en·ten′dre
dou′ble-head′er
dou′blet
dou′bling
dou·bloon′
dou′bly
doubt′ful
doubt′less
douche
douch′ing
dough′nut′
dough′ty
dough′y
doused
dous′ing
dove′cote′
dove′tail′
dow′a·ger

dow′di•ness
dow′dy
dow′el
dow′er
down′cast′
down′fall′
down′heart′ed
down′pour′
down′right′
down′stairs′
down′ward
down′y
dow′ry
dox′o•log′i•cal
dox•ol′o•gy
doz′en
doz′ing
drab′ness
drach′ma
draft
(*also:* draught)

draft•ee′
drafts′man
draft′y
dragged
drag′ging
drag′net′
drag′o•man
drag′on•fly
dra•goon′
drain′age
drain′pipe′
dra′ma
dra•mat′ic
dra•mat′i•cal•ly
dram′a•ti•za′tion
dram′a•tize
dram′a•tur′gy
dram′shop′
dra′per•y
drap′ing
dras′tic
dras′ti•cal•ly
draught
(*also:* draft)

draw′back′
draw′ing
drawl′ing
dray′age
dread′ful
dread′nought′
dream′ing
dream′y
drear′i•ly
drear′y
dredg′ing
dress′er
dress′ing room
dress′mak′er
dress′y
drib′ble
drib′bled
drib′let
dri′er
(*also:* dryer)

drift′wood′
drill′mas′ter
drink′a•ble
dripped
drip′ping
driv′el
driv′en
driv′er
drive′way′
driv′ing
driz′zle
driz′zly
drom′e•dar′y
dron′ing
droop′ing
droop′y
drop′let
dropped
drop′ping
drop′sy
drosh′ky
drought
(*or:* drouth)

dro′ver
drowned
drow′si•ness
drow′sy
drub′bing
drudge
drudg′er•y
drudg′ing
drugged
drug′gist
drug′store′
drummed
drum′mer
drum′ming
drum′stick′
drunk′ard
drunk′en
dry′ing
dry′ly

du′al
double *(see:* duel)

du′al·ly
dub′bing
du·bi′e·ty
du·bi·ous
du′cal
duc′at
duch′ess
duch′y
duck′ling
duc′tile
duct′less
dudg′eon
du′el
fight *(see:* dual)

du′el·ist
du·en′na
duf′fel
duff′er
dug′out′
duke′dom
dul′cet
dul′ci·mer
dull′ard
dull′ness
dul′ly
dull

du′ly
as due

dumb′bell′
dumb′wait′er
dum′found′
dum′my
dump′i·ness
dump′ling
dump′y
dunce
dun′ga·ree′
dun′geon
dung′hill′
Dun′kirk
dunned
dun′ning
du′o·dec′i·mal
du′o·de′nal
du′o·de′num
duped
dup′ing
du′plex
du′pli·cate
du′pli·ca′tion
du′pli·ca′tor
du·plic′i·ty
du′ra·bil′i·ty
du′ra·ble
du′rance
du·ra′tion
du·ress′
dur′ing
dusk′i·ness
dusk′y
dust′ bowl
dust′er
dust′i·ly
dust′pan′
dust′y
Dutch′man
du′te·ous
du′ti·a·ble
du′ti·ful
du′ty
Dvo′rak
dwarf′ish
dwell′ing
dwin′dle
dwelt
dyed
colored *(see:* died)

dye′ing
dye′stuff′
dy′ing
about to die

dyke
(also: dike)

dy·nam′ic
dy·nam′ics
dy′na·mite
dy′na·mit·ed
dy′na·mo
dy′na·mom′e·ter
dy′na·mo′tor
dy′nas·ty
Dy·nel′
dys′en·ter′ic
dys′en·ter′y
dys·pep′si·a
dys·pep′tic
dys·pro′si·um

E

ea′ger·ly
ea′gle
ea′glet
ear′ache′
ear′drum′
earl′dom
ear′li·er
ear′ly
ear′mark′
ear′muffs′
ear′nest
earn′ing
ear′phone′
ear′ring′
ear′shot′
earth′en
earth′en·ware′
earth′i·er
earth′i·ness
earth′li·ness
earth′ly
earth′quake′
earth′ward
earth′y
eased
ea′sel
ease′ment
eas′i·ly
eas′i·ness
eas′ing
East′er
east′er·ly
east′ern·er
East′er·tide′
east′ward
eas′y
eas′y·go′ing
eat′a·ble
eat′en
eat′ing
eaves
eaves′drop′ping
eb′on
eb′on·ite
eb′on·y
e·bul′lience
e·bul′lient
eb′ul·li′tion
ec′ce ho′mo
ec·cen′tric
ec·cen′tri·cal·ly
ec′cen·tric′i·ty
Ec·cle′si·as′tes
ec·cle′si·as′tic
ec·cle′si·as′ti·cal
ech′e·lon
ech′o
ech′oed
ech′o·ing
e·clair′
e·clat′
ec·lec′tic
ec·lec′ti·cism
e·clipse′
e·clips′ing
e·clip′tic
ec′logue
ec′o·log′i·cal
e·col′o·gist
e·col′o·gy
e′co·nom′ic
e′co·nom′i·cal
e·con′o·mist
e·con′o·mize
e·con′o·miz·ing
e·con′o·my
ec′ru
ec′sta·sy
ec·stat′ic
ec′to·derm
ec′to·der′mal
ec′to·plasm
ec′to·plas′mic
Ec′ua·dor
Ec′ua·do′re·an
ec′u·men′i·cal
ec′ze·ma
E′dam
ed′dies
ed′dy
e′del·weiss
e·de′ma
E′den
e·den′tate
edge′wise′
edg′ing
edg′y
ed′i·bil′i·ty
ed′i·ble
e′dict
ed′i·fi·ca′tion
ed′i·fice
ed′i·fied
ed′i·fy
ed′i·fy·ing

Ed'in·burgh'
ed'it
e·di'tion
ed'i·tor
ed'i·to'ri·al
ed'i·to'ri·al·ize
ed'u·ca·ble
ed'u·cate
ed'u·cat·ing
ed'u·ca'tion
ed'u·ca'tion·al·ly
ed'u·ca'tive
e·duce'
e·duc'i·ble
e·duc'tion
eel'grass'
ee'rie
ee'ri·ness
ef·face'
ef·face'a·ble
ef·fac'ing
ef·fect'
result *(see:* affect)

ef·fec'tive
ef·fec'tu·al
ef·fec'tu·al'i·ty
ef·fec'tu·ate
ef·fec'tu·a'tion
ef·fem'i·na·cy
ef·fem'i·nate
ef'fer·ent
ef'fer·vesce'
ef'fer·ves'cence
ef'fer·ves'cent
ef'fer·vesc'ing
ef·fete'
ef'fi·ca'cious
ef'fi·ca·cy
ef·fi'cien·cy
ef·fi'cient
ef·fi'gi·al
ef'fi·gy
ef'flo·resce'
ef'flo·res'cence
ef'flo·res'cent
ef'flu·ent
flowing *(see:* affluent)

ef·flu'vi·um
ef'fort
ef·fron'ter·y
ef·ful'gence
ef·ful'gent
ef·fuse'
ef·fu'sion
ef·fu'sive·ly
egg'head'
egg'nog'
egg'shell
e'gis
eg'lan·tine
e'go·ism
e'go·ist
e'go·is'tic
e'go·tism
e'go·tist
e'go·tis'tic
e'go·tis'ti·cal·ly
e·gre'gious
e'gress
e'gret
E'gypt
E·gyp'tian
E'gyp·tol'o·gist
E'gyp·tol'o·gy
ei'der
Eif'fel
eight'een
eight'fold'
eight'i·eth
eight'y
Ein'stein
Ei'sen·how'er
ei'ther
e·jac'u·late
e·jac'u·lat·ing
e·jac'u·la'tion
e·jac'u·la'tive
e·jac'u·la·to'ry
e·ject'
e·jec'tion
e·jec'tor
eked
ek'ing
e·lab'o·rate
e·lab'o·rat·ing
e·lab'o·ra'tion
e·lan'
e'land
e·lapse'
e·laps'ing
e·las'tic
e·las'ti·cal·ly
e·las'tic'i·ty
e·late'
e·lat'ed
e·la'tion
El'ba
island

El′be
river

el′bow
el′der·ber′ry
eld′er·ly
eld′est
El′do·ra′do
e·lect′
e·lec′tion
e·lec′tion·eer′
e·lec′tive
e·lec′tor·ate
E·lec′tra
e·lec′tric
e·lec′tri·cal·ly
e·lec′tri′cian
e·lec′tric′i·ty
e·lec′tri·fi·ca′tion
e·lec′tri·fied
e·lec′tri·fy
e·lec′tro·cute
e·lec′tro·cu′tion
e·lec′trode
e·lec′tro·dy·nam′ics
e·lec′trol′y·sis
e·lec′tro·lyte
e·lec′tro·lyt′i·cal
e·lec′tro·ly·za′tion
e·lec′tro·lyze
e·lec′tro·mag′net
e·lec′tro·mag·net′ic
e·lec′tro·mag′net·ism
e·lec′trom′e·ter
e·lec′tron
e·lec′tron′ic
e·lec′troph′o·rus
e·lec′tro·plate′
e·lec′tro·scope
e·lec′tro·scop′ic
e·lec′tro·stat′ics
e·lec′tro·ther′a·py
e·lec′tro·type
e·lec′trum
el′ee·mos′y·nar′y
el′e·gance
el′e·gant
el′e·gi′ac
el′e·gize
el′e·gy
el′e·ment
el′e·men′tal
el′e·men′ta·ri·ly
el′e·men′ta·ry
el′e·phant
el′e·phan·ti′a·sis
el′e·phan′tine
el′e·vate
el′e·vat·ed
el′e·va′tion
el′e·va′tor
e·lev′en
elf′in
e·lic′it
e·lic′i·ta′tion
e·lic′i·tor
e·lide′
e·lid′ing
el′i·gi·bil′i·ty
el′i·gi·ble
E·li′jah
e·lim′i·nate
e·lim′i·na′tion
E·li′sha
e·li′sion
e·lite′
e·lix′ir
E·liz′a·be′than
el·lipse′
el·lip′sis
(plural: -ses)

el·lip′ti·cal
el′o·cu′tion
el′o·cu′tion·ar′y
e·lon′gate
e·lon′ga′tion
e·lope′
e·lope′ment
e·lop′ing
el′o·quence
el′o·quent
else′where
e·lu′ci·date
e·lu′ci·da′tion
e·lu′ci·da′tive
e·lude′
e·lud′ing
e·lu′sion
an escape *(see:* illusion)

e·lu′sive
e·lu′so·ry
E·ly′sian
E·ly′si·um
e·ma′ci·ate
e·ma′ci·a′tion
em′a·nate

em'a·na'tion
e·man'ci·pate
e·man'ci·pa'tion
e·man'ci·pa'tor
e·mas'cu·late
e·mas'cu·la'tion
em·balm'
em·balm'er
em·bank'ment
em·bar'go
em·bar'goed
em·bark'
em'bar·ka'tion
em·bar'rass
em·bar'rass·ing·ly
em·bar'rass·ment
em'bas·sy
em·bat'tle
em·bed'
em·bed'ded
em·bel'lish
em·bel'lish·ment
em'ber
em·bez'zle
em·bez'zle·ment
em·bez'zler
em·bit'ter
em·bla'zon
em'blem
em'blem·at'ic
em'blem·at'i·cal·ly
em·bod'i·ment
em·bod'y
em·bold'en
em'bo·lism
em'bo·lis'mic
em'bo·lus
em·bos'om
em·bow'er
em·brace'
em·brace'a·ble
em·brac'ing
em·bra'sure
em'bro·cate
em·bro·ca'tion
em·broi'der
em·broi'der·y
em·broil'
em'bry·o
em'bry·o·log'i·cal
em'bry·ol'o·gist
em'bry·ol'o·gy
em'bry·on'ic
e·mend'
e'men·da'tion
em'er·ald
e·merge'
e·mer'gence
e·mer'gen·cy
e·mer'gent
e·mer'i·tus
e·mer'sion
emerging *(see:* immersion)
em'er·y
e·met'ic
em'i·grant
one leaving *(see:* immigrant)
em'i·grate
em'i·grat·ing
em'i·gra'tion
em'i·nence
em'i·nent
e·mir'
em'is·sar'y
e·mis'sion
e·mis'sive
e·mit'
e·mit'ted
e·mit'ting
Em·man'u·el
e·mol'u·ment
e·mote'
e·mot'ing
e·mo'tion
e·mo'tion·al·ism'
e·mo'tion·al·ly
em·pan'el
em·pan'el·ing
em·path'ic
em'pa·thy
em'per·or
em'pha·sis
(plural: -ses)
em'pha·size
em'pha·siz·ing
em·phat'ic
em·phat'i·cal·ly
em'phy·se'ma
em'pire
em·pir'ic
em·pir'i·cism
em·place'ment
em·ploy'ee
em·ploy'er
em·ploy'ment
em·po'ri·um
em·pow'er

em′press
emp′ti·er
emp′ty
em·pur′pled
em·pyr′e·al
em·pyr′e·an
e′mu
em′u·late
em′u·la′tion
em′u·la′tive
em′u·lous
e·mul′si·fi·ca′tion
e·mul′si·fied
e·mul′si·fy
e·mul′sion
en·a′ble
en·a′bling
en·act′
e·nam′el
e·nam′eled
e·nam′el·er
en·am′or
en·am′ored
en·camp′
en·camp′ment
en·case′
en·cas′ing
en·ceph′a·lit′ic
en·ceph′a·li′tis
en·ceph′a·lon
en·chain′
en·chant′ing
en·chant′ress
en·cir′cle
en·cir′cle·ment
en·cir′cling
en·close′
en·clos′ing
en·clo′sure
en·co′mi·ast
en·co′mi·um
en·com′pass
en′core
en·coun′ter
en·cour′age
en·cour′age·ment
en·cour′ag·ing
en·croach′ment
en·crust′
en·crus·ta′tion
en·cum′ber
en·cum′brance
en·cyc′li·cal
en·cy′clo·pe′di·a
en·cy′clo·pe′dic
en·cyst′
en·dan′ger
en·dear′
en·dear′ing·ly
en·deav′or
en·dem′ic
en·dem′i·cal·ly
end′ing
en′dive
en′do·carp
en′do·crine
en·dog′e·nous
en′do·plasm
en′do·plas′mic
en·dorse′
en·dorse′ment
en·dors′ing
en′do·sperm
en·dow′ment
en·due′
en·dur′ance
en·dure′
en·dur′ing
en′e·ma
en′e·my
en′er·get′ic
en′er·get′i·cal·ly
en′er·gize
en′er·gy
en′er·vate
en′er·va′tion
en′er·va′tor
en·fee′ble
en·fee′bling
en′fi·lade′
en·fold′
en·force′
en·for′ced·ly
en·forc′ing
en·fran′chise
en·fran′chise·ment
en·gage′
en·gage′ment
en·gag′ing
en·gen′der
en′gine
en′gi·neer′
en′gi·neer′ing
Eng′land
Eng′lish
en·graft′
en·grave′
en·grav′ing
en·gross′
en·gross′ing
en·gulf′

en·hance′
en·hance′ment
en·hanc′ing
e·nig′ma
en′ig·mat′i·cal·ly
En′i·we′tok
en·join′
en·joy′
en·joy′a·ble
en·joy′ment
en·kin′dle
en·kin′dling
en·large′
en·large′ment
en·light′en·ment
en·list′
en·list′ment
en·liv′en
en·mesh′
en′mi·ty
en·no′ble
en·no′bler
en·no′bling
en′nui
e·nor′mi·ty
e·nor′mous
e·nough′
en·rage′
en·rag′ing
en rap·port′
en·rap′ture
en·rich′
en·roll′
en·roll′ment
en·sconce′
en·sem′ble
en·shrine′
en·shroud′
en′sign
en′sign·cy
en′si·lage
en·slave′
en·slav′ing
en·snare′
en·sue′
en·su′ing
en·tab′la·ture
en·tail′
en·tan′gle
en·tente′
en′ter
en·ter′ic
en′ter·prise
en′ter·pris′ing
en′ter·tain′
en′ter·tain′ment
en·thrall′
en·thrall′ing·ly
en·throne′
en·thuse′
en·thu′si·asm
en·thu′si·ast
en·thu′si·as′tic
en·thu′si·as′ti·cal·ly
en·tice′
en·tic′ing
en·tire′
en·tire′ty
en·ti′tle
en′ti·ty
en·tomb′
en′to·mo·log′i·cal
en′to·mol′o·gist
en′to·mol′o·gy
en′tou·rage′
en′trails
en·train′
en′trance
en·tranc′ing
en′trant
en·trap′
en·trap′ment
en·trap′ping
en·treat′
en·treat′ing·ly
en·treat′y
en′tree
en·trench′
en·tre nous′
en′tre·pre·neur
en·trust′
en′try
en·twine′
e·nu′mer·ate
e·nu′mer·a′tion
e·nu′mer·a′tor
e·nun′ci·ate
e·nun′ci·a′tion
e·nun′ci·a′tor
en·vel′op, *v.*
en′ve·lope, *n.*
en·vel′op·ing
en·vel′op·ment
en·ven′om
en′vi·a·ble
en′vi·ous
en·vi′ron
en·vi′ron·ment
en·vi′ron·men′tal
en·vi′rons

en·vis′age
en′voy
en′vy
en′vy·ing·ly
en′zy·mat′ic
en′zyme
e′o·lith′ic
e′on
ep′au·let
e·phed′rine
e·phem′er·al
e·phem′er·id
E·phe′sians
Eph′e·sus
ep′ic
ep′i·cal·ly
ep′i·ca′lyx
ep′i·carp
ep′i·cen′ter
ep′i·cure
ep′i·cu·re′an
ep′i·dem′ic
ep′i·der′mal
ep′i·der′mis
ep′i·der′moid
ep′i·glot′tis
ep′i·gram
ep′i·gram·mat′
  i·cal
e·pig′ra·phy
ep′i·lep′sy
ep′i·lep′tic
ep′i·logue
E·piph′a·ny
e·pis′co·pa·cy
e·pis′co·pal
E·pis′co·pa′lian

e·pis′co·pate
ep′i·sode
ep′i·sod′ic
ep′i·sod′i·cal·ly
e·pis′te·mol′o·gy
e·pis′tle
e·pis′to·lar′y
ep′i·taph
ep′i·the′li·al
ep′i·the′li·um
ep′i·thet
e·pit′o·me
e·pit′o·mize
ep′i·zo·ot′ic
e plu′ri·bus u′num
ep′och
ep′och·al
ep′ode
ep′si·lon
Ep′som
eq′ua·bil′i·ty
eq′ua·ble
e′qual
e·qual′i·ty
e′qual·i·za′tion
e′qual·ize
e′qual·ly
e′qua·nim′i·ty
e·quate′
e·qua′tion
e·qua′tor
e′qua·to′ri·al
eq′uer·ry
e·ques′tri·an,
  masc.
e·ques′tri·enne′,
  fem.

e′qui·dis′tant
e′qui·lat′er·al
e·quil′i·brant
e′qui·li′brate
e′qui·li·bra′tion
e′qui·lib′ri·um
e′quine
e′qui·noc′tial
e′qui·nox
e·quip′
eq′ui·page
e·quip′ment
e′qui·poise
e·quip′ping
eq′ui·ta·ble
eq′ui·ty
e·quiv′a·lent
e·quiv′o·cal
e·quiv′o·cate
e·quiv′o·ca′tion
e·quiv′o·ca′tor
e′ra
e·rad′i·ca·ble
e·rad′i·cate
e·rad′i·ca′tion
e·rase′
e·ras′er
e·ras′ing
e·ra′sure
e·rect′
e·rec′tile
e·rec′tion
e·rec′tor
er′go
er′got
E′rie
Er′in

er′mine
e·rode′
e·rod′ing
E′ros
e·rose′
e·ro′sion
e·ro′sive
e·rot′ic
er′rand
er′rant
er·rat′ic
er·rat′i·cal·ly
er·ra′tum
erred
err′ing
er·ro′ne·ous
er′ror
er′satz
erst′while′
e·ruct′
e·ruc′tate
e·ruc′ta′tion
er′u·dite
er′u·di′tion
e·rupt′
e·rup′tion
e·rup′tive
er′y·sip′e·las
e·ryth′ro·my′cin
es′ca·drille′
es′ca·lade′
es′ca·la′tor
es·cal′lop
es′ca·pade
es·cape′
es·caped′
es′ca·pee′
es·cape′ment
es·cap′ing
es·cap′ist
es′ca·role
es·carp′ment
es·cheat′
es·chew′
es′cort, *n.*
es·cort′, *v.*
es′cri·toire′
es′crow
es′cu·lent
es·cutch′eon
Es′ki·mo
e·soph′a·gus
es′o·ter′ic
es′o·ter′i·cal·ly
es·pal′ier
es·pe′cial·ly
Es′pe·ran′to
es′pi·o·nage
es′pla·nade′
es·pous′al
es·pouse′
es·pous′ing
es·prit′
es·py′
es·quire′
es′say, *n.*
es·say′, *v.*
es′say·ist
es′sence
es·sen′tial
es·tab′lish
es·tab′lish·ment
es·tate′
es·teem′
es′ter
es′thete
es·thet′ics
es′ti·ma·ble
es′ti·mate
es′ti·ma′tion
es′ti·ma′tor
es·top′
es·top′ping
es·trange′
es·trang′ing
es′tro·gen
es′tro·gen′ic
es′tu·ar′y
et cet′er·a
etch′ing
e·ter′nal
e·ter′ni·ty
eth′ane
e′ther
e·the′re·al
e·the′re·al′i·ty
e·the′re·al·ize
e′ther·i·za′tion
e′ther·ize
eth′ic
eth′i·cal
eth′ics
E′thi·o′pi·a
eth′nic
eth′ni·cal·ly
eth′no·graph′i·cal
eth·nog′ra·phy
eth′no·log′i·cal
eth·nol′o·gy
eth′yl
eth′yl·ene

e'ti·o·log'i·cal
e'ti·ol'o·gy
et'i·quette
E·trus'can
e·tude'
et'y·mo·log'i·cal
et'y·mol'o·gist
et'y·mol'o·gy
eu'ca·lyp'tus
Eu'cha·rist
Eu'cha·ris'tic
eu'chre
Eu'clid
Eu·clid'e·an
eu·gen'i·cal
eu·gen'ics
eu'lo·gist
eu'lo·gis'tic
eu·lo'gi·um
eu'lo·gize
eu'lo·gy
eu'nuch
eu·pep'sia
eu'phe·mism
eu'phe·mis'tic
eu'phe·mize
eu·phon'ic
eu·pho'ni·ous
eu·pho'ni·um
eu'pho·ny
eu·phor'bi·a
eu·pho'ri·a
Eu·phra'tes
eu'phu·ism
eu'phu·is'tic
Eur·a'sian
eu·re'ka
Eu'rope
Eu'ro·pe'an
Eu·sta'chi·an
eu'tha·na'sia
eu·then'ics
e·vac'u·ate
e·vac'u·a'tion
e·vac'u·ee
e·vade'
e·vad'ing
e·val'u·ate
e·val'u·a'tion
ev'a·nesce'
ev'a·nes'cence
ev'a·nes'cent
e'van·gel'i·cal
e·van'ge·lism
e·van'ge·list
e·van'ge·lis'tic
e·van'ge·lize
e·vap'o·rate
e·vap'o·rat·ing
e·vap'o·ra'tion
e·va'sion
e·va'sive
eve'ning
e'ven·ly
e·vent'
e·vent'ful
e'ven·tide'
e·ven'tu·al
e·ven'tu·al'i·ty
e·ven'tu·ate
Ev'er·est
ev'er·glade'
ev'er·green'
ev'er·last'ing
ev'er·more'
e·ver'sion
e·vert'
eve'ry·day'
eve'ry·one
eve'ry·thing
eve'ry·where
e·vict'
e·vic'tion
ev'i·dence
ev'i·dent
e'vil·ly
e'vil-mind'ed
e·vince'
e·vin'ci·ble
e·vinc'ing
e·vis'cer·ate
e·vis'cer·a'tion
ev'o·ca'tion
e·voke'
e·vok'ing
ev'o·lu'tion
ev'o·lu'tion·ar'y
e·volve'
e·volv'ing
ex·act'ing
ex·ac'tion
ex·act'i·tude
ex·act'ly
ex·ag'ger·ate
ex·ag'ger·at'ed
ex·ag'ger·a'tion
ex·alt'
honor (*see:* exult)
ex'al·ta'tion
ex·am'i·na'tion

ex·am′ine
ex·am′in·er
ex·am′ple
ex·as′per·ate
ex·as′per·at′ing
ex·as′per·a′tion
ex ca·the′dra
ex′ca·vate
ex′ca·va′tion
ex·ceed′
surpass (*see:* accede)

ex·cel′
ex′cel·lence
ex′cel·len·cy
ex′cel·lent
ex·cel′ling
ex·cel′si·or
ex·cept′
leave out (*see:* accept)

ex·cep′tion
ex·cep′tion·a·ble
ex·cep′tion·al
ex′cerpt, *n.*
ex·cerpt′, *v.*
ex·cess′
surplus (*see:* access)

ex·ces′sive
ex·change′
ex·change′a·ble
ex·chang′ing
ex·cheq′uer
ex′cise, *n.*
ex·cise′, *v.*
ex·ci′sion
ex·cit′a·ble
ex′ci·ta′tion
ex·cite′
ex·cite′ment
ex·cit′ing
ex·claim′
ex′cla·ma′tion
ex·clam′a·to′ry
ex·clude′
ex·clud′ing
ex·clu′sive
ex′com·mu′ni·cate
ex′com·mu′ni·ca′tion
ex·co′ri·ate
ex·co′ri·a′tion
ex′cre·ment
ex·cres′cence
ex·cres′cent
ex·cre′ta
ex·crete′
ex′cre·to′ry
ex·cru′ci·ate
ex·cru′ci·at′ing
ex′cul·pate
ex′cul·pa′tion
ex·cur′sion
ex·cur′sive
ex·cus′a·ble
ex·cuse′
ex·cus′ing
ex′e·cra·ble
ex′e·crate
ex′e·cra′tion
ex′e·cute
ex′e·cu′tion
ex·ec′u·tive
ex·ec′u·tor
ex·ec′u·to′ri·al
ex·ec′u·trix
ex′e·ge′sis
ex·em′plar
ex·em′pla·ry
ex·em′pli·fi·ca′tion
ex·em′pli·fy
ex·empt′
ex·emp′tion
ex′er·cise
active use (*see:* exorcise)

ex·ert′
ex·er′tion
ex·hale′
ex′ha·la′tion
ex·haust′
ex·haus′tion
ex·haus′tive
ex·hib′it
ex′hi·bi′tion
ex·hib′i·tor
ex·hil′a·rate
ex·hil′a·ra′tion
ex·hort′
ex′hor·ta′tion
ex′hu·ma′tion
ex·hume′
ex′i·gen·cy
ex′i·gent
ex′ile
ex·ist′
ex·ist′ence
ex·ist′ent

ex′is·ten′tial·ism
ex′o·dus
ex·og′e·nous
ex·on′er·ate
ex·on′er·a′tion
ex·or′bi·tant
ex′or·cise
free from evil spirits
(*see:* exercise)
ex′or·cism
ex·ot′ic
ex·ot′i·cal·ly
ex·pand′
ex·panse′
ex·pan′si·ble
ex·pan′sion
ex·pan′sive
ex·pa′ti·ate
ex·pa′ti·a′tion
ex·pa′tri·ate
ex·pa′tri·a′tion
ex·pect′an·cy
ex·pect′ant
ex·pect′ant·ly
ex′pec·ta′tion
ex·pec′to·rant
ex·pec′to·rate
ex·pec′to·ra′tion
ex·pe′di·ency
ex·pe′di·ent
ex′pe·dite
ex′pe·dit·ing
ex′pe·di′tion
ex′pe·di′tious
ex·pelled′
ex·pel′ling
ex·pend′
ex·pend′a·ble
ex·pend′i·ture
ex·pense′
ex·pen′sive
ex·pe′ri·ence
ex·pe′ri·enc·ing
ex·per′i·ment
ex·per′i·men′tal
ex′pert
ex′pi·a·ble
ex′pi·ate
ex′pi·a′tion
ex′pi·ra′tion
ex·pir′a·to′ry
ex·pired′
ex·pir′ing
ex·plain′
ex′pla·na′tion
ex·plan′a·to′ry
ex′ple·tive
ex′pli·ca·ble
ex′pli·cate
ex′pli·ca′tion
ex·plic′it
ex·plode′
ex·plod′ing
ex′ploit, *n.*
ex·ploit′, *v.*
ex′ploi·ta′tion
ex′plo·ra′tion
ex·plor′a·to′ry
ex·plore′
ex·plor′er
ex·plor′ing
ex·plo′sion
ex·plo′sive
ex·po′nent
ex′port, *n.*
ex·port′, *v.*
ex′por·ta′tion
ex·pose′, *v.*
ex′po·sé, *n.*
ex·posed′
ex·pos′ing
ex′po·si′tion
ex·pos′i·to′ry
ex′ post′ fac′to
ex·pos′tu·late
ex·pos′tu·la′tion
ex·pos′tu·la·to′ry
ex·po′sure
ex·pound′
ex·press′
ex·press′i·ble
ex·pres′sion
ex·pres′sive
ex·press′way′
ex·pro′pri·ate
ex·pro′pri·a′tion
ex·pul′sion
ex·punge′
ex·pung′ing
ex′pur·gate
ex′pur·ga′tion
ex′qui·site
ex′tant
ex·tem′po·ra′
ne·ous
ex·tem′po·ra′ry
ex·tem′po·re
ex·tem′po·rize
ex·tend′
ex·tend′i·ble

ex·ten′si·bil′i·ty
ex·ten′si·ble
ex·ten′sion
ex·ten′sive
ex·ten′sor
ex·tent′
ex·ten′u·ate
ex·ten′u·at·ing
ex·ten′u·a′tion
ex·ten′u·a′tor
ex·te′ri·or
ex·ter′mi·nate
ex·ter′mi·na′tion
ex·ter′mi·na′tor
ex·ter′nal
ex·tinct′
ex·tinc′tion
ex·tin′guish
ex·tin′guish·er
ex′tir·pate
ex′tir·pa′tion
ex·tol′
ex·tolled′
ex·tol′ling
ex·tort′
ex·tor′tion
ex·tor′tion·ar′y
ex·tor′tion·ate
ex·tor′tion·ist
ex′tra
ex′tract, *n.*
ex·tract′, *v.*
ex·tract′a·ble
ex·trac′tion
ex′tra·cur·ric′u·lar
ex′tra·dite
ex′tra·dit·ing
ex′tra·di′tion
ex·tra′ne·ous
ex·traor′di·nar′i·ly
ex·traor′di·nar′y
ex′tra·sen′so·ry
ex·trav′a·gance
ex·trav′a·gant
ex·trav′a·gan′za
ex·treme′
ex·trem′ist
ex·trem′i·ty
ex′tri·ca·bil′i·ty
ex′tri·ca·ble
ex′tri·cate
ex′tri·ca′tion
ex·trin′sic
ex′tro·vert
ex·trude′
ex·trud′ing
ex·tru′sion
ex·tru′sive
ex·u′ber·ance
ex·u′ber·ant
ex′u·da′tion
ex·ude′
ex·ult′
rejoice *(see:* exalt)
ex·ult′ant
ex′ul·ta′tion
ex′ur′ban·ite
ex′ur′bi·a
eye′ball′
eye′brow′
eye′lash′
eye′let′
eye′lid′
eye′sight′
eye′sore′
eye′wit′ness
ey′rie
E·ze′ki·el

F

fa′ble
fa′bled
fab′ric
fab′ri·cate
fab′ri·ca′tion
fab′ri·ca′tor
fab′u·list
fab′u·lous
fa·cade′
faced
fac′et
fa·ce′tious
fa′cial
fac′ile
fa·cil′i·tate
fa·cil′i·ty
fac′ing
fac·sim′i·le

fac′tion
fac′tious
fac·ti′tious
fac′tor
fac′to·ry
fac·to′tum
fac′tu·al
fac′ul·ty
fad′dist
fade′-out′
fag′ot
Fahr′en·heit
fail′ing
faille
fail′ure
faint
dim *(see:* feint)
faint′ed
faint′heart′ed
fair′ly
fair′-mind′ed
fair′way′
fair′y
fair′y·land′
fait ac·com·pli′
faith′ful
faith′less
fak′er
fraud
fa·kir′
Hindu
fal′chion
fal′con
fal′con·ry
fal·la′cious
fal′la·cy
fall′en
fal′li·bil′i·ty
fal′li·ble
Fal·lo′pi·an
fall′-out′
fal′low
false′hood
false′ly
fal·set′to
fal′si·fi·ca′tion
fal′si·fied
fal′si·fy
fal′si·fy·ing
fal′si·ty
Fal′staff
fal′ter·ing·ly
famed
fa·mil′iar
fa·mil′iar′i·ty
fa·mil′iar·i·za′tion
fa·mil′iar·ize
fam′i·ly
fam′ine
fam′ish
fa′mous
fa·nat′ic
fa·nat′i·cal
fa·nat′i·cism
fan′cied
fan′ci·er
fan′ci·ful
fan′cy
fan′cy·ing
fan′cy·work′
fan·dan′go
fan′fare
fanged
fan′tail
fan′-tan′
fan·ta′si·a
fan·tas′tic
fan·tas′ti·cal·ly
fan′ta·sy
far′ad
far′a·way′
farce
far′ci·cal
fare′well′
far′-fetched′
fa·ri′na
far′i·na′ceous
farm′er
farm′house′
farm′ing
farm′yard′
far′o
far′ri·er
far′ri·er·y
far′row
far′-sight′ed
far′ther
far′thest
far′thing
far′thin·gale
fas′ces
fas′ci·cle
fas′ci·nate
fas′ci·nat′ing
fas′ci·na′tion
fas′cism
fas′cist
fash′ion
fash′ion·a·ble

fas′ten
fas′ten·ing
fas·tid′i·ous
fast′ness
fa′tal
fa′tal·ism
fa′tal·is′tic
fa·tal′i·ty
fat′ed
fate′ful
fa′ther·hood
fa′ther-in-law′
fa′ther·ly
fath′om
fath′om·less
fa·tigue′
fa·tigued′
fa·ti′guing
fat′ling
fat′ten
fat′ter
fat′ty
fa·tu′i·ty
fat′u·ous
fau′ces
fau′cet
fau′cial
fault′find′ing
fault′i·er
fault′less
fault′y
faun
Roman deity *(see:* fawn)

fau′na
faux′ pas′
fa′vor
fa′vor·a·ble
fa′vor·a·bly
fa′vor·ite
fa′vor·it·ism′
fawn
young deer *(see:* faun)

faze
disturb *(see:* phase)

fe′al·ty
fear′ful
fear′some
fea′si·bil′i·ty
fea′si·ble
feath′er
feath′er-bed′ding
feath′er·brain′
feath′ered
feath′er·edge′
feath′er·y
fea′ture
fea′tured
feb′ri·fuge
fe′brile
Feb′ru·ar′y
fe′cal
fe′ces
feck′less
fe′cund
fe·cun′di·ty
fed′er·al
fed′er·al·ism′
fed′er·al·is′tic
fed′er·al·i·za′tion
fed′er·al·ize
fed′er·ate
fed′er·a′tion
fe·do′ra
fee′ble
fee′ble-mind′ed
fee′bly
feed′ing
feel′er
feel′ing
feign
feign′ed
feint
deceptive movement *(see:* faint)

fe·lic′i·tate
fe·lic′i·ta′tion
fe·lic′i·tous
fe·lic′i·ty
fe′line
fe·lin′i·ty
fel′loe
fel′low
fel′low·ship
fel′on
fe·lo′ni·ous
fel′o·ny
fe′male
fem′i·nine
fem′i·nin′i·ty
fem′i·nism
fem′i·nist
femme fa·tale′
fem′o·ral
fe′mur
fence
fenced

fenc′ing
fend′er
fen′nel
fer-de-lance′
fer·ment′
fer′men·ta′tion
fer′mi·um
fern′er·y
fe·ro′cious
fe·roc′i·ty
fer′ret
fer′ric
fer′rous
fer·ru′gi·nous
fer′rule
metal ring *(see:* ferule)

fer′ry
fer′ry·boat
fer′tile
fer·til′i·ty
fer′ti·li·za′tion
fer′ti·lize
fer′ti·liz′er
fer′ule
stick *(see:* ferrule)

fer′ven·cy
fer′vent
fer′vid
fer′vor
fes′cue
fes′tal
fes′ter
fes′ti·val
fes′tive
fes·tiv′i·ty
fes·toon′
fe′tal
fetch′ing
fet′id
fe·tid′i·ty
fe′tish
fet′lock
fet′ter
fet′tle
fe′tus
(also: foetus)

feud
feu′dal
feu′dal·ism
feud′ist
fe′ver
fe′vered
fe′ver·ish
few′ness
fezzes
fi′an·cé′, *masc.*
fi′an·cée′, *fem.*
fi·as′co
fi′at
fib′bing
Fi′ber·glas′
fi′ber-glass′
fi′ber·board′
fi′bril
fi′brin·ous
fi′broid
fi′brous
fib′u·la
fib′u·lar
fich′u
fick′le
fic′tion
fic′tion·al
fic·ti′tious
fid′dle
fid′dler
fid′dle·sticks′
fid′dling
fi·del′i·ty
fidg′et
fidg′et·y
fi·du′ci·ar·y
field′er
field′piece′
fiend′ish
fierce′ly
fierc′er
fier′i·ness
fier′y
fi·es′ta
fif′teen′
fif′ti·eth
fif′ty
fight′er
fight′ing
fig′ment
fig′u·ra′tion
fig′u·ra·tive
fig′ure
fig′ured
fig′ure·head′
fig′ur·ine′
Fi′ji
fil′a·gree
(or: filigree)

fil′a·ment
fil′bert

filch′er
fi·let′
fil′i·al
fil′i·bus′ter
fil′ings
Fil′i·pi′no
fill′er
fil′let
fill′ing
fil′lip
fil′ly
film′i·er
film′y
fil′ter
strain (*see:* philter)

fil′ter·a·bil′i·ty
fil′ter·a·ble
filth′i·er
filth′y
fil′trate
fil·tra′tion
fi·na′gle
fi·na′gling
fi′nal
fi·na′le
fi′nal·ist
fi·nal′i·ty
fi′nal·ly
fi·nance′
fi·nan′cial
fi·nan′cial·ly
fin′an·cier′
fi·nanc′ing
fin′back′
find′er
find′ing
fine′ly
fin′er
fin′er·y
fi·nesse′
fin′ger
fin′ger·nail′
fin′ger·print′
fin′i·al
fin′i·cal
fin′ick·y
fi′nis
fin′ish
fi′nite
Fin′land
fin′nan had′die
Finn′ish
fiord
(*also:* fjord)

fire′arm′
fire′brand′
fire′crack′er
fire′fly′
fire′man
fire′place′
fire′proof′
fire′side′
fire′wa′ter
fire′wood′
fire′works′
fir′ing
fir′kin
fir′ma·ment
firm′ness
first′-born′
first′-class′
first′ling
first′ly
fis′cal
fis′cal·ly
fish′er
fish′er·man
fish′er·y
fish′-hook′
fish′ing
fish′mon′ger
fish′y
fis′sile
fis′sion
fis′sion·a·ble
fis′sure
fis′sur·ing
fist′ic
fist′i·cuffs′
fis′tu·la
fis′tu·lous
fitch′et
fit′ful
fit′ted
fit′ting·ly
five′fold′
fix·a′tion
fix′a·tive
fixed
fix′ed·ly
fix′ing
fix′i·ty
fix′ture
fiz′zle
fiz′zling
fiz′zy
fjord
(*also:* fiord)

flab′ber·gast
flab′bi·er
flab′bi·ness
flab′by
flac′cid
flac·cid′i·ty
flac′cid·ly
fla′con
flag′el·lant
flag′el·late
flag′el·la′tion
fla·gel′lum
flag′eo·let′
flagged
flag′ging
flag′on
flag′pole′
fla′gran·cy
fla′grant
flag′ship′
flag′stone′
flail
flair
talent (*see:* flare)

flaked
flak′i·er
flak′ing
flak′y
flam′beau
flam·boy′ance
flam·boy′ant
flamed
fla·men′co
flam′ing
fla·min′go
flam′ma·ble

flange
flanged
flang′ing
flank′er
flan′nel
flan′nel·et′
flap′jack′
flapped
flap′per
flap′ping
flare
light (*see:* flair)

flare′-up
flar′ing
flash′ing
flash′light′
flash′y
flat′boat′
flat′foot′ed
flat′i′ron
flat′ten
flat′ter
flat′ter·ing·ly
flat′ter·y
flat′top′
flat′u·lence
flat′u·lent
flaunt′ing·ly
flau′tist
(*also:* flutist)

fla′vor
fla′vor·ing
flaw′less
flax′en
flax′seed′
flay′er

flec′tion
fledged
fledg′ing
fledg′ling
fleece
fleec′i·er
fleec′y
flee′ing
fleet′ing
fleet′ly
Flem′ish
flesh′-col′ored
flesh′ly
flesh′pot′
flesh′y
fleur′-de-lis′
flex′i·bil′i·ty
flex′i·ble
flex′ion
flex′or
flex′ure
flib′ber·ti·gib′bet
flick′er
flick′er·ing·ly
fli′er
flight′i·ness
flight′less
flight′y
flim′si·ness
flim′sy
flinched
flinch′ing
flin′der
fling′ing
flint′lock′
flint′y
flip′pan·cy

flip′pant
flipped
flip′per
flip′ping
flir·ta′tion
flir·ta′tious
flirt′ing·ly
flit′ter
flit′ting
fliv′ver
float′a·ble
float′er
float′ing
floc′cu·lence
floc′cu·lent
flocked
flogged
flog′ging
flood′gate′
flood′light′
floor′ing
floor′walk′er
flopped
flop′pi·er
flop′ping
flop′py
flo′ra
flo′ral
Flor′ence
Flor′en·tine
flo·res′cence
flowering *(see:* fluorescence)

flo·res′cent
flo′ret
flo′ri·cul′tur·al
flo′ri·cul′ture
flor′id
Flor′i·da
Flo·rid′i·an
flo·rid′i·ty
flor′in
flo′rist
floss′y
flo·ta′tion
flo′til′la
flot′sam
flounced
flounc′ing
floun′dered
floun′der·ing
flour′ished
flour′ish·ing
flour′y
flout′ed
flout′ing
flow′er
flow′ered
flow′er·et
flow′er·ing
flow′er·pot′
flow′er·y
fluc′tu·ate
fluc′tu·at·ed
fluc′tu·at·ing
fluc′tu·a′tion
flu′en·cy
flu′ent
fluff′i·er
fluff′y
flu′id
flu·id′ic
flu·id′i·ty
fluk′y
flum′mer·y
flunk′y
flu′o·resce′
flu′o·res′cence
giving off light

flu′o·res′cent
having florescence

flu′o·resc′ing
fluor′i·date
fluor′i·da′tion
flu′o·ride
flu′o·rine
flu′o·rite
fluor′o·scope
flur′ried
flur′ry
flur′ry·ing
flus′ter
flus·tra′tion
flut′ed
flut′ing
flut′ist
(also: flautist)

flut′tered
flut′ter·ing
flux′ion
fly′catch′er
fly′er
fly′ing
fly′leaf′
fly′speck′
fly′weight′
fly′wheel′
foamed

foam′i • er
foam′ing
foam′y
fo′cal
fo′cal • i • za′tion
fo′cal • ize
fo′cused
fo′cus • ing
fod′der
foe′man
fog′gi • er
fog′gi • ly
fog′gy
misty
fog′horn′
fo′gy
(or: fogey) behind the times
foi′ble
foiled
foil′ing
foist • ed
fold′ed
fold′er
fo′li • a′ceous
fo′li • age
fo′li • ate
fo′li • a′tion
fo′li • o
folk′lore′
folk′sy
folk′way′
fol′li • cle
fol • lic′u • lar
fol′lowed
fol′low • ing
fol′ly
fo • ment′
fo′men • ta′tion
fon′dant
fon′dled
fon′dling
fond′ly
fon′due
Fon′taine • bleau
food′stuff′
fool′er • y
fool′har′di • ness
fool′har′dy
fool′ish
fool′proof′
fools′cap′
foot′age
foot′ball′
foot′board′
foot′bridge′
foot′hold′
foot′ing
foot′lights′
foot′note′
foot′man′
foot′print′
foot′step′
foot′stool′
fop′pish
for′aged
for′ag • ing
for′ay
for • bear′
for • bear′ance
for • bid′
for • bid′den
for • bid′ding
forced
force′ful
force′meat′
for′ceps
for′ci • ble
for′ci • bly
forc′ing
fore′arm′
fore • bode′
fore • bod′ing
fore′cast′
fore′cast′er
fore′cas • tle
fore • close′
fore • clo′sure
fore • doom′
fore′fa′ther
fore′fin′ger
fore′front′
fore • gath′er
fore • go′
fore′go′ing
fore • gone′
fore′ground′
fore′hand′
fore′hand′ed
fore′head
for′eign
for′eign • er
fore′leg′
fore′man
fore′mast′
fore′most
fore • noon′
fo • ren′sic
fore′or • dain′
fore′quar′ter

fore'run'ner
fore'sail'
fore·saw'
fore·see'
fore·shad'ow
fore'sight'
fore'skin
for'est
fore·stall'
for'est·a'tion
fore'stay'
for'est·er
for'est·ry
fore·tell'
fore·tell'ing
fore'thought'
fore·told'
for·ev'er
for·ev'er·more'
fore·warn'
fore'word'
preface *(see:* forward)

for'feit
for'fei·ture
for·gave'
forge
forge'a·ble
forg'er
for'ger·y
for·get'ful
for·get'ting
forg'ing
for·give'ness
for·giv'ing
for·go'ing
for·got'ten
forked
for·lorn'
for'mal
form·al'de·hyde
for'mal·ism
for'mal·is'tic
for·mal'i·ty
for'mal·ize
for'mal·iz·ing
for'mat
for·ma'tion
form'a·tive
for'mer
for'mic
for'mi·da·bil'i·ty
for'mi·da·ble
form'less
For·mo'sa
for'mu·la
for'mu·lar'y
for'mu·late
for'mu·la'tion
for'mu·la'tor
for'ni·cate
for'ni·ca'tion
for'ni·ca'tor
for·sake'
for·sak'en
for·swear'
for·sworn'
for·syth'i·a
fort
building

forte
strong point
for'te *(mus.)*
forth
forward *(see:* fourth)

forth'com'ing
forth'right'
forth'with'
for'ti·eth
for'ti·fi·ca'tion
for'ti·fied
for'ti·fy
for·tis'si·mo
for'ti·tude
fort'night
for'tress
for·tu'i·tous
for·tu'i·ty
for'tu·nate
for'tune
for'ty
fo'rum
for'ward
ahead *(see:* foreword)

fos'sa
fos'sil
fos'sil·i·za'tion
fos'sil·ize
fos'ter
foul
filthy *(see:* fowl)

fou·lard'
foul'ly
foun·da'tion
foun'der, *v.*
sink; fail

found′er, *n.*
one who founds

found′ling
found′ry
foun′tain
foun′tain·head′
four′-foot′ed
four′-post′er
four′score′
four′some
four′teen′
fourth
after third *(see:* forth)

fowl
bird *(see:* foul)

fox′glove′
fox′hole′
fox′-trot′
fox′y
foy′er
fra′cas
frac′tion
frac′tion·al
frac′tious
frac′ture
frag′ile
fra·gil′i·ty
frag′ment
frag·men′tal
frag′men·tar′y
frag′men·ta′tion
fra′grance
fra′grant
frail
frail′ty
framed
frame′work′
fram′ing
franc
monetary unit *(see:* frank)

fran′chise
Fran·cis′can
fran′gi·bil′i·ty
fran′gi·ble
frank
sincere *(see:* franc)

Frank′en·stein
frank′fur·ter
frank′in·cense
fran′tic
fran′ti·cal·ly
frap·pe′
fra·ter′nal
fra·ter′ni·ty
frat′er·ni·za′tion
frat′er·nize
frat′ri·cid′al
frat′ri·cide
fraud′u·lence
fraud′u·lent
frayed
fraz′zle
fraz′zling
freak′ish
freck′le
freck′led
free′born′
free′dom
free′hand′ed
free′ly
free′man
Free′ma′son·ry
fre′er
fre′est
free′stone′
free′think′er
free′way′
free′will′
freeze
turn to ice *(see:* frieze)

freez′er
freez′ing
freight′er
French′man
fre·net′ic
fre·net′i·cal·ly
fren′zied
fren′zy
fre′quen·cy
fre′quent
fre·quen′ta·tive
fres′co
fresh′en
fresh′et
fresh′man
fret′ful
fret′ted
fret′work′
fri′a·bil′i·ty
fri′a·ble
fri′ar
monk *(see:* fryer)

fri′ar·y
fric′as·see′

fric′tion
Fri′day
fried′cake′
friend′li·er
friend′li·ness
friend′ly
friend′ship
frieze
cloth *(see:* freeze)

frig′ate
fright′en
fright′en·ing
fright′ful
frig′id
fri·gid′i·ty
fringed
fring′ing
frip′per·y
frisk′i·er
frisk′y
frit′ter
fri·vol′i·ty
friv′o·lous
friz′zle
friz′zling
friz′zly
frock
frog′man
frol′ic
frol′icked
frol′ick·ing
frol′ic·some
front′age
fron′tal
fron·tier′
fron·tiers′man
fron′tis·piece
frost′bite′
frost′bit′ten
frost′ing
frost′y
froth′i·er
froth′y
fro′ward
frowned
frown′ing
frowz′i·er
frowz′i·ness
frowz′y
fro′zen
fruc′ti·fi·ca′tion
fruc′ti·fied
fruc′ti·fy
fruc′tose
fru′gal
fru·gal′i·ty
fruit′ful
fruit′i·ness
fru·i′tion
fruit′less
fruit′y
frump′ish
frump′y
frus′trate
frus′trat·ed
frus′trat·ing
frus·tra′tion
frus′tum
fry′er
one who fries; fowl *(see:* friar)

fuch′sia
fud′dle
fud′dling
fudge
fu′el
fu′gi·tive
fugue
Fu′ji·ya′ma
ful′crum
ful·fill′
ful·fill′ment
full′back′
full′er
full′ness
ful′ly
ful′mi·nate
ful′mi·nat·ing
ful′mi·na′tion
ful′some
ful′some·ness
fum′ble
fum′bling
fumed
fu′mi·gate
fu′mi·gat·ing
fu′mi·ga′tion
fu′mi·ga′tor
fum′ing
func′tion
func′tion·al
func′tion·ar′y
fun′da·men′tal
fun′da·men′tal·ism
fun′da·men′tal·ist
fun′da·men′tal·ly
fu′ner·al
fu·ne′re·al
fun′gi·cide

fun′gous, *adj.*
fun′gus, *n.*
fun′nel
fun′neled
fun′nel·ing
fun′ni·er
fun′ny
fur′be·low
fur′bish
fur′bish·er
fu′ri·ous
fur′long
fur′lough
fur′nace
fur′nish
fur′nish·ings
fur′ni·ture
fu′ror
furred
fur′ri·er
fur′ri·ness
fur′ring
fur′row
fur′ry
fur′ther
fur′ther·ance
fur′ther·more
fur′ther·most
fur′thest
fur′tive
fur′tive·ly
fu′ry
fused
fu′se·lage
fu′sel
fu′si·bil′i·ty
fu′si·ble
fu′sil·ier′
fu′sil·lade′
fus′ing
fu′sion
fuss′i·ly
fuss′y
fus′tian
fust′i·er
fust′y
fu′tile
fu′tile·ly
fu·til′i·ty
fu′ture
fu′tur·ism
fu′tur·ist
fu·tu′ri·ty
fuze
fuzz′i·ness
fuzz′y

G

gab′ar·dine
gab′bing
gab′ble
gab′by
ga′ble
ga′bled
Ga′bri·el
gad′a·bout′
gad′ding
gad′fly′
gadg′et
Gael′ic
gaf′fer
gage
pledge *(see:* gauge)
gagged
gag′ging
gai′e·ty
(also: gayety)
gai′ly
(also: gayly)
gain′er
gain′ful
gain·said′
gain·say′
gait
way of walking
(see: gate)
gai′ter
ga′la
ga·lac′tic
Gal′a·had
Ga·la′pa·gos
Ga·la′tians
gal′ax·y
ga·le′na
Gal′i·le′an
Gal′i·lee

Gal′i·le′o
gal′lant·ry
gal′le·on
gal′ler·y
gal′ley
Gal′lic
gal′li·na′ceous
gall′ing
gal′li·um
gal′li·vant
gal′lon
gal·loon′
gal′loped
gal′lows
gall′stone′
ga·losh′es
gal·van′ic
gal′va·nize
gal′va·niz·ing
gal′va·nom′e·ter
gal′va·no·met′ric
gal′va·nom′e·try
gal′va·no·scope
gal′va·no·scop′ic
gam′bit
gam′ble
  risk; bet
  (*see:* gambol)

gam′bler
gam′bling
gam′bol
  frolic (*see:* gamble)

gam′bol·ing
game′cock′
gam′ete
ga·me′to·phyte
gam′in
gam′i·ness
gam′ing
gam′ma glob′u·lin
gam′o·pet′al·ous
gam′o·sep′al·ous
gam′ut
gam′y
gan′der
gan′gling
gan′gli·on
gang′plank′
gan′grene
gan′gre·nous
gang′ster
gang′way′
gan′net
gan′oid
gant′let
  punishment
  (*see:* gauntlet)

gaped
  open-mouthed

gap′ing
gapped
  open

gap′ping
ga·rage′
Gar′and rifle
gar′bage
gar′bled
gar′bling
gar·con′
gar′den
gar·de′nia
gar′fish
Gar·gan′tu·an
gar′gled
gar′gling
gar′goyle
gar′ish
gar′land
gar′lic
gar′lick·y
gar′ment
gar′ner
gar′net
gar′nish
gar′nish·ee′
gar′nish·ee′ing
gar′nish·ment
gar′ni·ture
gar′ret
gar′ri·son
gar·rote′
gar·rot′ed
gar·rot′ing
gar·ru′li·ty
gar′ru·lous
gar′ter
Gas′co·ny
gas′e·ous
gashed
gas′i·fi·ca′tion
gas′i·fy
gas′ket
gas′o·line
gas·om′e·ter
gas′sy
gas′tric
gas·trit′ic
gas·tri′tis

gas′tro·nom′i·cal
gas·tron′o·my
gas′tro·pod
gas′tru·la
gate
movable barrier
(*see:* gait)

gate′way′
gath′ered
gath′er·ing
Gat′ling gun
gauche
gau′che·rie′
gaud′i·er
gaud′i·ly
gaud′y
gauge
measure (*see:* gage)

gauged
gaug′ing
Gau·guin′
gaunt′let
heavy glove
(*see:* gantlet)

gaunt′ly
gauze
gauz′i·ness
gauz′y
gav′el
ga·votte′
gawk′i·ness
gawk′y
gay′e·ty
(*also:* gaiety)

gay′ly
(*also:* gaily)

gazed
ga·zelle′
ga·zette′
gaz′et·teer′
gaz′ing
gear′shift′
gear′wheel′
Ge·hen′na
Gei′ger counter
gei′sha
gel
(*also:* jell)

gel′a·tin
ge·lat′i·nous
geld′ed
geld′ing
gel′id
ge·lid′i·ty
gelled
gel′ling
gem′i·nate
gem′i·na′tion
Gem′i·ni
gem′ma
gem′mate
gemmed
gen′darme
gen′der
ge′ne·a·log′i·cal
ge′ne·al′o·gist
ge′ne·al′o·gy
gen′er·al
gen′er·al·is′si·mo
gen′er·al′i·ty

gen′er·al·i·za′tion
gen′er·al·ize
gen′er·al·ly
gen′er·al·ship′
gen′er·ate
gen′er·at·ing
gen′er·a′tion
gen′er·a′tive
gen′er·a′tor
gen′er·a′trix
ge·ner′ic
ge·ner′i·cal·ly
gen′er·os′i·ty
gen′er·ous
Gen′e·sis
gen′et
(*also:* jennet)

ge·net′i·cist
ge·net′ics
Ge·ne′va
gen′ial
ge′ni·al′i·ty
ge′nie
gen′i·tals
gen′i·tive
gen′ius
Gen′o·a
gen′o·cide
Gen′o·ese′
gen′re
gen·teel′
gen′tian
gen′tile
gen·til′i·ty
gen′tle
gen′tle·man

gen′tly
gen′try
gen′u·flect
gen′u·flec′tion
gen′u·ine
gen′u·ine·ly
ge′nus
ge′o·cen′tric
ge·od′e·sy
ge′o·det′ic
ge·og′ra·pher
ge′o·graph′i·cal
ge·og′ra·phy
ge′o·log′i·cal
ge·ol′o·gist
ge·ol′o·gy
ge′o·met′ri·cal
ge·om′e·tri′cian
ge·om′e·try
ge′o·phys′i·cist
ge′o·phys′ics
ge′o·po·lit′i·cal
ge′o·pol′i·ti′cian
ge′o·pol′i·tics
Geor′gian
ge′o·tech′no·log′
i·cal
ge′o·tech·nol′o·gy
ge′o·trop′ic
ge·ot′ro·pism
ge·ra′ni·um
ger′i·at′rics
ger·mane′
Ger·man′ic
ger·ma′ni·um
Ger′ma·ny
ger′mi·cid′al
ger′mi·cide
ger′mi·nal
ger′mi·nant
ger′mi·nate
ger′mi·na′tion
ger′on·to·log′i·cal
ger′on·tol′o·gist
ger′on·tol′o·gy
ger′ry·man′der
ger′und
ge·run′dive
Ge·stalt′
Ge·sta′po
ges′tate
ges′tat·ing
ges·ta′tion
ges·tic′u·late
ges·tic′u·la′tion
ges·tic′u·la·to′ry
ges′ture
ges′tur·ing
get′a·way′
Geth·sem′a·ne
get′ting
Get′tys·burg
get′up′
gew′gaw
gey′ser
ghast′li·ness
ghast′ly
gher′kin
ghet′to
ghost′li·ness
ghost′ly
ghost′-write′
ghost′-writ′ten
ghoul′ish
gi′ant
gib′ber
gib′ber·ish
gib′bet
gib′bon
gibe
(*also:* jibe)
gib′ing
gib′lets
Gi·bral′tar
gid′di·ly
gid′dy
Gid′e·on
gift′ed
gi·gan′tic
gig′gle
gig′gling
gig′o·lo
gild
cover with gold (*see:* gilled; guild)
gilled
having gills (*see:* gild; guild)
gilt
layer of gold (*see:* guilt)
gilt′-edged′
gim′bals
gim′let
gim′mick
gin′ger·bread′
gin′ger·li·ness
gin′ger·ly
gin′ger·snap

ging′ham
gink′go
gi·raffe′
gird′er
gird′ing
gir′dle
gir′dling
girl′hood
girl′ish·ly
girth
gist
give′a·way′
giv′en
giv′ing
giz′zard
gla′brous
gla·ce′
gla′cial
gla′ci·a′tion
gla′cier
glad′den
glad′i·a′tor
glad′i·a·to′ri·al
glad′i·o′lus
(or: gladiola)

glad′ly
glad′some
glair
glaze *(see:* glare)

glam′or·ous
glam′our
(or: glamor)

glance
glanc′ing
glan′ders
glan′du·lar
glan′du·lous
glare
bright light *(see:* glair)

glar′ing
glar′y
Glas′gow
glass′es
glass′ful
glass′i·ly
glass′ware′
glass′y
glau·co′ma
glau·co′ma·tous
glau′cous
glazed
gla′zier
glaz′ing
gleam
glean′er
glee′ful
glen·gar′ry
glib′best
glib′ly
glide
glid′er
glid′ing
glim′mer
glim′mer·ing·ly
glimpse
glimps′ing
glis′ten
glit′ter
glit′ter·ing
gloam′ing
gloat′ing
glob′al
glob′al·ly
globe′trot′ter
glo′bose
glo·bos′i·ty
glob′u·lar
glob′u·lar′i·ty
glob′ule
glock′en·spiel′
glom′er·ate
glom′er·a′tion
gloom′i·ly
gloom′y
glo′ri·a
glo′ri·fi·ca′tion
glo′ri·fied
glo′ri·fy
glo′ri·fy·ing
glo′ri·ous
glo′ry
glos′sa·ry
gloss′er
gloss′i·ly
gloss′y
glot′tal
glot′tis
Glouces′ter·shire
gloved
glov′er
glov′ing
glow′er
glow′er·ing·ly
glow′ing
glow′worm′
glu·ci′num
glu′cose

glued
glue′y
glu′ing
glum′ly
glu′ten
glu′ti · nous
glut′ted
glut′ton
glut′ton · y
glyc′er · in
(*or:* -ine)

glyc′er · ol
gly′co · gen
gnarled
gnash
gnat′like′
gnawed
gnaw′ing
gnome
gno′mic
Gnos′tic
Gnos′ti · cism
gnu
goad′ed
goal′keep′er
goat · ee′
goat′skin′
gob′bet
gob′ble
gob′ble · dy · gook′
gob′bler
gob′bling
Go′bi
gob′let
gob′lin
go′cart′
god′child′
god′dess
god′fa′ther
God′head
god′less · ness
god′like′
god′li · ness
god′ly
god′moth′er
god′send′
God′speed′
Goe′the
go′-get′ter
gog′gle
gog′gle-eyed′
gog′gling
go′ing
goi′ter
gold′en · rod′
gold′fish′
gold′smith′
golf′er
Gol′go · tha
Go · li′ath
Go · mor′rah
gon′ad
go · na′di · al
gon′do · la
gon′do · lier′
gon′fa · lon
gon′or · rhe′a
gon′or · rhe′al
goo′ber
good′-by′
(*also:* -bye)

good′-heart′ed
good′ humor
good′-hum′ored
good′ies
good′-na′tured
good′ness
good′y
goose
(*plural:* geese)

goose′ber′ry
goose′neck′
goose′-step′
go′pher
gored
gorge
gor′geous
gor′get
gorg′ing
gor′gon
Gor′gon · zo′la
go · ril′la
ape (*see:* guerilla)

gor′ing
gor′mand
(*also:* gourmand)

gor′y
gos′hawk′
gos′ling
gos′pel
gos′sa · mer
gos′sip
Goth′am
Goth′ic
got′ten
goug′ing
gou′lash

gourd
gour′mand
(*also:* gormand)

gour·met′
gout′y
gov′ern
gov′ern·ance
gov′ern·ess
gov′ern·ment
gov′ern·men′tal
gov′er·nor
gowned
grab′bing
grace′ful
grac′ing
gra′cious
grack′le
gra·da′tion
grad′ed
grad′er
gra′di·ent
grad′ing
grad′u·al
grad′u·ate
grad′u·at·ing
grad′u·a′tion
graft′ing
gra′ham
grain′y
gram′mar
gram·mar′i·an
gram·mat′i·cal
gram′o·phone
gram′pus
gran′a·ry
grand′child′
gran·dee′
gran′deur
grand′fa′ther
gran·dil′o·quence
gran·dil′o·quent
gran′di·ose
gran′di·os′i·ty
grand′par′ent
grand′stand′
grang′er
gran′ite
gran′ny
grant′er
grant′or, *Law*
gran′u·lar
gran′u·lar′i·ty
gran′u·late
gran′u·lat·ing
gran′u·la′tion
gran′ule
grape′fruit′
grape′vine′
graph′ic
graph′i·cal·ly
graph′ite
gra·phit′ic
grap′nel
grap′ple
grap′pling
grasped
grass′hop′per
grass′land′
grass′y
grate
framework (*see:* great)

grate′ful
grat′i·fi·ca′tion
grat′i·fied
grat′i·fy
grat′i·fy′ing
grat′ing
grat′is
grat′i·tude
gra·tu′i·tous
gra·tu′i·ty
grav′el
grav′el·ly
grave′ly
grav′en
grave′yard′
grav′i·tate
grav′i·tat·ing
grav′i·ta′tion
grav′i·ty
gra·vure′
gra′vy
gray
(*also:* grey)

gray′beard′
gray′ish
gray mar′ket
graze
graz′ing
greas′i·ly
grease′wood′
greas′y
great
large (*see:* grate)

great′coat′
greave
armor (*see:* grieve)

grebe
Gre′cian
Gre′co-Ro′man
greed′i·ly
greed′y
green′er·y
green′gage′
green′horn′
green′house′
green′sward′
Green′wich
greet′ing
gre·gar′i·ous
Gre·go′ri·an
grem′lin
gre·nade′
gren′a·dier′
gren′a·dine′
grey
(*also:* gray)

grey′hound′
grid′dle·cake′
grid′i′ron
grief
griev′ance
grieve
to sorrow (*see:* greave)

griev′ing
griev′ous
grif′fin
(*also:* griffon; gryphon)

grill
broil

grille
screen

gri·mace′
grime
grim′i·er
grim′mer
grim′ness
grim′y
grind′ing
grind′stone′
grin′go
grinned
grin′ning
grip
seize

gripe
complain

grip′ing
complaining

grippe
influenza

grip′ping
holding

gris′li·er
gris′ly
gris′tle
gris′tly
grit′ting
grit′ty
griz′zled
griz′zly
groaned
groan′ing·ly
gro′cer
gro′cer·y
grog′gi·ness
grog′gy
grog′ram
grog′shop′
groin
grom′met
grooms′man
groove
groov′ing
grope
grop′ing
gros′beak′
gros′grain′
gross′ly
gro·tesque′
grot′to
grouch′i·ness
grouch′y
ground crew
ground′er
ground floor
ground′less
ground plan
ground′sill
ground′work′
group′er
grouse
grov′eled
grov′el·ing
grow′ing
grown′-up′
growth
grubbed
grub′bi·er
grub′bing
grub′stake′

grub′by
grudge
grudg′ing·ly
gru′el·ing
grue′some
gruff′ly
grum′ble
grum′bling
grump′i·ness
grump′y
grunt′ing
Gru·yere′
Gua′dal·ca·nal′
Gua′de·loupe′
gua′no
guar′an·tee′
guar′an·tee′ing
guar′an·tor
guar′an·ty
guard′ed
guard′house′
guard′i·an
guards′man
Gua′te·ma′la
gua′va
gu′ber·na·to′ri·al
gudg′eon
guer′don
Guern′sey
guer·ril′la
fighter; band of fighters (*see:* gorilla)

guess′ing
guess′work′
guest
guf·faw′
Gui·a′na
guid′ance
guide′book′
guid′ing
gui′don
guild
union (*see:* gild)

guil′der
guile′ful
guil′lo·tine
guilt
culpability (*see* gilt)

guilt′i·ly
guilt′y
guin′ea
guise
gui·tar′
gul′let
gul′li·bil′i·ty
gul′li·ble
gul′ly
gulped
gulp′ing
gum′bo
gum′drop′
gummed
gum′mi·ness
gum′my
gump′tion
gum′shoe′
gun′boat′
gun′fire′
gun′lock′
gun′nel
(*also:* gunwale)
gun′ner
gun′ner·y
gun′ning
gun′ny
gun′pow′der
gun′shot′
gun′smith′
gun′stock′
gun′wale
(*also:* gunnel)

gup′py
gur′gle
gur′gling
gush′er
gush′ing
gush′y
gus′set
gus′ta·to′ry
gust′i·ly
gus′to
gust′y
Gu′ten·berg
gut′ta-per′cha
gut′ted
gut′ter
gut′ter·snipe′
gut′ting
gut′tur·al
gut′tur·al′i·ty
guy′ing
guz′zle
guz′zling
gym·na′si·um
gym′nast
gym·nas′tics
gym′no·sperm

gym′no·sper′mous
gy′ne·co·log′i·cal
gy′ne·col′o·gist
gy′ne·col′o·gy
gy·noe′ci·um
gypped
gyp′ping
gyp·soph′i·la
gyp′sum
gyp′sy
gy′rate
gy′rat·ing
gy·ra′tion
gy′ra·to′ry
gy′ro·com′pass
gy′ro·scope
gy′ro·scop′ic
gy′ro·sta′bi·liz′er

H

ha′be·as cor′pus
hab′er·dash′er
hab′er·dash′er·y
ha·bil′i·ment
hab′it
hab′it·a·bil′i·ty
hab′it·a·ble
hab′it·ant
hab′i·tat
hab′i·ta′tion
ha·bit′u·al·ly
ha·bit′u·ate
ha·bit′u·a′tion
hab′i·tude
ha·bit′u·e′
ha′ci·en′da
hack′a·more
hack′ber′ry
hack′le
hack′ney
hack′neyed
hack′saw′
had′dock
Ha′des
haf′ni·um
hag′fish
hag′gard
hag′gis
hag′gle
hag′gling
hag′i·ol′o·gy
hag′rid′den
Hai′fa
hail′stone′
hair′cut′
hair′dress′er
hair′line′
hair′pin′
hair′split′ting
hair′y
Hai′ti
hal′berd
hal′cy·on
half
(*plural:* halves)
half′back′
half′-breed′
half′-heart′ed
half′-hour′
half′-mast′
half′pen·ny
half′-tone′
half′way′
half′-wit′ted
hal′i·but
Hal′i·fax
hal′i·to′sis
hal′le·lu′jah
hall′mark′
hal·loo′
hal′low
hal′lowed·ness
Hal′low·een′
hal·lu′ci·na′tion
hall′way′
ha′lo
hal′ter
halt′ing·ly
halve
halv′ing
hal′yard
(*also:* halliard)
ham′burg·er
ham′let
ham′mer
ham′mer·head′
ham′mock
ham′per
ham′string′

ham′strung′
hand′bag′
hand′ball′
hand′cuff′
hand′ful
hand′i·cap
hand′i·capped
hand′i·cap·ping
hand′i·craft
hand′i·crafts′man
hand′i·work′
hand′ker·chief
han′dle
han′dler
hand′made′
made by hand

hand′maid′
female servant

hand′out′
hand′shake′
hand′some
hand′some·ly
hand′spring′
hand′writ′ing
hand′y
hang′ar
airplane shed

hang′dog′
hang′er
one that hangs

hang′ing
hang′man
hang′out′
hang′o′ver
han′ker
Ha·noi′
Han′o·ver
Han′o·ve′ri·an
han′som
hap′haz′ard
hap′less
hap′pen
hap′pi·ness
hap′py
hap′py-go-luck′y
har′a-ki′ri
ha·rangue′
ha·rangu′ing
har′ass
har′ass·ment
har′bin·ger
har′bor
hard′-boiled′
hard′en
hard′-heart′ed
har′di·hood
har′di·ness
hard′ly
hard′ship
hard′tack′
hard′top′
hard′ware′
hard′wood′
har′dy
hare′brained′
hare′lip′
har′em
hark′en
(*also:* hearken)

Har′lem
har′le·quin
har′lot
harm′ful·ly
harm′less
har·mon′ic
har·mon′i·ca
har·mon′ics
har·mo′ni·ous
har·mo′ni·um
har′mo·ni·za′tion
har′mo·nize
har′mo·niz·ing
har′mo·ny
har′ness
harp′ist
har·poon′
harp′si·chord
har′py
har′que·bus
har′ri·dan
har′ri·er
har′row
har′ry
harsh′ly
har′te·beest
har′um-scar′um
har′vest
har′vest·er
hash′ish
has′sle
has′sock
has′ten
hast′i·ly
hast′ing
hast′y
hat′band′
hatch′er·y
hatch′et

hatch′ing
hatch′way′
hate′ful
hat′ing
ha′tred
hat′ter
haugh′ti·ly
haugh′ty
haunch
haunt′ed
hau·teur′
Ha·van′a
ha′ven
have′-not′
hav′er·sack
hav′oc
hav′ocked
hav′ock·ing
Ha·wai′i
Ha·wai′ian
hawk′-eyed′
haw′ser
haw′thorn
  thorny shrub
Haw′thorne
  Nathaniel: author
hay′field′
hay′mak′er
hay′seed′
hay′stack
hay′wire′
haz′ard·ous
ha′zel·nut′
ha′zi·ly
haz′ing
ha′zy

head′ache′
head′dress′
head′ed
head′ing
head′less
head′line
head′mas′ter
head′quar′ters
head′strong′
head′way′
head′y
heal′ing
health′ful
health′i·er
health′y
heaped
heard
hear′ing
heark′en
hear′say′
hearse
heart′beat′
heart′bro′ken
heart′burn′
heart′en
heart′felt′
hearth′stone′
heart′i·ly
heart′less
heart′-rend′ing
heart′y
heat′ed
heat′er
heath
hea′then
hea′then·ish
heath′er

heaved
heav′en
heav′en·ly
heav′i·er
heav′i·ly
heav′ing
heav′y
heav′y·weight′
He·bra′ic
He·bra′i·cal·ly
He′bra·ism
He′brew
Heb′ri·des
heck′le
heck′ler
heck′ling
hec′tare
hec′tic
hec′ti·cal·ly
hec′to·graph
hec′tor
Hec′u·ba
hedge′hog′
hedg′ing
he′don·ism
he′do·nis′ti·cal
heed′ful
heed′less
heft′i·er
heft′y
heg′e·mon′ic
he·gem′o·ny
Hei·del·berg
heif′er
height′en
hei′nous
heir′ess

heir′loom′
hel′i·cal
hel′i·cop′ter
he′li·o·cen′tric
he′li·o·graph′
he′li·og′ra·phy
he′li·o·scope′
he′li·o·trope
he′li·ot′ro·pism
hel′i·port
he′li·um
he′lix
hell′-bent′
hell′cat′
Hel·len′ic
Hel′len·is′tic
hel′lion
hell′ish
hel·lo′
hel′met
hel′minth
helms′man
help′ful
help′less
help′mate′
Hel′sin·ki
hel′ter-skel′ter
hem′a·tite
hem′i·sphere
hem′i·spher′
i·cal·ly
hem′lock
he′mo·glo′bin
he′mo·phil′i·a
he′mo·phil′i·ac
hem′or·rhage
hem′or·rhag′ic
hem′or·rhoids
hem′or·rhoi′dal
hemp′en
hem′stitch′
hence′forth′
hench′man
hen′house′
hen′na
hen′naed
hen′na·ing
hen′ner·y
hen′peck′
hen′ry, *elec.*
he·pat′ic
he·pat′i·ca
hep′ta·gon
hep·tag′o·nal
hep·tam′e·ter
her′ald
he·ral′dic
her′ald·ry
her·ba′ceous
herb′age
herb′al
her·bar′i·um
her·biv′o·rous
her·cu′le·an
Her′cu·les
herds′man
here′a·bouts′
here·af′ter
here·by′
he·red′i·ta·bil′i·ty
he·red′i·ta·ble
he·red′i·tar′i·ly
he·red′i·tar′y
he·red′i·ty
Her′e·ford
here·in′
her′e·sy
her′e·tic
here′to·fore′
here′up·on′
her′it·a·bil′i·ty
her′it·a·ble
her′it·age
her·maph′ro·dite
her·met′ic
her·met′i·cal·ly
her′mit
her′mit·age
her′ni·a
Her′od
he·ro′ic
her′o·in
drug
her′o·ine
great woman
her′o·ism
her′on
her′pes
her′pe·to·log′i·cal
her′pe·tol′o·gy
her′ring
her′ring·bone′
her·self′
hes′i·tan·cy
hes′i·tant
hes′i·tate
hes′i·tat′ing
hes′i·ta′tion
Hes′per·us
Hes′sian

het′er·o·dox
het′er·o·dox′y
het′er·o·dyne′
het′er·o·ge·ne′i·ty
het′er·o·ge′ne·ous
hew′ing
hex′a·gon
hex·ag′o·nal
hex′a·gram
hex′a·he′dron
hex·am′e·ter
hex′a·met′ric
hex′a·pod
hey′day′
hi·a′tus
hi·ber′nal
hi′ber·nate
hi′ber·nat·ing
hi′ber·na′tion
Hi·ber′ni·a
hi·bis′cus
hic′cup
(*also:* hiccough)

hick′o·ry
hi·dal′go
hid′den
hide′bound′
hid′e·ous
hid′ing
hi′er·ar′chi·cal
hi′er·ar′chy
hi′er·at′ic
hier′o·glyph′ic
hi′-fi′
high′ball′
high′boy′
high′-fi·del′i·ty
high′-fre′quen·cy
high′hat′
high′land
High′land·er
high′light′
high′ness
high′-spir′it·ed
high′-strung′
high′way′man
hi′jack′
hik′ing
hi·lar′i·ous
hi·lar′i·ty
hill′bil′ly
hill′ock
hill′side′
hill′y
hi′lum
Him′a·la′yas
him·self′
hin′der, *v.*
prevent

hind′er, *adj.*
rear

hind′most
hind′quar′ter
hin′drance
hind′sight′
Hin′du
Hin′du·stan′
hing′ing
hin′ter·land′
Hip·poc′ra·tes
Hip′po·crat′ic
hip′po·drome
hip′po·pot′a·mus
hir′cine
hire′ling
hir′ing
Hir′o·shi′ma
hir′sute
His′pan·io′la
his′ta·mine
his′to·log′i·cal
his·tol′o·gy
his·to′ri·an
his·tor′i·cal
his′to·ry
his′tri·on′i·cal
his′tri·on′ics
hitch′hike′
hitch′hik′er
hith′er·to′
hit′ting
Hit′tite
hoard
save (*see:* horde)

hoar′frost′
hoar′hound′
(*also:* hore-)

hoar′i·ness
hoarse
rough-sounding
(*see:* horse)

hoar′y
hoax
hob′ble
hob′bling
hob′by
hob′by·horse′

hob'gob'lin
hob'nail'
hob'nob'bing
ho'bo
hock'ey
ho'cus-po'cus
hodge'podge'
hog'ging
hog'gish
hogs'head
hog'tie'
hoi' pol·loi'
ho'kum
hold'er
hol'i·day
ho'li·ness
Hol'land
hol'low
hol'ly
hol'ly·hock
hol'o·caust
hol'o·graph
Hol'stein
hol'ster
hom'age
hom'burg
home'land'
home'li·ness
home'ly
home'made'
ho'me·o·path'ic
ho'me·op'a·thist
ho'me·op'a·thy
home'sick'
home'stead
home'y
hom'i·cid'al
hom'i·cide
hom'i·let'ics
hom'i·ly
hom'i·ny
ho'mo·ge·ne'i·ty
ho'mo·ge'ne·ous
ho·mog'e·nize
ho·mog'e·niz·ing
hom'o·graph
ho·mol'o·gous
ho·mol'o·gy
hom'o·nym
hom'o·phone
ho·moph'o·ny
Ho'mo sa'pi·ens
ho'mo·sex'u·al
ho'mo·sex'u·al'
i·ty
ho·mun'cu·lus
Hon·du'ras
honed
hon'est
hon'es·ty
hon'ey
hon'ey·bee'
hon'ey·dew'
hon'ey·moon'
hon'ey·suck'le
hon'ing
honk'y-tonk'
Hon'o·lu'lu
hon'or
hon'or·a·ble
hon'o·rar'i·um
hon'or·ar'y
hon'or·if'ic
hood'lum
hoo'doo
hood'wink
hoof'beat'
hook'ah
hook'up'
hook'worm'
hook'y
hoo'li·gan
hoo·ray'
hoose'gow
Hoo'sier
hope'ful
Ho'pi
hop'per
hop'scotch'
horde
crowd (*see:* hoard)

hore'hound'
(*also:* hoar-)

ho·ri'zon
hor'i·zon'tal
hor·mo'nal
hor'mone
horn'bill'
hor'net
horn'pipe'
horn'swog'gle
horn'y
ho·rol'o·ger
(*also:* horologist)

ho·rol'o·gy
hor'o·scope
hor·ren'dous
hor'ri·ble
hor'rid

hor′ri·fied
hor′ri·fy
hor′ror-strick′en
hors d′oeu′vre
horse
animal *(see:* hoarse)

horse′back′
horse′fly′
horse′man
horse′play′
horse′pow′er
horse′rad′ish
horse′shoe′
horse′whip′
hors′y
hor′ta·to′ry
hor′ti·cul′ture
hor′ti·cul′tur·ist
ho·san′na
ho′sier·y
hos′pice
hos′pi·ta·ble
hos′pi·tal
hos′pi·tal′i·ty
hos′pi·tal·i·za′tion
hos′pi·tal·ize
hos′tage
hos′tel
lodging *(see:* hostile)

hos′tel·ry
host′ess
hos′tile
unfriendly *(see:* hostel)

hos·til′i·ty
hos′tler
hot′bed′
hot′box′
ho·tel′
hot′-head′ed
hot′house′
hot′-tem′pered
Hot′ten·tot
hound
hour′glass′
house′boat′
house′bro′ken
house′hold
house′keep′er
house′warm′ing
house′wife′
house′work′
hous′ing
Hous′ton
hov′el
hov′er
how·ev′er
how′itz·er
howl′er
hoy′den
hub′bub
huck′le·ber′ry
huck′ster
hud′dle
hud′dling
huff′i·ness
huff′y
huge′ly
hugged
hug′ging
Hu′gue·not
hu′la-hu′la
hulk′ing
hul′la·ba·loo′
hu′man
hu·mane′
hu′man·ism
hu′man·is′tic
hu·man′i·tar′i·an
hu·man′i·ty
hu′man·ize
hu′man·kind′
hum′ble
hum′bly
hum′bug′
hum′drum′
hu′mer·al
hu′mer·us
upper arm bone *(see:* humorous)

hu′mid
hu·mid′i·fi·ca′tion
hu·mid′i·fied
hu·mid′i·fy
hu·mid′i·ty
hu′mi·dor
hu·mil′i·ate
hu·mil′i·at′ing
hu·mil′i·a′tion
hu·mil′i·ty
hu′mit
hu′mi·ture
hum′ming·bird′
hum′mock
hu′mor
hu′mor·esque′
hu′mor·ist

hu′mor·ous
funny *(see:* humerus)

hump′back′
hump′y
hu′mus
hunch′back′
hun′dred
hun′dredth
hun′dred·weight′
Hun·gar′i·an
Hun′ga·ry
hun′ger·ing
hun′gri·er
hun′gri·ly
hun′gry
hunt′er
hunts′man
hur′dle
barrier *(see:* hurtle)

hur′dler
hur′dy-gur′dy
hurl′er
hurl′y-burl′y
Hu′ron
hur·rah′
hur′ri·cane
hur′ried
hur′ry
hur′ry-scur′ry
hurt′ful
hurt′ing
hur′tle
dash *(see:* hurdle)

hus′band
hus′band·ry
husk′er
husk′i·ness
husk′ing
husk′y
hus·sar′
hus′sy
hus′tings
hus′tle
hus′tling
hy′a·cinth
hy′brid
hy′brid·i·za′tion
hy′dra
hy·dran′gea
hy′drant
hy′drate
hy·dra′tion
hy·drau′lic
hy·drau′li·cal·ly
hy′dride
hy′dro·car′bon
hy′dro·chlo′ric
hy′dro·cor′ti·sone
hy′dro·cy·an′ic
hy′dro·dy·nam′ics
hy′dro·e·lec′tric
hy′dro·flu·or′ic
hy′dro·gen
hy′dro·gen·a′tion
hy′dro·gen·ize
hy·drog′e·nous
hy′dro·graph′ic
hy·drog′ra·phy
hy′droid
hy′dro·lyt′ic
hy·drol′y·sis
hy′dro·lyze
hy·drom′e·ter
hy·drom′e·try
hy·drop′a·thy
hy′dro·pho′bi·a
hy′dro·pho′bic
hy′dro·phyte
hy′dro·plane
hy′dro·sphere
hy′dro·stat
hy′dro·stat′ics
hy′dro·ther′a·peu′tics
hy′dro·ther′a·py
hy′drous
hy·drox′ide
hy·drox′yl
hy′dro·zo′an
hy·e′na
hy′giene
hy′gi·en′ic
hy′gi·en′i·cal·ly
hy′gien·ist
hy′gro·met′ric
hy·grom′e·try
hy′gro·scope
hy′men
hy′me·ne′al
hy′me·nop′ter·ous
hym′nal
hym·nol′o·gy
hy′per·ac′id
hy′per·a·cid′i·ty
hy·per′bo·la
curve

hy·per′bo·le
exaggeration

hy′per·bol′ic
hy′per·crit′i·cal
hy′per·sen′si·tive
hy′per·ten′sion
hy′per·troph′ic
hy·per′tro·phy
hy′phen
hy′phen·a′tion
hyp·no′sis
hyp·not′ic
hyp·not′i·cal·ly
hyp′no·tism
hyp′no·tize
hyp′no·tiz·ing
hy′po·chlo′rite
hy′po·chlo′rous
hy′po·chon′dri·a
hy′po·chon′dri·ac
hy·poc′ri·sy
hyp′o·crite
hyp′o·crit′i·cal·ly
hy′po·der′mic
hy′po·der′mi·cal·ly
hy′po·phos′phite
hy′po·sul′fite
hy·pot′e·nuse
hy·poth′e·cate
hy·poth′e·ca′tion
hy·poth′e·sis
(*plural:* -ses)
hy·poth′e·size
hy′po·thet′i·cal
hys′sop
hys′ter·ec′to·my
hys·te′ri·a
hys·ter′i·cal

I

i′amb
i-am′bic
I·be′ri·a
i′bex
i′bis
ice′berg′
ice′box′
ice′break′er
ice′cap′
Ice′land
ich·neu′mon
ich′thy·o·log′i·cal
ich′thy·ol′o·gist
ich′thy·ol′o·gy
i′ci·cle
ic′ing
i′con
(*also:* ikon)
i·con′o·clast
i·con′o·clas′tic
I′da·ho
i·de′a
i·de′al
i·de′al·ism
i·de′al·is′tic
i·de′al·i·za′tion
i·de′al·ize
i·de′al·ly
i·den′ti·cal
i·den′ti·fi′able
i·den′ti·fi·ca′tion
i·den′ti·fied
i·den′ti·ty
id′e·o·graph′
(*also:* ideogram)
i′de·o·log′i·cal
i′de·ol′o·gist
i′de·ol′o·gy
id′i·o·cy
id′i·om
id′i·o·mat′ic
id′i·o·syn′cra·sy
id′i·ot
id′i·ot′ic
i′dling
i′dly
i·dol′a·ter
i·dol′a·trous
i·dol′a·try
i′dol·i·za′tion
i′dol·ize
i′dyl
i·dyl′lic
ig′loo
ig′ne·ous
ig·nite′
ig·nit′ing
ig·ni′tion

ig′no·bil′i·ty
ig·no′ble
ig′no·min′i·ous
ig′no·min′y
ig′no·ra′mus
ig′no·rance
ig·nore′
i·gua′na
i′kon
(*also:* icon)

il′e·i′tis
il′e·um
lower small intestine
(*see:* ilium)

i′lex
il′i·ac
Il′i·ad
il′i·um
upper hipbone
(*see:* ileum)

ill′-ad·vised′
il·le′gal
il′le·gal′i·ty
il·leg′i·bil′i·ty
il·leg′i·ble
il′le·git′i·ma·cy
il′le·git′i·mate
ill′-got′ten
ill′-hu′mored
il·lic′it
il·lim′it·a·ble
Il′li·nois′
il·lit′er·a·cy
il·lit′er·ate
ill′-man′nered
ill′ness
il·log′i·cal
ill′-suit′ed
il·lu′mi·nant
il·lu′mi·nate
il·lu′mi·nat′ing
il·lu′mi·na′tion
il·lu′mine
il·lu′min·ing
il·lu′sion
false idea
(*see:* elusion)

il·lu′sive
il·lu′so·ri·ly
il·lu′so·ry
il′lus·trate
il′lus·trat·ing
il′lus·tra′tion
il·lus′tra·tive
il·lus′tri·ous
im′age
im′age·ry
i·mag′i·na·ble
i·mag′i·nar′y
i·mag′i·na′tion
i·mag′i·na′tive
i·mag′ine
i·mag′in·ing
im′ag·ism
im′ag·ist
i·ma′go
im′ag·is′tic
im′be·cile
im′be·cil′i·ty
im·bed′
im·bibe′
im·bib′er
im′bri·cate
im′bri·ca′tion
im·bro′glio
im·brue′
im·bru′ing
im·bue′
im·bu′ing
im′i·ta·bil′i·ty
im′i·ta·ble
im′i·tate
im′i·ta′tion
im′i·ta′tive
im′i·ta′tor
im·mac′u·la·cy
im·mac′u·late
im′ma·nence
im′ma·nent
dwelling within (*see:* imminent)

Im·man′u·el
(*also:* Emmanuel)

im′ma·te′ri·al
im′ma·ture′
im′ma·tur′i·ty
im·meas′ur·a·bly
im·me′di·a·cy
im·me′di·ate
im·me′di·ate·ly
im′me·mo′ri·al
im·mense′
im·men′si·ty
im·merse′
im·mer′sion
dipping
(*see:* emersion)

im′mi·grant
one entering *(see:* emigrant)

im′mi·grate
im′mi·gra′tion
im′mi·nence
im′mi·nent
impending
(see: immanent)

im·mis′ci·ble
im·mo′bile
im′mo·bil′i·ty
im·mo′bi·li·za′tion
im·mo′bi·lize
im·mod′er·ate
im·mod′est
im′mo·late
im′mo·la′tion
im·mor′al
im·mor′al·ly
im·mor′tal
im′mor·tal′i·ty
im·mor′tal·i·za′tion
im·mor′tal·ize
im·mov′a·bil′i·ty
im·mov′a·ble
im·mune′
im′mo·ral′i·ty
im·mu′ni·ty
im′mu·ni·za′tion
im′mu·nize
im′mu·nol′o·gy
im·mure′
im·mur′ing
im·mu′ta·bil′i·ty
im·mu′ta·ble
im′pact
im·pac′tion
im·pair′
im·pale′
im·pal′ing
im·pal′pa·bil′i·ty
im·pal′pa·ble
im·pan′el
im·pan′eled
im·part′
im·par′tial
im′par·ti·al′i·ty
im·part′i·ble
im·pass′a·bil′i·ty
im·pass′a·ble
not passable *(see:* impassible)

im·passe′
im·pas′si·bil′i·ty
im·pas′si·ble
without feeling *(see:* impassable)

im·pas′sioned
im·pas′sive
im′pas·siv′i·ty
im·pa′tience
im·pa′tient
im·peach′
im·peach′a·bil′i·ty
im·peach′ment
im·pec′ca·bil′i·ty
im·pec′ca·ble
im′pe·cu′ni·os′i·ty
im′pe·cu′ni·ous
im·ped′ance
im·pede′
im·ped′i·ment
im·ped′i·men′ta
im·ped′i·men′ta·ry
im·ped′ing
im·pel′
im·pelled′
im·pel′ling
im·pend′
im·pen′e·tra·bil′i·ty
im·pen′e·tra·ble
im·pen′i·tence
im·pen′i·tent
im·per′a·tive
im′pe·ra′tor
im·per′a·to′ri·al
im′per·cep′ti·ble
im·per′fect
im′per·fec′tion
im·per′fo·rate
im·per′fo·ra′tion
im·pe′ri·al
im·pe′ri·al·ism′
im·pe′ri·al·is′tic
im·per′il
im·per′il·ing
im·pe′ri·ous
im·per′ish·a·ble
im·per′ma·nence
im·per′ma·nent
im·per′me·a·bil′i·ty
im·per′me·a·ble
im·per′son·al
im·per′son·ate
im·per′son·a′tion

im·per′ti·nence
im·per′ti·nent
im′per·turb′a·bil′i·ty
im′per·turb′a·ble
im·per′vi·ous
im′pe·ti′go
im·pet′u·os′i·ty
im·pet′u·ous
im′pe·tus
im·pi′e·ty
im·pinge′
im·ping′ing
im′pi·ous
imp′ish
im·pla′ca·bil′i·ty
im·pla′ca·ble
im·plant′
im′plan·ta′tion
im′ple·ment
im′ple·men′tal
im′pli·cate
im′pli·ca′tion
im·plic′it
im·plied′
im·pli′ed·ly
im·plor′a·to′ry
im·plore′
im·plor′ing·ly
im·ply′
im′po·lite′
im·pon′der·a·ble
im·port′, *v.*
im′port, *n.*
im·por′tance
im·por′tant
im′por·ta′tion
im·por′tu·nate
im′por·tune′
im′por·tun′ing
im′por·tu′ni·ty
im·pose′
im·pos′ing
im′po·si′tion
im·pos′si·bil′i·ty
im·pos′si·ble
im′post
im·pos′tor
im·pos′ture
im′po·tence
im′po·tent
im·pound′
im·pov′er·ish
im·pow′er
im·prac′ti·ca·bil′i·ty
im·prac′ti·ca·ble
im·prac′ti·cal
im·prac′ti·cal′i·ty
im′pre·cate
im′pre·ca′tion
im′pre·ca·to′ry
im·preg′na·bil′i·ty
im·preg′na·ble
im·preg′nate
im′preg·na′tion
im′pre·sa′ri·o
im′pre·scrip′ti·ble
im·press′, *v.*
im′press, *n.*
im·pres′sion
im·pres′sion·a·ble
im·pres′sion·ism
im·pres′sion·is′tic
im·pres′sive
im′pri·ma′tur
im′print, *n.*
im·print′, *v.*
im·pris′on
im·prob′a·bil′i·ty
im·prob′a·ble
im·promp′tu
im·prop′er
im′pro·pri′e·ty
im·prove′
im·prove′ment
im·prov′ing
im·prov′i·dence
im·prov′i·dent
im′pro·vi·sa′tion
im′pro·vise
im′pro·vis·ing
im·pru′dence
im·pru′dent
im′pu·dence
im′pu·dent
im·pugn′
im′pug·na′tion
im·pugn′er
im′pulse
im·pul′sion
im·pul′sive
im·pu′ni·ty
im·pure′
im·pu′ri·ty
im′pu·ta′tion
im·pute′
im·put′ing
in′a·bil′i·ty
in ab·sen′tia
in′ac·ces′si·bil′i·ty

in′ac·ces′si·ble
in·ac′cu·ra·cy
in·ac′cu·rate
in·ac′tion
in′ac·ti·va′tion
in·ac′ti·vate
in·ac′tive
in·ad′e·qua·cy
in·ad′e·quate
in′ad·mis′si·ble
in′ad·ver′tence
in′ad·ver′tent
in′ad·vis′a·ble
in·al′ien·a·ble
in·am′o·ra′ta
in·ane′
in·an′i·mate
in′a·ni′tion
in·an′i·ty
in·ap′pli·ca·ble
in′ap·pro′pri·ate
in′ar·tic′u·late
in′at·ten′tion
in′at·ten′tive
in·au′di·ble
in·au′gu·ral
in·au′gu·rate
in·au′gu·rat·ing
in·au′gu·ra′tion
in′aus·pi′cious
in′born′
in′breed′ing
In′ca
in·cal′cu·la·ble
in′can·des′cence
in′can·des′cent
in′can·ta′tion
in·ca′pa·bil′i·ty
in·ca′pa·ble
in′ca·pac′i·tate
in′ca·pac′i·ta′tion
in′ca·pac′i·ty
in·car′cer·ate
in·car′cer·a′tion
in·car′na·dine
in·car′nate
in′car·na′tion
in·cau′tious
in·cen′di·a·rism′
in·cen′di·ar′y
in′cense, *n.*
in·cense′, *v.*
in·cens′ing
in·cen′tive
in·cep′tion
in·cer′ti·tude
in·ces′san·cy
in·ces′sant
in′cest
in·ces′tu·ous
in·cho′ate
in·cho′ate·ly
inch′worm′
in′ci·dence
in′ci·dent
in′ci·den′tal
in·cin′er·ate
in·cin′er·a′tion
in·cin′er·a′tor
in·cip′i·ence
in·cip′i·ent
in·cise′
in·ci′sion
in·ci′sive
in·ci′sor
in′ci·ta′tion
in·cite′
in·cit′ing
in′ci·vil′i·ty
in·clem′en·cy
in·clem′ent
in′cli·na′tion
in·cline′, *v.*
in′cline, *n.*
in·clin′ing
in′cli·nom′e·ter
in·close′
in·clude′
in·clud′ing
in·clu′sion
in·clu′sive
in·cog′ni·to
in′co·her′ence
in′co·her′ent
in′com·bus′ti·ble
in′come
in′com′ing
in′com·men′
su·ra·ble
in′com·men′
su·rate
in′com·mode′
in′com·mo′di·ous
in′com·mu′
ni·ca·ble
in′com·mu′ni·ca′
do
in·com′pa·ra·ble
in′com·pat′i·bil′
i·ty
in′com·pat′i·ble

in·com′pe·tence
in·com′pe·tent
in′com·plete′
in′com·plete′ly
in′com·pre·hen′
si·ble
in′com·press′i·ble
in′con·ceiv′a·ble
in′con·clu′sive
in′con·gru′i·ty
in·con′gru·ous
in·con′se·quent
in′con·se·quen′tial
in′con·sid′er·a·ble
in′con·sid′er·ate
in′consid′er·a′tion
in′con·sist′en·cy
in′con·sist′ent
in′con·sol′a·ble
in·con′so·nance
in·con′so·nant
in′con·spic′u·ous
in·con′stan·cy
in·con′stant
in′con·test′a·bil′
i·ty
in′con·test′a·ble
in·con′ti·nence
in·con′ti·nent
in′con·tro·vert′
i·ble
in′con·ven′ience
in′con·ven′ient
in′con·vert′i·ble
in·cor′po·rate
in·cor′po·rat·ed
in·cor′po·ra′tion
in·cor′po·ra′tive
in′cor·po′re·al
in′cor·rect′
in·cor′ri·gi·ble
in·cor′ri·gi·bil′i·ty
in′cor·rupt′i·bil′
i·ty
in′cor·rupt′i·ble
in·crease′, *v.*
in′crease, *n.*
in·creas′ing·ly
in·cred′i·ble
in′cre·du′li·ty
in·cred′u·lous
in′cre·ment
in·crim′i·nate
in·crim′i·na′tion
in·crim′i·na·to′ry
in·crust′
in′crus·ta′tion
in′cu·bate
in′cu·ba′tion
in′cu·ba′tor
in′cu·bus
in·cul′cate
in′cul·ca′tion
in·cul′pate
in′cul·pa′tion
in·cum′ben·cy
in·cum′bent
in·cum′ber
(*also:* encumber)
in′cu·nab′u·la
in·cur′
in·cur′a·ble
in·cu′ri·ous
in·cur′sion
in·debt′ed
in·de′cen·cy
in·de′cent
in′de·ci′pher·a·ble
in′de·ci′sion
in′de·ci′sive
in·dec′o·rous
in′de·co′rum
in·deed′
in′de·fat′i·ga·bil′
i·ty
in′de·fat′i·ga·ble
in′de·fea′si·ble
in′de·fen′si·ble
in′de·fin′a·ble
in·def′i·nite
in·def′i·nite·ly
in′de·his′cent
in·del′i·bil′i·ty
in·del′i·ble
in·del′i·ca·cy
in·del′i·cate
in·dem′ni·fi·ca′
tion
in·dem′ni·fied
in·dem′ni·fy
in·dem′ni·ty
in·dent′, *v.*
in′dent, *n.*
in′den·ta′tion
in·den′tion
in·den′ture
in′de·pend′ence
in′de·pend′en·cy
in′de·pend′ent
in′de·scrib′a·ble

in′de·struct′i·ble
in′de·ter′mi·nate
in′de·ter′mi·na′
tion
in′dex
(plural: -dexes;
-dices)

In′di·a
In′di·an
In′di·an′a
In′di·an·ap′o·lis
in′di·cate
in′di·ca′tion
in·dic′a·tive
in′di·ca′tor
in·dict′
accuse of crime
(see: indite)

in·dict′ment
in·dif′fer·ence
in·dif′fer·ent
in′di·gence
in′di·gen′i·ty
in·dig′e·nous
in′di·gent
in′di·gest′i·ble
in′di·ges′tion
in·dig′nant
in′dig·na′tion
in·dig′ni·ty
in′di·go
in′di·rect′
in′dis·cern′i·ble
in′dis·creet′
in′dis·cre′tion
in′dis·crim′i·nate
in′dis·pen′sa·ble
in′dis·pose′
in′dis·po·si′tion
in·dis·put′a·ble
in′dis·sol′u·ble
in′dis·tinct′
in′dis·tin′
guish·a·ble
in·dite′
write *(see:* indict)

in·dite′ment
in′di·vid′u·al
in′di·vid′u·al·is′tic
in′di·vid′u·al′i·ty
in′di·vid′u·al·ly
in′di·vis′i·bil′i·ty
In′do-Chi′na
in·doc′tri·nate
in·doc′tri·na′tion
In′do-Eu′ro·pe′an
in′do·lence
in′do·lent
in·dom′i·ta·ble
In′do·ne′sia
in′doors′
in·dorse′
in′dor·see′
in·dorse′ment
in·dors′er
in·du′bi·ta·ble
in·duce′
in·duce′ment
in·duc′i·ble
in·duc′ing
in·duct′
in·duct′ance
in·duc′tee
in·duc′tile
in′duc·til′i·ty
in·duc′tion
in·duc′tive
in′duc·tiv′i·ty
in·duc′tor
in·due′
in·dulge′
in·dul′gence
in·dul′gent
in·dulg′ing
in′du·rate
in·dus′tri·al
in·dus′tri·al·ism′
in·dus′tri·al·ist
in·dus′tri·al·i·za′
tion
in·dus′tri·al·ize
in·dus′tri·ous
in′dus·try
in·dwell′ing
in·e′bri·ate
in·e′bri·a′tion
in·ed′i·bil′i·ty
in·ed′i·ble
in·ef′fa·bil′i·ty
in·ef′fa·ble
in′ef·face′a·ble
in′ef·fec′tive
in′ef·fec′tive·ly
in′ef·fec′tu·al
in′ef·fec′tu·al′i·ty
in′ef·fi·ca′cious
in·ef′fi·ca·cy
in′ef·fi′cien·cy
in′ef·fi′cient

in′e·las′tic
in′e·las·tic′i·ty
in·el′e·gance
in·el′e·gant
in·el′i·gi·bil′i·ty
in·el′i·gi·ble
in′e·luc′ta·ble
in·ept′
in·ept′i·tude
in′e·qual′i·ty
in·eq′ui·ta·ble
in·eq′ui·ty
in′e·rad′i·ca·ble
in·ert′
in·er′tia
in·er′tial
in′es·cap′a·ble
in·es′ti·ma·ble
in·ev′i·ta·bil′i·ty
in·ev′i·ta·ble
in′ex·act′
in′ex·cus′a·ble
in′ex·haust′i·ble
in·ex′o·ra·bil′i·ty
in·ex′o·ra·ble
in′ex·pe′di·en·cy
in′ex·pe′di·ent
in′ex·pen′sive
in′ex·pe′ri·ence
in·ex′pert
in·ex′pi·a·ble
in·ex′pli·ca·bil′
i·ty
in·ex′pli·ca·ble
in′ex·press′i·ble
in′ex·pres′sive
in ex·tre′mis
in·ex′tri·ca·bil′i·ty
in·ex′tri·ca·ble
in·fal′li·bil′i·ty
in·fal′li·ble
in′fa·mous
in′fa·my
in′fan·cy
in′fant
in·fan′ti·cide
in′fan·tile
in·fan′ti·lism
in′fan·try
in′fan·try·man
in·fat′u·ate
in·fat′u·at·ed
in·fat′u·a′tion
in·fect′
in·fec′tion
in·fec′tious
in·fec′tive
in′fe·lic′i·tous
in′fe·lic′i·ty
in·fer′
in′fer·ence
in′fer·en′tial
in·fe′ri·or
in·fe′ri·or′i·ty
in·fer′nal
in·fer′no
in·ferred′
in·fer′ring
in·fer′tile
in′fer·til′i·ty
in·fest′
in′fes·ta′tion
in′fi·del
in′fi·del′i·ty
in′field′
in·fil′trate
in′fil·tra′tion
in′fi·nite
in′fi·nite·ly
in′fin·i·tes′i·mal
in·fin′i·tive
in·fin′i·ty
in·firm′
in·fir′ma·ry
in·fir′mi·ty
in·flame′
in·flam′ing
in·flam′ma·bil′i·ty
in·flam′ma·ble
in′flam·ma′tion
in·flam′ma·to′ry
in·flate′
in·flat′ing
in·fla′tion
in·fla′tion·ar′y
in·flect′
in·flec′tion
in·flex′i·ble
in·flict′
in′flo·res′cence
in′flo·res′cent
in′flow′
in′flu·ence
in′flu·en′tial
in′flu·en′za
in′flux
in·fold′
(*also:* enfold)
in·form′
in·for′mal

in'for·mal'i·ty
in·form'ant
in'for·ma'tion
in·form'a·tive
in·frac'tion
in'fra·red'
in·fre'quen·cy
in·fre'quent
in·fringe'
in·fringe'ment
in·fring'ing
in·fu'ri·ate
in·fu'ri·at'ing
in·fu'ri·a'tion
in·fuse'
in·fu'si·ble
in·fu'sion
in·gen'ious
skillful *(see:* ingenuous)

in'ge·nue
in'ge·nu'i·ty
in·gen'u·ous
simple *(see:* ingenious)

in·gest'
in·ges'tion
in·glo'ri·ous
in'got
in·grained'
in'grate
in·gra'ti·ate
in·gra'ti·at'ing
in·gra'ti·a'tion
in·grat'i·tude
in·gre'di·ent

in'gress
in'grown'
in'gui·nal
in·hab'it
in·hab'it·ant
in'hab·i·ta'tion
in·hal'ant
in·hale'
in·hal'er
in·hal'ing
in'har·mon'ic
in'har·mo'ni·ous
in·here'
in·her'ent
in·her'it
in·her'it·ance
in·her'i·tor
in·hib'it
in'hi·bi'tion
in·hib'i·to'ry
in·hos'pi·ta·ble
in·hos'pi·tal'i·ty
in·hu'man
in'hu·mane'
in'hu·man'i·ty
in·im'i·cal
in·im'i·cal·ly
in·im'i·ta·ble
in·iq'ui·tous
in·iq'ui·ty
i·ni'tial
i·ni'tial·ly
i·ni'ti·ate
i·ni'ti·a'tion
i·ni'ti·a·tive
in·ject'
in·jec'tion

in'ju·di'cious
in·junc'tion
in'jure
in'jur·ing
in·ju'ri·ous
in'ju·ry
in·jus'tice
ink'i·er
ink'ling
ink'well'
ink'y
in'laid'
in'land
in'-law'
in'lay'
in'let
in'mate
in me·mo'ri·am
in'most
in·nate'
in·nate'ly
in'ner
in'ner·most
in'ning
inn'keep'er
in'no·cence
in'no·cent
in·noc'u·ous
in'no·vate
in'no·va'tion
in'no·va'tor
in·nox'ious
in'nu·en'do
in·nu'mer·a·ble
in·oc'u·late
in·oc'u·lat·ing
in·oc'u·la'tion

in·oc′u·la′tor
in′of·fen′sive
in·op′er·a′tive
in′op·por·tune′
in·or′di·na·cy
in·or′di·nate
in′or·gan′ic
in′or·gan′i·cal·ly
in′quest
in·qui′e·tude
in·quire′
in·quir′ing
in·quir′y
in′qui·si′tion
in·quis′i·tive
in·quis′i·tor
in·quis′i·to′ri·al
in′road′
in·sane′
in·san′i·tar′y
in·san′i·ty
in·sa′tia·bil′i·ty
in·sa′tia·ble
in·sa′ti·ate
in·scribe′
in·scrib′ing
in·scrip′tion
in·scru′ta·ble
in′sect
in·sec′ti·cide
in·sec′ti·vore
in′se·cure′
in′se·cu′ri·ty
in·sem′i·nate
in·sem′i·na′tion
in·sen′sate
in·sen′si·ble
in·sen′si·tive
in·sen′ti·ent
in·sep′a·ra·ble
in·sert′, *v.*
in′sert, *n.*
in·ser′tion
in′set′
in′side′, *n., adj.*
in′side′, *adv., pr.*
in·sid′i·ous
in′sight′
in·sig′ni·a, *pl.*
(sing.: insigne)

in′sig·nif′i·cance
in′sig·nif′i·cant
in′sin·cere′
in′sin·cere′ly
in′sin·cer′i·ty
in·sin′u·ate
in·sin′u·a′tion
in·sip′id
in·sist′ence
in′sole′
in′so·lence
in′so·lent
in·sol′u·bil′i·ty
in·sol′u·ble
in·sol′ven·cy
in·sol′vent
in·som′ni·a
in′so·much′
in·sou′ci·ance
in·sou′ci·ant
in·spect′
in·spec′tion
in·spec′tor
in′spi·ra′tion
in·spire′
in·spir′ing
in·spis′sate
in′sta·bil′i·ty
in·stall′
in′stal·la′tion
in·stall′ment
in′stance
in′stant
in′stan·ta′ne·ous
in·stead′
in′step
in′sti·gate
in′sti·gat·ing
in′sti·ga′tion
in′sti·ga′tor
in·still′
(also: instil)

in′stinct, *n.*
in·stinct′, *adj.*
in·stinc′tive
in′sti·tute
in′sti·tu′tion
in·struct′
in·struc′tion
in·struc′tive
in·struc′tor
in′stru·ment
in′stru·men′tal
in′stru·men·tal′
i·ty
in′stru·men·ta′tion
in′sub·or′di·nate
in′sub·or·di·na′
tion

in'sub·stan'tial
in·suf'fer·a·ble
in'suf·fi'cien·cy
in'suf·fi'cient
in'su·lar
in'su·lar'i·ty
in'su·late
in'su·la'tion
in'su·la'tor
in'su·lin
in·sult', *v.*
in'sult, *n.*
in·su'per·a·ble
in'sup·port'a·ble
in·sur'a·ble
in·sur'ance
in·sure'
in·sured'
in·sur'er
in·sur'gen·cy
in·sur'gent
in·sur'ing
in'sur·mount'a·ble
in'sur·rec'tion
in'sus·cep'ti·ble
in·tact'
in·tagl'io
in'take'
in·tan'gi·bil'i·ty
in·tan'gi·ble
in'te·ger
in'te·gral
in'te·grate
in'te·gra'tion
in·teg'ri·ty
in·teg'u·ment
in'tel·lect
in'tel·lec'tu·al
in·tel'li·gence
in·tel'li·gent
in·tel'li·gent'si·a
in·tel'li·gi·bil'i·ty
in·tel'li·gi·ble
in·tem'per·ance
in·tem'per·ate
in·tend'
in·tend'ant
in·tense'
in·ten'si·fi·ca'tion
in·ten'si·fied
in·ten'si·fy
in·ten'si·ty
in·ten'sive
in·tent'
in·ten'tion
in·ten'tion·al·ly
in·ter'
in'ter·act'
in'ter·ac'tion
in'ter·cede'
in'ter·ced'ing
in'ter·cept'
in'ter·cep'tion
in'ter·ces'sion
in'ter·ces'so·ry
in'ter·change', *v.*
in'ter·change', *n.*
in'ter·change'a·ble
in'ter·com'
in'ter·com·mu'
ni·cate
in'ter·cos'tal
in'ter·course
in'ter·de·pend'ent
in'ter·dict', *v.*
in'ter·dict, *n.*
in'ter·dic'tion
in'ter·est
in'ter·est·ed
in'ter·est·ing
in'ter·fere'
in'ter·fer'ence
in'ter·fuse'
in'ter·fu'sion
in'ter·im
in·te'ri·or
in'ter·ject'
in'ter·jec'tion
in'ter·lace'
in'ter·lay'
in'ter·lin'e·ar
in'ter·lin'ing
in'ter·lock'
in'ter·loc'u·tor
in'ter·loc'u·to'ry
in'ter·lop'er
in'ter·lude
in'ter·me'di·ar'y
in'ter·me'di·ate
in·ter'ment
in'ter·mez'zo
in·ter'mi·na·ble
in'ter·min'gle
in'ter·min'gling
in'ter·mis'sion
in'ter·mit'tent
in'ter·mix'
in·tern', *v.*
in'tern, *n.*
(*also:* interne)

in·ter′nal
in·ter′nal·ly
in′ter·na′tion·al
in′ter·na′
tion·al·ist
in′ter·na′
tion·al·ize
in′tern·ee′
in′ter·pel′late
in′ter·plan′e·tar′y
in′ter·play′
in·ter′po·late
in·ter′po·la′tion
in′ter·pose′
in′ter·pos′ing
in·ter′pret
in·ter′pre·ta′tion
in·ter′pret·er
in·ter′pre·tive
in′ter·ra′cial
in′ter·re·late′
in′ter·re·lat′ed
in′ter·re·la′tion
in·ter′ro·gate
in·ter′ro·ga′tion
in′ter·rog′a·tive
in′ter·rog′a·to′ry
in′ter·rupt′
in′ter·rup′tion
in′ter·sect′
in′ter·sec′tion
in′ter·sperse′
in′ter·sper′sion
in′ter·state′
between states *(see:* intrastate)
in′ter·stel′lar
in·ter′stice
in′ter·twine′
in′ter·ur′ban
in′ter·val
in′ter·vene′
in′ter·ven′tion
in′ter·view
in·tes′ta·cy
in·tes′tate
in·tes′ti·nal
in·tes′tine
in′ti·ma·cy
in′ti·mate
in′ti·ma′tion
in·tim′i·date
in·tim′i·da′tion
in·tol′er·a·ble
in·tol′er·ance
in·tol′er·ant
in′to·na′tion
in·tone′
in·ton′ing
in·tox′i·cant
in·tox′i·cat′ing
in·tox′i·ca′tion
in·trac′ta·ble
in′tra·mu′ral
in·tran′si·gent
in·tran′si·tive
in′tra·state′
within a state *(see:* interstate)
in′tra·ve′nous
in·trep′id
in′tre·pid′i·ty
in′tri·ca·cy
in′tri·cate
in·trigue′
in·tri′guing
in·trin′sic
in·trin′si·cal·ly
in′tro·duce′
in′tro·duc′tion
in′tro·duc′to·ry
in′tro·spec′tion
in′tro·spec′tive
in′tro·ver′sion
in′tro·vert′, *v.*
in′tro·vert′, *n., adj.*
in·trude′
in·tru′sion
in·tru′sive
in·trust′
in′tu·i′tion
in·tu′i·tive
in′un·date
in′un·da′tion
in·ure′
in·ur′ing
in·vade′
in′va·lid, *n.*
in·val′id, *adj.*
in·val′i·date
in·val′i·da′tion
in′va·lid·ism′
in′va·lid′i·ty
in·val′u·a·ble
in·var′i·a·bly
in·va′sion
in·vec′tive
in·veigh′
in·vei′gle

in·vei′gling
in·vent′
in·ven′tion
in·ven′tive
in·ven′tor
in′ven·to′ry
in·verse′
in·ver′sion
in·vert′, *v.*
in′vert, *n.*
in·ver′te·brate
in·vest′
in·ves′ti·gate
in·ves′ti·ga′tion
in·ves′ti·ga′tor
in·ves′ti·ture
in·vest′ment
in·vet′er·a·cy
in·vet′er·ate
in·vid′i·ous
in·vig′or·ate
in·vig′or·at′ing
in·vig′or·a′tion
in·vin′ci·bil′i·ty
in·vin′ci·ble
in·vi′o·la·ble
in·vi′o·la·cy
in·vi′o·late
in·vis′i·bil′i·ty
in·vis′i·ble
in′vi·ta′tion
in·vite′
in·vit′ing
in′vo·ca′tion
in′voice
in·voke′
in·vok′ing
in·vol′un·tar′i·ly
in·vol′un·ta′ry
in′vo·lut′ed
in′vo·lu′tion
in·volve′ment
in·volv′ing
in·vul′ner·a·ble
in′ward
i′o·dide
i′o·dine
i·o′do·form
i′on
I·on′ic
i·o′ni·um
i′o·ni·za′tion
i′on·ize
i·on′o·sphere
i·o′ta
ip′e·cac
ip′so fac′to
i·ras′ci·bil′i·ty
i·ras′ci·ble
i′rate
ire′ful·ly
ir′i·des′cence
ir′i·des′cent
i·rid′i·um
i′ris
irk′some
i′ron·clad′
i·ron′i·cal
i′ron·ing
i′ron·mon′ger
i′ron·work′
i′ro·ny
Ir′o·quois
ir·ra′di·ate
ir·ra′di·a′tion
ir·ra′tion·al
ir′re·claim′a·ble
ir·rec′on·cil′a·ble
ir′re·cov′er·a·ble
ir′re·deem′a·ble
ir′re·duc′i·bil′i·ty
ir′re·duc′i·ble
ir·ref′u·ta·bil′i·ty
ir·ref′u·ta·ble
ir·reg′u·lar
ir·reg′u·lar′i·ty
ir·rel′e·vance
ir·rel′e·vant
ir′re·me′di·a·ble
ir·rep′a·ra·bil′i·ty
ir·rep′a·ra·ble
ir′re·place′a·ble
ir′re·press′i·ble
ir′re·proach′a·ble
ir′re·sis′i·ble
ir·res′o·lute
ir′re·spec′tive
ir′re·spon′si·ble
ir′re·triev′a·ble
ir·rev′er·ence
ir·rev′er·ent
ir′re·vers′i·bil′i·ty
ir′re·vers′i·ble
ir·rev′o·ca·bil′i·ty
ir·rev′o·ca·ble
ir′ri·ga·ble
ir′ri·gate
ir′ri·ga′tion
ir′ri·ta·bil′i·ty
ir′ri·ta·ble
ir′ri·tant

ir′ri·tate
ir′ri·tat′ing
ir′ri·ta′tion
I·sai′ah
Is·car′i·ot (Judas)
Ish′ma·el
i′sin·glass′
is′land·er
i′so·bar
i·soch′ro·nous
i′so·gon′ic
i′so·late
i′so·la′tion·ist
i′so·mer
i′so·mer′ic
i′so·met′ric
i′so·mor′phic
i·sos′ce·les
i′so·therm
i′so·tope
i′so·top′ic
i′so·trop′ic
Is′ra·el
Is·rae′li
Is′ra·el·ite
is′su·ance
is′su·ing
isth′mus
I·tal′ian
i·tal′i·cize
i·tal′i·ciz·ing
i·tal′ics
It′a·ly
itch′i·ness
itch′y
i′tem·i·za′tion
i′tem·ize
it′er·ate
it′er·a′tion
it′er·a′tive
i·tin′er·a·cy
i·tin′er·ant
i·tin′er·ar′y
i·tin′er·ate
its
  belonging to it
it′s
  it is
it·self′
i′vied
i′vo·ry

J

jabbed
jab′ber
jab′bing
ja·bot′
ja′cinth
jack′al
jack′a·napes
jack′ass′
jack′daw′
jack′knife′
jack′-o-lan′tern
jack′straw′
Jac′o·bin
jad′ed
jae′ger
jag′ged
jag′uar
jail′bird′
jail′break′
jail′er
  (*also:* jailor)
ja·lop′y
Ja·mai′ca
jam′bo·ree′
jam′ming
jam′packed′
jan′gle
jan′gling
jan·i·to′ri·al
Jan′u·ar′y
Ja·pan′
Jap′a·nese′
jar′di·niere′
jar′gon
jar′ring
jas′mine
jas′per
jaun′dice
jaun′ti·ly
jaun′ty
Jav′a·nese′
jave′lin
jaw′bone′
jay′walk′er

jeal′ous·y
Jef′fer·son
Je·ho′vah
je·june′
je·ju′num
jell
(*also:* gel)
jel′lied
jel′ly·fish′
jen′net
(*also:* genet)
jen′ny
jeop′ard·ize
jeop′ard·iz·ing
jeop′ard·y
jer′e·mi′ad
Jer′e·mi′ah
Jer′i·cho
jerk′i·ly
jer′kin
jer′ry·built′
jer′sey
Je·ru′sa·lem
jes′sa·mine
jest′er
jest′ing·ly
Jes′u·it
Je′sus (Christ)
jet′lin·er
jet′sam
jet′ting
jet′ti·son
jet′ty
jew′eled
jew′el·er
jew′el·ry
jew′fish′
Jew′ish
jews′′-harp′
Jez′e·bel
jib′bing
jif′fy
jig′ger
jig′gle
jig′gling
jig′saw′
jilt′ed
jim′mied
jim′my
jin′gle
jin′gling
jin′go·ism
jin·rik′i·sha
jit′ney
jit′ter·bug′
jit′ter·y
job′ber
job′hold′er
jock′ey
jo·cose′
jo·cos′i·ty
joc′u·lar
joc′u·lar′i·ty
joc′und
jo·cun′di·ty
jodh′purs
jog′ging
jog′gle
jog′gling
Jo·han′nes·burg
join′er
joint′ly
join′ture
joist
joked
jok′er
jok′ing·ly
jol′li·ty
jol′ly
Jo′nah
jon′quil
Josh′u·a
jos′tle
jos′tling
jot′ted
jot′ting
jounce
jounc′ing
jour′nal·ism
jour′nal·ist
jour′nal·is′ti·cal·ly
jour′ney·man
joust
jo′vi·al
jo′vi·al′i·ty
joy′ful
joy′ous·ly
joy′-ride′
ju′bi·lance
ju′bi·lant
ju′bi·la′tion
ju′bi·lee
Ju′da·ism
judge′ship
judg′ing
judg′ment
ju′di·ca·to′ry
ju·di′cial
ju·di′ci·ar′y
ju·di′cious

jug′ger·naut
jug′gle
jug′gler
jug′gling
Ju′go·sla′vi·a
jug′u·lar
juic′y
ju·jit′su
ju′lep
ju′li·enne′
jum′bled
jum′bling
jum′bo
jump′ing
jump′y
junc′tion
junc′ture
Ju′neau
jun′gle
jun′ior
ju′ni·per
jun′ket
junk′man′
jun′ta
Ju′pi·ter
ju′ries
ju′ris·dic′tion
ju′ris·pru′dence
ju′rist
ju′ror
ju′ry·man
jus′tice
jus′ti·fi′a·ble
jus′ti·fi·ca′tion
jus′ti·fied
jus′ti·fy
Jus·tin′i·an
jut′ting
ju′ve·nile
jux′ta·pose′
jux′ta·po·si′tion

K

kai′ser
ka·lei′do·scope
kal′so·mine
kal′so·min·ing
kan′ga·roo′
ka′pok
kar′a·kul
kar′at
(also: carat)
ka′ty·did
kay′ak
keel′haul′
keen′ness
keep′sake′
ken′nel
Ken·tuck′y
ker′a·tin
ker′chief
ker′nel
ker′o·sene
ketch′up
ket′tle·drum′
key′board′
keyed
key′hole′
key′note′
key′stone′
khak′i
kib′itz·er
kick′back′
kick′off′
kid′ded
kid′ding
kid′nap·er
kid′nap·ing
kid′ney
Kil′i·man·ja′ro
Kil·lar′ney
kill′deer′
kill′ing
kill′-joy′
kiln
kil′o·cy′cle
kil′o·gram
kil′o·me′ter
kil′o·met′ric
kil′o·ton
kil′o·watt′
kil′ter
Kim′ber·ly
ki·mo′no
kin′der·gar′ten
kind′-heart′ed
kin′dle
kind′li·ness
kin′dling

kind′ness
kin′dred
kin′e·mat′ics
kin′e·mat′o·graph
kin′e·scope
kin′es·thet′ic
ki·net′ic
kin′folk′
king′dom
king′fish′er
king′li·ness
king′pin′
kin′ka·jou
kink′y
kin′ship
kins′man
ki·osk′
Kip′ling
kis′met
kiss′a·ble
kitch′en
kitch′en·ette′
kitch′en·ware′
kit′ten·ish
kit′ty
klep′to·ma′ni·ac
klys′tron
knap′sack′
knav′er·y
knee′cap′
knee′-deep′
kneel′ing
Knick′er·bock′er
knick′ers
knick′knack′
knife
(*plural:* knives)
knight′-er′rant
knight′hood
knit′ting
knob′by
knock′a·bout′
knock′out′
knoll
knot′hole′
knot′ting
knot′ty
knowl′edge
knowl′edge·a·ble
knuck′le
knuck′ling
ko·a′la
kohl′ra′bi
ko·lin′sky
ko′peck
Ko·re′a
ko′sher
kow′tow′
Krem′lin
kryp′ton
kum′quat

L

la′beled
la′bel·ing
la′bi·al
la′bi·o·den′tal
la′bi·um
lab′o·ra·to′ry
la′bored
la·bo′ri·ous
Lab′ra·dor
la·bur′num
lab′y·rinth
lab′y·rin′thine
lac′er·ate
lac′er·at·ing
lac′er·a′tion
lace′work′
lach′ry·mal
lach′ry·mose
lac′ing
lack′a·dai′si·cal
lack′ey
lack′lus′ter
la·con′i·cal·ly
lac′quer
lac′ri·mal
la·crosse′
lac′tate
lac·ta′tion
lac′te·al
lac′tic
lac′tose
la·cu′na
lac′y
lad′der
lad′die
lad′ing

lad′le·ful′
la′dy·bug′
la′dy·like′
la′ger
lag′gard
lag′ging
la·gniappe′
la·goon′
lais′sez faire′
la′i·ty
la′ma
Buddhist monk
(see: llama)

la′ma·ser′y
lam·baste′
lam′ben·cy
lam′bent
lamb′kin
lamb′skin′
la·mel′la
lam′en·ta·ble
lam′en·ta′tion
la·ment′ed
lam′i·na
lam′i·nate
lam′i·na′tion
lamp′black′
lam·poon′
lam′prey
Lan′ca·shire
Lan′cas·ter
lan′ce·o·late
lanc′er
lan′cet
lance′wood′
lanc′ing

lan′dau
land′ed
land′hold′er
land′ing
land′la′dy
land′locked′
land′lord′
land′lub′ber
land′mark′
land′own′er
land′scape
land′slide′
lang′syne′
lan′guage
lan′guid
lan′guished
lan′guish·ing
lan′guor·ous
lank′i·er
lank′y
lan′o·lin
lan′tern
lan′yard
la·pel′
lap′i·dar′y
lap′in
lap′is laz′u·li
Lap′land
lap′pet
lapsed
laps′ing
lar′board
lar′ce·nous
lar′ce·ny
lard′er
large′ly

lar′gess
(also: -gesse)

lar·ghet′to
lar′go
lar′i·at
lark′spur
lar′rup
lar′va
(plural: -vae)

la·ryn′ge·al
lar′yn·gi′tis
lar′ynx
las·civ′i·ous
lash′ing
las′sie
las′si·tude
las′so
last′ing
latch′key′
la·teen′
late′ly
la′ten·cy
la′tent
lat′er·al
lat′er·al·ly
Lat′er·an
la′tex
lath
board

lathe
machine

lath′er
lath′ing
lath′work′
Lat′in

lat′i·tude
lat′i·tu′di·nal
la·trine′
lat′ter
lat′tice·work′
laud′a·bil′i·ty
laud′a·ble
lau′da·num
laud′a·to′ry
laugh′a·ble
laugh′ing
laugh′ing·stock′
laugh′ter
launched
laun′der
laun′dress
laun′dry
laun′dry·man
lau′re·ate
lau′rel
la′va
lav′a·liere′
lav′a·to′ry
lav′en·der
lav′ing
lav′ish
law′break′er
law′ful·ly
law′less
law′mak′er
law′suit′
law′yer
lax′a·tive
lax′i·ty
lay′er
lay·ette′
lay′man
lay′off′
laz′ar
laz′a·ret′to
la′zi·er
la′zi·ly
la′zy
leach
dissolve *(see:* leech)

lead′en
lead′er
lead′ing
leaf′let
leaf′y
league
leak′age
leak′y
lean
incline *(see:* lien)

lean′ing
lean′-to′
leap′frog′
leap′ing
leap′ year′
learn′ed
learn′ing
leased
leas′ing
leath′er·neck′
leav′en
leav′ing
Leb′a·nese′
Leb′a·non
lech′er·ous
lech′er·y
lec′tern
lec′tured
lec′tur·ing
ledg′er
leech
bloodsucking worm
(see: leach)

leer′ing·ly
leer′y
lee′ward
lee′way′
left′-hand′ed
left′ist
left′o′ver
leg′a·cy
le′gal
le·gal′i·ty
le′gal·i·za′tion
le′gal·ize
le′gal·ly
leg′ate
leg′a·tee′
le·ga′tion
le·ga′to
leg′end
leg′end·ar′y
leg′er·de·main′
leg′gings
leg′horn
leg′i·bil′i·ty
leg′i·ble
le′gion
le′gion·ar′y
le′gion·naire′
leg′is·late
leg′is·la′tion
leg′is·la′tive
leg′is·la′tor

leg′is·la′ture
le·git′i·ma·cy
le·git′i·mate
le·git′i·miz·ing
leg′ume
le·gu′mi·nous
lei′sure
leit′mo·tif′
lem′ming
lem′on
lem′on·ade′
le′mur
lend′er
lend′ing
length′en
length′wise′
length′y
len′ien·cy
len′ient
len′i·ty
Lent′en
len′til
vegetable *(see:* lintel)

le′o·nine
leop′ard
lep′er
lep′re·chaun
lep′ro·sy
lep′rous
Les′bi·an
lese′-maj′es·ty
le′sion
les·see′
less′en
decrease

less′er
smaller

les′son
thing studied

les′sor
one granting a lease

let′down′
le′thal
le·thar′gic
leth′ar·gy
let′ter
let′tered
let′ter·head′
let′ter·press′
let′tuce
let′up′
leu′co·cyte
leu·ke′mi·a
lev′ee
riverbank *(see:* levy)

lev′eled
lev′el·ing
lev′er·age
lev′er·et
le·vi′a·than
lev′i·tate
lev′i·ta′tion
Le′vite
Le·vit′i·cus
lev′i·ty
lev′u·lose
lev′y
order to be paid
(see: levee)

lev′y·ing

lewd′ness
lex′i·cog′ra·pher
lex′i·cog′ra·phy
lex′i·con
li′a·bil′i·ty
li′a·ble
likely *(see:* libel)

li′ai·son′
li′ar
one who tells lies
(see: lyre)

li·ba′tion
li′bel
damaging written
statement *(see:*
liable)

li′bel·ous
lib′er·al
lib′er·al·ism′
lib′er·al·is′tic
lib′er·al′i·ty
lib′er·al·ize
lib′er·ate
lib′er·a′tion
lib′er·a′tor
Li·be′ri·a
lib′er·tine
lib′er·ty
li·bid′i·nous
li·bi′do
li·brar′i·an
li′brar·y
li·bret′to
li′cense
li′cen·see′
li′cens·ing

li·cen′ti·ate
li·cen′tious
li′chen
lic′it
lic′o·rice
lie′der·kranz
liege
lien
legal claim
(*see:* lean)

lieu·ten′an·cy
lieu·ten′ant
life
(*plural:* lives)

life′boat′
life′guard′
life′sav′er
life′time′
lift′er
lig′a·ment
lig′a·ture
light′ed
light′en
light′-heart′ed
light′house′
light′ning
light′ship′
light′-year′
lig′ne·ous
lig′nite
lik′a·ble
like′li·hood
like′ly
lik′en
like′ness
like′wise′
lik′ing
li′lac
lil′i·a′ceous
Lil′li·pu′tian
lil′y
lim′ber
lim′bo
Lim′bur·ger
lime′light′
lim′er·ick
lime′stone′
lim′it
lim′i·ta′tion
lim′it·ed
lim′it·less
lim′ou·sine′
lim′pet
lim′pid
lim·pid′i·ty
limp′ly
lim′y
lin′age
Lin′coln
lin′den
lin′e·age
lin′e·al
lin′e·a·ment
lin′e·ar
line′man
lin′en
lin′er
lin′ger
lin′ge·rie′
lin′go
lin′gual
lin′guist
lin·guis′tic
lin′i·ment
lin′ing
link′ing
lin′net
li·no′le·um
lin′o·type
lin′seed′
lin′tel
door beam
(*see:* lentil)

li′on·ess
li′on·ize
lip′stick′
liq′ue·fac′tion
liq′ue·fied
liq′ue·fy
li·ques′cence
li·ques′cent
li·queur′
liq′uid
liq′ui·date
liq′ui·da′tion
liq′uor
lisp′ing·ly
lis′some
lis′ten·er
list′less
lit′a·ny
li′ter
lit′er·a·cy
lit′er·al
lit′er·al·ly
lit′er·ar′y
lit′er·ate
lit′e·ra′ti
lit′er·a·ture

lith′arge
lithe′some
lith′i·um
lith′o·graph
li·thog′ra·pher
li·thog′ra·phy
lith′o·sphere
Lith′u·a′ni·a
lit′i·ga·ble
lit′i·gant
lit′i·gate
lit′i·ga′tion
lit′i·ga′tor
lit′mus
lit′ter
lit′tle
lit′to·ral
lit′ur·gy
liv′a·ble
live′li·hood
live′long′
live′ly
liv′en
liv′er
liv′er·ied
liv′er·wurst′
liv′er·y
live′stock′
liv′id
liv′ing
liz′ard
lla′ma
animal (*see:* lama)

load′star
(*also:* lode-)

load′stone′
(*also:* lode-)

loaf
(*plural:* loaves)

loam′y
loath, *adj.*
loathe, *v.*
loath′ing
loath′some
lo′bar
lo′bate
lobbed
lob′bing
lob′by
lob′ster
lob′ule
lo′cal
lo·cale′
lo·cal′i·ty
lo′cal·i·za′tion
lo′cal·ize
lo′cate
lo′cat·ing
lo·ca′tion
loc′a·tive
lock′er
lock′et
lock′jaw′
lock′smith′
lo′co·mo′tion
lo′co·mo′tive
lo′co·weed′
lo′cus
lo′cust
lo·cu′tion
lodg′ing

loft′i·ly
loft′y
lo′gan·ber′ry
log′a·rithm
log′a·rith′mi·cal
log′book′
log′ger·head′
log′gia
log′ging
log′ic
log′i·cal
lo·gi′cian
lo·gis′tics
log′roll′ing
lo′gy
Lo′hen·grin
loin′cloth′
loi′ter
lol′li·pop
Lon′don
lone′li·ness
lone′ly
lone′some
long′-dis′tance
lon·gev′i·ty
long′hand′
lon′gi·tude
lon′gi·tu′di·nal
long′-range′
long′shore′man
long′-suf′fer·ing
look′ing
look′out′
loon′y
loop′hole′
loose′-leaf′
loos′en

lop′sid′ed
lo·qua′cious
lo·quac′i·ty
lord′li·ness
lord′ship
lor·gnette′
Los An′ge·les
los′ing
Lo·thar′i·o
lo′tion
lot′ter·y
lo′tus
loud′ness
loud′-speak′er
Lou·i′si·an′a
lounged
loung′ing
louse
(*plural:* lice)
lous′y
lout′ish
lou′ver
Lou′vre
lov′a·ble
love′bird′
love′li·er
love′lorn′
love′ly
lov′er
love′sick′
lov′ing-kind′ness
low′boy′
low′bred′
low′-down′
low′er-case′
low′er·ing
low′land
low′li·ness
low′ly
low′-spir′it·ed
loy′al·ly
loy′al·ty
loz′enge
lub′ber
lu′bri·cant
lu′bri·cate
lu′bri·ca′tion
lu′bri·ca′tor
lu·bric′i·ty
lu′cen·cy
lu′cent
Lu·cerne′
lu′cid
lu·cid′i·ty
Lu′ci·fer
Lu′cite
luck′i·ly
luck′y
lu′cra·tive
lu′cre
lu′di·crous
lug′gage
lug′ging
lu·gu′bri·ous
luke′warm′
lul′la·by
lum·ba′go
lum′bar
of the loins
lum′ber
timber
lum′ber·jack′
lu′men
lu′mi·nar′y
lu′mi·nes′cence
lu′mi·nes′cent
lu′mi·nos′i·ty
lu′mi·nous
lum′mox
lump′i·er
lump′y
lu′na·cy
lu′nar
lu′na·tic
lunch′eon
lunch′eon·ette′
lunged
lung′ing
lu′pine
lurched
lured
lu′rid
lur′ing
lurk′ing
lus′cious
lush′ly
lus′ter
lust′ful
lust′i·er
lus′trate
lus·tra′tion
lus′tra·tive
lus′trous
lus′trum
lust′y
Lu′ther·an
Lux′em·burg
lux·u′ri·ance
lux·u′ri·ant

lux·u′ri·ate
lux·u′ri·at·ing
lux·u′ri·a′tion
lux·u′ri·ous
lux′u·ry
ly·ce′um
ly′ing
ly′ing-in′
lymph
lym·phat′ic
lym′pho·cyte
lynch′ing
lynx′-eyed′
ly′on·naise′
lyr′i·cal
ly′sin

M

ma·ca′bre
ma·cad′am
ma·caque′
mac′a·ro′ni
mac′a·roon′
ma·caw′
Mac′e·do′ni·a
mac′er·ate
mac′er·at′er
mac′er·a′tion
ma·chet′e
Mach′i·a·vel′li·an
ma·chic′o·la′tion
mach′i·nate
mach′i·na′tion
ma·chine′
ma·chin′er·y
ma·chin′ist
mack′er·el
Mack′i·nac
mack′i·naw
mack′in·tosh
mac′ro·cosm
mac′ra·cos′mic
ma′cron
Mad′a·gas′car
mad′den·ing
mad′dest
mad′e·moi·selle′
mad′ness
Ma·don′na
mad′ras
mad′ri·gal
mael′strom
maes′tro
mag′a·zine′
mag′da·lene
ma·gen′ta
mag′got
mag′ic
ma·gi′cian
mag′is·te′ri·al
mag′is·trate
mag′na cum lau′de
mag′na·nim′i·ty
mag·nan′i·mous
mag′nate
mag·ne′sia
mag·ne′si·um
mag′net
mag·net′ic
mag′net·ism
mag′net·ize
mag·ne′to
mag′ni·fi·ca′tion
mag·nif′i·cence
mag′nified
mag′ni·fy·ing
mag·nil′o·quence
mag′ni·tude
mag·no′lia
mag′num
mag′pie
ma′ha·ra′ja
ma·hat′ma
ma·hog′a·ny
ma·hout′
maid′en·head
maid′en·hood
maid′ser′vant
main′land′
main′spring′
main′stay′
main·tain′
main′te·nance
mai′tre d'ho·tel′
maize
corn (*see:* maze)
ma·jes′tic
maj′es·ty

ma·jol′i·ca
ma′jor-do′mo
ma·jor′i·ty
(plural: -ties)

make′shift′
Ma·lac′ca
mal′a·chite
mal′ad·just′ed
mal′ad·just′ment
mal′ad·min′is·ter
mal′a·droit′
mal′a·dy
ma·laise′
mal′a·prop·ism
ma·lar′i·a
Ma·lay′a
mal′con·tent
mal de mer′
mal′e·dic′tion
mal′e·fac′tion
mal′e·fac′tor
ma·lef′i·cence
ma·lef′i·cent
ma·lev′o·lent
mal·fea′sance
mal′for·ma′tion
mal·formed′
mal′ice
ma·li′cious·ly
ma·lign′
ma·lig′nan·cy
ma·lig′nant
ma·lig′ni·ty
ma·line′
ma·lin′ger
mal′lard
mal′le·a·bil′i·ty
mal′le·a·ble
mal′let
mal′low
mal′nu·tri′tion
mal·o′dor·ous
mal·prac′tice
malt′ose
mal·treat′
mam′bo
mam′mal
mam·ma′li·an
mam′ma·ry
mam′mon
mam′moth
man′a·cle
man′a·cling
man′age
man′age·a·bil′i·ty
man′age·a·ble
man′age·ment
man′ag·er
man′a·ge′ri·al
man′a·tee′
man·da′mus
man′da·rin
man′da·tar′y
mandated nation
(see: mandatory)

man′date
man′da·to′ry
required *(see:* mandatary)

man′di·ble
man′do·lin
man′drake
man′drel
spindle

man′drill
baboon

ma·neu′ver
ma·neu′ver·a·bil′i·ty
man′ful·ly
man′ga·nese
man′ger
man′gi·er
man′gi·ness
man′gle
man′gling
man′go
man′grove
man′gy
man′han′dle
Man·hat′tan
man′hole
man′hood
man′-hour′
ma′ni·a
ma′ni·ac
ma·ni′a·cal
man′ic-de·pres′sive
man′i·cure
man′i·cur′ist
man′i·fest
man′i·fes·ta′tion
man′i·fes′to
man′i·fold
Ma·nil′a
man′i·oc
ma·nip′u·late
ma·nip′u·la′tion

ma·nip′u·la′tor
Man′i·to′ba
man′kind′
man′li·ness
man′ly
man′na
man′ne·quin
man′ner·ism
man′ner·ly
man′-of-war′
ma·nom′e·ter
man′or
ma·no′ri·al
man′pow′er
man′sard
man′serv′ant
man′sion
man′slaugh′ter
man′tel
shelf *(see:* mantle)
man·til′la
man′tis
man′tle
cloak *(see:* mantel)
man′tling
man′u·al·ly
man′u·fac′ture
man′u·fac′tur·ing
man′u·mis′sion
man′u·mit′
ma·nure′
man′u·script
man′za·ni′ta
ma′ple
mar′a·schi′no
mar′a·thon
ma·raud′er
mar′ble
mar′bling
mar′ca·site
mar·cel′
mar·celled′
mar′chion·ess
Mar·co′ni
Mar′co Po′lo
Mar′di Gras′
mar′ga·rine
mar′gin·al
mar′grave
mar′gue·rite′
mar′i·gold
mar′i·jua′na
ma·rim′ba
mar′i·nate
mar′i·nat·ing
mar′i·na′tion
ma·rine′
mar′i·ner
mar′i·o·nette′
mar′i·tal
mar′i·tal·ly
mar′i·time
mar′jo·ram
mar′ket
mar′ket·a·bil′i·ty
mar′lin
fish
mar′line
cord
mar′ma·lade
mar′mo·set
mar′mot
ma·roon′
mar·quee′
mar′que·try
mar′quis
mar·quise′
mar′qui·sette′
mar′riage
mar′riage·a·ble
mar′ried
mar′row
mar′ry
Mar′seil·laise′
Mar·seilles′
mar′shal
marsh′mal′low
mar·su′pi·al
mar′ten
animal *(see:* martin)
mar′tial
mar′tin
bird *(see:* marten)
mar′ti·net′
mar′tin·gale
mar·ti′ni
Mar′ti·nique′
mar′tyr·dom
mar′vel
mar′vel·ous·ly
Mar′y·land
mar′zi·pan
mas·car′a
mas′cot
mas′cu·line
mas′cu·lin′i·ty
mash′ie
mas′och·ism

mas′och·ist
mas′och·is′tic
ma′son
ma·son′ic
ma′son·ry
mas′quer·ade′
Mas′sa·chu′setts
mas′sa·cre
mas′sa·cred
mas′sa·cring
mas·sage′
mas·seur′
mas·seuse′
mas′sive
mas′ter·ful
mas′ter·piece′
mas′ter·y
mast′head′
mas′tic
mas′ti·cate
mas′ti·ca′tion
mas′ti·ca′tor
mas′tiff
mas′to·don
mas′toid
mas′toid·i′tis
mas′tur·ba′tion
mat′a·dor
match′less
match′mak′er
match′mak′ing
ma′té (tea)
ma′ter
ma·te′ri·al
matter (*see:* materiel)
ma·te′ri·al·ism′
ma·te′ri·al·ist
ma·te′ri·al·is′ti-
c·al·ly
ma·te′ri·al·ize
ma·te′ri·al·ly
ma·té′ri·el′
equipment (*see:* material)

ma·ter′nal
ma·ter′nal·ly
ma·ter′ni·ty
math′e·mat′i·cal
math′e·ma·ti′cian
math′e·mat′ics
mat′i·née′
ma′tins
ma′tri·arch
ma′tri·ar′chal
ma′tri·ar′chy
ma′tri·cide
ma′tri·cid′al
ma·tric′u·late
ma·tric′u·la′tion
mat′ri·mo′ni·al
mat′ri·mo′ny
ma′trix
ma′tron·li·ness
mat′ted
mat′ter
mat′ting
mat′tock
mat′tress
mat′u·rate
mat′u·ra′tion
ma·ture′
ma·ture′ness
ma·tu′ri·ty
ma·tu′ti·nal
matz′oth
maud′lin
maun′der
Mau·pas·sant′
mau′so·le′um
mav′er·ick
ma′vis
mawk′ish
max·il′la
max′im
max′i·mum
May′flow′er
may′hem
may′on·naise′
may′or
may′or·al·ty
may′pole′
maze
network (*see:* maize)

ma·zur′ka
mead′ow
mea′ger
mea′ger·ly
meal′i·ness
meal′time
meal′y
meal′y-mouthed′
me·an′der
mean′ing
mean′ing·ful
mean′time′
mea′sles
mea′sly

meas'ur·a·bil'i·ty
meas'ur·a·ble
meas'ure
meas'ure·ment
meat'y
me·chan'ic
me·chan'i·cal
mech'a·ni'cian
mech'a·nism
mech'a·nist
mech'a·nis'tic
mech'a·ni·za'tion
mech'a·nize
med'al
decoration *(see:* meddle)

me·dal'lion
med'dle
interfere *(see:* medal)

med'dler
me'di·an
me'di·ate
me'di·a'tion
me'di·a'tive
me'di·a'tor
med'ic
med'i·cal
med'i·cal·ly
me·dic'a·ment
med'i·cate
med'i·ca'tion
me·dic'i·nal
med'i·cine man'
me'di·e'val
me'di·e'val·ism
me'di·o'cre
me'di·oc'ri·ty
med'i·tate
med'i·ta'tion
med'i·ta'tive
med'i·ta'tor
Med'i·ter·ra'ne·an
me'di·um
(plural: -diums; -dia)

med'lar
med'ley
me·dul'la
me·dul'la ob'
lon·ga'ta
med'ul·lar'y
me·du'sa
meer'schaum
meet'ing
meg'a·cy'cle
meg'a·lo·ma'ni·a
meg'a·phone
meg'a·ton
me'grim
mel'an·cho'li·a
mel'an·chol'ic
mel'an·chol'y
mé·lange'
me'lee
mel'io·rate
mel'io·ra'tion
mel'io·ra'tor
mel·lif'lu·ence
mel·lif'lu·ent
mel·lif'lu·ous
mel'low
me·lo'de·on
me·lod'ic
me·lod'i·cal·ly
me·lo'di·ous
mel'o·dra'ma
mel'o·dra·mat'ic
mel'o·dram'a·tist
mel'o·dy
mel'on
mem'ber
mem'brane
mem'bra·nous
me·men'to
mem'oir
mem'o·ra·bil'i·a
mem'o·ra·bil'i·ty
mem'o·ra·ble
mem'o·ran'dum
(plural: -dums; -da)

me·mo'ri·al
me·mo'ri·al·ize
mem'o·ri·za'tion
mem'o·rize
mem'o·riz·ing
mem'o·ry
Mem'phis
men'ace
men'ac·ing
mé·nage'
me·nag'er·ie
men·da'cious
men·dac'i·ty
Men'dels·sohn
men'di·cant
me'ni·al
me·nin'ge·al
me·nin'ges
men'in·gi'tis

Men′non·ite
men′o·pause
men′ses
men′stru·al
men′stru·ate
men′stru·a′tion
men′sur·a·bil′i·ty
men′sur·a·ble
men′su·ra′tion
men′tal
men·tal′i·ty
men′thol
men′tho·lat′ed
men′tion
men′tor
men′u
me·phit′ic
mer′can·tile
mer′can·til·ism
mer′ce·nar′y
mer′cer
mer′cer·ize
mer′cer·iz·ing
mer′chan·dise
mer′chan·dis′er
mer′chan·dis·ing
mer′chant
mer′chant·man
mer′ci·ful
mer′ci·ful·ly
mer′ci·ful·ness
mer′ci·less
mer·cu′ri·al
mer·cu′ric
mer·cu′ro·chrome
mer·cu′rous
mer′cu·ry
mer′cy
mer′est
mere′ly
mer′e·tri′cious
merg′er
me·rid′i·an
me·ringue′
me·ri′no
mer′it
mer′i·to′ri·ous
mer′maid
mer′ri·ly
mer′ri·ment
mer′ry-go-round′
mer′ry mak′ing
me′sa
mé·sal′li·ance
(*also:* misalliance)

mes·cal′
mes·dames′
mes′mer·ism
mes′mer·i·za′tion
mes′mer·ize
mes′mer·iz·ing
mes′o·carp
mes′o·derm
mes′o·der′mal
mes′on
mes′o·tron
mes·quite′
mes′sage
mes′sa·line′
mes′sen·ger
Mes·si′ah
Mes·si·an′ic
mes′sieurs
mess′i·ness
mess′y
mes·ti′zo
met′a·bol′ic
me·tab′o·lism
met′a·car′pus
met′al
mineral (*see:* mettle)

me′tal·ing
me·tal′lic
met′al·lif′er·ous
met′al·lur′gi·cal
met′al·lur′gist
met′al·lur′gy
met′al·work′ing
met′a·mor′phic
met′a·mor′phism
met′a·mor′phose
met′a·mor′pho·sis
met′a·phor
met′a·phor′i·cal
met′a·phys′i·cal
met′a·phy·si′cian
met′a·phys′ics
met′a·tar′sal
met′a·tar′sus
me·tath′e·sis
met′a·thet′ic
Met′a·zo′a
me′te·or′ic
me′te·or·ite
me′te·or·o·log′
i·cal
me′te·or·ol′o·gist
me′te·or·ol′o·gy
me′ter

meth′ane
meth′od
me·thod′i·cal
Meth′od·ism
Meth′od·ist
meth′od·ize
Me·thu′se·lah
meth′yl
me·tic′u·lous
me·ton′y·my
met′ric
met′ri·cal
me·trol′o·gy
met′ro·nome
met′ro·nom′ic
me·trop′o·lis
met′ro·pol′i·tan
met′tle
courage *(see:* metal)
Mex′i·can
Mex′i·co
mez′za·nine
mez′zo
mez′zo·so·pran′o
mez′zo·tint′
Mi·am′i
mi·as′ma
Mich′ael·mas
Mi′chel·an′ge·lo
Mich′i·gan
mi′crobe
mi·cro′bi·al
mi·cro′bic
mi′cro·cop′y
mi′cro·cosm
mi′cro·cos′mic
mi′cro·film′
mi′cro·groove′
mi·crom′e·ter
mi′cron
mi′cro·or′gan·ism
mi′cro·phone
mi′cro·scope
mi′cro·scop′ic
mi·cros′co·py
mi′cro·wave′
mid′brain′
mid′day′
mid′dle
mid′dle-aged′
mid′dle·man′
mid′dle-of-the-road′
mid′dle·weight′
mid′dling
mid′dy
midg′et
mid′i·ron
mid′land
mid′night
mid′riff
mid′ship′man
mid′ships′
mid′stream′
mid′sum′mer
mid′-Vic·to′ri·an
mid′way
Mid′west′
Mid′west′ern·er
mid′wife′
mid′win′ter
might
might′i·er
might′i·ly
might′i·ness
might′y
mi′gnon·ette′
mi′graine
mi′grant
mi′grate
mi′grat·ing
mi·gra′tion
mi′gra·to′ry
mi·ka′do
mi·la′dy
mil′dew
mile′age
mile′stone′
mi·lieu′
mil′i·tan·cy
mil′i·tant
mil′i·tant·ly
mil′i·tar′i·ly
mil′i·ta·rism′
mil′i·ta·ris′tic
mil′i·ta·ri·za′tion
mil′i·ta·rize
mil′i·ta·riz·ing
mil′i·tar′y
mil′i·tate
mil′i·tat·ing
mi·li′tia
milk′sop
milk′weed′
Milk′y Way′
mill′dam′
mil·len′ni·um
mil′le·pede
mill′er
mil′let

mil'li·am'pere
mil'liard
mil'li·gram
mil'li·me'ter
mil'li·ner
mil'li·ner'y
mil'lion
mil'lion·aire'
mil'lionth
mill'pond'
mill'stone'
mill'stream'
mill wheel
mill'wright'
mi·lord'
milque'toast'
Mil·wau'kee
mim'e·o·graph'
mi·met'ic
mim'ic
mim'i·cry
mim'ing
mi·mo'sa
min'a·ret'
min'a·to'ri·ly
min'a·to'ry
mince'meat'
minc'ing
mind'ful
min'er
mine worker (*see:* minor)
min'er·al
min'er·al'o·gy
min'e·stro'ne
min'gle
min'gling
min'i·a·ture
min'i·a·tur·ist
min'im
min'i·mi·za'tion
min'i·mize
min'i·mi'zer
min'i·mum
min'ing
min'ion
min'is·ter
min'is·te'ri·al
min'is·trant
min'is·tra'tion
min'is·try
min'i·ver
Min'ne·ap'o·lis
Min'ne·so'ta
min'now
mi'nor
lesser (*see:* miner)
mi·nor'i·ty
min'strel
mint'age
min'u·end
min·u·et'
mi'nus
min'ute, *n.*
sixty seconds
mi·nute', *adj.*
very small
min'ute hand
min'ute·man'
mi·nu'ti·ae
mir'a·cle
mi·rac'u·lous
mi·rage'
mired
mir'ing
mir'ror
mirth'ful
mirth'less
mir'y
mis'ad·ven'ture
mis'al·li'ance
mis'an·thrope
mis'an·throp'ic
mis'an·throp'i·cal·ly
mis·an'thro·pist
mis·an'thro·py
mis'ap·pli·ca'tion
mis'ap·plied'
mis'ap·ply'
mis'ap·pre·hend'
mis'ap·pre·hen'sion
mis'ap·pro'pri·ate
mis'ap·pro'pri·a'tion
mis'be·got'ten
mis'be·have'
mis'be·hav'ing
mis'be·hav'ior
mis'be·lief'
mis'be·lieve'
mis'be·liev'er
mis·cal'cu·late
mis'cal·cu·la'tion
mis·call'
mis·car'riage
mis·car'ried

mis·car′ry
mis·car′ry·ing
mis′ce·ge·na′tion
mis′cel·la′ne·ous
mis′cel·la′ny
mis·chance′
mis′chief
mis′chie·vous
mis′ci·bil′i·ty
mis′ci·ble
mis′con·ceive′
mis′con·cep′tion
mis·con′duct
mis′con·struc′tion
mis′con·strue′
mis′cre·ant
mis·cue′
mis·deal′
mis·deed
mis′de·mean′or
mis·do′er
mis·do′ing
mi′ser
mis′er·a·ble
mi′ser·li·ness
mi′ser·ly
mis′er·y
mis·fea′sance
mis·fire′
mis′fit, *n.*
mis·fit′, *v.*
mis·for′tune
mis·give′
mis·giv′ing
mis·gov′ern
mis·guid′ed
mis·han′dle
mis·han′dling
mis′hap
mis′in·form′
mis′in·for·ma′tion
mis′in·ter′pret
mis′in·ter′pre·ta′tion
mis·judge′
mis·judg′ment
mis·laid′
mis·lay′ing
mis·lead′
mis·led′
mis·man′age
mis·man′age·ment
mis·match′
mis·mate′
mis·mat′ing
mis·no′mer
mi·sog′a·mist
mi·sog′a·my
mi·sog′y·nist
mi·sog′y·ny
mis·place′
mis·place′ment
mis′print
mis·pri′sion
mis′pro·nounce′
mis′pro·nun′ci·a′tion
mis′pro·nounc′ing
mis′quo·ta′tion
mis·quote′
mis·quot′ing
mis′rep·re·sent′
mis′rep·re·sen·ta′tion
mis·rule′
mis·rul′ing
mis′sal
prayerbook *(see:* missile)
mis·shape′
mis·shap′en
mis′sile
object for hurling *(see:* missal)
miss′ing
mis′sion
mis′sion·ar′y
(plural: -aries)
Mis′sis·sip′pi
mis′sive
Mis·sou′ri
mis·speak′
mis·spell′
mis·spelled′
mis·spell′ing
mis·spelt′
mis·spend′
mis·spent′
mis·state′
mis·step′
mis·tak′a·ble
mis·take′
mis·tak′en
mis·tak′ing
mis·took′
mis′ter
mis′tle·toe
mis′tral
mis·treat′ment

mis′tress
mis·tri′al
mis·trust′ful
mist′i·ness
mist′y
mis′un·der·stand′
mis′un·der·stood′
mis·us′age
mis·use′
mis·us′ing
mi′ter
mit′i·ga·ble
mit′i·gate
mit′i·gat·ing
mit′i·ga′tion
mit′i·ga′tor
mi·to′sis
mi·tot′ic
mit′ten
mix′er
mix′ture
mix′-up
miz′zen·mast′
mne·mon′ic
moan′ing
mobbed
mob′bing
mo′bile
mo·bil′i·ty
mo′bi·li·za′tion
mo′bi·lize
moc′ca·sin
mock′er·y
mock′ing
mock′ing·bird′
mo′dal
mo·dal′i·ty
mod′el
mod′eled
mod′el·ing
mod′er·ate
mod′er·ate·ly
mod′er·at·ing
mod′er·a′tion
mod′er·a′to
mod′er·a′tor
mod′ern
mod′ern·ism
mod′ern·is′tic
mo·der′ni·ty
mod′ern·i·za′tion
mod′ern·ize
mod′ern·ness
mod′est
mod′es·ty
mod′i·cum
mod′i·fi′a·ble
mod′i·fi·ca′tion
mod′i·fied
mod′i·fi′er
mod′i·fy
mod′i·fy·ing
mod′ish
mo·diste′
mod′u·late
mod′u·la′tion
mod′u·la′tor
mod′u·la·to·ry
mod′ule
mo′dus o′pe·ran′di
mo′gul
mo′hair
Mo·ham′med
Mo·ham′med·an
moil′ing
moi·re′
moist′en
moist′ly
mois′ture
mo′lar
mold′a·ble
mold′ing
mold′y
mo·lec′u·lar
mol′e·cule
mole′hill′
mole′skin′
mo·lest′
mo′les·ta′tion
mo·lest′er
mol′li·fied
mol′li·fy
mol′li·fy·ing
mol′lusk
Mo·lo·kai′
mol′ly·cod′dle
molt′en
mo·lyb′de·num
mo′ment
mo′men·tar′i·ly
mo′men·tar′y
mo·men′tous
mo·men′tum
Mon′a·co
mon′ad
mon′arch
mo·nar′chic
mon′ar·chist
mon′ar·chy
mon′as·te′ri·al
mon′as·ter′y

mo•nas′tic
mo•nas′ti•cism
mon′a•tom′ic
Mon′day
mon′e•tar′i•ly
mon′e•tar′y
mon′e•ti•za′tion
mon′e•tize
mon′ey
(plural: moneys)

mon′ey•bags′
mon′eyed
money order
mon′ger
Mon′gol
Mon•go′li•a
Mon′gol•oid
mon′goose
mon′grel
mon′ism
mon′ist
mo•nis′tic
mo•ni′tion
mon′i•tor
mon′i•to′ri•al
mon′i•to′ry
mon′key•shine
mon′key wrench
monk′ish
monks′hood′
mon′o•bas′ic
mon′o•chro•mat′ic
mon′o•chrome
mon′o•cle
mo•nod′ic
mo•nod′i•cal•ly
mon′o•dy
mo•nog′a•mist
mo•nog′a•mous
mo•nog′a•my
mon′o•gram
mon′o•gram•mat′ic
mon′o•grammed
mon′o•graph
mo•nog′ra•pher
mon′o•graph′ic
mon′o•lith
mon′o•lith′ic
mon′o•logue
or: monolog

mon′o•log′ist
mon′o•ma′ni•a
mon′o•ma′ni•ac
mon′o•ma•ni′a•cal
mo•no′mi•al
mon′o•plane
mo•nop′o•list
mo•nop′o•li•za′tion
mo•nop′o•lize
mo•nop′o•ly
mon′o•rail′
mon′o•syl•lab′ic
mon′o•syl′la•ble
mon′o•the•ism′
mon′o•the•is′tic
mon′o•tone
mo•not′o•nous
mo•not′o•ny
mon′o•treme
mon′o•type
mon•ox′ide
Monroe Doctrine
mon•sieur′
(plural: messieurs)

Mon•si′gnor
(plural: -gnors; -gnori)

mon•soon′
mon′ster
mon•stros′i•ty
mon′strous
mon•tage′
Mon•taigne′
Mon•tan′a
Mon′te Car′lo
Mon′ter•rey′
Mon′te•vi•de′o
Mon′te•zu′ma
Mont•gom′er•y
month′ly
Mon′ti•cel′lo
Mont•pel′ier
Mont′re•al′
mon′u•ment
mon′u•men′tal
mood′i•ly
mood′y
mooed
moo′ing
moon′beam′
moon′calf′
moon′light
moon′shine′
moon′shin′er
moon′stone′
moon′strick′en

moon′struck′
moor′ings
moor′land′
moped
mop′ing
mop′pet
mo·raine′
mor′al
mo·rale′
mor′al·ist
mor′al·is′tic
mo·ral′i·ty
mor′al·i·za′tion
mor′al·ize
mor′al·ly
mo·rass′
mor′a·to′ri·um
mor′bid
mor·bid′i·ty
mor′bid·ly
mor′dan·cy
mor′dant
more·o′ver
mo′res
mor′ga·nat′ic
morgue
mor′i·bund
mor′i·bun′di·ty
mo′ri·on
Mor′mon
Mor′mon·ism
morn′ing
morn′ing-glo′ry
mo·roc′co
leather

Morocco
country

mo′ron
mo·ron′ic
mo·rose′
mo·rose′ly
Mor′pheus
mor′phine
mor·pho·log′ic
mor·phol′o·gist
mor·phol′o·gy
mor′ris
mor′sel
mor·tal′i·ty
mor′tal·ly
mor′tar
mor′tar·board′
mort′gage
mort·ga·gee′
mort′ga·gor
mor·ti′cian
mor′ti·fi·ca′tion
mor′ti·fied
mor′ti·fy
mor′ti·fy·ing
mor′tise
mor′tis·ing
mor′tu·ar′y
mo·sa′ic
Mos′cow
Mo·selle′
Mos′lem
mosque
mos·qui′to
moss′back′
moss′i·er

moss′y
most′ly
mo·tel′
moth′-eat·en
moth′er
moth′er·hood
moth′er-in-law′
(plural: mothers-)

moth′er·land′
moth′er·li·ness
moth′er·ly
moth′er-of-pearl′
mo·tif′
mo′tile
mo·til′i·ty
mo′tion·less
mo′ti·vate
mo′ti·vat·ing
mo′ti·va′tion
mo′tive
mot′ley
mo′tor·boat′
mo′tor·cade
mo′tor·car′
mo′tor·cy′cle
mo′tor·cy′clist
mo′tor·ist
mo′tor·i·za′tion
mo′tor·ize
mo′tor·man
mot′tle
mot′tling
mot′to
mou·jik′
moun′tain
moun′tain·eer′

moun′tain•ous
moun′te•bank
mount′ing
Mount Ver′non
mourn′er
mourn′ful
mourn′ing
mous′er
mous′y
mouth′ful
mouth′piece′
mov′a•bil′i•ty
mov′a•ble
move′ment
mov′er
mov′ie
mowed
mown
mow′ing
Mo′zart
mu′ci•lage
muck′er
muck′rake′
muck′y
mu′cous, *adj.*
mu′cus, *n.*
mud′di•ly
mud′di•ness
mud′dle
mud′dy
mud′guard′
muf′fin
muf′fle
muf′fler
muf′fling
muf′ti
mug′gi•ness
mug′ging
mug′gy
mug′wump′
mu•lat′to
mul′ber′ry
mu′le•teer′
mul′ish
mul′let
mul′li•gan
mul′li•ga•taw′ny
mul′lion
mul′ti•cel′lu•lar
mul′ti•col′ored
mul′ti•far′i•ous
mul′ti•form
mul′ti•for′mi•ty
mul′ti•graph
mul′ti•lat′er•al
mul′ti•mil′lion•aire′
mul′ti•ple
mul′ti•pli•cand′
mul′ti•pli•ca′tion
mul′ti•plic′i•ty
mul′ti•plied
mul′ti•pli′er
mul′ti•ply
mul′ti•ply•ing
mul′ti•tude
mul′ti•tu′di•nous
mum′ble
mum′bling
mum′mer
mum′mer•y
mum′mi•fy
mum′my
mun′dane
mu•nic′i•pal
mu•nic′i•pal′i•ty
mu•nic′i•pal•ly
mu•nif′i•cence
mu•nif′i•cent
mu•ni′tion
mu′ral
mur′der
mur′der•er
mur′der•ess
mur′der•ous
murk′i•er
murk′i•ly
murk′y
mur′mur
mur′mur•ing
mur′rain
mus′ca•dine
mus′cat
mus′ca•tel′
mus′cle
mus′cle-bound′
mus′cu•lar
mus′cu•lar′i•ty
mus′cu•la•ture
mused
mu•se′um
mush′room
mush′y
mu′sic
mu′si•cal
mu•si•cale′
mu•si′cian
mus′ing
mus′kel•lunge
mus′ket
mus′ket•eer′

mus′ket·ry
musk′mel′on
musk ox
musk′rat′
musk′y
mus′lin
mus′sel
Mus′so·li′ni
muss′y
mus′tache
mus′tang
mus′tard
mus′ter
mus′ti·ness
mus′ty
mu′ta·bil′i·ty
mu′ta·ble
mu′tant
mu′tate
mu′tat·ing
mu·ta′tion
mut′ed
mu′ti·late
mu′ti·la′tion
mu′ti·la′tor
mu′ti·neer′
mut′ing
mu′ti·nous
mu′ti·ny
mu′ti·ny·ing
mut′ter
mut′ter·ing
mut′ton
mu′tu·al
mu′tu·al′i·ty
mu′tu·al·ly
muz′zle
muz′zle·load′er
my·ce′li·um
my·col′o·gist
my·col′o·gy
my′na
my·o′pi·a
my·op′ic
myr′i·ad
myr′i·a·pod′
myrrh
myr′tle
my·self′
mys·te′ri·ous
mys′ter·y
mys′tic
mys′ti·cal
mys′ti·cism
mys′ti·fi·ca′tion
mys′ti·fy
mys′ti·fy′ing·ly
myth′i·cal
myth′o·log′i·cal
my·thol′o·gist
my·thol′o·gy

N

nab′bing
na′bob
na·celle′
na′cre
na′cre·ous
na′dir
nag′ging
Na′ga·sa′ki
nai′ad
nail′er
nain′sook
Nai·ro′bi
na·ive′
na·ive′té′
na′ked
name′ly
name′sake′
nam′ing
nan·keen′
Nan·king′
Nan·tuck′et
na·palm′
nape
na′per·y
naph′tha
naph′tha·lene
nap′kin
Na′ples
Na·po′le·on
nap′ping
nar·cis′sism
nar·cis′sus
nar·co′sis
nar·cot′ic
nar′co·tism
nard

Nar′ra·gan′sett
nar·rate′
nar·ra′tion
nar′ra·tive
nar·ra′tor
nar′row-mind′ed
nar′whal
na′sal
na·sal′i·ty
nas′cen·cy
nas′cent
Nash′ville
Nas′sau
nas′ti·ly
na·stur′tium
nas′ty
na′tal
Na·tal′
na′tant
na′ta·to′ri·al
na′ta·to′ri·um
na′ta·to·ry
na′tion
na′tion·al
na′tion·al·ism′
na′tion·al·is′tic
na′tion·al′i·ty
na′tion·al·i·za′tion
na′tion·al·ize
na′tion-wide′
na′tive-born′
na·tiv′i·ty
nat′ti·ly
nat′ty
nat′u·ral
nat′u·ral·ism′
nat′u·ral·ist
nat′u·ral·is′tic
nat′u·ral·i·za′tion
nat′u·ral·ize
nat′u·ral·ly
na′ture
Nau′gha·hyde
naught
naugh′ti·ness
naugh′ty
nau′sea
nau′se·ate
nau′se·at·ed
nau′seous
nau′ti·cal
nau′ti·cal·ly
nau′ti·lus
Nav′a·ho (-jo)
na′val
of the navy

na′vel
abdominal mark

nav′i·ga·bil′i·ty
nav′i·ga·ble
nav′i·gate
nav′i·ga′tion
nav′i·ga′tor
na′vy
Naz′a·rene′
Naz′a·reth
Na′zi
Na′zi·ism
Ne·an′der·thal
Ne′a·pol′i·tan
neap tide
near′by′
near′ly
near′ness
near′-sight′ed
neat′ly
neat′ness
Ne·bras′ka
Neb′u·chad·nez′
zar
neb′u·la
(plural: -lae; -las)

neb′u·lar
neb′u·los′i·ty
neb′u·lous
nec′es·sar′i·ly
nec′es·sar·y
ne·ces′si·tate
ne·ces′si·tous
ne·ces′si·ty
neck′er·chief
neck′lace
neck′piece′
neck′tie′
ne·crol′o·gy
nec′ro·man′cy
ne·crop′o·lis
ne·cro′sis
ne·crot′ic
nec′tar
nec·tar′e·ous
nec′tar·ine′
need′ful
need′i·er
nee′dle
nee′dle-point′
need′less
nee′dle·work′
need′y

ne′er′-do-well′
ne·far′i·ous
ne·gate′
ne·ga′tion
neg′a·tive
neg′a·tive·ly
neg′a·tiv·ism′
neg′a·tiv·is′tic
neg′a·tiv′i·ty
neg·lect′ful
neg′li·gee′
neg′li·gence
neg′li·gent
neg′li·gi·bil′i·ty
neg′li·gi·ble
ne·go′tia·bil′i·ty
ne·go′tia·ble
ne·go′ti·ate
ne·go′ti·at·ing
ne·go′ti·a′tion
ne·go′ti·a′tor
Ne′gress
Ne·gri′to
Ne′gro
(plural: -groes)
Ne′groid
Neh′ru
neigh
whinny
neigh′bor
neigh′bor-hood
neigh′bor·ing
neigh′bor·li·ness
nei′ther
nem′a·tode
nem′e·sis
(plural: -ses)
ne′o·lith′ic
ne·ol′o·gy
ne·o·my′cin
ne′on
ne′o·phyte
ne·pen′the
neph′ew
ne·phrit′ic
ne·phri′tis
nep′o·tism
Nep′tune
ner·va′tion
nerve′less
nerv′ing
nerv′ous
nerv′ous·ness
nerv′y
nes′cience
nes′cient
nes′tle
nes′tling
p.p. of nestle
nest′ling, *n.*
young bird
neth′er
Neth′er·lands
neth′er·most
net′ting
net′tle
net′work′
neu′ral
neu·ral′gia
neu·ral′gic
neu′ras·the′ni·a
neu′ras·then′ic
neu·rit′ic
neu·ri′tis
neu′ro·log′i·cal
neu·rol′o·gist
neu·rol′o·gy
neu′ron
neu·ron′ic
neu′ro·path′ic
neu′ro·path′
i·cal·ly
neu·rop′a·thy
neu·ro′sis
neu·rot′ic
neu′ter
neu′tral
neu′tral·ism
neu·tral′i·ty
neu′tral·i·za′tion
neu′tral·ize
neu′tron
Ne·vad′a
nev′er·more′
nev′er·the·less′
New′ark
new′born
New′cas′tle
new′com·er
new′el
new′fan′gled
New′found·land′
New Hamp′shire
New Jer′sey
new′ly
new′ness
New Or′le·ans

news′cast′
news′cast′er
news′deal′er
news′let′ter
news′pa′per
news′print′
news′reel′
news′stand′
news′y
New Zea′land
nex′us
ni′a·cin
Ni·ag′a·ra
nib′ble
nib′bling
nib′lick
Nic′a·ra′gua
nic′est
ni′ce·ty
niche
nick′el
nick′el·o′de·on
nick′el-plate′
nick′name′
nic′o·tine
nic′ti·tate
nic′ti·ta′tion
niece
Nie′tzsche
nif′ty
Ni·ge′ri·a
nig′gard·ly
night′cap′
night′fall′
night′gown′
night′hawk′
night′in·gale
night′ly
night′mare′
night′shirt′
night′time′
ni′hil·ism
ni′hil·is′tic
Ni′ke
nim′ble
nim′ble·ness
nim′bly
nim′bus
Nim′rod
nin′com·poop
nine′fold
nine′pins′
nine′teen′
nine′ti·eth
nine′ty
nin′ny
ninth′ly
nip′per
nip′ping
nip′ple
Nip·pon′
nip′py
nir·va′na
Ni′sei′
ni′ter
ni′trate
ni′tric
ni′trite
ni′tro·gen
ni·trog′e·nous
ni′tro·glyc′er·in
ni′trous
nit′wit′
No·bel′
no·bil′i·ty
no′ble·man
no′ble·ness
no·blesse′ o·blige′
no′ble·wom′an
no′bly
no′bod·y
noc·tur′nal
noc′turne
nod′al
nod′ding
nod′dle
nod′u·lar
nod′ule
no·el′
nog′gin
no′how′
nois′ing
noise′less
noi′some
nois′y
no′mad
no·mad′ic
no′mad·ism
nom′ de plume′
no′men·cla′ture
nom′i·nal
nom′i·nate
nom′i·na′tion
nom′i·na·tive
nom′i·na′tor
nom·i·nee′
non′ac·cept′ance
nonage
non′a·ge·nar′i·an
non′ag·gres′sion
non′a·gon

non′cha·lance
non′cha·lant
non′com·bat′ant
non′com·mis′
sioned
non′com·mit′tal
non′ com′pos
men′tis
non′con·duc′tor
non′con·form′ist
non′con·form′i·ty
non′de·script
non·en′ti·ty
non′es·sen′tial
none′such′
non·fic′tion
non′ful·fill′ment
non′me·tal′lic
non′pa·reil′
non·par′ti·san
non·plus′
non·plus′ing
non·plussed′
non′pro·duc′tive
non·prof′it
non′sec·tar′i·an
non′sense
non·sen′si·cal
non se′qui·tur
non′stop′
non′sup·port′
noo′dle
noon′day′
noon′time′
Nor′dic
Nor′folk
nor′mal
nor′mal·cy
nor·mal′i·ty
nor′mal·ize
Nor′man·dy
Norse′man
North A·mer′i·ca
North Car′o·li′na
North Da·ko′ta
north′east′
north′east′er·ly
north′er·ly
north′ern
north′land
north′ward·ly
north′west′
north′west′er·ly
Nor′way
Nor·we′gian
nose′-dive′
nose′gay′
nos′ing
nos·tal′gia
nos·tal′gic
nos′tril
nos′trum
nos′y
no′ta be′ne
no′ta·bil′i·ty
no′ta·ble
no·tar′i·al
no′ta·rize
no′ta·ry pub′lic
(*plural:* notaries)
no·ta′tion
notched
note′book′
not′ed
note′wor′thi·ness
note′wor·thy
noth′ing
no′tice
no′tice·a·ble
no′tic·ing
no′ti·fi·ca′tion
no′ti·fi′er
no′ti·fy
no′ti·fy·ing
not′ing
no′tion
no′to·ri′e·ty
no·to′ri·ous
not′with·stand′ing
nou′gat
nour′ish
nour′ish·ing
nour′ish·ment
nou·veau riche′
No′va Sco′tia
nov′el
nov′el·ette′
nov′el·ist
no·vel′la
nov′el·ty
(*plural:* -ties)
No·vem′ber
no·ve′na
nov′ice
no·vi′ti·ate
no′vo·caine
now′a·days′
no′where
no′wise

nox′ious
noz′zle
nu·ance′
nub′bin
nu′bile
nu·bil′i·ty
nu′cle·ar
nu′cle·o′nics
nu′cle·ons
nu′cle·us
(plural: -cleuses; -clei)
nude′ness
nudged
nudg′ing
nud′ism
nud′ist
nu′di·ty
nug′get
nui′sance
nul′li·fi·ca′tion
nul′li·fied
nul′li·fi·er
nul′li·fy
nul′li·fy·ing
nul′li·ty
num′ber
num′ber·er
num′ber·less
numb′ing·ly
numb′ly
numb′ness
nu′mer·a·ble
nu′mer·al
nu′mer·ate
nu′mer·a′tion
nu′mer·a′tor
nu·mer′i·cal
nu·mer′i·cal·ly
nu′mer·ous
nu′mis·mat′ics
nu·mis′ma·tist
num′skull′
nun′ci·o
nun′ner·y
nup′tial
Nu′rem·berg
nurs′er·y
nurs′er·y·man
nurs′ing
nurs′ling
nur′ture
nur′tur·ing
nut′crack′er
nut′hatch′
nut′meg
nu′tri·a
nu′tri·ent
nu′tri·ment
nu·tri′tion
nu·tri′tion·al
nu·tri′tion·ist
nu·tri′tious
nu′tri·tive
nut′shell′
nut′ti·er
nut′ti·ness
nuz′zle
ny′lon
nymph
nym′pho·ma′ni·a

O

O·a′hu
oak′en
Oak′land
oa′kum
oar′lock′
oars′man
o·a′sis
(plural: oases)
oat′en
oat′meal′
ob′bli·ga′to
ob′du·ra·cy
ob′du·rate
o·be′di·ence
o·be′di·ent
o·bei′sance
o·bei′sant
ob′e·lisk
O′ber·am′mer·gau′
o·bese′
o·bes′i·ty
o·bey′ing
ob′fus′cate
ob′fus·ca′tion

ob·fus′ca·tor
ob′i·ter dic′tum
o·bit′u·ar·y
ob′ject, *n.*
ob·ject′, *v.*
ob·ject′i·fi·ca′tion
ob·jec′ti·fy
ob·ject′ing
ob·jec′tion
ob·jec′tion·a·ble
ob·jec′tive
ob′jec·tiv′i·ty
ob·jec′tor
ob·jet d'art′
(*plural:* objets)

ob′jur·gate
ob′jur·ga′tion
ob′jur·ga′tor
ob′late
ob·la′tion
ob′li·gate
ob′li·gat·ing
ob′li·ga′tion
ob′li·ga′tor
ob·lig′a·to′ry
o·blige′
o·blig′ing·ly
ob·lique′
ob·lique′ly
ob·lique′ness
ob·liq′ui·ty
ob·lit′er·ate
ob·lit′er·a′tion
ob·lit′er·a′tive
ob·lit′er·a′tor
ob·liv′ion
ob·liv′i·ous
ob′long
ob′lo·quy
ob·nox′ious
o′boe
o′bo·ist
ob·scene′
ob·scene′ly
ob·scen′i·ty
ob·scur′ant
ob′scu·ra′tion
ob·scure′
ob·scure′ly
ob·scur′ing·ly
ob·scu′ri·ty
ob′se·quies
ob·se′qui·ous
ob·serv′a·ble
ob·serv′ance
ob·serv′ant
ob′ser·va′tion
ob·serv′a·to′ry
ob·serve′
ob·serv′er
ob·serv′ing·ly
ob·sess′
ob·ses′sion
ob·ses′sive
ob·ses′sor
ob·sid′i·an
ob′so·les′cence
ob′so·les′cent
ob′so·lete
ob′so·lete·ness
ob′sta·cle
ob·stet′ri·cal
ob′ste·tri′cian
ob·stet′rics
ob′sti·na·cy
ob′sti·nance
ob′sti·nate
ob·strep′er·ous
ob·struct′
ob·struct′er
ob·struc′tive
ob·struc′tion
ob·struc′tion·ism
ob·struc′tion·ist
ob·tain′
ob·tain′a·ble
ob·tain′ment
ob·trude′
ob·trud′ing
ob·tru′sion
ob·tru′sive
ob·tru′sive·ly
ob·tuse′
ob·verse′ly
ob′vi·ate
ob′vi·at·ing
ob′vi·a′tion
ob′vi·a′tor
ob′vi·ous
ob′vi·ous·ly
oc′a·ri′na
oc·ca′sion
oc·ca′sion·al·ly
Oc′ci·dent
oc′ci·den′tal
oc·cip′i·tal
oc′ci·put
oc·clude′
oc·clud′ing
oc·clu′sive·ly

oc·clu′sion
oc·cult′
oc·cult′ism
oc′cu·pan·cy
oc′cu·pant
oc′cu·pa′tion
oc′cu·pi·er
oc′cu·py·ing
oc·cur′
oc·curred′
oc·cur′rence
oc·cur′rent
oc·cur′ring
o′cean
O′ce·an′i·a
o′ce·an′ic
o′cean·og′ra·pher
o′cean·o·graph′ic
o′cean·og′ra·phy
o′ce·lot
o′cher
o′cher·ous
o′clock′
oc′ta·gon
oc·tag′o·nal
oc′ta·he′dral
oc′ta·he′dron
oc′tane
oc·ta′val
oc′tave
oc·ta′vo
oc·tet′
Oc·to′ber
oc′to·ge·nar′i·an
oc·tog′e·nar′y
oc′to·pus
oc·to·roon′
oc′tu·ple
oc′u·lar
oc′u·list
odd′i·ty
odd′ly
od′ic
o′di·ous
od′ist
o′di·um
o′dor
o′dor·if′er·ous
o′dor·ous
Od′ys·sey
Oed′i·pus
of′fal
off′beat′
off′-col′or
off·end′
of·fend′er
of·fend′ing
of·fense′
of·fen′sive
of′fer·ing
of′fer·to′ri·al
of′fer·to′ry
off′hand′ed·ly
of′fice·hold′er
of′fi·cer
of·fi′cial·dom
of·fi′cial·ly
of·fi′ci·ate
of·fi′ci·a′tion
of·fic′i·nal
of·fi′cious
off′ing
off′set′
off′set′ting
off′shoot′
off′shore′
off′side′
off′spring′
off′stage′
off′-the-cuff′
of′ten
of′ten·times′
o·gee′
o′gle
o′gling
o′gre
ohm′ic
ohm′me′ter
oil′cloth′
oil′skin′
oil′y
oint′ment
o·ka′pi
o′kay′
O′ki·na′wa
O′kla·ho′ma
o′kra
old′en
old′-fash′ioned
old′-line′
old′ster
old′-tim′er
old′-world′
o·le·ag′i·nous
o′le·an′der
o′le·in
o′le·o·mar′ga·rine
ol·fac′tion
ol·fac′tive
ol·fac′to·ry
ol′i·garch

ol′i·gar′chy
ol′ive
ol′la
o·lym′pi·ad
O·lym′pi·an
O·lym′pics
O·lym′pus
O′ma·ha
O′mar Khay·yam′
o·meg′a
om′e·let
o′men
om′i·cron
om′i·nous
o·mis′sion
o·mit′
o·mit′tance
o·mit′ted
om′ni·bus
om′ni·far′i·ous
om·nip′o·tence
om·nip′o·tent
om′ni·pres′ence
om′ni·pres′ent
om·nis′cience
om·nis′cient
om·niv′o·rous
o′nan·ism
o′nan·ist
once′o·ver
on′com′ing
one′-horse′
one′ness
on′er·ous
one·self′
one′-sid′ed
one′step
one′-track′
one′-way′
one′-world′er
on′ion·skin′
on′look′er
on′o·mat′o·poe′ia
on′o·mat′o·po·et′
ic
on′rush′
on′set′
on′shore′
on′slaught′
On·tar′i·o
o′nus
on′ward
on′yx
oo′long
oozed
ooz′ing
o·pac′i·ty
o′pal
o′pal·esce′
o′pal·es′cence
o′pal·es′cent
o′pal·ine
o·paque′
o′pen·er
o′pen-hand′ed
o′pen·ing
o′pen-mind′ed
o′pen·ness
o′pen·work′
op′er·a
op′er·a·ble
o′pe·ra bouffe′
op′er·at′a·ble
op′er·ate
op′er·at′ic
op′er·a′tion
op′er·a′tion·al
op′er·a′tive
op′er·a′tor
o·per′cu·lum
op′er·et′ta
oph·thal′mi·a
oph·thal′mic
oph·thal′mo·log′
i·cal
oph′thal·mol′o·gist
oph′thal·mol′o·gy
o′pi·ate
o·pi·at′ic
o·pine′
o·pin′ion
o·pin′ion·at′ed
o·pin′ion·a′tive
o′pi·um
o·pos′sum
op·po′nent
op′por·tune′
op′por·tune′ly
op′por·tune′ness
op′por·tun′ism
op′por·tun′ist
op′por·tun·is′tic
op′por·tu′ni·ty
op·pos′a·ble
op·pose′
op·pos′ing
op′po·site
op′po·si′tion
op′press′
op·pres′sion
op·pres′sive

op·pres′sor
op·pro′bri·ous
op·pro′bri·um
op′tic
op′ti·cal
op·ti′cian
op′tics
op′ti·mal
op′ti·mism
op′ti·mist
op′ti·mis′tic
op′ti·mum
op′tion
op′tion·al
op·tom′e·trist
op·tom′e·try
op′u·lence
op′u·len·cy
op′u·lent
or′a·cle
o·rac′u·lar
o·rac′u·lar′i·ty
o′ral·ly
or′ange
or′ange·ade′
o·rang′u·tan
o·rate′
o·ra′tion
or′a·tor
or′a·tor′i·cal
or′a·to′ri·o
or′a·to′ry
or·bic′u·lar
or·bic′u·lar′i·ty
or·bic′u·late
or′bit
or′chard
or′ches·tra
or·ches′tral
or′ches·trate
or′ches·tra′tion
or′chid
or·dain′
or·deal′
or′der·li·ness
or′der·ly
or′di·nal
or′di·nance
rule or law
or′di·nar′i·ly
or′di·nar′y
or′di·nate
ord′nance
military weapons
Or′e·gon
or′gan·dy
or·gan′ic
or·gan′i·cal·ly
or′gan·ism
or′gan·ist
or′gan·i·za′tion
or′gan·ize
or′gan·iz·ing
or′gasm
or·gas′tic
or′gi·ac
or′gi·as′tic
o′ri·ent
o′ri·en′tal
o′ri·en·tate
o′ri·en·ta′tion
or′i·fice
or′i·fi′cial
or′i·gin
o·rig′i·nal
o·rig′i·nal′i·ty
o·rig′i·nate
o·rig′i·na′tion
o·rig′i·na′tor
o′ri·ole
O·ri′on
or′i·son
Or′lon
or′mo·lu
or′na·ment
or′na·men′tal
or′na·men·ta′tion
or·nate′ness
or′ner·y
or′ni·tho·log′i·cal
or′ni·thol′o·gist
or′ni·thol′o·gy
o′ro·tund
o′ro·tun′di·ty
or′phan·age
Or′phe·us
or′ris·root′
or′tho·don′tia
or′tho·don′tic
or′tho·don′tist
or′tho·dox
or′tho·dox′y
or′tho·ep′i·cal
or·tho′e·pist
or·tho′e·py
or·thog′ra·pher
or′tho·graph′ic
or·thog′ra·phy
or′tho·pe′dic
or′tho·pe′dics

or'tho·pe'dist
or'to·lan
o'ryx
os'cil·late
os'cil·la'tion
os'cil·la'tor
os'cil·la·to·ry
os'cu·late
os'cu·la'tion
os'cu·la·to'ry
os'mi·um
os·mo'sis
os·mot'ic
os'prey
os'se·ous
os'si·fi·ca'tion
os'si·fied
os'si·fy
os'si·fy·ing
os·ten'si·ble
os'ten·ta'tion
os'ten·ta'tious
os'te·ol'o·gist
os'te·ol'o·gy
os'te·o·path
os'te·o·path'ic
os'te·op'a·thy
ost'ler
os'tra·cism
os'tra·cize
os'tra·ciz·ing
os'trich
O·thel'lo
oth'er·wise'
o'to·log'i·cal
o·tol'o·gy
Ot'ta·wa

ot'ter
ot'to·man
ought
should *(see:* aught)

Oui'ja
ounce
our·selves'
oust'er
out·bid'
out'board'
out'bound'
out'break'
out'burst'
out'cast'
out'come'
out'crop'ping
out'cry'
out·dis'tance
out·do'
out·doors'
out'er
out'field'
out'fit
out'go'
out'go'ing
out·grow'
out'ing
out'lan'der
out·land'ish
out·last'
out'law'
out'lay'
out'let
out'line'
out·live'
out'look'

out'ly'ing
out'ma·neu'ver
out·mod'ed
out·num'ber
out'-of-date'
out'-of-doors'
out'-of-the-way'
out'pa'tient
out'post'
out'pour'ing
out'put'
out'rage
out·ra'geous
out·rank'
ou·tré'
out'rig'ger
out'right'
out'set'
out'side'
out'sid'er
out'size'
out'skirts'
out·smart'
out'spo'ken
out'spread'
out·stand'ing
out'stretched'
out-stripped'
out'ward
out·wear'
out·weigh'
out·wit'ted
ou'zel
o'va, *pl.*
o'val
o·var'i·an
o'va·ry

o′vate
o·va′tion
o′ver·ac·tiv′i·ty
o′ver·all′
o′ver·awe′
o′ver·bal′ance
o′ver·bear′ing
o′ver·bid′
o′ver·board′
o′ver·came′
o′ver·cast′
o′ver·charge′
o′ver·coat′
o′ver·come′
o′ver·do′
o′ver·dose′
o′ver·draft′
o′ver·draw′
o′ver·drive′
o′ver·due′
o′ver·flow′
o′ver·grow′
o′ver·hang′
o′ver·haul′
o′ver·head′
o′ver·hear′
o′ver·joy′
o′ver·land′
o′ver·lap′ping
o′ver·load′
o′ver·look′
o′ver·ly
o′ver·night′
o′ver·pass′
o′ver·pow′er
o′ver·reach′
o′ver·ride′
o′ver·rule′
o′ver·run′
o′ver·seas′
o′ver·see′
o′ver·se′er
o′ver·shoe′
o′ver·shoot′
o′ver·sight′
o′ver·size′
o′ver·stay′
o′ver·stuffed
o·vert′
o′ver·take′
o′ver·took′
o′ver·throw′
o′ver·time′
o′ver·tone′
o′ver·ture
o′ver·turn′
o′ver·weight′
o′ver·whelm′
o′ver·work′
o′ver·wrought′
o′vi·duct
o′vi·form
o′vi·par′i·ty
o·vip′a·rous
o′vi·pos′i·tor
o′void
o′vu·lar
o′vule
o′vum
(*plural:* ova)

ow′ing
owl′et
owl′ish
own′er
own′er·ship
ox·al′ic
ox′cart′
ox′en
ox′ford
ox′i·da′tion
ox′ide
ox′i·di·za′tion
ox′i·dize
ox′i·diz′er
Ox·o′ni·an
ox′y·a·cet′y·lene
ox′y·gen
ox′y·gen·ate
ox′y·gen·a′tion
ox′y·gen′ic
oys′ter
O′zarks
o′zone
o′zo·nif′er·ous

P

pab′u·lum
paced
pace′mak′er
pac′ing
pach′y·derm
pa·cif′ic
pa·cif′i·cal·ly
pac′i·fi·ca′tion
pac′i·fied
pac′i·fi′er
pac′i·fism
pac′i·fist
pac′i·fis′tic
pac′i·fy
pac′i·fy′ing
pack′age
pack′ag·ing
pack′et
pack′sad′dle
pad′ding
pad′dle
pad′dling
pad′dy
Pad′e·rew′ski
pad′lock′
pa′dre
pae′an
  joyful song *(see:* peon)

pa′gan·ism
paged
pag′eant
pag′eant·ry
pag′i·na′tion
pag′ing
pa·go′da
pail′ful
pain′ful·ly
pain′less·ly
pains′tak′ing
paint′er
paint′ing
pais′ley
pa·ja′mas
Pak′i·stan
pal′ace
pal′a·din
pal′an·quin′
pal′at·a·bil′i·ty
pal′at·a·ble
pal′a·tal
pal′ate
  roof of mouth *(see:* palette; pallet)

pa·la′tial
pal′a·tine
pa·lav′er
pale′face′
pa′le·og′ra·pher
pa′le·o·graph′ic
pa′le·og′ra·phy
pa′le·o·lith′ic
pa′le·on·tol′o·gist
pa′le·on·tol′o·gy
Pal′es·tine
pal′ette
  color board *(see:* palate; pallet)

pal′frey
pal′imp·sest
pal′i·sade′
pal·la′di·um
Pal′las
pall′bear′er
pal′let
  bed *(see:* palate; palette)

pal′li·ate
pal′li·at·ing
pal′li·a′tion
pal′li·a′tive
pal′lid
pal′lor
pal′mate
pal·met′to
palm′ist
palm′is·try
pal′o·mi′no
pal′pa·bil′i·ty
pal′pa·ble
pal′pi·tate
pal′pi·tat·ing
pal′pi·ta′tion
pal′pus
pal′sied
pal′sy
pal′ter
pal′tri·ness
pal′try
pam′pas
pam′per
pam′phlet

pam'phlet·eer'
pan'a·ce'a
Pan'a·ma
Pan'a·ma'ni·an
Pan'-A·mer'i·can
pan'cake'
pan'chro·mat'ic
pan'cre·as
pan'cre·at'ic
pan'de·mo'ni·um
pan'der
Pan·do'ra
pan·dow'dy
pan'e·gyr'ist
pan'eled
pan'el·ing
pan'han'dle
pan'han'dling
Pan'hel·len'ic
pan'ic
pan'icked
pan'ick·ing
pan'ick·y
pan'ic-strick'en
pan'ni·er
pan'ning
pan'o·ply
pan'o·ram'a
pan'o·ram'ic
pan'sy
pan'ta·lets'
pan'ta·loon'
pan'the·ism
pan'the·ist
pan'the·is'tic
Pan'the·on
Pan'the·on'ic
pan'ther
pan'to·graph
pan'to·mime
pan'to·mim'ic
pan'to·mim'ist
pan'try
pan'zer
pa'pa·cy
pa'pal
pa'paw
pa·pa'ya
pa'per·back'
pa'per·like'
pa'per·weight'
pa'pier-ma·che'
pa·pil'la
pap'il·lar'y
pap'il·lose
pap'il·los'i·ty
pa'pist
pa·poose'
pap·ri'ka
pa·py'rus
par'a·ble
pa·rab'o·la
par'a·bol'ic
par'a·chute
par'a·chut'ist
pa·rade'
pa·rad'ing
par'a·digm
par'a·dise
par'a·dox
par'af·fin
par'a·gon
par'a·graph
par'a·graph'
i·cal·ly
Par'a·guay
par'a·keet
par'al·lac'tic
par'al·lax
par'al·leled
par'al·lel·ing
par'al·lel·ism'
par'al·lel'o·gram
pa·ral'y·sis
(plural: -ses)
par'a·lyt'ic
par'a·ly·za'tion
par'a·lyze
par'a·lyz·ing
par'a·me'ci·um
pa'ram·e·ter
para'met·ric
par'a·mount
par'a·noi'a
par'a·noi'ac
par'a·pet
par'a·pher·nal'ia
par'a·phrase
par'a·phras·ing
par'a·ple'gi·a
par'a·ple'gic
par'a·site
par'a·sit'ic
par'a·sol
par'a·thy'roid
par'a·troop'er
par'boil'
par'celed
par'cel·ing

par·chee′si
parch′ment
par′don·a·ble
pared
par′e·gor′ic
par′ent·age
pa·ren′tal
pa·ren′the·sis
(*plural:* -ses)
pa·ren′the·size
par′en·thet′i·cal
par′ent·hood
pa·re′sis
pa·ret′ic
par ex′cel·lence
par·fait′
par·he′li·on
pa·ri′ah
pa·ri′e·tal
par′i·mu′tu·el
par′ing
Par′is
par′ish
pa·rish′ion·er
Pa·ri′si·an
par′i·ty
par′ka
park′way′
par′lance
par′lay
bet
par′ley
discuss
par′lia·ment
par′lia·men·tar′i·an
par′lia·men′ta·ry
par′lor
Par′me·san′
pa·ro′chi·al
par′o·died
par′o·dist
par′o·dy·ing
pa·role′
pa·roled′
pa·rol′ing
pa·rot′id
par′ox·ysm
par′ox·ys′mal
par·quet′
par′quet·ry
par′ri·cid′al
par′ri·cide
par′ried
par′rot
par′ry·ing
parse
par′si·mo′ni·ous
par′si·mo′ny
pars′ing
pars′ley
pars′nip
par′son
par′son·age
par·take′
par·tak′en
part′ed
par·terre′
par′the·no·gen′e·sis
par′the·no·ge·net′ic
Par′the·non
par′tial
par′ti·al′i·ty
par·tic′i·pant
par·tic′i·pate
par·tic′i·pa′tion
par′ti·cip′i·al
par′ti·ci′ple
par′ti·cle
par′ti-col′ored
par·tic′u·lar·ly
par·tic′u·lar′i·ty
par·tic′u·lar·ize
part′ing
par′ti·san
par′ti·san·ship′
par·ti′tion
par·ti′tion·ment
par′ti·tive
part′ly
part′ner
part′ner·ship
par′tridge
par·tu′ri·ent
par′tu·ri′tion
par′ty
par′ve·nu
Pas′a·de′na
pas′chal
pa·sha′
pass′a·ble
pass′a·bly
pas′sage
pas′sage·way′
pas·sé′

pas′sen•ger
pass′er-by′
pass′ing
pas′sion
pas′sion•ate•ly
pas′sion•less
pas′sive
pas′sive•ly
pas•siv′i•ty
Pass′o•ver
pass′port
pass′word′
paste′board′
past′ed
pas•tel′
pas′tern
Pas•teur′
pas′teur•i•za′tion
pas′teur•ize
pas•tille′
pas′time
past′ing
pas′tor
pas′tor•al
pas′tor•ate
pas•tra′mi
pas′try
pas′tur•age
pas′ture
past′i•ness
past′y
Pat′a•go′ni•a
patch′i•ness
patch′work′
patch′y
pa•té′ de foie gras′
pa•tel′la
pat′ent
pat′ent•a•ble
pat′ent•ee′
pat′en•tor
pa′ter
pa•ter′nal
pa•ter′nal•ism
pa•ter′nal•is′tic
pa•ter′ni•ty
pat′er•nos′ter
pa•thet′ic
pa•thet′i•cal•ly
path′find′er
path′o•gen′ic
path′o•log′i•cal
pa•thol′o•gist
pa•thol′o•gy
pa′thos
path′way′
pa′tience
pa′tient
pat′i•na
pat′i•o
pat′ois
pa′tri•arch
pa′tri•ar′chal
pa′tri•ar′chy
pa•tri′cian
pat′ri•cid′al
pat′ri•cide
pat′ri•mo′ni•al
pat′ri•mo′ny
pa′tri•ot
pa′tri•ot′ic
pa′tri•ot′i•cal•ly
pa′tri•ot•ism′
pa•tris′tic
pa•tris′ti•cal•ly
pa•trol′
pa•trol′ler
pa•trol′man
pa′tron
pa′tron•age
pa′tron•ess
pa′tron•ize
pa′tron•iz′ing
pat′ro•nym′ic
pat′ter
pat′tern
pat′tern•mak′er
pat′ting
pat′ty
pau′ci•ty
paunch′i•ness
paunch′y
pau′per
pau′per•ism
pau′per•ize
paus′ing
pave′ment
pa•vil′ion
pav′ing
pawn′bro′ker
Paw•nee′
pawn′shop′
pay′a•ble
pay•ee′
pay′ing
peace′a•ble
peace′a•bly
peace′ful
peace′mak′er
peace′time′
peach′y

pea′cock′
pea′hen′
peak′ed
pea′nut′
pearl′i·ness
pearl′y
peas′ant
peas′ant·ry
peat′y
pea′vey
peb′ble
peb′bled
peb′bling
peb′bly
pe·can′
pec′ca·dil′lo
pec′ca·ry
pec′tin
pec′to·ral
pec′u·late
pec′u·lat·ing
pec′u·la′tion
pec′u·la′tor
pe·cul′iar
pe·cu′li·ar′i·ty
pe·cu′ni·ar′i·ly
pe·cu′ni·ar′y
ped′a·gog′ic
ped′a·gogue
ped′a·go′gy
ped′al
ped′ant
pe·dan′tic
pe·dan′ti·cism
ped′ant·ry
ped′dle
ped′dler
ped′es·tal
pe·des′tri·an
pe′di·a·tri′cian
pe′di·at′rics
pe′di·at′rist
ped′i·cel
ped′i·gree
ped′i·ment
ped′lar
pe·dom′e·ter
pe·dun′cle
pe·dun′cu·lar
peel′ing
peep′hole′
peer′age
peer′ess
peer′less
pee′vish
Peg′a·sus
peg′ging
peign·oir′
Pei′ping′
Pe′king·ese′
pe′koe
pel′i·can
pe·lisse′
pel·lag′ra
pel·lag′rous
pel′let
pell′-mell′
pel·lu′cid
pel′lu·cid′i·ty
pelt′ry
pel′vic
pel′vis
pem′mi·can
pe′nal
pe′nal·ize
pe′nal·iz·ing
pen′al·ty
pen′ance
pe·na′tes
pen′chant
pen′cil
pen′cil·ing
pend′ant, *n.*
hanging ornament
pend′ent, *adj.*
hanging
pend′ing
pen′du·lous
pen′du·lum
pen′e·tra·bil′i·ty
pen′e·tra·ble
pen′e·trate
pen′e·trat·ing
pen′e·tra′tion
pen′e·tra′tive
pen′guin
pen′i·cil′lin
pen′i·cil′li·um
pen·in′su·la
pe′nis
pen′i·tence
pen′i·tent
pen′i·ten′tial
pen′i·ten′tia·ry
pen′knife′
pen′man
pen′man·ship
pen′nant
pen′ni·less
pen′ning

pen′non
Penn′syl·va′ni·a
pen′ny
pen′ny·roy′al
pen′ny·weight′
pen′ny-wise′
pe′no·log′ic
pe·nol′o·gist
pe·nol′o·gy
pen′sile
pen′sion
pen′sion·ar′y
pen′sion·er
pen′sive
pen′sive·ly
pen′ta·gon
pen·tag′o·nal
pen·tam′e·ter
Pen′ta·teuch
pen·tath′lon
Pen′te·cost
Pen′te·cos′tal
pent′house′
pent′-up′
pe′nult
pe·nul′ti·mate
pe·num′bra
pe·nu′ri·ous
pen′u·ry
pe′on
laborer (*see:* paean)
pe′on·age
pe′o·ny
peo′ple
peo′pling
pep′lum
pep′per
pep′per·mint
pep′per·y
pep′py
pep′sin
pep′tic
pep′tone
pep·ton′ic
per′ad·ven′ture
per·am′bu·late
per·am′bu·lat·ing
per·am′bu·la′tion
per·am′bu·la′tor
per an′num
per·cale′
per cap′i·ta
per·ceiv′a·ble
per·ceive′
percent′
per·cent′age
per·cen′tile
per′cept
per·cep′ti·bil′i·ty
per·cep′ti·ble
per·cep′ti·bly
per·cep′tion
per·cep′tive
per·chance′
Per′che·ron
per·cip′i·ence
per·cip′i·ent
per′co·late
per′co·la′tion
per′co·la′tor
per·cus′sion
per di′em
per·di′tion
per′e·gri·nate
per′e·gri·na′tion
per′e·gri·na′tor
per′e·grine
per·emp′to·ri·ly
per·emp′to·ry
per·en′ni·al
per′fect, *adj.*
per·fect′, *v.*
per·fect′i·bil′i·ty
per·fect′i·ble
per·fec′tion
per·fec′tive
per′fect′ly
per·fec′to
per·fid′i·ous·ness
per′fi·dy
per′fo·rate
per′fo·ra′tion
per′fo·ra′tive
per′fo·ra′tor
per·force′
per·form′
per·form′ance
per·form′er
per′fume
per·fum′er·y
per·func′to·ri·ly
per·func′to·ry
per′go·la
per·haps′
per′i·car′di·ac
per′i·car·di′tis
per′i·car′di·um
per′i·ge′al
per′i·gee
per′i·he′li·on

per′il•ing
per′il•ous
pe•rim′e•ter
per′i•met′ric
per′i•met′ri•cal
per′i•ne′um
pe′ri•od
pe′ri•od′ic
pe′ri•od′i•cal
pe′ri•o•dic′i•ty
per′i•os′te•al
per′i•os′te•um
per′i•pa•tet′ic
pe•riph′er•al
pe•riph′er•y
per′i•phrase
pe•riph′ra•sis
per′i•phras′tic
per′i•scope
per′i•scop′ic
per′ish
per′ish•a•ble
per′i•stal′sis
per′i•stal′tic
per′i•style
per′i•to•ne′al
per′i•to•ne′um
per′i•to•ni′tis
per′i•wig
per′i•win′kle
per′jure
per′jur•er
per′jur•ing
per′ju•ry
perk′i•ness
perk′y
per′ma•nence
per′ma•nent
per•man′ga•nate
per′me•a•bil′i•ty
per′me•a•ble
per′me•ate
per′me•a′tion
per′me•a′tive
per•mis′si•bil′i•ty
per•mis′si•ble
per•mis′sion
per•mis′sive
per•mit′, *v.*
per′mit, *n.*
per•mit′ting
per′mu•ta′tion
per•ni′cious
per′o•ra′tion
per•ox′ide
per′pen•dic′u•lar
per′pe•trate
per′pe•tra′tion
per′pe•tra′tor
per•pet′u•al
per•pet′u•ate
per•pet′u•a′tion
per′pe•tu′i•ty
per•plex′
per•plex′i•ty
per′qui•site
per se′
per′se•cute
per′se•cu′tion
per′se•cu′tor
per′se•ver′ance
per′se•vere′
per′se•ver′ing
per′si•flage
per•sim′mon
per•sist′
per•sist′ence
per•sist′ent
per′son
per′son•a•ble
per′son•age
per′son•al
per′son•al′i•ty
per′son•al•ize
per′son•al•ly
per•so′na non
gra′ta
per′son•ate
per′son•a′tion
per•son′i•fi•ca′tion
per•son′i•fi′er
per•son′i•fy
per•son′i•fy•ing
per′son•nel′
per•spec′tive
per′spi•ca′cious
per′spi•cac′i•ty
per′spi•cu′i•ty
per•spic′u•ous
per′spi•ra′tion
per•spire′
per•spir′ing
per•suad′a•ble
per•suade′
per•suad′ing
per•sua′sion
per•sua′sive
per•tain′
per′ti•na′cious
per′ti•nac′i•ty
per′ti•nence

per′ti·nent
pert′ly
per·turb′
per·turb′a·ble
per′tur·ba′tion
per·turb′ed·ly
Pe·ru′vi·an
pe·ruke′
pe·rus′a·ble
pe·rus′al
pe·ruse′
pe·rus′ing
per·vade′
per·vad′er
per·vad′ing
per·va′sion
per·va′sive·ly
per·verse′
per·ver′sion
per·ver′si·ty
per·vert′, *v.*
per′vert, *n.*
per·vert′i·ble
per′vi·ous
pes′si·mism
pes′si·mist
pes′si·mis′tic
pes′si·mis′ti·cal·ly
pes′ter
pest′house′
pes·tif′er·ous
pes′ti·lence
pes′ti·len′tial
pes′tle
pet′al
pet′aled
pe·tard′
pet′cock′
pe′tered
pet′i·ole
pe·tite′
pet′it four′
(*plural:* petits fours)

pe·ti′tion
pe·ti′tion·ar·y
pet·rel
pet′ri·fac′tion
pet′ri·fi·ca′tion
pet′ri·fy
pe·trog′ra·phy
pet′rol
pet′ro·la′tum
pe·tro′le·um
pet′ro·log′i·cal
pe·trol′o·gist
pe·trol′o·gy
pet′ti·coat
pet′ti·fog
pet′ti·fog′ger
pet′ti·ly
pet′tish·ness
pet′ty
pet′u·lance
pet′u·lant
pe·tu′ni·a
pe′wee
pe′wit
pew′ter
pha′e·ton
phag′o·cyte
pha·lan′ger
pha′lanx
phal′lic
phal′lus
phan′tasm
phan·tas′mal
phan·tas′ma·go′
ri·a
phan·tas′ma·gor′ic
phan′tom
Phar′aoh
phar′i·sa′ic
Phar′i·see
phar′ma·ceu′ti·cal
phar′ma·ceu′tics
phar′ma·cist
phar′ma·co·log′
i·cal
phar′ma·col′o·gist
phar′ma·col′o·gy
phar′ma·co·poe′ia
phar′ma·cy
pha·ryn′ge·al
phar′yn·gi′tis
phar′ynx
phase
aspect (*see:* faze)

pheas′ant
phe′no·bar′bi·tal
phe′nol
phe·nol′ic
phe·nom′e·nal
phe·nom′e·non
(*plural:* -na; -nons)

phi′al
Phi′ Be′ta Kap′pa
Phil′a·del′phi·a
phi·lan′der
phi·lan′der·er

phil′an·throp′ic
phi·lan′thro·pist
phi·lan′thro·py
phil′a·tel′ic
phi·lat′e·list
phi·lat′e·ly
phil′har·mon′ic
Phil′ip·pines
Phi·lis′tine
phil′o·log′i·cal
phi·lol′o·gist
phi·lol′o·gy
phil′o·mel
phi·los′o·pher
phil′o·soph′i·cal
phi·los′o·phize
phi·los′o·phiz′er
phi·los′o·phy
phil′ter
potion *(see:* filter)
phle·bit′ic
phle·bi′tis
phlegm
phleg·mat′ic
phlox
pho′bi·a
pho′bic
phoe′be
Phoe·ni′cia
phoe′nix
pho′neme
pho·ne′mics
pho·net′i·cal·ly
pho′ne·ti′cian
pho·net′ics
phon′ic
pho′no·gen′ic
pho′no·gram
pho′no·graph
pho′no·log′i·cal
pho·nol′o·gist
pho·nol′o·gy
pho′ny
phos′phate
phos′phide
phos′pho·resce′
phos′pho·res′cence
phos′pho·res′cent
phos·phor′ic
phos′pho·rous, *adj.*
phos′pho·rus, *n.*
pho′to·e·lec′tric
pho′to·en·grav′ing
pho′to·flash′
pho′to·gen′ic
pho′to·graph
pho·tog′ra·pher
pho′to·graph′ic
pho·tog′ra·phy
pho′to·gra·vure′
pho·tom′e·ter
pho·to·met′ric
pho·tom′e·try
pho′ton
pho′to·sen′si·tive
pho′to·stat
pho′to·syn′the·sis
pho′to·tran·sis′tor
phrase
phra′se·ol′o·gy
phras′ing
phre·net′ic
phre·nol′o·gist
phre·nol′o·gy
phthis′ic
phthi′sis
phy·lac′ter·y
phy′lo·ge·net′ic
phy·log′e·ny
phy′lum
phys′ic
phys′i·cal
phy·si′cian
phys′i·cist
phys′ics
phys′icked
phys′ick·ing
phys′i·og′no·my
phys′i·og′ra·pher
phys′i·o·graph′ic
phys′i·og′ra·phy
phys′i·o·log′i·cal
phys′i·ol′o·gist
phys′i·ol′o·gy
phys′i·o·ther′a·py
phy·sique′
pi′a·nis′si·mo
pi·an′ist
pi·an′o
pi·an′o·for′te
pi·as′ter
pi·az′za
pi′ca
pic′a·dor
pic′a·resque′
Pi·cas′so
pic′a·yune′
Pic′ca·dil′ly
pic′ca·lil′li
pic′co·lo

pick′a·back′
pick′a·nin′ny
pick′ax′
pick′er·el
pick′et
pick′et·ing
pick′ings
pick′le
pick′ling
pick′pock′et
pick′up′
pic′nic
pic′nicked
pic′nick·ing
pi′cot
pic′ric
pic′to·graph
pic′to·graph′i·cal
pic·tog′ra·phy
pic·to′ri·al
pic′ture
pic′tur·esque′
pic′tur·ing
pid′dling
pie′bald′
pieced
piece de
re·sis·tance′
piece′meal′
piece′work′
piec′ing
pie′plant′
pierced
pierc′ing
pi′e·tism
pi′e·tis′tic
pi′e·ty
pif′fle
pi′geon
pi′geon·hole′
pi′geon-toed′
pig′ger·y
pig′gish
pig′-head′ed
pig′ment
pig′men·tar′y
pig′men·ta′tion
pig′skin′
pig′sty′
pig′tail′
pik′er
pike′staff′
pi·laf′
pi·las′ter
pil′chard
pil′fer
pil′grim
pil′grim·age
pil′ing
pil′lage
pil′lar
pill′box′
pil′lion
pil′lo·ried
pil′lo·ry
pil′low
pil′low·slip′
pil′low·y
pi′lot
pi·men′to
pim′per·nel
pim′ple
pim′ply
pin′a·fore′
pin′ball′
pince′-nez′
pin′cers
(or: pinchers)
pinch′-hit′
pin′cush′ion
pin′e·al
pine′ap′ple
pine′y
pin′feath′er
Ping′-Pong′
pin′head′
pin′ion
pink′eye′
pink′ish
pin′na
pin′nace
pin′na·cle
pin′nate
pin′ning
pi′noch′le
pin′point′
pin′to
pin′wheel′
pin′worm′
pi′o·neer′
pi′ous
pipe′ful
pipe′-line′
pi·pette′
pip′ing
pip′pin
pi′quan·cy
pi′quant
pique
piqued

pi′quing
pi′ra·cy
pi′rate
pi·rat′i·cal
pir′ou·ette′
pir′ou·et′ted
pir′ou·et′ting
pis′ca·to′ri·al
pis′ca·to′ry
Pis′ces
pis·ta′chi·o
pis′til
flower part
pis′til·late
pis′tol
gun
pis′ton
pitch′blende′
pitch′er
pitch′fork′
pitch′ing
pit′e·ous
pit′fall′
Pith′e·can·thro′pus
pith′y
pit′i·a·ble
pit′i·ful
pit′i·less
pit′tance
pit′ted
pit′ting
Pitts′burgh
pi·tu′i·tar′y
pit′y
piv′ot
piv′ot·al
pix′i·lat′ed
pix′y
piz′zi·ca′to
pla′ca·bil′i·ty
pla′ca·ble
plac′ard
pla′cate
pla′cat·er
pla′cat·ing
pla·ca′tion
pla′ca·tive
pla′ca·to′ry
place′ment
pla·cen′ta
plac′id
pla·cid′i·ty
plac′ing
plack′et
pla′gia·rism
pla′gia·rist
pla′gia·ris′tic
pla′gia·rize
pla′gia·riz·ing
pla′gia·ry
plagued
pla′guing
plains′man
plain′tiff
legal term
plain′tive
mournful
plan′er
plan′et
plan′e·tar′i·um
plan′e·tar′y
plank′ing
plan′ned
plan′ning
Plan·tag′e·net
plan′tain
plan·ta′tion
plant′er
plan′ti·grade
plant′ing
plaque
plas′ma
plas′mic
plas′ter
plas′ter·er
plas′ter·work′
plas′tic
plas·tic′i·ty
pla·teau′
plat′ed
plat′en
plat′form
plat′ing
plat′i·num
plat′i·tude
plat′i·tu′di·nous
Pla′to
pla·ton′ic
pla·toon′
plat′ter
plat′y·pus
plau′dit
plau′si·bil′i·ty
plau′si·ble
play′a·ble
play′bill′
play′boy′
play′er

play′fel′low
play′ful
play′ground′
play′mate′
play′thing′
play′wright′
pla′za
plead′er
plead′ing
pleas′ant
pleas′ant·ry
pleas′ing
pleas′ur·a·ble
pleas′ure
pleat′ed
ple·be′ian
pleb′i·scite
pleb′i·scit′ic
plec′trum
pledg′er
pledg′ing
Ple′ia·des
ple′na·ry
plen′i·po·ten′
  ti·ar′y
plen′i·tude
plen′i·tu′di·nous
plen′te·ous
plen′ti·ful·ly
plen′ty
pleth′o·ra
ple·thor′ic
pleu′ra
pleu′ri·sy
pleu·rit′ic
Plex′i·glas
plex′us

pli′a·bil′i·ty
pli′a·ble
pli′an·cy
pli′ant
plied
pli′ers
plight
plinth
plod′ded
plod′ding
plot′less
plot′ting
plov′er
plow′ing
plow′man
pluck′er
pluck′i·er
pluck′y
plug′ging
plum
  fruit
plum′age
plumb
  weight
plumb′er
plumb′ing
plum′ing
plum′met
plu′mose
plump′ness
plum′y
plun′der
plun′der·er
plun′der·ous
plung′er
plung′ing

plu′per′fect
plu′ral
plu·ral′i·ty
plu′ral·ize
plu′ral·ly
plush′y
Plu′tarch
Plu′to
plu·toc′ra·cy
plu′to·crat
plu′to·crat′ic
Plu·to′ni·an
plu·to′ni·um
plu′vi·al
plu′vi·ous
ply′ing
Plym′outh
ply′wood′
pneu·mat′ic
pneu·mat′i·cal·ly
pneu·mo′nia
pneu·mon′ic
poach′er
Po′ca·hon′tas
pock′et·book′
pock′et·ful
pock′mark′
pod′ding
podg′i·ness
podg′y
po·di′a·trist
po·di′a·try
po′di·um
po′em
po′e·sy
po′et
po′et·as′ter

po′et·ess
po·et′ic
po·et′i·cal·ly
po·et′ics
po′et·ry
po·grom′
poign′an·cy
poign′ant
poin·set′ti·a
point′-blank′
point′ed·ly
point′er
point′less
poised
pois′ing
poi′son
poi′son·ous
pok′er
pok′ing
pok′y
Po′land
po′lar
Po·lar′is
po·lar′i·ty
po′lar·i·za′tion
po′lar·ize
po′lar·iz·ing
pole′cat′
po·lem′ic
po·lem′i·cal·ly
pole′star′
po·lice′
po·lice′man
po·lic′ing
pol′i·cy
(plural: policies)

po′li·o
po′li·o·my′e·li′tis
pol′ish
Po·lit′bu′ro
po·lite′
po·lite′ness
pol′i·tic
po·lit′i·cal·ly
pol′i·ti′cian
pol′i·tic·ly
pol′i·tics
pol′ka
pol′kaed
pol′len
pol′li·nate
pol′li·nat·ing
pol′li·na′tion
pol′li·wog
poll′ster
pol·lute′
pol·lut′ing
pol·lu′tion
pol′o·naise′
po·lo′ni·um
pol·troon′
pol′y·an′drous
pol′y·an′dry
pol′y·eth′yl·ene′
po·lyg′a·mist
po·lyg′a·mous
po·lyg′a·my
pol′y·glot
pol′y·gon
po·lyg′o·nal
pol′y·he′dron
pol′y·mer′ic
pol′y·mor′phism

pol′y·mor′phous
Pol′y·ne′sia
pol′y·no′mi·al
pol′yp
pol′y·phon′ic
po·lyph′o·ny
pol′y·pro′pyl·ene′
pol′y·syl·lab′ic
pol′y·syl′la·ble
pol′y·tech′nic
pol′y·the·ism′
pol′y·the·is′tic
pol′y·u′re·thane′
pol′y·vi′nyl
po·made′
pome′gran′ate
Pom′er·a′ni·an
pom′mel
saddle part *(see:* pummel)

pom′pa·dour
pom′pa·no
pom′pon
pom·pos′i·ty
pom′pous
pon′cho
pon′der
pon′der·a·bil′i·ty
pon′der·a·ble
pon′der·os′i·ty
pon′der·ous
pon·gee′
pon′iard
pon′tiff
pon·tif′i·cal
pon·tif′i·cate

pon·toon′
po′ny
poo′dle
pool′room′
poor′house′
poor′ly
pop′corn′
pop′gun′
pop′in·jay
pop′lar
pop′lin
Po′po·cat′e·pet′l
pop′o·ver
pop′per
pop′ping
pop′py
pop′py·cock′
pop′u·lace
pop′u·lar
pop′u·lar′i·ty
pop′u·lar·i·za′tion
pop′u·lar·ize
pop′u·late
pop′u·la′tion
pop′u·lous
por′ce·lain
por′cine
por′cu·pine
por′gy
pork′er
pork′y
por′no·graph′ic
por·nog′ra·phy
po·ros′i·ty
po′rous
por′phy·rit′ic
por′phy·ry
por′poise
por′ridge
por′rin·ger
port′a·bil′i·ty
port′a·ble
por′tage
por′tal
port·cul′lis
por·tend′
por′tent
por·ten′tous
por′ter
por′ter·house
port·fo′li·o
port′hole′
por′ti·co
por·tiere′
por′tion
port′li·er
port′li·ness
port′ly
port·man′teau
por′trait
por′trai·ture
por·tray′
por·tray′al
Ports′mouth
Por′tu·gal
Por′tu·guese′
posed
pos′ing
po·si′tion
pos′i·tive
pos′i·tive·ly
pos′i·tiv·ism′
pos′i·tiv·is′tic
pos′i·tron
pos′se
pos·sess′
pos·ses′sion
pos·ses′sive·ly
pos·ses′sor
pos′set
pos′si·bil′i·ty
pos′si·ble
pos′sum
post′age
post′al
post′date′
post′er
pos·te′ri·or
pos·ter′i·ty
pos′tern
post·grad′u·ate
post′haste′
post′hu·mous
post′hu·mous·ly
pos·til′ion
post′man
post′mark′
post′mas′ter
post′me·rid′i·an, *adj.*
post me·rid′i·em (*p.m.*)
post′mis′tress
post-mor′tem
post′paid′
post·pone′
post·pone′ment
post′script
pos′tu·late
pos′tu·lat·ing
pos′tu·la′tion

pos′tu·la′tor
pos′tur·al
pos′ture
pos′tur·ing
post′war′
po′sy
po′ta·bil′i·ty
po′ta·ble
pot′ash′
po·tas′si·um
po·ta′tion
po·ta′to
pot′boil′er
po′ten·cy
po′tent
po′ten·tate
po·ten′tial
po·ten′ti·al′i·ty
po′tent·ly
pot′hook
po′tion
pot′luck′
Po·to′mac
pot′pie′
pot′pour·ri′
pot′tage
pot′ted
pot′ter
pot′ter·y
poul′tice
poul′try
pounc′ing
pound′age
pound′-fool′ish
poured
pour′ing
pout′ing·ly

pout′y
pov′er·ty
pow′der
pow′der·y
pow′er
pow′er·ful
pow′er·house′
pow′er·less
pow′wow′
prac′ti·ca·bil′i·ty
prac′ti·ca·ble
prac′ti·cal·ly
prac′ti·cal′i·ty
prac′tice
prac′ticed
prac′tic·ing
prac·ti′tion·er
prag·mat′ic
prag·mat′i·cal·ly
prag′ma·tism
prag′ma·tist
prai′rie
praise′wor′thy
prais′ing
pra′line
pranced
pranc′ing
prank′ish
prank′ster
prat′ing
prat′tle
prayed
prayer
prayer′ful
preached
preach′er
preach′ing

preach′ment
preach′y
pre′am′ble
pre′ar·range′
pre′ar·range′ment
pre·car′i·ous
pre·car′i·ous·ness
pre·cau′tion
pre·cau′tion·ar′y
pre·cede′
go before *(see:* proceed)
prec′e·dence
prec′e·dent
example *(see:* president)
pre·ced′ing
pre′cept
pre·cep′tor
pre′cep·to′ri·al
pre·ces′sion
pre′cinct
pre′ci·os′i·ty
pre′cious
prec′i·pice
pre·cip′i·tance
pre·cip′i·tant
pre·cip′i·tate
pre·cip′i·ta′tion
pre·cip′i·ta′tive
pre·cip′i·tous
pré·cis′
pre·cise′
pre·ci′sion
pre·clude′
pre·clud′ing

pre·clu′sion
pre·clu′sive
pre·co′cious
pre·coc′i·ty
pre′con·ceive′
pre′con·ceiv′ing
pre′con·cep′tion
pre·cur′sor
pre·cur′so·ry
pre·da′cious
pre·dac′i·ty
pred′a·to′ri·ly
pred′a·to′ry
pred′e·ces′sor
pre·des′ti·nate
pre′des·ti·na′tion
pre·des′tine
pre′de·ter′mi·
na·ble
pre′de·ter′mi·na′
tion
pre′de·ter′mine
pre′de·ter′min·ing
pred′i·ca·bil′i·ty
pred′i·ca·ble
pre·dic′a·ment
pred′i·cate
pred′i·cat·ing
pred′i·ca′tion
pred′i·ca′tive
pre·dict′
pre·dict′a·ble
pre·dic′tion
pre·dic′tive
pre·dic′tor
pre′di·lec′tion
pre′dis·pose′
pre′dis·pos′ing
pre′dis·po·si′tion
pre·dom′i·nance
pre·dom′i·nant
pre·dom′i·nate
pre·dom′i·na′tion
pre-em′i·nence
pre-em′i·nent
pre-empt′
pre-emp′tion
pre-emp′tive
pre-emp′tor
preened
pre·fab′ri·cate
pre′fab·ri·ca′tion
pref′ace
pref′ac·ing
pref′a·to′ri·ly
pref′a·to′ry
pre′fect
pre·fec′to·ral
pre·fec′ture
pre·fer′
pref′er·a·bil′i·ty
pref′er·a·bly
pref′er·ence
pref′er·en′tial
pre·fer′ment
pre·fer′ring
pre′fig·u·ra′tion
pre·fig′u·ra·tive
pre·fig′ure
pre′fix
preg′na·bil′i·ty
preg′na·ble
preg′nan·cy
preg′nant
pre·hen′sile
pre′hen·sil′i·ty
pre′his·tor′ic
pre′his·tor′i·cal·ly
pre·judge′
pre·judg′ment
prej′u·dice
prej′u·di′cial
prel′a·cy
prel′ate
pre·lim′i·nar′y
prel′ude
pre′ma·ture′
pre′ma·tu′ri·ty
pre·med′i·cal
pre·med′i·tate
pre′med·i·ta′tion
pre·med′i·ta′tor
pre·mier′
prime minister
pre·miere′
first performance
prem′ise
pre′mi·um
pre′mo·ni′tion
pre·mon′i·to′ry
pre·na′tal
pre·oc′cu·pan·cy
pre·oc′cu·pa′tion
pre·oc′cu·py
pre′or·dain′
pre′or·di·na′tion
pre·paid′
prep′a·ra′tion
pre·par′a·to′ry
pre·pare′

pre·par'ed·ly
pre·par'ed·ness
pre·pay'
pre·pay'ment
pre·pon'der·ance
pre·pon'der·ant
pre·pon'der·ate
prep'o·si'tion
pre'pos·sess'
pre'pos·ses'sing
pre'pos·ses'sion
pre·pos'ter·ous
pre·req'ui·site
pre·rog'a·tive
pres'age, *n.*
pres·age', *v.*
pre·sag'er
pres'by·ter
pres·byt'er·al
Pres'by·te'ri·an
Pres'by·te'
ri·an·ism
pres'by·ter'y
pre'school'
pre'sci·ence
pre'sci·ent
pre·scribe'
pre·scrib'ing
pre'script
pre·scrip'tion
pre·scrip'tive
pres'ence
pres'ent, *n; adj.*
pre·sent', *v.*
pre·sent'a·ble
pres'en·ta'tion
pres'ent-day'
pre·sen'ti·ment
pres'ent·ly
pres'er·va'tion
pre·serv'a·tive
pre·serve'
pre·side'
pres'i·den·cy
pres'i·dent
chief officer *(see: precedent)*

pres'i·den'tial
pres'i·dent-e·lect'
pre·sid'ing
pre·sid'i·um
press'ing
pres'sure
pres'sur·ize
pres'ti·dig'i·ta'tion
pres'ti·dig'i·ta'tor
pres·tige'
pres'to
pre·sum'a·ble
pre·sume'
pre·sum'ed
pre·sump'tion
pre·sump'tive
pre·sump'tu·ous
pre·sup·pose'
pre'sup·po·si'tion
pre·tend'
pre·tend'er
pre·tense'
pre·ten'sion
pre·ten'tious
pre'ter·nat'u·ral
pre'text
pret'ti·fied
pret'ti·fy
pret'ti·ly
pret'ti·ness
pret'ty
pret'zel
pre·vail'
pre·vail'ing
prev'a·lence
prev'a·lent
pre·var'i·cate
pre·var'i·ca'tion
pre·var'i·ca'tor
pre·vent'
pre·vent'a·ble
pre·vent'a·tive
pre·ven'tion
pre·ven'tive
pre'view
pre'vi·ous
pre·vi'sion
price'less
pric'ing
prick'ing
prick'le
prick'ling
prick'ly
pride'ful
prid'ing
priest'ess
priest'hood
priest'ly
prig'gish
pri'ma·cy
pri'ma don'na
pri'ma fa'ci·e
pri'mal

pri'ma'ri·ly
pri'ma·ry
pri'mate
prim'er
pri·me'val
prim'ing
prim'i·tive
prim'i·tiv·ism
prim'ness
pri'mo·gen'i·tal
pri'mo·gen'i·tor
pri'mo·gen'i·ture
pri·mor'di·al
prim'rose'
prince'li·ness
prince'ly
prin'cess
prin'ci·pal
main *(see:* principle)
prin'ci·pal'i·ty
prin'ci·pal·ly
prin'ci·pate
prin'ci·ple
rule *(see:* principal)
print'a·ble
print'er
print'ing
pri'or
pri'or·ess
pri·or'i·ty
pri'o·ry
prism
pris·mat'ic
pris'on
pris'on·er
pris'sy
pris'tine
pri'va·cy
pri'vate
pri'va·teer'
pri·va'tion
priv'a·tive
priv'et
priv'i·lege
priv'i·leged
priv'i·ly
priv'y
priz'ing
prob'a·bil'i·ty
prob'a·ble
pro'bate
pro'bat·ing
pro·ba'tion
pro·ba'tion·a'ry
pro·ba'tion·er
prob'ing
pro'bi·ty
prob'lem
prob'lem·at'ic
pro·bos'cis
pro·ce'dur·al
pro·ce'dure
pro·ceed'
go on *(see:* precede)
pro·ceed'ing
proc'ess
pro·ces'sion
pro·ces'sion·al
pro·claim'
proc'la·ma'tion
pro·clam'a·to'ry
pro·cliv'i·ty
pro·con'sul
pro·con'su·late
pro·cras'ti·nate
pro·cras'ti·na'tion
pro'cre·ate
pro'cre·a'tion
pro'cre·a'tive
pro'cre·a'tor
proc'tor
proc·to'ri·al
pro·cum'bent
pro·cur'a·ble
proc'u·ra'tor
pro·cured'
pro·cure'ment
pro·cur'ing
prod'ding
prod'i·gal
prod'i·gal'i·ty
pro·di'gious
prod'i·gy
pro·duce'
pro·duc'er
pro·duc'i·ble
pro·duc'ing
prod'uct
pro·duc'tion
pro·duc'tive
pro'duc·tiv'i·ty
prof'a·na'tion
pro·fan'a·to'ry
pro·fane'
pro·fan'er
pro·fan'ing
pro·fan'i·ty
pro·fess'
pro·fessed'

pro·fess′ed·ly
pro·fes′sion
pro·fes′sion·al
pro·fes′sor
pro′fes·so′ri·al
prof′fer
pro·fi′cien·cy
pro·fi′cient
pro′file
prof′it
prof′it·a·ble
prof′it·eer′
prof′it·less
prof′li·gate
pro·found′
pro·fun′di·ty
pro·fuse′
pro·fuse′ly
pro·fu′sion
pro·fu′sive
pro·gen′i·tor
pro·gen′i·to′ri·al
pro·gen′i·ture
prog′e·ny
pro·ges′ter·one
prog′na·thous
prog·no′sis
prog·nos′tic
prog·nos′ti·cate
prog·nos′ti·ca′tion
pro′gram
pro′gram·ming
prog′ress
pro·gres′sion
pro·gres′sive
pro·gres′sive·ly
pro·hib′it
pro′hi·bi′tion
pro′hi·bi′tion·ist
pro·hib′i·tive
pro·hib′i·to′ry
proj′ect, *n.*
pro·ject′, *v.*
pro·ject′ed
pro·jec′tile
pro·jec′tion
pro·jec′tor
pro′late
pro′le·tar′i·an
pro′le·tar′i·an·ism
pro′le·tar′i·at
pro·lif′ic
pro·lif′i·ca·cy
pro·lif′i·cal·ly
pro·lix′
pro·lix′i·ty
pro′logue
pro·long′
pro′long·a′tion
pro·longed′
prom′e·nade′
Pro·me′the·an
Pro·me′the·us
prom′i·nence
prom′i·nent
prom′is·cu′i·ty
pro·mis′cu·ous
prom′ise
prom′is·ing
prom′is·so′ry
prom′on·to′ri·al
prom′on·to′ry
pro·mote′
pro·mot′ing
pro·mo′tion
pro·mo′tive
prompt′er
prompt′ness
pro·mul′gate
pro′mul·ga′tion
pro·mul′ga·tor
prone′ness
pro′noun
pro·nounce′
pro·nounce′a·ble
pro·nounce′ment
pro·nun′ci·a′tion
pro·nounc′ing
proof′read′er
prop′a·gan′da
prop′a·gan′dist
prop′a·gan′dize
prop′a·gate
prop′a·ga·bil′i·ty
prop′a·ga′tion
prop′a·ga′tive
prop′a·ga′tor
pro·pel′
pro·pel′lent
pro·pel′ler
pro·pen′si·ty
prop′er
prop′er·ly
prop′er·tied
prop′er·ty
proph′e·cy, *n.*
proph′e·sied
proph′e·sy, *v.*
proph′et
proph′et·ess
pro·phet′ic

pro′phy·lac′tic
pro′phy·lax′is
pro·pin′qui·ty
pro·pi′ti·ate
pro·pi′ti·a′tion
pro·pi′ti·a·to′ry
pro·pi′tious
pro·po′nent
pro·por′tion
pro·por′tion·ate
pro·por′tioned
pro·pos′al
pro·pose′
pro·pos′ing
prop′o·si′tion
prop′o·si′tion·al
pro·pound′
pro·pound′er
pro·pri′e·tar′y
pro·pri′e·tor
pro·pri′e·tor·ship
pro·pri′e·to′ry
pro·pri′e·tress
pro·pri′e·ty
pro·pul′sion
pro·pul′sive
pro·pul′so·ry
pro·rat′a·ble
pro·rate′
pro′ro·ga′tion
pro·rogue′
pro·sa′ic
pro·sa′i·cal·ly
pro·sce′ni·um
pro·scribe′
pro·scrip′tion
pro·scrip′tive·ly
pros′er
pros′e·cute
pros′e·cu′tion
pros′e·cu′tor
pros′e·lyte
pros′e·lyt′ism
pros′e·lyt·ize′
pros′e·lyt·iz′er
pro·sod′ic
pros′o·dist
pros′o·dy
pros′pect
pro·spec′tive
pros′pec·tor
pro·spec′tus
pros′per
pros·per′i·ty
pros′per·ous
pros′tate
pro·stat′ic
pros′ti·tute
pros′ti·tu′tion
pros′trate
pros′strat·ing
pros·tra′tion
pros′i·er
pros′y
pro·tag′o·nist
pro′te·an
pro·tect′
pro·tect′ing·ly
pro·tec′tion
pro·tec′tive·ly
pro·tec′tor
pro·tec′tor·ate
pro′té·gé, *masc.*
pro′té·gée, *fem.*
pro′tein
pro tem′po·re
pro′test, *n.*
pro·test′, *v.*
Prot′es·tant
Prot′es·tant·ism′
prot′es·ta′tion
pro·test′ing
pro′to·col
pro′ton
pro′to·plasm
pro′to·plas′mic
pro′to·type
pro′to·typ′i·cal
pro′to·zo′al
pro′to·zo′an
pro·tract′
pro·tract′ed
pro·trac′tile
pro·trac′tion
pro·trac′tive
pro·trac′tor
pro·trude′
pro·tru′sion
pro·tru′sive
pro·tu′ber·ance
pro·tu′ber·ant
pro·tu′ber·an′tial
proud′ly
prov′a·ble
proved
prov′en·der
prov′erb
pro·ver′bi·al
pro·vide′
pro·vid′ed
prov′i·dence

prov'i·dent
prov'i·den'tial
pro·vid'er
pro·vid'ing
prov'ince
pro·vin'cial
pro·vin'cial·ism
prov'ing
pro·vi'sion
pro·vi'sion·al·ly
pro·vi'sion·er
pro·vi'so
pro·vi'so·ri·ly
pro·vi'so·ry
prov'o·ca'tion
pro·voc'a·tive
pro·voke'
pro·vok'ing·ly
prov'ost
prow'ess
prowl'er
prox'i·mal
prox'i·mate
prox·im'i·ty
prox'y
prude
pru'dence
pru'dent
pru·den'tial
prud'er·y
prud'ish
prun'er
prun'ing
pru'ri·ence
pru'ri·ent
Prus'sia
prus'sic

pry'ing
psalm
psal'mo·dy
psal'ter·y
pseu'do
pseu'do·nym
psit'ta·co'sis
pso·ri'a·sis
psy'che
psych'e·del'ic
psy'chi·at'ric
psy·chi'a·trist
psy·chi'a·try
psy'chic
psy'chi·cal·ly
psy'cho·a·nal'y·sis
psy'cho·an'a·lyst
psy'cho·an'a·lyt'ic
psy'cho·an'a·lyt'i·cal
psy'cho·an'a·lyze
psy'cho·log'i·cal
psy·chol'o·gist
psy·chol'o·gy
psy'cho·neu·ro'sis
psy'cho·neu·rot'ic
psy'cho·path'ic
psy·chop'a·thy
psy·cho'sis (*plural:* -ses)
psy'cho·so·mat'ic
psy'cho·ther'a·py
psy'chot'ic
ptar'mi·gan
pter'o·dac'tyl
Ptol'e·ma'ic

Ptol'e·my
pto'maine
pu'ber·ty
pu·bes'cence
pu'bic
pu'bis
pub'lic
pub'li·can
pub'li·ca'tion
pub'li·cist
pub·lic'i·ty
pub'li·cize
pub'lish
pub'lish·er
puck'er
puck'ish
pud'ding
pud'dle
pud'dler
pud'dling
pudg'i·ness
pudg'y
pueb'lo
pu'er·ile
pu'er·il'i·ty
pu·er'per·al
Puer'to Ri'co
puff'er
puf'fin
puff'i·ness
puff'y
pu'gi·lism
pu'gi·list
pu'gi·lis'tic
pug·na'cious
pug·nac'i·ty
pul'chri·tude

pul'chri·tu'di·nous
Pu'litz·er
pul'let
pul'ley
pull'ing
pull'-o'ver
pul'mo·nar'y
Pul'mo'tor
pulp'i·ness
pul'pit
pulp'wood'
pulp'y
pul'sate
pul·sa'tion
pul'sa·tive
pulsed
puls'ing
pul'ver·i·za'tion
pul'ver·ize
pul'ver·iz'er
pu'ma
pum'ice
pum'mel
beat *(see:* pommel)

pump'er
pum'per·nick'el
pump'kin
punch'er
pun'chi·nel'lo
punc·til'i·o
punc·til'i·ous
punc'tu·al
punc'tu·al'i·ty
punc'tu·ate
punc'tu·a'tion
punc'ture
punc'tur·ing
pun'dit
pun'gen·cy
pun'gent
pun'ish
pun'ish·ment
pu'ni·tive
pu'ni·to'ry
punned
pun'ning
pun'ster
punt'er
pu'ni·ness
pu'ny
pu'pa
pu'pil
pup'pet
pup'py
pur'blind
pur'chas·a·ble
pur'chased
pur'chas·er
pur'chas·ing
pu·rée'
pure'ly
pur'ga·tive
pur'ga·to'ri·al
pur'ga·to'ry
purg'ing
pu'ri·fi·ca'tion
pu'ri·fy
pur'ist
pu·ris'tic
Pu'ri·tan
pu·ri·tan'i·cal
pu'ri·tan·ism
pu'ri·ty
pur'lieu
pur·loin'
pur'ple
pur'pling
pur'plish
pur·port'
pur'pose
pur'pose·ful·ly
pur'pose·ly
purs'er
purs'ing
pur·su'ance
pur·su'ant
pur·sued'
pur·su'er
pur·su'ing
pur·suit'
pur'sy
pu'ru·lence
pu'ru·lent
pur·vey'
pur·vey'ance
pur·vey'or
push'cart'
push'ing
push'-o'ver
pu'sil·la·nim'i·ty
pu'sil·lan'i·mous
pus'sy
containing pus

puss'y
cat

puss'y·foot'
pus'tu·lar
pus'tule
pu'tre·fac'tion

pu′tre·fied
pu′tre·fy·ing
pu·tres′cence
pu·tres′cent
pu′trid
put′ter, *v.*
putt′er, *n.*
put′ting
(to put)
putt′ing
(to putt)
puz′zle
puz′zling
py·e′mi·a
Pyg·ma′li·on
pyg′my
py·lo′rus
py′or·rhe′a
pyr′a·mid
Pyr′e·nees
py·ret′ic
py·ri′tes
py′ro·graph′ic
py·rog′ra·phy
py′ro·ma′ni·a
py′ro·tech′ni·cal
py′ro·tech′nics
Py·thag′o·ras
py′thon

Q

quack′er·y
quad′ran·gle
quad·ran′gu·lar
quad′rant
quad′rate
quad·rat′ic
quad·ren′ni·al
quad′ri·lat′er·al
qua·drille′
quad·ril′lion
quad·roon′
quad′ru·ped
quad′ru·ple
quad′ru·plet
quad·ru′pli·cate
quad′ru·pling
quaff
quag′mire′
quaint′ly
quaked
Quak′er
quak′ing
qual′i·fi·ca′tion
qual′i·fied
qual′i·fy
qual′i·fy′ing
qual′i·ta′tive
qual′i·ty
quan′da·ry
quan′ti·ta′tive
quan′ti·ty
quan·ti·za′tion
quan·tize′
quan′tum
quar′an·tine
quar′reled
quar′rel·ing
quar′rel·some
quar′ry
quar′ter·back′
quar′ter·deck′
quar′tered
quar′ter·ly
quar′ter·mas′ter
quar·tet′
quar′to
quartz
qua′si
quat′rain
qua′ver·ing
qua′ver·y
quea′si·ly
quea′si·ness
quea′sy
Que·bec′
queen′li·ness
queer′ly
quelled
Que·moy′
quenched
que′ried
quer′u·lous
que′ry

que′ry·ing
ques′tion·a·ble
ques′tion·er
ques′tion·ing
ques′tion·naire′
queue
quib′ble
quib′bling
quick′en
quick′lime′
quick′ly
quick′sand′
quick′sil′ver
quick′-tem′pered
quick′-wit′ted
quid′di·ty
qui·es′cence
qui·es′cent
qui′et·ly
qui′e·tude
qui·e′tus
quilt′ed
qui′na·ry
qui′nine
quin′tal
quin·tes′sence
quin·tet′
quin·til′lion
quin′tu·ple
quin′tu·plet
quin′tu·pling
quipped
quip′ping
quis′ling
quit′claim
quit′tance
quit′ted
quit′ting
quiv′er·ing
qui vive′
quix·ot′ic
quix·ot′i·cal·ly
quizzed
quiz′zi·cal
quiz′zing
quoit
quon′dam
Quon′set
quo′rum
quo′ta
quot′a·bil′i·ty
quot′a·ble
quo·ta′tion
quot′ed
quo·tid′i·an
quo′tient
quot′ing

R

rab′bet
slot; groove (*see:* rabbit)
rab′bi
rab·bin′i·cal
rab′bit
rodent (*see:* rabbet)
rab′ble
Rab′e·lais
rab′id
ra·bid′i·ty
ra′bies
rac·coon′
Rach·ma′ni·noff
ra′cial
ra′cial·ly
rac′ing
rac′ism
rack′et
rack′et·eer′
rac′on·teur′
ra′dar
ra′di·al
ra′di·an
ra′di·ance
ra′di·ant·ly
ra′di·ate
ra′di·a′tion
ra′di·a′tor
rad′i·cal
rad′i·cal·ism
ra′di·o·ac′tive
ra′di·o·gram′
ra′di·o·graph′
ra′di·o·i′so·tope
ra′di·o·tel′e·graph
ra′di·o·tel′e·phone
ra′di·o·te·leph′o·ny
ra′di·o·ther′a·py
rad′ish

ra'di•um
ra'di•us
raf'fi•a
raf'fle
raf'fling
raft'er
rag'a•muf'fin
rag'ged
rag'ing
ra•gout'
rag'time'
rag'weed'
raid'er
rail'er
rail'ing
rail'ler•y
rail'road'
rai'ment
rain'bow'
rain'coat'
rain'drop'
rain'fall'
Rai•nier', Mt.
rain'mak'er
rain'storm'
rain'y
rai'sin
rais'ing
ra'jah
raked
rak'ing
rak'ish
ral'lied
ral'ly
ram'ble
ram'bler
ram'bling
ram•bunc'tious
ram'e•kin
ram'i•fi•ca'tion
ram'i•fy
ram'i•fy•ing
ram'jet'
rammed
ram'ming
ram'page
ram'pag•ing
ramp'ant
ram'part
ram'rod'
ram'shack'le
ranch'er
ran'cid
ran•cid'i•ty
ran'cor
ran'cor•ous
ran'dom
ranged
rang'er
rang'ing
Ran•goon'
rang'y
ran'kle
rank'ness
ran'sack
ran'som
rant'ing
ra•pa'cious
ra•pac'i•ty
ra•pid'i•ty
rap'i•dly
ra'pi•er
rap'ine
rapped
rap'ping
rap•port'
rap•proche•ment'
rap•scal'lion
rapt'ly
rap'ture
rap'tur•ous
rare'bit
rar'e•fac'tion
rar'e•fied
rar'e•fy
rare'ly
rar'i•ty
ras'cal
ras•cal'i•ty
rash'ness
rasp'ber'ry
rasp'ing
rat'a•bil'i•ty
rat'a•ble
ratch'et
rat'ed
rath'er
raths'kel'ler
rat'i•fi•ca'tion
rat'i•fied
rat'i•fy•ing
rat'ing
ra'ti•o
ra'ti•oc'i•nate
ra'ti•oc'i•na'tion
ra'tion
ra'tion•al
ra'tion•al•ly
ra'tion•al•ism'
ra'tion•al'i•ty
ra'tion•ali•za'tion

ra′tion • al • ize
rat′tan
rat′tle
rat′tler
rat′tle • snake′
rau′cous
rav′age
rav′ag • ing
rav′eled
rav′el • ing
rav′en • ing
rav′en • ous
ra • vine′
rav′ing
rav′i • o′li
rav′ish • ing
rav′ish • ment
raw′hide′
ray′on
ra′zor • back′
raz′zle-daz′zle
re • act′ance
re • ac′tion
re • ac′tion • ar′y
re • ac′tor
read′a • bil′i • ty
read′a • ble
read′i • ly
read′i • ness
re • a′gent
re′al • ist
re′al • is′tic
re′al • is′ti • cal • ly
re • al′i • ty
re′al • i • za′tion
re′al • ize
re′al • ly
realm
re′al • tor
re′al • ty
reap′er
re • arm′
re • ar′ma • ment
re′ar • range′
re′ar • range′ment
re′ar • rang′ing
rear′ward
rea′son
rea′son • a • ble
rea′son • a • bly
rea′son • ing
re′as • sur′ance
re′as • sure′
re′as • sur′ing
re′bate
reb′el, *n. and adj.*
re • bel′, *v.*
re • belled′
re • bel′ling
re • bel′lion
re • bel′lious
re′bound, *n.*
re • bound′, *v.*
re • buff′
re • buke′
re • buk′ing
re′bus
re • but′
re • but′tal
re • but′ted
re • but′ting
re • cal′ci • trance
re • cal′ci • trant
re • call′
re • call′ment
re • cant′
re′can • ta′tion
re′ca • pit′u • late
re′ca • pit′u • la′tion
re′capped′
re′cap′ping
re • cap′ture
re • cede′
re • ced′ed
re • ced′ing
re • ceipt′
re • ceiv′a • ble
re • ceive′
re • ceiv′er
re • ceiv′er • ship
re • ceiv′ing
re′cent • ly
re • cep′ta • cle
re • cep′tion
re • cep′tion • ist
re • cep′tive
re′cep • tiv′i • ty
re • cep′tor
re • cess′
re • ces′sion
re • ces′sion • al
re • ces′sive
rec′i • pe
re • cip′i • ent
re • cip′ro • cal
re • cip′ro • cate
re • cip′ro • ca′tion
rec′i • proc′i • ty
re • cit′al
rec′i • ta′tion
rec′i • ta • tive′

re·cite′
re·cit′ing
reck′less·ly
reck′on·ing
re·claim′
re·claim′a·ble
rec′la·ma′tion
re·cline′
re·clin′ing
rec′luse
rec′og·ni′tion
rec′og·niz′a·ble
re·cog′ni·zance
rec′og·nize
re·coil′
rec′ol·lect′
rec′ol·lec′tion
rec′om·mend′
rec′om·men·da′tion
re′com·mit′
re′com·mit′ment
rec′om·pense
rec′om·pens·ing
rec′on·cil′a·ble
rec′on·cile′ment
rec′on·cil·ing
rec′on·cil′i·a′tion
rec′on·dite
re′con·di′tion
re·con′nais·sance
rec′on·noi′ter
re′con·sid′er
re′con·sid′er·a′tion
re′con·struct′
re′con·struc′tion
rec′ord, *n., adj.*
re·cord′, *v.*
re·cord′able
re·count′
re·coup′
re′course
re·cov′er
re·cov′er·a·ble
re·cov′er·y
rec′re·ant
rec′re·ate
refresh
re′-cre·ate′
create anew
rec′re·a′tion
rec′re·a′tive
re·crim′i·nate
re·crim′i·nat·ing
re·crim′i·na′tion
re·crim′i·na·to′ry
re′cru·des′cence
re′cru·des′cent
re·cruit′
re·cruit′ment
rec′tal
rec′tan·gle
rec·tan′gu·lar
rec′ti·fi′a·ble
rec′ti·fi·ca′tion
rec′ti·fied
rec′ti·fy
rec′ti·lin′e·ar
rec′ti·tude
rec′tor
rec′to·ry
rec′tum
re·cum′ben·cy
re·cum′bent
re·cu′per·ate
re·cu′per·a′tion
re·cu′per·a′tive
re·cur′
re·curred′
re·cur′rence
re·cur′rent
re·cur′ring
re·dact′
re·dac′tion
red′den
re·deem′
re·deem′a·ble
re·deem′er
re·demp′tion
re·demp′tive
re·demp′to·ry
re′de·ploy′
re′de·ploy′ment
red′-hand′ed
red′head′
red′-hot′
red′in·gote
red·in′te·grate
re′di·rect′
re·dis′trict
red′-let′ter
red′ness
red′o·lence
red′o·lent
re·dou′ble
re·dou′bling
re·doubt′
re·doubt′a·ble
re·dound′
re·dress′

red′skin'
re·duce′
re·duc′i·ble
re·duc′ing
re·duc′tion
re·duc′tive
re·dun′dan·cy
re·dun′dant
red′wood'
re'e·lect′
re'en·force′
re'en·force′ment
re'en·list′
re'en′ter
re'es·tab′lish
re'ex·am′ine
re·fer′
ref′er·a·ble
ref′er·ee
ref′er·ence
ref'er·en′dum
ref′er·ent
ref'er·en′tial
re·ferred′
re·fer′ring
re·fine′ment
re·fin′er
re·fin′er·y
re·fin′ing
re·flect′
re·flec′tion
re·flec′tive
re·flec′tor
re′flex
re·flex′ive
ref′lu·ent
re′flux
re'for·est·a′tion
re·form′
ref'or·ma′tion
re·form′a·tive
re·form′a·to'ry
re·form′er
re·fract′
re·frac′tion
re·frac′to·ry
re·frain′
re·fran′gi·ble
re·fresh′
re·fresh′ing
re·fresh′ment
re·frig′er·ant
re·frig′er·ate
re·frig'er·a′tion
re·frig′er·a'tor
ref′uge
ref'u·gee′
re·ful′gence
re·ful′gent
re·fur′bish
re·fus′al
re·fuse′, *v.*
ref′use, *n.*
re·fus′ing
ref′u·ta·ble
ref'u·ta′tion
re·fute′
re·fut′ing
re·gain′
re′gal
re·gale′
re·ga′li·a
re·gal′ing
re′gal·ly
re·gard′
re·gard′ing
re·gard′less
re·gat′ta
re′gen·cy
re·gen′er·a·cy
re·gen′er·ate
re·gen'er·a′tion
re′gent
reg′i·cide
re·gime′
reg′i·men
reg′i·ment
reg'i·men′tal
reg'i·men·ta′tion
re′gion
re′gion·al
reg′is·ter
reg′is·tered
reg′is·tra·ble
reg′is·trar
reg'is·tra′tion
reg′is·try
reg′nant
re·gress′
re·gres′sion
re·gret′ful
re·gret′ta·ble
re·gret′ting
reg′u·lar·ly
reg'u·lar′i·ty
reg′u·lat'a·ble
reg′u·late
reg'u·la′tion
reg′u·la'tive
reg′u·la'tor
reg′u·la·to'ry

re·gur′gi·tate
re·gur′gi·ta′tion
re′ha·bil′i·tate
re′ha·bil′i·ta′tion
re·hears′al
re·hearse′
re·hears′ing
reign
re′im·burse′
re′im·burse′ment
re′im·port′
re′im·por·ta′tion
re′in·car′nate
re′in·car·na′tion
rein′deer′
re′in·force′ment
re′in·state′ment
re·it′er·ate
re·it′er·a′tion
re·it′er·a′tive
re·ject′
re·jec′tion
re·joice′
re·joic′ing
re·join′
re·join′der
re·ju′ve·nate
re·ju′ve·na′tion
re·ju′ve·na′tor
re·lapse′
re·lapsed′
re·laps′ing
re·late′
re·lat′ed
re·lat′ing
re·la′tion
re·la′tion·ship
rel′a·tive
rel′a·tive·ly
rel′a·tiv′i·ty
re′lax·a′tion
re·lax′ed·ly
re·lay′
re·lease′
re·leased′
re·leas′ing
rel′e·gate
rel′e·gat·ed
rel′e·ga′tion
re·lent′
re·lent′ing·ly
re·lent′less
rel′e·van·cy
rel′e·vant
re·li′a·bil′i·ty
re·li′a·ble
re·li′a·bly
re·li′ance
re·li′ant
rel′ic
rel′ict
re·lied′
re·lief′
re·liev′a·ble
re·lieve′
re·lieved′
re·liev′ing
re·li′gion
re·li′gi·os′i·ty
re·li′gious
re·li′gious·ly
re·lin′quish
rel′i·quar′y
rel′ish
rel′ish·a·ble
rel′ish·ing·ly
re·luc′tance
re·luc′tant
re·ly′
re·ly′ing
re·main′
re·main′der
re·main′ing
re·mand′
re·mand′ment
re·mark′
re·mark′a·ble
Rem′brandt
re·me′di·a·ble
re·me′di·al
rem′e·died
rem′e·dy
re·mem′ber
re·mem′brance
re·mind′er
rem′i·nisce′
rem′i·nis′cence
rem′i·nis′cent
rem′i·nisc′ing
re·miss′
re·mis′si·bil′i·ty
re·mis′si·ble
re·mis′sion
re·mit′
re·mit′tance
re·mit′ted
re·mit′ting
rem′nant
re·mod′el·ing
re·mon′strance
re·mon′strant

re•mon′strate
re′mon•stra′tion
re•morse′ful•ly
re•mote′ly
re•mot′est
re•mov′a•bil′i•ty
re•mov′a•ble
re•mov′al
re•move′
re•mov′ing
re•mu′ner•ate
re•mu′ner•a′tion
re•mu′ner•a′tive
ren′ais•sance′
re′nal
re•nas′cence
re•nas′cent
ren′der
ren′dez•vous
rend′ing
ren•di′tion
ren′e•gade
re•nege′
re•neg′ing
re•new′
re•new′a•ble
re•new′al
re•new′ed•ly
ren′net
ren′nin
Re•noir′
re•nounce′
re•nounce′ment
re•nounc′ing
ren′o•vate
ren′o•vat•ing
ren′o•va′tion
ren′o•va′tor
re•nown′
re•nowned′
rent′a•ble
rent′al
rent′ing
re•nun′ci•a′tion
re′or•gan•i•za′tion
re•or′gan•ize
re•paid′
re•pair′
re•pair′a•ble
re•pair′man
rep′a•ra•ble
rep′a•ra′tion
re•par′a•to′ry
rep′ar•tee′
re•past′
re•pa′tri•ate
re•pa′tri•a′tion
re•pay′
re•pay′ing
re•peal′
re•peal′a•ble
re•peat′a•ble
re•peat′ed•ly
re•peat′er
re•pel′
re•pelled′
re•pel′lent
re•pel′ling
re•pent′
re•pent′ance
re•pent′ant
re′per•cus′sion
re′per•cus′sive
rep′er•toire
rep′er•to′ry
rep′e•ti′tion
rep′e•ti′tious
re•pet′i•tive
re•pine′
re•place′
re•place′a•ble
re•plac′ing
re•plen′ish
re•plen′ish•ment
re•plete′
re•ple′tion
rep′li•ca
re•plied′
re•ply′ing
re•port′
re•port′er
rep′or•to′ri•al
re•pose′
re•pose′ful
re•pos′ing
re•pos′i•to′ry
re′pos•sess′
re′pos•ses′sion
rep′re•hend′
rep′re•hen′si•bil′i•ty
rep′re•hen′si•ble
rep′re•hen′sion
rep′re•sent′
rep′re•sent′a•ble
rep′re•sen•ta′tion
rep′re•sent′a•tive
re•press′
re•press′i•ble
re•pres′sion
re•pres′sive

re·prieve′
rep′ri·mand
re·print′
re·pris′al
re·proach′
re·proach′ful
re·proach′ing
rep′ro·bate
rep′ro·ba′tion
re′pro·duce′
re′pro·duc′i·ble
re′pro·duc′ing
re′pro·duc′tion
re′pro·duc′tive
re·proof′
re·prov′al
re·prove′
re·prov′ing·ly
rep′tile
rep·til′i·an
re·pub′lic
re·pub′li·can
re·pub′li·can·ism′
re·pu′di·ate
re·pu′di·a′tion
re·pu′di·a′tor
re·pug′nance
re·pug′nant
re·pulse′
re·puls′ing
re·pul′sion
re·pul′sive
rep′u·ta·ble
rep′u·ta·bly
rep′u·ta′tion
re·pute′
re·put′ed
re·put′ing
re·quest′
req′ui·em
re·quire′
re·quire′ment
re·quir′ing
req′ui·site
req′ui·si′tion
re·quit′al
re·quite′
re·quit′ed
re·quit′ing
re·scind′
re·scind′a·ble
re·scind′ment
res′cue
res′cued
res′cu·er
res′cu·ing
re·search′
re·search′er
re·sem′blance
re·sem′ble
re·sem′bling
re·sent′
re·sent′ful
re·sent′ment
res′er·va′tion
re·serve′
re·served′
re·serv′ed·ly
re·serv′ist
res′er·voir
re·set′
re·set′ting
re·side′
res′i·dence
res′i·den·cy
res′i·dent
res′i·den′tial
re·sid′ing
re·sid′u·al
re·sid′u·ar′y
res′i·due
re·sid′u·um
re·sign′
res′ig·na′tion
re·signed′
re·sign′ed·ly
re·sil′i·en·cy
re·sil′i·ent
res′in
res′in·ous
re·sist′ance
re·sist′er
one who resists
re·sist′i·bil′i·ty
re·sist′i·ble
re·sist′less
re·sis′tor
elect. conductor
res′o·lute
res′o·lu′tion
re·solve′
re·solved′
re·solv′ed·ly
re·solv′ing
res′o·nance
res′o·nant
res′o·na′tor
re·sort′
re·sound′
re·sound′ed

re•sound′ing•ly
re•source′
re•source′ful•ly
re•spect′
re•spect′a•bil′i•ty
re•spect′a•ble
re•spect′a•bly
re•spect′ful
re•spect′ing
re•spec′tive•ly
res′pi•ra′tion
res′pi•ra′tor
res′pi•ra•to′ry
re•spite′
re•spir′ing
res′pite
re•splend′ence
re•splend′ent
re•spond′
re•spond′ent
re•sponse′
re•spon′si•bil′i•ty
re•spon′si•ble
re•spon′si•bly
re•spon′sive
re•spon′sive•ly
res′tau•rant
res′tau•ra•teur′
rest′ful
res′ti•tu′tion
res′tive
rest′less
res′to•ra′tion
re•stor′a•tive
re•store′
re•stor′ing
re•strain′
re•strain′ed
re•straint′
re•strict′ed
re•stric′tion
re•stric′tive
re•sult′
re•sult′ant
re•sume′, *v.*
begin again

rés′u•mé′, *n.*
summary

re•sum′ing
re•sump′tion
re•sur′gence
re•sur′gent
res′ur•rect′
res′ur•rec′tion
re•sus′ci•tate
re•sus′ci•ta′tion
re•sus′ci•ta′tor
re′tail
re•tain′er
re•tain′ment
re•tal′i•ate
re•tal′i•a′tion
re•tal′i•a′tive
re•tal′i•a•to′ry
re•tard′
re′tar•da′tion
retch
vomit (*see:* wretch)

re•ten′tion
re•ten′tive
ret′i•cence
ret′i•cent
re•tic′u•la′tion
ret′i•na
ret′i•nal
ret′i•nue
re•tired′
re•tire′ment
re•tir′ing
re•tort′
re•touch′
re•trace′
re•trace′a•ble
re•trac′ing
re•tract′
re•tract′a•bil′i•ty
re•tract′a•ble
re•trac′tive
re•trac′tor
re•trac′tile
re′trac•til′i•ty
re•trac′tion
re•tread′
re•treat′
re•trench′
re•trench′ment
ret′ri•bu′tion
re•trib′u•tive
re•trib′u•to•ry
re•triev′a•ble
re•trieve′
re•triev′er
re•triev′ing
ret′ro•ac′tive
ret′ro•cede′
ret′ro•grade
ret′ro•gress
ret′ro•gres′sion
ret′ro•gres′sive

ret′ro•spect
ret′ro•spec′tion
ret′ro•spec′tive
re•turn′a•ble
re•turn•ee′
re•un′ion
re′u•nite′
re′u•nit′ing
re•vamp′
re•veal′
re•veal′a•ble
rev′eil•le
rev′el
rev′e•la′tion
rev′eled
rev′el•ing
rev′el•ry
re•venge′
re•venge′ful
re•venge′ful•ness
re•veng′ing
rev′e•nue
re•ver′ber•ant
re•ver′ber•ate
re•ver′ber•a′tion
re•vere′
rev′er•ence
rev′er•end
rev′er•ent
rev′er•en′tial
rev′er•ie
re•ver′ing
re•ver′sal
re•verse′
re•vers′i•bil′i•ty
re•vers′i•ble
re•vers′ing
re•ver′sion
re•vert′
re•vert′i•ble
re•view′
survey *(see:* revue)

re•view′er
re•vile′
re•vile′ment
re•vil′ing
re•vise′
re•vi′sion
re•vi′so•ry
re•viv′al
re•viv′al•ist
re•vive′
re•viv′i•fy
re•viv′ing
rev′o•ca•bil′i•ty
rev′o•ca•ble
rev′o•ca′tion
rev′o•ca•to′ry
re•voke′
re•vok′ing
re•volt′
re•volt′ing•ly
rev′o•lu′tion
rev′o•lu′tion•ar′y
rev′o•lu′tion•ist
rev′o•lu′tion•ize
re•volv′a•ble
re•volve′
re•volv′er
re•volv′ing
re•vue′
entertainment *(see:* review)
re•vul′sion
re•ward′
re•ward′a•ble
rhap•sod′ic
rhap′so•dist
rhap′so•dize
rhap′so•diz•ing
rhap′so•dy
rhe′ni•um
rhe′o•stat
rhe′o•stat′ic
rhe′sus
rhet′o•ric
rhe•tor′i•cal
rhet′o•ri′cian
rheum
rheu•mat′ic
rheu′ma•tism
rhi′nal
rhine′stone′
rhi•ni′tis
rhi•noc′er•os
Rho•de′sia
rho′di•um
rho′do•den′dron
rhom′boid
rhom′bus
rhu′barb
rhum′ba
rhyme
sound alike *(see:* rime)

rhyme′ster
rhym′ing
rhythm′
rhyth′mi•cal

Ri·al′to
rib′ald
rib′ald·ry
ribbed
rib′bing
rib′bon
ri′bo·fla′vin
Rich′e·lieu
rich′es
rich′ness
rick′ets
rick′et·y
rick′shaw
ric′o·chet′
ric′o·cheted′
rid′dance
rid′ding
rid′dle
ride′a·ble
rid′er
ridge
ridg′ing
rid′i·cule
ri·dic′u·lous
rid′ing
rife′ness
rif′fle
rif′fling
riff′raff′
ri′fle·man
ri′fling
rig′ging
right′-an′gled
right′eous
right′eous·ness
right′ful
right′ist
right′ly
rig′id
ri·gid′i·ty
rig′id·ly
rig′ma·role
rig′or
rig′or mor′tis
rig′or·ous
rime
frost (*see:* rhyme)
rim′less
rimmed
rim′ming
ring′er
ring′ing
ring′lead′er
ring′let
ring′mas′ter
ring′side′
ring′worm′
rinsed
rins′ing
Ri′o de Ja·nei′ro
Ri′o Grande′
ri′ot·ous
ri′ot·ous·ly
ri·par′i·an
rip′en
ripe′ness
rip′ping
rip′ple
rip′pling
ris′en
ris′i·ble
ris′ing
risk′i·ness
risk′y
ris·que′
rit′u·al
rit′u·al·is′tic
ri′val
ri′valed
ri′val·ing
ri′val·ry
riv′er·side
riv′et·er
Riv′i·er′a
riv′u·let
road′bed′
road′side′
road′way′
Ro′a·noke
roast′ed
roast′er
robbed
rob′ber
rob′ber·y
rob′bing
rob′in
rob′ing
ro′bot
ro·bust′
Roch′es·ter
rock′-bound′
rock′er
rock′et
rock′et·ry
rock′ing
rock′y
ro·co′co
ro′dent
ro′de·o
roe′buck′

roent′gen
rogue
ro′guer·y
ro′guish·ness
rois′ter
rois′ter·ous
roll′er
rol′lick·ing
roll′ing
ro′ly-po′ly
ro·maine′
ro·mance′
ro·manc′ing
Ro′man·esque′
Ro·ma′ni·a
ro·man′tic
ro·man′ti·cal·ly
ro·man′ti·cism
Rom′a·ny
Ro′me·o
romp′ers
romp′ish
ron′deau *(poet.)*
ron′del
ron′do *(mus.)*
roof′ing
roof′less
rook′er·y
rook′ie
room′er
room·ette′
room′ful
room′mate′
room′y
roost′er
root′ed
root′er
root′less
root′let
root′stock′
roped
rop′ing
Roque′fort
Ror′schach
ro′sa·ry
ro′se·ate
rose′bud′
rose′bush′
rose′mar′y
ro·sette′
rose′wood′
Rosh′ Ha·sha′na
ros′i·er
ros′ter
ros′trum
ros′y
ro′ta·ry
ro′tate
ro·ta′tion
ro′ta·tor
rote
ro′to·gra·vure′
ro′tor
rot′ten·ness
Rot′ter·dam′
rot′ting
ro·tund′
ro·tun′da
ro·tun′di·ty
rou·é′
rouged
roug′ing
rough′age
rough′-dry′
rough′en
rough′neck′
rough′shod′
rou·lette′
round′a·bout′
roun′de·lay
round′house′
round′ness
round′up′
roused
rous′ing·ly
Rous·seau′
roust′a·bout′
route
rout′ed
rou·tine′
rout′ing
rov′ing
row′boat′
row′di·ness
row′dy
row′el
roy′al·ist
roy′al·ly
roy′al·ty
rubbed
rub′ber
rub′ber·ize
rub′bing
rub′bish
rub′ble
rub′down′
Ru′bi·con
ru′bi·cund
ru′bi·cun′di·ty
ru′ble
ru′bric

ruche
ruch′ing
ruck′us
rud′der
rud′di·ness
rud′dy
rude′ness
rud′est
ru′di·ment
ru′di·men′ta·ry
rue′ful
ruf′fi·an
ruf′fle
ruf′fled
ruf′fling
rug′ged
ru′in·a′tion
ru′in·ous
ruled
rul′er
rul′ing
rum′ble
rum′bling
ru′mi·nant
ru′mi·nate
ru′mi·na′tion
rum′mage
rum′mag·ing
ru′mor
rum′ple
rum′pling
rum′pus
run′a·round′
run′a·way′
run′-down′
run′ner
run′ning
runt′y
run′way′
ru·pee′
rup′ture
rup′tur·ing
ru′ral
rush′ing
rus′set
Rus′sia
Rus′sian
rust′a·ble
rus′tic
rus′ti·cate
rus′ti·ca′tion
rus·tic′i·ty
rust′i·ly
rus′tle
rus′tler
rus′tling
rust′proof′
rust′y
ru′ta·ba′ga
ru·the′ni·um
ruth′less
ruth′less·ly
rut′ted
rut′ty

S

Sab′bath
sab·bat′i·cal
sa′ber (·bre)
sab′o·tage
sab′o·teur′
sac′cha·rin, *n.*
sac′cha·rine, *adj.*, *n.*
sac′er·do′tal
sa·chet′
sack′cloth′
sack′ful
sack′ing
sac′ra·ment
sac′ra·men′tal
Sac′ra·men′to
sa′cred
sac′ri·fice
sac′ri·fi′cial
sac′ri·fic·ing
sac′ri·lege
sac′ri·le′gious
sac′ris·tan
sac′ris·ty
sa′cro·il′i·ac
sac′ro·sanct
sac′ro·sanc′ti·ty
sa′crum
sad′den
sad′der
sad′dle
sad′dler·y
Sad′du·cee

sa′dism
sa′dist
sa·dis′ti·cal·ly
sa·fa′ri
safe′guard′
safe′keep′ing
safe′ly
saf′est
safe′ty
saf′fron
sa′ga
sa·ga′cious
sa·gac′i·ty
sag′a·more
sage′brush′
sagged
sag′ging
Sag′it·tar′i·us
sa′go
Sa·har′a
sa′hib
Sai·gon′
sailed
sail′cloth′
sail′fish′
sail′or
saint′ed
saint′hood
saint′ly
Sai·pan′
sake
cause
sa′ke
rice wine
sa·laam′
sal′a·bil′i·ty
sal′a·ble
sa·la′cious
sa·lac′i·ty
sal′ad
sal′a·man′der
sa·la′mi
sal′a·ried
sal′a·ry
Sa′lem
sal′e·ra′tus
sales′man·ship
sales′wom′an
sal′i·cyl′ic
sa′li·ence
sa′li·ent
sa′line
sa·lin′i·ty
sa·li′va
sal′i·var′y
sal′i·vate
sal′i·va′tion
sal′lied
sal′low
sal′ly·ing
sal′ma·gun′di
salm′on
Sa·lo′me
sa·lon′
sa·loon′
sal′si·fy
salt′cel′lar
salt′i·er
salt′pe′ter
salt′y
sa·lu′bri·ous
sa·lu′bri·ty
sal′u·tar′i·ly
sal′u·tar′y
sal′u·ta′tion
sa·lu′ta·to′ri·an
sa·lu′ta·to′ry
sa·lute′
sa·lut′ing
Sal′va·dor
sal′vage
sal·va′tion
salved
sal′ver
salv′ing
sal′vo
Sa·mar′i·a
Sa·mar′i·tan
sam′ba
Sa·mo′a
sam′o·var
sam′pan
sam′ple
sam′pler
sam′pling
sam′u·rai
san′a·tive
san′a·to′ri·um
san′a·to′ry
sanc′ti·fi·ca′tion
sanc′ti·fied
sanc′ti·fy
sanc′ti·fy·ing
sanc′ti·mo′ni·ous
sanc′ti·mo′ny
sanc′tion
sanc′ti·ty
sanc′tu·ar·y
sanc′tum
san′dal

san′daled
san′dal·wood′
sand′bag′
San Di·e′go
sand′i·er
sand′pa′per
sand′stone′
sand′wich
sand′y
san′er
sane′ly
San Fran·cis′co
sang-froid′
san′gui·nar′i·ly
san′gui·nar′y
san′guine
san′i·tar′i·an
san′i·tar′i·um
san′i·tar′i·ly
san′i·tar′y
san′i·ta′tion
san′i·ty
San′skrit
San′ta Claus′
San′ta Fe′
San′ti·a′go
sa′pi·ence
sa′pi·ent
sap′ling
sa·pon′i·fi·ca′tion
sa·pon′i·fy
sap′per
sap′ping
sap′phire
sap′py
sap′suck′er
sap′wood′
Sar′a·cen
Sar′a·to′ga
sar′casm
sar·cas′tic
sar·cas′ti·cal·ly
sar·co′ma
sar·co′ma·toid
sar·coph′a·gus
sar·dine′
Sar·din′i·a
sar·don′ic
sar·don′i·cal·ly
sa′ri
sa·rong′
sar′sa·pa·ril′la
sar·to′ri·al
sa·shay′
Sas·katch′e·wan
sas′sa·fras
Sa′tan
sa·tan′ic
sa·tan′i·cal·ly
satch′el
sat′ed
sa·teen′
sat′el·lite
sa′ti·a·bil′i·ty
sa′ti·a·ble
sa′ti·ate
sa′ti·a′tion
sa·ti′e·ty
sat′in
sat′in·wood′
sat′in·y
sat′ire
sa·tir′i·cal
sat′i·rist
sat′i·rize
sat′i·riz·ing
sat′is·fac′tion
sat′is·fac′to·ri·ly
sat′is·fac′to·ry
sat′is·fy
sat′is·fy′ing·ly
sa′trap
sat′u·ra·bil′i·ty
sat′u·ra·ble
sat′u·rate
sat′u·rat·ing
sat′u·ra′tion
Sat′ur·day
Sat′urn
Sat′ur·na′li·an
sat′ur·nine
sat′ur·nin′i·ty
sat′yr
sauce′pan′
sau′cer
sau′ci·ly
sau′cy
sauer′kraut′
saun′ter
saun′ter·ing
sau′ri·an
sau′sage
sau′té′
sau·téed′
sau·té′ing
sau·terne′
sav′age
sav′age·ly
sav′age·ry
Sa·van′nah
sa′vant

saved
sav'ing
sav'ior
sa'voir-faire'
sa'vor
sa'vor·ous
sa'vor·y
Sa·voy'
sav'vy
saw'dust'
saw'horse'
saw'yer
sax'i·frage
Sax'on·y
sax'o·phone
sax'o·phon'ist
say'ing
scab
scab'bard
scabbed
scab'bing
scab'by
sca'bies
sca'brous
scaf'fold
scaf'fold·ing
scal'a·wag
scald'ed
scaled
sca·lene'
scal'ing
scal'lion
scal'lop
scal'pel
scalp'er
scal'y
scam'per
scamp'ish
scan'dal
scan'dal·i·za'tion
scan'dal·ize
scan'dal·mon'ger
scan'dal·ous
Scan'di·na'vi·a
scanned
scan'ner
scan'ning
scan'sion
scant'ling
scant'i·ly
scant'ly
scant'y
scape'goat'
scape'grace'
scap'u·la
scap'u·lar
scar'ab
scarce'ly
scar'ci·ty
scare'crow'
scared
afraid

scar'i·fi·ca'tion
scar'i·fied
scar'i·fy
scar'ing
scar'la·ti'na
scar'let
scarred
marked

scar'ring
scar'y
scathe
scathed
scath'ing
scat'ter
scav'en·ger
scav'eng·ing
sce·nar'i·o
sce·nar'ist
scen'er·y
sce'nic
sce'ni·cal·ly
scent'ed
scep'ter
scep'tic
scep'ti·cal
scep'ti·cism
sched'ule
sched'uled
sched'ul·ing
sche·mat'ic
scheme
schem'er
schem'ing
Sche·nec'ta·dy
scher'zo
schism
schis·mat'ic
schiz'oid
schiz'o·phre'ni·a
schiz'o·phren'ic
schnau'zer
schol'ar
schol'ar·ly
schol'ar·ship
scho·las'tic
scho·las'ti·cal·ly
scho·las'ti·cism
school'boy'

school′ing
school′mas′ter
school′mate′
school′teach′er
schoon′er
schot′tische
sci·at′ic
sci·at′i·ca
sci′ence
sci′en·tif′ic
sci′en·tif′i·cal·ly
sci′en·tist
scim′i·tar
scin·til′la
scin′til·late
scin′til·lat′ing
scin′til·la′tion
sci′on
scis′sors
scle·ro′sal
scle·ro′sis
scle·rot′ic
scoff′er
scold′ing
sconce
scone
scoop′ful
scoot′er
scope
sco·pol′a·mine
scor·bu′tic
scorch′ing
scored
scor′ing
scorn′ful
Scor′pi·o
scor′pi·on
Scotch′man
scot′-free′
Scot′land
Scots′man
Scot′tish
scoun′drel
scourge
scourg′ing
scout′ing
scout′mas′ter
scowl′ing·ly
scrab′ble
scrab′bling
scrag′gly
scrag′gy
scram′ble
scram′bling
Scran′ton
scrap′book′
scraped
  rubbed
scrap′ing
scrapped
  threw away
scrap′ping
scrap′ple
scrap′py
scratch′i·ness
scratch′y
scrawl′y
scraw′ni·ness
scraw′ny
scream′ing
screech′y
screen
screw′dri′ver
scrib′ble
scrib′bler
scrib′bling
scribe
scrim′mage
scrimp′i·ly
scrimp′y
scrip
  certificate
script
  writing
scrip′tur·al
scrip′ture
scrive′ner
scrof′u·la
scrof′u·lous
scroll
scro′tum
scrounge
scroung′ing
scrubbed
scrub′bing
scrump′tious
scru′ple
scru′pu·los′i·ty
scru′pu·lous
scru′ti·nize
scru′ti·niz′ing
scru′ti·ny
scud′ded
scuf′fle
scuf′fling
scull
  oar *(see:* skull)
scul′ler·y

scul′lion
sculp′tor
sculp′tur·al
sculp′ture
scum′my
scurf′y
scur·ril′i·ty
scur′ri·lous
scur′ried
scur′ry·ing
scur′vi·ly
scur′vy
scut′tle
scut′tle·butt′
scut′tling
scythe
scyth′ing
sea′board′
sea′coast′
sea′far′er
sea′far′ing
sea′food′
seal′a·ble
seal′er
seal′skin
Sea′ly·ham
sea′man
sea′man·ship
seam′i·ness
seam′stress
seam′y
se′ance
search′ing
search′light′
sea′shore′
sea′sick′ness
sea′son
sea′son·a·ble
sea′son·al
sea′son·ing
seat′ed
Se·at′tle
sea′ward
sea′way′
sea′weed′
sea′wor′thy
se·ba′ceous
se′cant
se·cede′
se·ced′ed
se·ced′ing
se·ces′sion
se·ces′sion·ist
se·clude′
se·clud′ed
se·clud′ing
se·clu′sion
se·clu′sive
sec′ond
sec′ond·ar′i·ly
sec′ond·ar′y
sec′ond-hand′
not new

second hand
clock hand

se′cre·cy
se′cret
sec′re·tar′i·al
sec′re·tar′i·at
sec′re·tar′y
se·crete′
se·cret′ed
se·cre′tion
se·cre′tive
se′cret·ly
se·cre′to·ry
sect
sec·tar′i·an
sec·tar′i·an·ism
sec′tion
sec′tion·al
sec′tor
sec·to′ri·al
sec′u·lar
sec′u·lar·ism
sec′u·lar·i·za′tion
sec′u·lar·ize
se·cure′
se·cure′ly
se·cu′ri·ty
se·dan′
se·date′
se·date′ness
sed′a·tive
sed′en·tar′i·ly
sed′en·tar′y
sed′i·ment
sed′i·men′ta·ry
sed′i·men·ta′tion
se·di′tion
se·di′tion·ar′y
se·di′tious
se·duce′
se·duc′i·ble
se·duc′ing
se·duc′tion
se·duc′tive
se·du′li·ty
sed′u·lous
seed′ing

seed′ling
seed′y
see′ing
seem′ing
seem′ly
seep′age
seer′suck′er
see′saw′
seethe
seethed
seeth′ing
seg′ment
seg·men′tal·ly
seg′men·tar′y
seg′men·ta′tion
seg′re·gate
seg′re·ga′tion
seg′re·ga′tion·ist
seg′re·ga′tive
seign′ior
lord *(see:* senior)

seis′mic
seis′mo·graph
seis·mog′ra·pher
seis′mo·graph′ic
seis′mo·log′i·cal
seis·mol′o·gist
seis·mol′o·gy
seize
seiz′ing
sei′zure
sel′dom
se·lect′
se·lect′ee′
se·lec′tion
se·lec′tive
se·lec′tiv′i·ty
se·lec′tor
sel′e·nite
se·le′ni·um
self′-cen′tered
self′-con′fi·dence
self′-con′scious
self′-con·trol′
self′-de·fense′
self′-es·teem′
self′im·por′tant
self′ish
self′ish·ness
self′less
self′-pres′er·va′tion
self′-re·spect′
self′same′
self′-suf·fi′cient
sell′er
sell′ing
Selt′zer
sel′vage
se·man′tic
se·man′tics
sem′a·phore
sem′a·phor′ic
sem′blance
se′men
se·mes′ter
se·mes′tral
sem′i·an′nu·al
sem′i·cir′cle
sem′i·cir′cu·lar
sem′i·co′lon
sem′i·fi′nal
sem′i·nal
sem′i·nar
sem′i·nar′y
sem′i·na′tion
Sem′i·nole
sem′i·pre′cious
Sem′ite
Se·mit′ic
sem′o·li′na
sem′pi·ter′nal
sem′pi·ter′ni·ty
sen′ate
sen′a·tor
sen′a·to′ri·al
send′ing
Sen′e·ca
se·nes′cence
se·nes′cent
sen′es·chal
se′nile
se·nil′i·ty
sen′ior
older *(see:* seignior)

sen·ior′i·ty
sen′na
se·nor′
se·no′ra
se′no·ri′ta
sen·sa′tion
sen·sa′tion·al
sensed
sense′less
sen′si·bil′i·ty
sen′si·ble
sens′ing
sen′si·tive
sen′si·tiv′i·ty
sen′si·ti·za′tion

sen′si·tize
sen·so′ri·al
sen′so·ry
sen′su·al
sen′su·al·is′tic
sen′su·al′i·ty
sen′su·ous·ly
sen′tence
sen·ten′tial
sen·ten′tious
sen′tience
sen′tient
sen′ti·ment
sen′ti·men′tal
sen′ti·men·tal′i·ty
sen′ti·men′tal·ize
sen′ti·nel
sen′try
se′pal
sep′a·ra·bil′i·ty
sep′a·ra·ble
sep′a·rate
sep′a·rate·ly
sep′a·ra′tion
se′pi·a
sep′sis
Sep·tem′ber
sep·ten′ni·al
sep·tet′
sep′tic
sep′ti·ce′mi·a
sep·tic′i·ty
sep·til′lion
sep′tu·a·ge·nar′
i·an
sep′tum
sep·tu′ple
sep′ul·cher
se·pul′chral
se′quel
se′quence
se′quent
se·quen′tial
se·ques′ter
se·ques′trate
se′ques·tra′tion
se′quin
se′quined
se·quoi′a
se·ragl′i·o
se·ra′pe
ser′aph
(plural: -aphs;
-aphim)
ser′e·nade′
ser′e·nad′ing
se·rene′
se·rene′ly
se·ren′i·ty
serf′dom
serge
cloth *(see:* surge)
ser′geant
se′ri·al
se′ri·al′ly
se′ries
se′ri·o·com′ic
se′ri·ous
se′ri·ous·ness
ser′mon
ser·mon′ic
ser′mon·ize
se′ro·log′i·cal
se·rol′o·gist
se·rol′o·gy
se′rous
ser′pent
ser′pen·tine
ser′rate
ser′rat·ed
ser·ra′tion
ser′ried
se′rum
serv′ant
served
serv′er
serv′ice
serv′ice·a·ble
ser′vi·ette′
ser′vile
ser·vil′i·ty
serv′ing
ser′vi·tor
ser′vi·tude
ses′a·me
ses′qui·cen·ten′
ni·al
ses′sion
set′back′
set·tee′
set′ter
set′ting
set′tle
set′tle·ment
set′tler
set′tling
set′-to′
sev′en
sev′en·fold′
sev′en·teen′

sev′enth
sev′en·ti·eth
sev′en·ty
sev′er·a·ble
sev′er·al
sev′er·al·ly
sev′er·ance
se·vere′
sev′ered
se·vere′ly
se·ver′i·ty
Se·ville′
sew′age
sew′er
sew′er·age
sew′ing
sex′a·ge·nar′i·an
sex′tant
sex·tet′
sex·til′lion
sex′ton
sex′tu·ple
sex′tu·plet
sex′u·al
sex′u·al′i·ty
shab′bi·ness
shab′by
shack′le
shack′ling
shade
shad′ed
shad′i·er
shad′ing
shad′ow
shad′ow·i·ness
shad′ow·y
shad′y
shagged
shag′ging
shag′gy
shah
shake
shak′en
Shake·spear′e·an
Shake′speare
shak′i·ly
shak′ing
shak′o
shak′y
shal′lop
shal′lot
shal′low
sham′ble
shamed
shame′ful
shame′less
shammed
sham′ming
sham·poo′
sham·pooed′
sham′rock
Shang′hai′
Shan′gri-La′
Shan′non
shan′tung
shan′ty
shaped
shap′ing
shape′less
shape′li·ness
shape′ly
share′crop′per
share′hold′er
shar′ing
shark′skin′
sharp′en
sharp′ly
sharp′shoot′er
shat′ter
shaved
shav′en
shav′er
shav′ing
Shaw·nee′
sheaf
(*plural:* sheaves)

shear
clip off (*see:* sheer)

shear′ing
sheath, *n.*
sheathe, *v.*
sheathed
sheath′ing
She′ba
shed′ding
sheep′herd′er
sheep′ish
sheep′skin′
sheer
swerve (*see:* shear)

sheer′ness
sheet′ing
sheik
shek′el
shelf
(*plural:* shelves)

shel·lac′
shel·lacked′
shel·lack′ing

Shel′ley
shell′fish′
shel′ter
shel′ter•ing
shelve, *v.*
shelv′ing
she•nan′i•gans
shep′herd
shep′herd•ess
sher′bet
sher′iff
sher′ry
shib′bo•leth
shield′er
shift′i•er
shift′y
shil•le′lagh
shil′ling
shim′mer
shim′mer•y
shim′my
shine
shin′gle
shin′i•er
shin′ing
Shin′to
shin′y
ship′board′
ship′ment
shipped
ship′per
ship′ping
ship′shape′
ship′wreck′
shirk′er
shirred
shirt′ing
shirt′waist′
shiv′er
shiv′er•y
shoal
shoat
shock′er
shock′ing
shod′di•ness
shod′dy
shoe′horn′
shoe′ing
shoe′lace′
shoe′mak′er
shoe′string′
shoot′ing
shopped
shop′ping
shop′talk′
shop′worn′
shore′line′
shor′ing
short′age
short′cake′
short′com′ing
short′en•ing
short′hand′
short′ly
short′-sight′ed
short′stop′
short′-wave′
shot′gun′
should
shoul′der
shout′ed
shoved
shov′el
shov′eled
shov′el•ful
shov′el•ing
shov′ing
show′down′
showed
show′er
show′ing
show′man
show′man•ship
show′y
shrap′nel
shred′ded
shred′ding
shrewd′ly
shrew′ish
shrieked
shriek′ing
shrill′ness
shril′ly
shrimp
shrined
shrink′a•ble
shrink′age
shriv′el
shriv′eled
shriv′el•ing
shroud′ed
Shrove′tide′
shrub′ber•y
shrub′bi•ness
shrub′by
shrugged
shrug′ging
shrunk′en
shuck′ing
shud′der
shuf′fle•board′

shuf′fling
shunned
shun′ning
shut′out′
shut′ter
shut′ting
shut′tle
shy′ness
Shy′lock
shy′ster
Si′a•mese′
Si•be′li•us
Si•be′ri•a
sib′i•lance
sib′i•lant
sib′ling
sib′yl
si•byl′ic
Si•cil′ian
Sic′i•ly
sick′en•ing•ly
sick′le
sick′li•er
sick′ly
sick′ness
side′board′
side′burns′
sid′ed
si•de′re•al
side′swiped
side′swip•ing
side′walk′
side′ways′
sid′ing
si′dle
si′dling
siege
sieg′ing
si•en′na
si•er′ra
si•es′ta
sieve
sift′er
sigh′ing
sight′less
sight′ly
sight′see′ing
sig′nal
sig′naled
sig′nal•ing
sig′nal•ize
sig′nal•ly
sig′na•to′ry
sig′na•ture
sig′net
sign (*see:* cygnet)

sig•nif′i•cance
sig•nif′i•cant
sig′ni•fi•ca′tion
sig′ni•fied
sig′ni•fy
sig′ni•fy•ing
sign′post′
si′lage
si′lence
si′lenc•er
si′lenc•ing
si′lent•ly
si′lex
sil′hou•ette′
sil′hou•et′ted
sil′i•ca
sil′i•cate
sil′i•con
sil′i•co′sis
silk′en
silk′i•er
silk′worm′
silk′y
sil′li•ness
sil′ly
si′lo
sil′ver-plat′ed
sil′ver•smith′
sil′ver•ware′
sil′ver•y
sim′i•an
sim′i•lar
sim′i•lar′i•ty
sim′i•le
si•mil′i•tude
sim′mer
si•mo′le•on
si′mon-pure′
si′mo•ny
si•moom′
sim′pered
sim′per•ing
sim′ple
sim′plest
sim′ple•ton
sim•plic′i•ty
sim′pli•fi•ca′tion
sim′pli•fied
sim′pli•fy
sim′pli•fy•ing
sim′ply
sim′u•la′crum
sim′u•late
sim′u•lat•ing

sim′u·la′tion
sim′u·la′tive
sim′u·la′tor
si′mul·cast′
si′mul·ta′ne·ous
Si′nai
sin·cere′
sin·cer′est
sin·cere′ly
sin·cer′i·ty
si′ne·cure
si′ne di′e
sin′ew
sin′ew·y
sin′ful
Sin′ga·pore
singed
singe′ing
sing′er
sing′ing
sin′gle
sin′gle·ton
sin′gling
sin′gly
sing′song′
sin′gu·lar
sin′gu·lar′i·ty
sin′is·ter
sink′er
sink′ing
sin′less
sinned
sin′ner
sin′ning
sin′u·os′i·ty
sin′u·ous
si′nus

si′nus·i′tis
Sioux
si′phon
sipped
sip′ping
sired
si′ren
sir′ing
sir′loin
si·roc′co
sis′al
sis′sy
sis′ter·ly
sit′ter
sit′ting
sit′u·ate
sit′u·at′ed
sit′u·a′tion
six′pence
six′teen′
sixth
six′ti·eth
six′ty
siz′a·ble
sized
siz′ing
siz′zle
siz′zling
skat′ed
skat′er
skat′ing
skein
skel′e·tal
skel′e·ton
skep′tic
(also: sceptic)

sketch′book′
sketched
sketch′i·ly
sketch′y
skew′er
skid′ded
skid′ding
skied
ski′ing
skilled
skil′let
skill′ful·ly
skimmed
skim′mer
skim′ming
skimp′i·ly
skimp′ing
skimp′y
skinned
skin′ni·ness
skin′ning
skin′ny
skip′per
skip′ping
skir′mish
skit′tish
skit′tles
skul·dug′ger·y
skulk′er
skulk′ing·ly
skull
bones of head *(see:* scull)
skull′cap′
skunk
sky′lark′

sky′line′
sky′rock′et
sky′scrap′er
slack′en
slag′gy
slake
slaked
slak′ing
slam′-bang′
slammed
slam′ming
slan′der
slan′der•ous
slang′y
slant′ing
slant′wise′
slapped
slap′ping
slap′stick′
slash′ing
slate
slat′ed
nominated
slat′ing
slat′ted
slat covered
slat′tern
slat′ting
slaugh′ter
slav′er•y
Slav′ic
slav′ish
slay′ing
slea′zy
sled′ding
sledge
sleek′ly
sleep′i•ly
sleep′ing
sleep′walk′ing
sleep′y
sleet′i•ness
sleet′y
sleeve′less
sleigh
sleight
skill (*see:* slight)
slen′der•ize
slen′der•ness
slept
sleuth
sliced
slic′ing
slick′er
slick′ness
slide
slid′ing
slight
small (*see:* sleight)
slight′ing
slight′ly
slim′i•ness
slim′ness
slim′y
sling′shot′
slink′ing
slipped
slip′per
slip′per•i•ness
slip′per•y
slip′ping
slip′shod′
slith′er
slit′ting
sliv′er
slob′ber
slob′ber•ing
slo′gan
slog′ging
sloped
at an angle
slop′ing
slopped
spilled
slop′pi•ly
slop′ping
slop′py
slosh′y
sloth′ful
slot′ted
slouch′ing
slouch′y
Slo′vak
Slo•va′ki•a
slov′en•li•ness
slov′en•ly
slow′ly
slug′gard
slug′gish
sluice
sluic′ing
slum′ber
slum′ming
slurred
slur′ring
slush′i•ness
slush′y
slut′tish

sly′ly
sly′ness
smack′ing
small′ness
small′pox′
smart′en
smart′ly
smashed
smat′ter
smat′ter·ing
smeared
smell′ing
smell′y
smelt
smelt′er
smi′lax
smiled
smil′ing
smirch
smirk′ing
smite
smith′er·eens′
smith′y
smit′ten
smoke′house′
smok′er
smok′i·er
smok′ing
smok′y
smol′der·ing
smooth′ly
smor′gas·bord
smoth′er
smudge
smudg′ing
smudg′y
smug′gle
smug′gler
smug′ly
smut′ti·ness
smut′ty
snaf′fle
sna·fu′
snagged
snag′ging
snak′i·ly
snak′y
snap′drag′on
snap′per
snap′pi·ly
snap′py
snap′shot′
snared
snar′ing
snarled
snarl′ing
snatch′y
sneaked
sneak′i·ly
sneak′ing
sneak′y
sneer′ing
sneezed
sneez′ing
snick′ered
snick′er·ing
sniff′er
sniff′ing
snif′fle
snip′ing
snipped
snip′pet
snip′pi·er
snip′ping
snip′py
sniv′el
sniv′el·ing
snob′ber·y
snob′bish
snoop′er
snored
snor′ing
snor′kel
snort′ing
snout
snow′ball′
snow′bank′
snow′flake′
snow′i·er
snow′shoe′
snow′y
snubbed
snub′bing
snuff′er
snuf′fle
snug′gle
snug′gling
snug′ly
soak′ing
soap′box′
soap′i·er
soap′suds′
soap′y
soar′ing
sob′bing
so′ber
so·bri′e·ty
so′bri·quet
soc′cer
so′cia·bil′i·ty
so′cia·ble

so′cial·ism
so′cial·ist
so′cial·ite
so′cial·i·za′tion
so′cial·ize
so′cial·ly
so·ci′e·ty
so′ci·o·log′i·cal
so′ci·ol′o·gist
so′ci·ol′o·gy
sock′et
Soc′ra·tes
So·crat′ic
so′da
so·dal′i·ty
sod′den
sod′ding
so′di·um
sod′om·y
so′fa
soft′en
soft′ly
sog′gi·ness
sog′gy
soiled
soi·ree′
so·journ′, *v.*
so′journ, *n.*
sol′aced
sol′ac·ing
so′lar
so·lar′i·um
sol′der
sol′dier
sol′e·cism
sol′e·cist
sole′ly
sol′emn
so·lem′ni·ty
sol′em·ni·za′tion
sol′em·nize
so·lic′it
so·lic′i·ta′tion
so·lic′i·tor
so·lic′it·ous
so·lic′i·tude
so·lic′i·tu′di·nous
sol′id
sol′i·dar′i·ty
so·lid′i·fi·ca′tion
so·lid′i·fied
so·lid′ify
so·lid′i·ty
so·lil′o·quist
so·lil′o·quize
so·lil′o·quy
sol′ing
sol′i·taire
sol′i·tar′i·ly
sol′i·tar′y
sol′i·tude
so′lo·ist
Sol′o·mon
So′lon
sol′stice
sol′u·bil′i·ty
sol′u·ble
so·lu′tion
solv′a·ble
solved
sol′ven·cy
sol′vent
solv′ing
so·mat′ic
so·mat′i·cal·ly
som′ber·ness
som·brer′o
some′bod′y
some′how
some′one
som′er·sault
some′thing
some′times
some′what
som·nam′bu·late
som·nam′bu·lism
som·nam′bu·list
som·nam′bu·lis′tic
som·nif′er·ous
som′no·lence
som′no·lent
so′nance
so′nant
so·nan′tal
so·na′ta
song′ster
son′ic
son′net
son′net·eer′
so·nor′i·ty
so·no′rous·ly
soon′er
soothe
soothed
sooth′er
sooth′ing·ly
sooth′say′er
soot′i·ness
soot′y
soph′ism
soph′ist

so·phis′tic
so·phis′ti·cate
so·phis′ti·cat·ed
so·phis′ti·ca′tion
soph′ist·ry
Soph′o·cles
soph′o·more
so′po·rif′ic
sop′ping
sop′py
so·pran′o
Sor·bonne′
sor′cer·er
sor′cer·ess
sor′cer·y
sor′did
sore′ness
sor′ghum
so·ror′i·ty
sor′rel
sor′row·ful·ly
sor′ry
sort′er
sor′tie
sot′tish
sot′to vo′ce
sou·brette′
souf·fle′
soul′ful·ly
soul′less
sound′ing
sound′less
sound′ly
soup·con′
soup′i·er
soup′y
source
sour′ness
South Da·ko′ta
south′east′
south′east′er·ly
south′er·ly
south′ern
south′ern·er
south′land
south′west′
south′west′er·ly
sou′ve·nir
sov′er·eign
sov′er·eign·ty
so′vi·et
so′vi·et·ism′
soy′a
soy′bean′
spaced
spac′ing
spa′cious
spad′ed
spad′ing
spa·ghet′ti
span′gle
span′gly
Span′iard
span′iel
Span′ish
spank′ing
spanned
span′ner
span′ning
spared
spare′ness
spare′rib′
spar′ing
spar′kle
spar′kler
spar′kling
sparred
spar′ring
spar′row
sparse′ly
spar′si·ty
Spar′ta
Spar′tan
spasm
spas·mod′ic
spas·mod′i·cal·ly
spas′tic
spate
spa′tial
spa′ti·al′i·ty
spa′tial·ly
spat′ter
spat′ting
spat′u·la
spav′ined
spawned
speak′a·ble
speak′er
speak′ing
spear′head′
spear′man
spear′mint′
spe′cial
spe′cial·ist
spe′ci·al′i·ty
spe′cial·i·za′tion
spe′cial·ize
spe′cial·ly
spe′cial·ty
spe′cie (*coin*)
spe′cies (*kind*)

spe·cif′ic
spe·cif′i·cal·ly
spec′i·fi·ca′tion
spec′i·fied
spec′i·fy
spec′i·fy·ing
spec′i·men
spe′cious
speck′le
speck′ling
spec′ta·cle
spec·tac′u·lar
spec·tac′u·lar′i·ty
spec′ta·tor
spec′ta·to′ri·al
spec′ter
spec′tral
spec′tro·scope
spec′tro·scop′i·cal
spec·tros′co·pist
spec·tros′co·py
spec′trum
spec′u·late
spec′u·lat′ing
spec′u·la′tion
spec′u·la′tive
spec′u·la′tor
spec′u·lum
sped
speech′less
speed′er
speed′i·ly
speed′ing
speed·om′e·ter
speed′way′
speed′y
spe′le·ol′o·gist
spe′le·ol′o·gy
spell′bound′
spell′ing
spend′ing
spend′thrift′
spent
sper′me·cet′i
sper·mat′ic
sper′ma·to·phyte′
sper′ma·to·phyt′ic
sper′ma·to·zo′ic
sper′ma·to·zo′on
sphere
spher′i·cal
spher′i·cal′i·ty
sphe′roid
sphe·roi′dal
sphinc′ter
sphinx
spiced
spic′i·ness
spic′ing
spic′y
spi·der
spig′ot
spiked
spike′let
spike′nard
spik′ing
spilled (or: spilt)
spill′ing
spill′way
spin′ach
spi′nal
spin′dle
spin′dling
spin′dly
spin′drift′
spine′less
spin′et
spin′na·ker
spin′ner
spin′ner·et
spin′ning
Spi·no′za
spin′ster
spin′y
spi′ra·cle
spi·rac′u·lar
spi·rae′a
spi′ral
spi′raled
spi′ral·ing
spi′ral·ly
spi′rant
spir′it
spir′it·ed
spir′it·less
spir′it·u·al
spir′it·u·al·ism′
spir′it·u·al·is′tic
spir′it·u·al′i·ty
spir′it·u·al·ly
spir′i·tu·os′i·ty
spir′it·u·ous
spi′ro·chete
spite
spit′ed
spite′ful
spit′fire′
spit′ing
spit′ting
spit′tle
spit·toon′

splash'ing
splash'y
splat'ter
spleen'ish
splen'did
splen'did·ly
splen·dif'er·ous
splen'dor
splen'dor·ous
sple·net'ic
spliced
splic'ing
splin'ter
split'-lev'el
split'ting
splotch'y
splurge
splut'ter
spoil'age
spoiled (or: spoilt)
spoil'er
spoil'ing
Spo·kane'
spo'ken
spokes'man
spo'li·a'tion
spo'li·a'tive
spon·da'ic
spon'dee
sponged
spon'gi·ness
spong'ing
spon'gy
spon'sor
spon·so'ri·al
spon'ta·ne'i·ty
spon·ta'ne·ous

spook'y
spoon'ful
spoor
animal track
spo·rad'ic
spore
seed
spo'ro·phyte
spor'ran
sport'ing
spor'tive
sports'cas·ter
sports'man
sports'man·ship
sport'y
spot'less
spot'light'
spot'ted
spot'ter
spot'ti·er
spot'ting
spot'ty
spous'al
spouse
spout'er
sprained
sprawl'ing
sprayed
spread'ing
sprig'gy
spright'li·ness
spright'ly
spring'board'
spring'ing
spring'time'
spring'y

sprin'kle
sprin'kling
sprint'er
sprite
sprit'sail'
sprock'et
sprout
spruced
spruce'ly
spruc'ing
spry'er
spry'ly
spume
spu·mo'ne
spu'mous
spum'y
spunk'i·ness
spunk'y
spu'ri·ous·ly
spurn'ing
spurred
spur'ring
spurt'ed
sput'ter
sput'ter·ing
spu'tum
spy'glass'
spy'ing
squab'ble
squab'bling
squad
squad'ron
squal'id
squa·lid'i·ty
squal'or
squan'der
squan'der·ing

square
squared
squar′er
squar′ing
squash′ing
squash′i·ness
squash′y
squat′ted
squat′ting
squat′ty
squaw
squawked
squeak′i·ly
squeak′ing
squeak′y
squeal′ing
squeam′ish
squee′gee
squeezed
squeez′ing
squelched
squid
squint′ed
squint′ing
squire
squir′ing
squirm′y
squir′rel
squirt′ed
squirt′ing
stabbed
stab′bing
sta·bil′i·ty
sta′bi·li·za′tion
sta′bi·lize
sta′bi·liz′er
sta′ble

sta′bling
stac·ca′to
stacked
stack′er
sta′di·um
staffed
stage′coach′
staged
stage′hand′
stag′ger
stag′ger·ing·ly
stag′ing
stag′nan·cy
stag′nant
stag′nate
stag′nat·ing
stag·na′tion
stag′y
staid
sedate *(see:* stayed)
stain′less
stair′case′
stair′way′
staked
stak′ing
sta·lac′tite
sta·lag′mite
stale′ness
stal′er
Sta′lin
stalk′er
stalk′ing
stal′lion
stal′wart
sta′men
stam′i·na

stam′mer
stamped
stam·pede′
stamp′er
stance
stan′chion
stand′ard
stand′ard·i·za′tion
stand′ard·ize
stand′-by′
stand·ee′
stand′ing
stand′point′
stan′nic
stan′nous
stan′num
stan′za
sta′pes
sta′pled
sta′pling
star′board
starch′i·ness
starch′y
stared
star′fish′
star′ing
stark′ly
star′ling
star′lit′
starred
star′ring
star′ry
start′er
star′tle
star′tling
star·va′tion
starved

starve′ling
starv′ing
state′craft′
stat′ed
state′hood
state′li·ness
state′ly
state′ment
state′room′
states′man·ship
stat′ic
stat′i·cize
sta′tion·ar′y
fixed
sta′tion·er
sta′tion·er′y
writing paper
stat′ism
sta·tis′tic
sta·tis′ti·cal·ly
stat′is·ti′cian
sta·tis′tics
stat′u·ar′y
stat′ue
stat′u·esque′
stat′u·ette′
stat′ure
sta′tus
stat′ute
stat′u·to′ry
staunch
staunch′ly
stayed
remained *(see:* staid)
stay′ing
stead′fast
stead′i·ly
stead′y
steal
take
stealth′i·ly
stealth′y
steam′er
steam′y
ste′a·rin
steel
metal
steel′works′
steel′y
stee′ple
stee′ple·chase′
stee′ple·jack′
steep′ly
steer′age
stel′lar
stel′late
stem′less
stemmed
stem′ming
sten′cil
sten′ciled
sten′cil·ing
ste·nog′ra·pher
sten′o·graph′ic
ste·nog′ra·phy
sten′o·typ′ist
sten′o·typ′y
sten·to′ri·an
step′lad′der
step′ping
step′son′
ster′e·o·phon′ic
ster′e·op′ti·con
ster′e·op′tics
ster′e·o·scope′
ster′e·o·scop′ic
ster′e·os′co·pist
ster′e·o·type′
ster′e·o·typ′ing
ster′ile
ste·ril′i·ty
ster′i·li·za′tion
ster′i·lize
ster′ling
stern′ly
ster′num
ster′to·rous
steth′o·scope
steth′o·scop′ic
ste·thos′co·py
ste′ve·dore
stew′ard
stew′ard·ess
stick′er
stick′ing
stick′i·ness
stick′le
stick′ler
stick′y
stiff′en·ing
stiff′ly
sti′fle
sti′fling
stig′ma
stig′ma·ti·za′tion
stig′ma·tize
sti·let′to
still′born′

stilt'ed
stim'u·lant
stim'u·late
stim'u·la'tion
stim'u·la'tive
stim'u·lus
(plural: -li)

stin'gi·er
stin'gi·ness
sting'ing
stin'gy
stink'ing
stint'ing
sti'pend
sti·pen'di·ar'y
stip'ple
stip'pling
stip'u·late
stip'u·la'tion
stip'u·la'tor
stip'u·la·to'ry
stip'ule
stirred
stir'ring
stir'rup
stitch'ing
stock·ade'
stock'bro'ker
stock'hold'er
Stock'holm
stock'ing
stock'pile
stock'y
stock'yard'
stodg'i·ness
stodg'y
sto'gy
Sto'ic
sto'i·cal
sto'i·cism
stoked
stok'er
stok'ing
sto'len
stol'id
sto·lid'i·ty
sto'ma
stom'ach
stom'ach·er
sto·mach'ic
stone'cut'ter
stoned
ston'ing
ston'y
stop'gap'
stop'page
stopped
stop'per
stop'ping
stor'age
stored
store'house'
store'room'
sto'ried
stor'ing
stork
storm'i·ly
storm'y
sto'ry
stove'pipe'
stow'age
stow'a·way'
stra·bis'mal
stra·bis'mus
strad'dle
strad'dling
Strad'i·var'i·us
strafed
straf'ing
strag'gle
strag'gler
strag'gling
straight
continuous *(see:* strait)

straight'en
straight'for'ward
strained
strain'er
strait
channel *(see:* straight)

strait'en
strait'laced'
strange'ly
strang'er
stran'gle
stran'gler
stran'gling
stran'gu·late
stran'gu·la'tion
strapped
strap'ping
strat'a·gem
stra·te'gic
strat'e·gist
strat'e·gy
strat'i·fi·ca'tion
strat'i·fied

strat'i·fy
strat'i·fy·ing
strat'o·sphere
strat'o·spher'ic
stra'tum
straw'ber'ry
stray'ing
streak'i·ness
streak'y
stream'er
stream'let
stream'lined'
street
strength'en
strength'less
stren'u·ous
strep'to·coc'cic
strep'to·coc'cus
(plural: -cocci)
strep'to·my'cin
stressed
stretch'er
strewed
strewn
stri'at·ed
strick'en
strict'ly
stric'ture
stri'den·cy
stri'dent
strid'ing
strid'u·late
strid'u·la'tion
strife
strik'er
strik'ing
stringed
strin'gen·cy
strin'gent
string'ing
string'y
striped
with stripes
strip'ing
strip'ling
stripped
removed
strip'ping
strive
striv'en
striv'ing
stroked
strok'ing
stroll'er
strong'hold'
strong'ly
stron'ti·um
stro'phe
stroph'ic
strop'ping
struc'tur·al
struc'tur·al·ly
struc'ture
stru'del
strug'gle
strug'gling
strum'ming
strum'pet
strut'ted
strut'ting
strych'nine
stubbed
stub'bi·ness
stub'bing
stub'ble
stub'bly
stub'born
stub'born·ness
stub'by
stuc'co
stud'ded
stud'ding
stu'dent
stud'ied
stu'di·o
stu'di·ous
stud'y
stud'y·ing
stuffed
stuff'i·ness
stuff'ing
stuff'y
stul'ti·fi·ca'tion
stul'ti·fied
stul'ti·fy
stul'ti·fy·ing
stum'ble
stum'bling
stump'y
stunned
stun'ning
stunt'ed
stu'pe·fac'tion
stu'pe·fied
stu'pe·fi'er
stu'pe·fy
stu'pe·fy·ing
stu·pen'dous
stu·pid'i·ty

stu'pid·ly
stu'por
stu'por·ous
stur'di·ness
stur'dy
stur'geon
stut'ter
stut'ter·ing
styled
styl'ing
styl'ish
styl'ist
sty·lis'tic
styl'i·za'tion
styl'ize
sty'lus
sty'mied
sty'mie·ing
styp'tic
Sty'ro·foam
sua'sion
sua'sive·ness
suave'ly
sua'vi·ty
sub·al'tern
sub'a·tom'ic
sub'com·mit'tee
sub·con'scious
sub'cu·ta'ne·ous
sub'di·vide'
sub'di·vid'ing
sub'di·vi'sion
sub·due'
sub·du'ing
sub·ja'cen·cy
sub·ja'cent
sub'ject, *n., adj.*
sub·ject', *v.*
sub·jec'tion
sub'jec'tive
sub'jec·tiv'i·ty
sub·join'
sub'ju·gate
sub'ju·gat·ing
sub'ju·ga'tion
sub·junc'tive
sub'lease'
sub'les·see'
sub·les'sor
sub·let'
sub·let'ting
sub'li·mate
sub'li·mat·ing
sub'li·ma'tion
sub·lime'
sub·lime'ly
sub·lim'i·ty
sub'ma·rine'
sub·max'il·lar'y
sub·merge'
sub·mer'gence
sub·mer'gi·ble
sub·merse'
sub·mers'ing
sub·mer'sion
sub·mis'sion
sub·mis'sive
sub·mit'
sub·mit'ted
sub·mit'ting
sub·nor'mal
sub'nor·mal'i·ty
sub·or'di·nate
sub·or'di·nate·ly
sub·or'di·na'tion
sub·or'di·na'tive
sub·orn'
sub'or·na'tion
sub·poe'na
sub·poe'naed
sub·poe'na·ing
sub'ro·ga'tion
sub ro'sa
sub·scribe'
sub·scrib'er
sub·scrib'ing
sub·scrip'tion
sub'scrip'tive
sub'se·quence
sub'se·quent
sub'se·quen'tial
sub·serve'
sub·ser'vi·ence
sub·ser'vi·ent
sub·serv'ing
sub·side'
sub·sid'ence
sub·sid'i·ar'y
sub·sid'ing
sub'si·di·za'tion
sub'si·dize
sub'si·dy
sub·sist'
sub·sist'ence
sub·sist'ent
sub·son'ic
sub'stance
sub·stan'tial
sub·stan'ti·al'i·ty
sub·stan'ti·ate
sub·stan'ti·a'tion

sub′stan·tive
sub′sta′tion
sub′sti·tute
sub′sti·tut·ed
sub′sti·tut·ing
sub′sti·tu′tion
sub·tend′
sub′ter·fuge
sub′ter·ra′ne·an
sub′ti′tle
sub′tle
sub′tle·ty
sub′tly
sub·tract′
sub·trac′tion
sub′tra·hend
sub′urb
sub·ur′ban
sub·ur′ban·ite
sub·ven′tion
sub·ver′sion
sub·ver′sion·a·ry
sub·ver′sive
sub·vert′
sub·vert′i·ble
sub′way′
suc·ceed′
suc·cess′
suc·cess′ful·ly
suc·ces′sion
suc·ces′sive
suc·ces′sor
suc·cinct′
suc′cor
suc′co·tash
suc′cu·lence
suc′cu·lent
suc·cumb′
suck′er
suck′le
suck′ling
su′crose
suc′tion
suc·to′ri·al
Su′da·nese′
sud′den·ly
suds′y
suede
su′et
su′et·y
suf′fer
suf′fer·a·ble
suf′fer·ance
suf′fer·ing
suf·fice′
suf·ficed′
suf·fi′cien·cy
suf·fi′cient
suf·fic′ing
suf′fix
suf′fo·cate
suf′fo·cat′ing
suf′fo·ca′tion
suf′fra·gan
suf′frage
suf′fra·gette′
suf′fra·gist
suf·fuse′
suf·fus′ing
suf·fu′sion
suf·fu′sive
sug′ar
sug′ar·i·ness
sug′ar·y
sug·gest′
sug·gest′i·bil′i·ty
sug·gest′i·ble
sug·ges′tion
sug·ges′tive
su′i·cid′al
su′i·cide
su′ing
suit′a·bil′i·ty
suit′a·ble
suite
suit′ing
suit′or
su′ki·ya′ki
sul′fa
sul′fa·nil′a·mide
sul′fate
sul′fa·thi′a·zole
sul′fide
sul′fite
sulk′i·ness
sulk′y
sul′len
sul′lied
sul′ly
sul′phur
sul′phu·rate
sul·phu′re·ous
sul·phu′ric
sul′phur·ous
sul′tan
sul·tan′a
sul′tan·ate
sul·tan′ic
sul′tri·er
sul′tri·ness
sul′try

su′mac
Su·ma′tra
sum′ma cum lau′de
sum′ma·ri·ly
sum′ma·ri·za′tion
sum′ma·rize
sum′ma·ry
sum·ma′tion
sum′mer
sum′mer·y
sum′ming
sum′mit
sum′moned
sum′mon·ing
sump′ter
sump′tu·ar′y
sump′tu·os′i·ty
sump′tu·ous
sun′beam′
sun′burn′
sun′dae
Sun′day
sun′der
sun′der·ance
sun′di′al
sun′dries
sun′dry
sunk′en
sun′light′
sun′ni·er
sun′ning
sun′ny
sun′rise′
sun′set′
sun′shine′
su′per
su′per·a·bil′i·ty
su′per·a·ble
su′per·a·bun′dant
su′per·an′nu·ate
su′per·an′nu·at′ed
su′per·an′nu·a′tion
su·perb′ly
su′per·car′go
su′per·cil′i·ous
su′per·er′o·ga′tion
su′per·fi′cial
su′per·fi′ci·al′i·ty
su′per·fi′cial·ly
su′per·flu′i·ty
su·per′flu·ous
su′per·hu′man
su′per·im·pose′
su′per·im′po·si′tion
su′per·in·tend′
su′per·in·tend′en·cy
su′per·in·tend′ent
su·pe′ri·or
su·pe′ri·or′i·ty
su·per′la·tive
su′per·man′
su·per′nal
su′per·nat′u·ral
su′per·nat′u·ral·is′tic
su′per·nu′mer·ar′y
su′per·sede′
su′per·sed′ence
su′per·sed′ing
su′per·sen′si·tive
su′per·son′ic
su′per·sti′tion
su′per·sti′tious
su′per·struc′ture
su′per·vene′
su′per·ven′ing
su′per·ven′tion
su′per·vise
su′per·vis·ing
su′per·vi′sion
su′per·vi′sor
su′per·vi′so·ry
su·pine′
sup′per
sup·plant′
sup′plan·ta′tion
sup·plant′er
sup′ple
sup′ple·ment
sup′ple·men′ta·ri·ly
sup′ple·men′ta·ry
sup′ple·men·ta′tion
sup′pli·ant
sup′pli·cant
sup′pli·cate
sup′pli·cat′ing
sup′pli·ca′tion
sup′pli·ca·to′ry
sup·plied′
sup·pli′er
sup·ply′
sup·ply′ing
sup·port′
sup·port′a·bil′i·ty
sup·port′a·ble
sup·port′ing
sup·pos′a·ble

sup·pose′
sup·posed′
sup·pos′ing
sup′po·si′tion
sup′po·si′tion·al·ly
sup·press′
sup·press′i·ble
sup·pres′sion
sup·pres′sive
sup′pu·rate
sup′pu·rat·ing
sup′pu·ra′tion
sup′pu·ra′tive
su′pra
su·prem′a·cy
su·preme′
su′rah
sur·cease′
sur′charge′, *n.*
sur·charge′, *v.*
sur′cin·gle
sure′ly
sur′er
sur′est
sur′e·ty
sur′face
sur′faced
sur′fac·ing
sur′feit
surge
rise and fall *(see:* serge)
sur′geon
sur′ger·y
sur′gi·cal
surg′ing
sur′li·ness
sur′ly
sur·mise′
sur·mis′ing
sur′mount′
sur·mount′a·ble
sur′name′
sur·pass′
sur·pass′ing
sur′plice
clergyman's gown
sur′plus
excess
sur·prise′
sur·prised′
sur·pris′ed·ly
sur·pris′ing
sur·re′al·ism
sur·re′al·is′tic
sur·ren′der
sur′rep·ti′tious
sur′rey
sur′ro·gate
sur′ro·gat′ed
sur′ro·gat′ing
sur·round′ed
sur·round′ing
sur′tax′
sur·veil′lance
sur·veil′lant
sur′vey, *n.*
sur·vey′, *v.*
sur·vey′ing
sur·vey′or
sur·viv′al
sur·vive′
sur·viv′or
sus·cep′ti·bil′i·ty
sus·cep′ti·ble
sus′pect, *n.*
sus·pect′, *v.*
sus·pend′
sus·pend′ed
sus·pense′
sus·pen′sion
sus·pen′so·ry
sus·pi′cion
sus·pi′cious
Sus′que·han′na
sus·tain′
sus·tain′ed
sus·tain′ment
sus′te·nance
sut′ler
sut·tee′
su′ture
su′tur·ing
su′ze·rain
svelte
swabbed
swab′bing
swad′dle
swad′dling
swag′ger
swal′low
swal′low-tailed′
swa′mi
swamp′land′
swamp′y
swan′like′
swank′i·ness
swank′y
swarmed

swarth′i·ness
swarth′y
swash′buck′ler
swas′ti·ka
swatch
swath
sway′-backed
sway′ing
swear′ing
sweat′er
sweat′i·ness
sweat′y
Swe′den
Swed′ish
sweep′er
sweep′stakes′
sweet·bread′
sweet′en·ing
sweet′heart′
sweet′ly
sweet′meats′
swelled
swell′ing
swel′ter
swel′ter·ing
swerved
swerv′ing
swift′ly
swim′mer
swim′ming
swin′dle
swin′dler
swin′dling
swine′herd′
swing′ing
swin′ish
swiped
swip′ing
swirl′ing
switch′board′
Switz′er·land
swiv′el
swiv′eled
swiv′el·ing
swol′len
swoon′ing
sword′fish′
sword′play′
swords′man·ship
sworn
syb′a·rite
syc′a·more
syc′o·phan·cy
syc′o·phant
Syd′ney
syl·lab′ic
syl·lab′i·cate
syl·lab′i·cat·ing
syl·lab′i·ca′tion
syl·lab′i·fi·ca′tion
syl·lab′i·fied
syl·lab′i·fy
syl·lab′i·fy·ing
syl′la·ble
syl′la·bus
syl′lo·gism
sylph′like′
syl′van
sym′bol
sign (*see:* cymbal)
sym·bol′ic
sym′bol·ism
sym′bol·is′tic
sym′bol·i·za′tion
sym′bol·ize
sym·met′ri·cal
sym′me·try
sym′pa·thet′ic
sym′pa·thize
sym′pa·thiz′ing
sym′pa·thy
sym·phon′ic
sym′pho·ny
sym·po′si·um
symp′tom
symp′to·mat′ic
syn′a·gogue
syn·apse′
syn′chro·nism
syn′chro·nis′tic
syn′chro·ni·za′tion
syn′chro·nize
syn′chro·niz·ing
syn′chro·nous
syn′co·pate
syn′co·pat′ed
syn′co·pat′ing
syn′co·pa′tion
syn′co·pe
syn·cop′ic
syn′dic
syn′di·cal·ism′
syn′di·cate
syn′di·cat·ing
syn′di·ca′tion
syn′di·ca′tor
syn·ec′do·che
syn′ec·doch′i·cal
syn′od
syn·od′i·cal

syn'o·nym
syn'o·nym'ic
syn'o·nym'i·ty
syn·on'y·mous
syn·on'y·my
syn·op'sis
(plural: -ses)
syn·op'tic
syn·tac'ti·cal
syn'tax
syn'the·sis
(plural: -ses)
syn'the·sist
syn'the·size
syn'the·siz·ing
syn·thet'ic
syn·thet'i·cal·ly
syph'i·lis
syph'i·lit'ic
sy'phon
Syr'a·cuse
Syr'i·a
sy·rin'ga
sy·ringe'
syr'inx
syr'up
sys'tem
sys'tem·at'ic
sys'tem·a·ti·za'tion
sys'tem·a·tize
sys·tem'ic
sys'tem·i·za'tion
sys'tem·ize
sys'to·le
sys·tol'ic

T

Ta·bas'co
tabbed
tab'bing
tab'er·nac'le
tab'er·nac'u·lar
ta'ble
tab'leau
ta'ble·cloth'
ta'ble d'hote'
ta'ble·land'
ta'ble·spoon'
ta'ble·spoon'fuls
tab'let
ta'ble·ware'
ta'bling
tab'loid
ta·boo'
tab'o·ret
tab'u·lar
tab'u·late
tab'u·lat·ing
tab'u·la'tor
ta·chom'e·ter
tac'it·ly
tac'i·turn
tac'i·tur'ni·ty
tack'le
tack'ling
tack'y
tact'ful
tac'ti·cal
tac·ti'cian
tac'tics
tac'tile
tac·til'i·ty
tact'less
tad'pole'
taf'fe·ta
tagged
tag'ging
Ta·hi'ti
tail'board'
tai'lor
taint
take'-off'
tak'ing
tal'cum
tal'ent
tal'is·man
talk'a·tive
Tal'la·has'see
tal'lied
tal'low
tal'ly
Tal'mud
tal'on
ta·ma'le
tam'a·rack
tam'a·rind
tam'bou·rine'

tame′a·ble
tamed
tam′ing
Tam′ma·ny
tam′-o'-shan′ter
tam′per
tam′pon
tan′a·ger
tan′bark′
tan′dem
Tan′gan·yi′ka
tan′gent
tan·gen′tial
tan′ge·rine′
tan′gi·ble
tan′gle
tan′gling
tan′go
tan′goed
tang′y
tank′ard
tank′er
tanned
tan′ner
tan′ner·y
tan′nic
tan′ning
tan′tal·ize
tan′ta·lum
tan′ta·mount
tan′trum
taped
ta′per
tap′es·try
tape′worm′
tap′i·o′ca
ta′pir
tapped
tap′ping
tar′an·tel′la
ta·ran′tu·la
tar′di·ness
tar′dy
tar′get
tar′iff
tar′nish
tar·pau′lin
tar′pon
tarred
tar′ried
tar′ring
tar′ry
tar′sal
tar′tan
tar′tar
task′mas′ter
Tas·ma′ni·a
tas′sel
tas′seled
tas′sel·ing
taste′ful
tast′ing
tast′y
tat′ter
tat′tle
tat·too′
taught
taunt′er
taunt′ing·ly
taupe
Tau′rus
tau·tol′o·gy
tav′ern
taw′dri·ness
taw′dry
taw′ni·er
taw′ny
tax′a·ble
tax·a′tion
tax′i·cab′
tax′i·der′mic
tax′i·der′my
tax′ied
tax′o·nom′ic
tax·on′o·my
tax′pay′er
Tchai·kov′sky
teach′a·ble
teach′er
tea′cup′
tea′ket′tle
team′ster
team′work′
tea′pot′
tear′ful
tear′ing
teased
tea′sel
teas′ing
tea′spoon·fuls′
tech′ni·cal
tech′ni·cal′i·ty
tech·ni′cian
Tech′ni·col′or
tech′nics
tech·nique′
tech·noc′ra·cy
tech′no·log′i·cal
tech·nol′o·gy
te′di·ous
te′di·um

teen′ag′er
teethe, *v.*
teeth′ing
tee·to′tal·er
teg′u·ment
Te′he·ran′ (also Tehran)
Tel′ A·viv′
tel′e·cast′
tel′e·gram
tel′e·graph
te·leg′ra·phy
tele′me·ter
te·lem′e·try
tel′e·ol′o·gy
tel′e·path′ic
te·lep′a·thy
tel′e·phone
te′leph′o·ny
tel′e·pho′to
Tel′e·prompt′er
tel′e·scope
tel′e·scop′ic
te·les′co·py
tel′e·type
tel′e·vise
tel′e·vi′sion
tel·lu′ri·um
tem·blor′
te·mer′i·ty
tem′per
tem′per·a
tem′per·a·ment
tem′per·a·men′tal
tem′per·ance
tem′per·ate
tem′per·a·ture
tem′pered
tem′pest
tem·pes′tu·ous
tem′ple
tem′po
tem′po·ral
tem′po·rar′i·ly
tem′po·rar′y
tem′po·rize
temp·ta′tion
tempt′ing
tem′pus fu′git
ten′a·ble
te·na′cious
te·nac′i·ty
ten′an·cy
ten′ant
tend′en·cy
ten′der·foot′
ten′der·loin′
ten′don
ten′dril
ten′e·ment
ten′et
ten′fold′
Ten′nes·see′
ten′nis
Ten′ny·son
ten′on
ten′or
ten′pins′
ten′sile
ten·sil′i·ty
ten′sion
ten′sor
ten′ta·cle
ten′ta·tive
ten′ter·hook′
ten·u′i·ty
ten′u·ous
ten′ure
te′pee
tep′id
te·pid′i·ty
ter·cen′te·nar′y
ter′ma·gant
ter′mi·na·ble
ter′mi·nal
ter′mi·nate
ter′mi·na′tion
ter′mi·nol′o·gy
ter′mi·nus
ter′mite
Terp·sich′o·re
terp′si·cho·re′an
ter′race
ter′ra cot′ta
ter′ra fir′ma
ter·rain′
ter′ra·my′cin
ter′ra·pin
ter·rar′i·um
ter·res′tri·al
ter′ri·ble
ter′ri·er
ter·rif′ic
ter′ri·fied
ter′ri·fy
ter′ri·to′ri·al
ter′ri·to′ry
ter′ror·ize
terse′ness
ter′ti·ar′y
tes′sel·late

tes′sel·la′tion
tes′ta·ment
tes′ta·men′ta·ry
tes′tate
tes′ta·tor
tes·ta′trix
tes′ti·cle
tes′ti·fi·ca′tion
tes′ti·fy
tes′ti·mo′ni·al
tes′ti·mo′ny
tes′tis
tes′ty
te·tan′ic
tet′a·nus
tête′-à-tête′
teth′er
tet′ra·he′dron
te·tral′o·gy
te·tram′e·ter
tet′rarch
te·trox′ide
Teu·ton′ic
text′book′
tex′tile
tex′tu·al
tex′ture
Thai′land
tha·lam′ic
thal′a·mus
thal′lo·phyte
thal′lus
thank′ful
thanks·giv′ing
thatch′er
thau′ma·tur′gy
the′a·ter
the·at′ri·cal
the′ism
the·is′tic
the·mat′ic
them·selves′
thence′forth′
the·oc′ra·cy
the′o·crat′ic
the·od′o·lite
the′o·lo′gian
the′o·log′i·cal
the·ol′o·gy
the′o·rem
the′o·ret′i·cal
the′o·re·ti′cian
the′o·rist
the′o·rize
the′o·ry
the′o·soph′ic
the·os′o·phy
ther′a·peu′tic
ther′a·peu′ti·cal·ly
ther′a·pist
ther′a·py
there′a·bouts′
there·af′ter
there′fore
there′up·on′
ther′mal
ther′mi·cal·ly
ther′mo·dy·nam′ic
ther·mom′e·ter
ther′mo·met′ric
ther′mo·nu′cle·ar
ther′mos
ther′mo·stat
ther′mo·stat′ic
the·sau′rus
the′sis
Thes′pi·an
Thes′sa·lo′ni·ans
the′ta
thi′a·mine
thick′en
thick′et
thief
(*plural:* thieves)
thiev′er·y
thigh′bone′
thim′ble
think′ing
thin′ner
third′ly
thirst′i·ly
thirst′y
thir′teen′
thir′ti·eth
thir′ty
this′tle·down′
thith′er
thong
tho·rac′ic
tho′rax
thor′ic
tho′ri·um
thorn′y
thor′ough
thor′ough·bred′
thor′ough·fare′
though
thought′ful
thou′sand
thrash′er

thread′bare′
thread′er
threat′en
three′some
thren′o·dy
thresh′er
thresh′old
thrift′i·er
thrift′y
thrill′er
thriv′ing
throat′i·ness
throat′y
throb′bing
throm·bo′sis
throm·bot′ic
throng
thros′tle
throt′tle
through
throw
thrush
thrust′ing
thud′ding
thumb′nail′
thump′er
thun′der·ous·ly
thun′der·storm′
Thurs′day
thwart
thy′mol
thy′mus
thy′roid
thy·rox′in
ti·ar′a
tib′i·a
tick′et
tick′le
tid′bit′
tid′dly·winks′
tide′wa′ter
ti′di·ness
ti′dings
tif′fin
ti′ger
tight′en
tight′rope′
tight′wad′
ti′gress
tiled
til′ing
till′er
tilt′er
tim′bal
kettledrum
tim′bale
food
tim′ber
wood
tim′bre
sonic quality
tim′brel
Tim·buk′tu
time′li·ness
time′ly
time′piece′
tim′id
ti·mid′i·ty
tim′ing
tim′or·ous
tim′o·thy
tim′pa·ni, *pl.*
tinc′ture
tin′der
tinge′ing
tin′gle
ti′ni·er
tink′er
tin′kle
tin′ner
tin′ni·er
tin′ny
tin′sel
tin′smith′
ti′ny
tip′-off′
tip′per
tip′pet
tip′ping
tip′ple
tip′si·ly
tip′sy
tip′toe′
ti′rade
tire′some
tir′ing
tis′sue
ti′tan
ti·tan′ic
ti·ta′ni·um
tithe
tith′ing
ti′tian
tit′il·late
tit′i·vate
ti′tle
tit′mouse′
Ti′to·ism
ti′trate

tit′ter
tit′u·lar
toad′stool′
toast′er
toast′mas′ter
to·bac′co
to·bac′co·nist
to·bog′gan
toc·ca′ta
toc′sin
alarm *(see:* toxin)

tod′dle
tod′dy
tof′fee
to′ga
to·geth′er
tog′ging
toil′er
toi′let·ry
to′ken
tol′er·a·ble
tol′er·ance
tol′er·ant
tol′er·ate
toll′gate′
Tol′stoy
(also: -stoi)

tol′u·ene
tom′a·hawk
to·ma′to
tom′boy′
tomb′stone′
tom′cat′
to·mor′row
ton′al
to·nal′i·ty
tone′less
tongue
ton′ic
to·night′
ton′nage
ton·neau′
ton′sil
ton′sil·lec′to·my
ton′sil·li′tis
ton·so′ri·al
ton′sure
ton′tine
tool′ing
tooth′ache′
tooth′some
to′paz
top′coat′
top′flight′
top′-hea′vy
top′ic
top′i·cal
top′-notch′
to·pog′ra·phy
top′per
top′ping
top′ple
top′pling
top′side′
top′soil′
top′sy-tur′vy
toque
to′rah
torch′bear′er
tor′e·a·dor
tor·ment′, *v.*
tor′ment, *n.*
tor·men′tor
tor·na′do
To·ron′to
tor·pe′do
tor′pid
tor′por
torque
tor′rent
tor·ren′tial
tor′rid
tor′sion
tor′so
tort
civil wrong

torte
cake

tor·til′la
tor′toise
tor′tu·ous
tor′ture
tor′tur·ing·ly
toss′ing
toss′-up′
to′tal·i·tar′i·an
to·tal′i·ty
to′tem
tot′ing
tot′ter
tou′can
touch′down′
touch′ing
touch′y
tough′en
tou·pee′
tour′ist
tour′na·ment
tour′ney

tour'ni·quet
tou'sle
tou'sled
tout'er
to·ward'
tow'el·ing
tow'er·ing
tow'head'
tow'line'
town'ship
towns'peo'ple
tox·e'mi·a
tox·e'mic
tox'ic
tox·ic'i·ty
tox'i·co·log'i·cal
tox'i·col'o·gy
tox'in
poison (*see:* tocsin)

trac'er·y
tra'che·a
tra·cho'ma
tra·chom'a·tous
track'er
trac'ta·bil'i·ty
trac'ta·ble
trac'tile
trac'tion
trac'tor
trade'mark'
trad'er
trades'man
tra·di'tion
tra·di'tion·al
tra·duce'
Tra·fal'gar
traf'fic
traf'ficked
tra·ge'di·an, *masc.*
tra·ge'di·enne', *fem.*
trag'e·dy
trag'ic
trag'i·cal·ly
trag'i·com'e·dy
trail'er
train·ee'
train'load'
trai'tor
tra·jec'to·ry
tram'mel
tram'mel·ing
tram'ple
tran'quil
tran'quil·iz'er
tran·quil'li·ty
trans·act'
trans·ac'tion
trans'at·lan'tic
tran·scend'
tran·scend'en·cy
tran·scend'ent
trans'con·ti·nen'tal
tran·scribe'
tran'script
tran·scrip'tion
tran'sept
trans·fer'able
trans·fer'ence
trans'ferred
trans'fer·ring
trans·fig'u·ra'tion
trans·fig'ure
trans·fix'
trans·fix'ion
trans·form'
trans'for·ma'tion
trans·form'a·tive
trans·form'er
trans·fuse'
trans·fu'sion
trans·gress'
trans·gres'sion
trans·gres'sor
tran'sien·cy
tran'sient
tran·sis'tor
trans'it
tran·si'tion
tran'si·tive
tran'si·to'ry
trans·late'
trans·la'tion
trans·lu'cence
trans·lu'cent
trans'mi·gra'tion
trans·mis'si·ble
trans·mis'sion
trans·mit'
trans·mit'tal
trans·mit'ter
trans·mut'a·ble
trans'mu·ta'tion
trans·mute'
trans'o·ce·an'ic
tran'som
trans·par'en·cy
trans·par'ent
tran'spi·ra'tion
tran·spire'

trans·plant′
trans′plan·ta′tion
trans·port′, *v.*
trans′port, *n.*
trans′por·ta′tion
trans′po·si′tion
trans·ship′ping
trans·son′ic
trans·ver′sal
trans·verse′
tra·peze′
tra·pe′zi·um
trap′e·zoid
trap′pings
Trap′pist
trap′shoot′ing
trau′ma
trau·mat′ic
trav′ail
trav′el·ing
trav′e·logue
trav′erse
trav′es·ty
trawl′er
treach′er·ous
treach′er·y
trea′cle
tread′ing
trea′dle
tread′mill′
trea′son
trea′son·ous
treas′ure
treas′ur·er
treas′ur·y
trea′tise
treat′ment

trea′ty
tre′ble
tree′ing
tre′foil
trek′king
trel′lis
trem′a·tode
trem′ble
trem′bling·ly
tre·men′dous
trem′o·lo
trem′or
trem′u·lous
trench′ant
tre·pan′
tre·pan′ning
tre·phine′
trep′i·da′tion
tres′pass
tres′tle
tri′ad
tri′an′gle
tri·an′gu·lar
tri·an′gu·late
trib′al
tribes′man
trib′u·la′tion
tri·bu′nal
trib′une
trib′u·tar′y
trib′ute
tri′ceps
tri·chi′na
trich′i·no′sis
trick′er·y
trick′le
trick′y

tri′col′or
tri′cot
tri·cus′pid
tri′cy·cle
tri′dent
tri·en′ni·al
Tri·este′
tri′fle
tri′fo′cal
tri·fo′li·ate
trig′ger
trig′o·nom′e·try
tri·he′dral
tri·he′dron
tri·lat′er·al
tril′lion
tril′li·um
tril′o·gy
trim′e·ter
trim′ming
Trin′i·dad
Trin′i·tar′i·an
tri·ni′tro·tol′u·ene
(*also:* -toluol; TNT)
Trin′i·ty
trin′ket
tri·no′mi·al
tri·par′tite
tri′par·ti′tion
tri′ple
tri′plet
trip′li·cate
tri′pod
Trip′o·li
trip′ping·ly
trip′tych

tri′reme
tri·sec′tion
Tris′tram
(*also:* Tristan)
tri·syl′la·ble
trite′ness
trit′i·um
tri′ton
trit′u·rate
tri′umph
tri·um′phant
tri·um′vi·rate
tri′une
tri·va′lence
tri·va′lent
triv′et
triv′i·a
triv′i·al′i·ty
tro·cha′ic
tro′che
lozenge
tro′chee
poetic foot
trod′den
trog′lo·dyte
Tro′jan
troll′er
trol′ley
trol′lop
trom′bone
troop
group (*see:* troupe)
troop′ship′
tro′phy
trop′ic
trop′i·cal
tro′pism
trop′o·sphere
trot′ting
trou′ba·dour
trou′ble
trou′blous
trough
trounce
troupe
group of actors (*see:* troop)
trou′sers
trous′seau
trow′el
tru′an·cy
tru′ant
truck′er
truck′le
truc′u·lence
truc′u·lent
trudge
trudg′ing
tru′est
truf′fle
tru′ism
tru·is′tic
tru′ly
trump′er·y
trum′pet
trun′cate
trun·ca′tion
trun′cheon
trun′dle
trun′nion
trus·tee′, *n.*
trust′ful
trust′wor′thi·ness
trust′wor′thy
trust′y, *adj.*
truth′ful
try′ing
try′out′
tryp′sin
tryst
tsar
(*also* czar)
tset′se
tu′ber
tu′ber·cle
tu·ber′cu·lar
tu·ber′cu·lo′sis
tu·ber′cu·lous
tube′rose′
tu′ber·os′i·ty
tu′ber·ous
tub′ing
tu′bu·lar
tuck′er
Tu′dor
Tues′day
tuft′ed
tug′boat′
tu·i′tion
tu′la·re′mi·a
tu′lip
tulle
tum′ble
tum′brel
(*also:* -bril)
tu′me·fac′tion
tu′me·fy

tu′mid
tu′mor
tu′mult
tu·mul′tu·ous
tun′dra
tune′ful
tung′sten
tu′nic
tun′ing
Tu·ni′sia
tun′nel
tun′ny
tu′pe·lo
tur′ban
tur′bid
tur′bine
tur′bo·jet′
tur′bo·prop′
tur′bot
tur′bu·lence
tur′bu·lent
tu·reen′
turf′man′
tur·ges′cence
tur·ges′cent
tur′gid
tur′key
Turk′ish
tur′mer·ic
tur′moil
turn′coat′
tur′nip
turn′key′
turn′o′ver
turn′pike′
tur′pen·tine
tur′pi·tude
tur′quoise
tur′ret
tur′tle·dove′
tus′sle
tus′sock
tu′te·lage
tu′te·lar′y
tu′tor
tu·to′ri·al·ly
tut′ti-frut′ti
tux·e′do
tweez′ers
twelfth
twen′ti·eth
twen′ty
twid′dle
twi′light′
twing′ing
twi′night′
twin′ing
twin′kle
twin′ning
twist′er
twitch′er
twit′ting
two′fold′
two′pence
two′some
two′step′
ty·coon′
ty′ing
tym·pan′ic
tym′pa·nist
tym′pa·num
type′set′ter
type′writ′er
ty′phoid
ty·phoon′
ty′phous, *adj.*
ty′phus, *n.*
typ′i·cal
typ′i·fi·ca′tion
typ′i·fy
typ′ist
ty·pog′ra·pher
ty′po·graph′ic
ty·pog′ra·phy
ty·ran′ni·cal
tyr·an·nize
tyr′an·nous
tyr′an·ny
ty′rant

U

u·biq′ui·tous
u·biq′ui·ty
ud′der
U·gan′da
ug′li·ness
ug′ly
u·kase′
U·kraine′
u′ku·le′le

ul′cer
ul′cer·ate
ul′cer·ous
ul′na
ul′nar
ul·te′ri·or
ul′ti·mate
ul′ti·ma′tum
ul′tra
ul′tra·son′ic
ul′tra·vi′o·let
ul′u·late
U·lys′ses
um′ber
um·bil′i·cal
um·bil′i·cus
um′bra
um′brage
um·bra′geous
um·brel′la
um′laut
um′pire
un·a′ble
un′ac·count′a·ble
un′ac·cus′tomed
un′af·fect′ed
un′-Amer′i·can
u′na·nim′i·ty
u·nan′i·mous
un·an′swer·a·ble
un′as·sum′ing
un′a·void′a·ble
un′a·ware′
un·bal′anced
un·bear′a·ble
un′be·com′ing
un′be·liev′er
un·bend′
un·bi′ased
un·bid′den
un·bind′
un·blush′ing
un·bolt′ed
un·born
un·bri′dled
un·bro′ken
un·buck′le
un·bur′den
un·but′ton
un·can′ny
un′cer·e·mo′
ni·ous
un·cer′tain
un·cer′tain·ty
un·change′a·ble
un·char′i·ta·ble
un·chaste′
un·chris′tian
un′ci·al
un·civ′il
un·civ′i·lized
un·clad′
un′cle
un·clean′
un·com′fort·a·ble
un·com′mon
un′com·mu′ni·ca′
tive
un′con·cerned′
un′con·di′tion·al
un·con′quer·a·ble
un·con′scion·a·ble
un·con′scious
un′con·sti·tu′
tion·al
un′con·ven′tion·al
un·count′ed
un·cou′ple
un·couth′
un·cov′er
unc′tion
unc′tu·ous
un′de·cid′ed
un′de·fined′
un′de·ni′a·ble
un′der·brush′
un′der·clothes′
un′der·cov′er
un′der·cur′rent
un′der·cut′
un′der·es′ti·mate
un′der·foot′
un′der·go′
un′der·grad′u·ate
un′der·ground′
un′der·growth′
un′der·hand′ed
un′der·line′
un′der·ling
un′der·ly′ing
un′der·mine′
un′der·neath′
un′der·paid′
un′der·pass′
un′der·priv′i·leged
un′der·score′
un′der·sec′re·tar·y
un′der·signed′
un′der·stand′
un′der·state′ment

un′der·stud′y
un′der·tak′er
un′der·tak′ing
un′der·tone′
un′der·tow′
un′der·wear′
un′der·weight′
un′der·went′
un′der·world′
un′der·write′
un′der·writ′ten
un′de·sir′a·ble
un·dis′ci·plined
un·do′ing
un·doubt′ed·ly
un·dress′
un′du·lant
un′du·late
un′du·la′tion
un·du′ly
un·dy′ing
un·earth′
un·earth′ly
un·eas′i·ly
un·eas′y
un′em·ployed′
un′em·ploy′ment
un·e′qual
un′e·quiv′o·cal
un·err′ing
un·e′ven·ness
un′e·vent′ful
un′ex·am′pled
un′ex·cep′tion·al
un′ex·pec′ted
un·fail′ing
un·fair′
un·faith′ful
un′fa·mil′iar
un·fas′ten
un·fa′vor·a·ble
un·feel′ing
un·feigned′
un·fin′ished
un·fit′ted
un·flag′ging
un·fledged′
un′fore·seen′
un′for·get′ta·ble
un·for′tu·nate
un·found′ed
un·friend′ly
un·furl′
un·gain′ly
un·god′ly
un·gov′ern·a·ble
un·gra′cious
un·grate′ful
un·ground′ed
un·guard′ed
un′guent
un′gu·la
un′gu·late
un·hal′lowed
un·hap′pi·ness
un·health′y
un·hinge′
un·ho′ly
un·horse′
u′ni·cam′er·al
u′ni·cel′lu·lar
u′ni·corn
u′ni·fi·ca′tion
u′ni·fied
u′ni·form
u′ni·form′i·ty
u′ni·fy
u′ni·fy·ing
u′ni·lat′er·al
un′im·peach′a·ble
un′im·por′tance
un′in·tel′li·gi·ble
un′in·ter·rupt′ed
un′ion·ism
un′ion·ize
u·nique′
u′ni·son
u′nit
U′ni·tar′i·an
u·nite′
u·nit′ing
u′ni·ty
u′ni·va′lence
u′ni·va′lent
u′ni·ver′sal
U′ni·ver′sal·ist
u′ni·ver·sal′i·ty
u′ni·verse
u′ni·ver′si·ty
un·just′
un·kempt′
un·kind′li·ness
un·known′
un·law′ful
un·learn′ed
un·leav′ened
un·let′tered
un·like′
un·lim′ber
un·lim′it·ed
un·load′

un·lock′
un·loose′
un·luck′y
un·man′ly
un·man′ner·ly
un·men′tion·a·ble
un·mer′ci·ful
un′mis·tak′a·ble
un·mor′al
un·nat′u·ral
un·nec′es·sar′y
un·nerve′
un·oc′cu·pied
un·or′gan·ized
un·pal′at·a·ble
un·par′al·leled
un·pleas′ant
un·pop′u·lar
un·prac′ti·cal
un·prec′e·dent′ed
un·prej′u·diced
un′pre·ten′tious
un·prin′ci·pled
un·print′a·ble
un′pro·fes′sion·al
un′pro·voked′
un·qual′i·fied
un·ques′tion·a·ble
un·quote′
un·rav′el
un·read′y
un′re·al′i·ty
un·rea′son·a·ble
un′re·gen′er·ate
un′re·lent′ing
un′re·li′a·ble
un′re·mit′ting
un′re·served′
un·rest′
un·ripe′
un·ri′valed
un·roll′
un·ruf′fled
un·ru′ly
un·safe′
un·san′i·tar·y
un·sa′vor·y
un·scathed′
un′sci·en·tif′ic
un·scram′ble
un·scru′pu·lous
un·sea′son·a·ble
un·seat′
un·seem′ly
un·self′ish
un·sheathe′
un·shod′
un·sight′ly
un·skilled′
un·snarl′
un·so′cia·ble
un′so·phis′ti·cat′ed
un·sound′
un·spar′ing
un·speak′a·ble
un·sta′ble
un·stead′y
un·strung′
un·stud′ied
un·suit′ed
un·tan′gle
un·taught′
un·think′ing
un·ti′dy
un·time′ly
un·tir′ing
un·touch′a·ble
un·to·ward′
un·tram′meled
un·tu′tored
un·u′su·al
un·ut′ter·a·ble
un·veil′
un·war′rant·a·ble
un·war′y
un·whole′some
un·wield′y
un·will′ing
un·wit′ting
un·wor′thy
un·writ′ten
up·braid′
up′bring′ing
up′coun′try
up·date′
up·end′
up′grade′
up·heav′al
up′hill′
up·hold′
up·hol′ster·y
up′keep′
up·lift′, *v.*
up′lift′, *n.*
up·on′
up′per·most
up′right′
up′ris′ing
up′roar′
up·roar′i·ous

up·set′, *v., adj.*
up′set′, *n.*
up′si·lon
up′stage′
up′stairs′
up·stand′ing
up′start′
up′state′
up′stream′
up′thrust′
up′-to-date′
up′ward
U′ral
u·ra′ni·um
U·ra′nus
ur′ban
ur·bane′
ur·ban′i·ty
ur′chin
u·re′a
u·re′mi·a
u·re′mic
u·re′ter
u·re′thra
ur′gen·cy
ur′gent
urg′ing
u′ric
u′ri·nal
u′ri·nal′y·sis
u′ri·nar′y
u′ri·na′tion
u′rine
u·ros′co·py
ur′sine
U′ru·guay
us′a·bil′i·ty
us′a·ble
us·age
use′ful
ush′er
u′su·al·ly
u′su·rer
u·su′ri·ous
u·surp′
u′sur·pa′tion
u·surp′er
u′su·ry
u·ten′sil
u′ter·ine
u′ter·us
u·til′i·tar′i·an
u·til′i·ty
u′ti·lize
ut′most
U·to′pi·a
ut′ter·ance
u′vu·la
ux·o′ri·ous

V

va′can·cy
va′cant
va′cate
va′cat·ing
va·ca′tion
vac′ci·nate
vac′ci·na′tion
vac′cine
vac′il·late
vac′il·lat′ing
vac′il·la′tion
va·cu′i·ty
vac′u·ole
vac′u·ous
vac′u·um
vag′a·bond
va·gar′i·ous
va·gar′y
va·gi′na
va′gran·cy
va′grant
vague′ly
vain′glo′ri·ous
val′ance
drapery *(see:* valence)
val′e·dic·to′ri·an
val′e·dic′to·ry
va′lence
atomic capacity *(see:* valance)
val′en·tine
va·le′ri·an
val′e·tu′di·nar′i·an
val′iant

val′id
val′i·date
val′i·da′tion
va·lid′i·ty
va·lise′
val′ley
val′or·ous·ly
Val′pa·rai′so
val′u·a·ble
val′u·a′tion
val′ued
val′u·ing
valve
val′vu·lar
vam′pire
va·na′di·um
Van·cou′ver
van′dal
van·dyke′
van′guard′
va·nil′la
van′ish
van′i·ty
van′quish
van′tage
vap′id
va·pid′i·ty
va′por·i·za′tion
va′por·ize
va′por·ous
va·que′ro
var′i·a·bil′i·ty
var′i·a·ble
var′i·ance
var′i·ant
var′i·a′tion
var′i·col′ored
var′i·cos′i·ty
var′i·cose
var′ied
var′i·e·gate
var′i·e·gat′ed
var′i·e·ga′tion
va·ri′e·ty
var′i·ous
va′ri·typ′er
var′let
var′nish
var′si·ty
var′y
vas′cu·lar
vas′cu·lar′i·ty
vas′o·mo′tor
vas′sal
vast′ly
Vat′i·can
vau′de·ville
vault′ing
vaunt′ing
vec·to′ri·al
veer′ing·ly
veg′e·ta·ble
veg′e·tal
veg′e·tar′i·an
veg′e·tate
veg′e·ta′tion
ve′he·mence
ve′he·ment
ve′hi·cle
ve·hic′u·lar
ve′lar
veldt
vel′lum
paper
ve·loc′i·pede
ve·loc′i·ty
ve·lours′
ve′lum
the palate
vel′vet
vel′vet·een′
ve′nal
ve·nal′i·ty
vend′er
(also: vendor)
ven·det′ta
vend′i·ble
ve·neer′
ven′er·a·ble
ven′er·ate
ven′er·a′tion
ve·ne′re·al
ven′er·y
Ve·ne′tian
Ven′e·zue′la
venge′ance
venge′ful
ve′ni·al
Ven′ice
ve·ni′re
ven′i·son
ven′om·ous
ve·nos′i·ty
ve′nous
ven′ti·late
ven′ti·la′tion
ven′ti·la′tor
ven′tral
ven′tri·cle
ven·tric′u·lar

ven·tril'o·quist
ven·tril'o·quy
ven'ture·some
ven'tur·ing
ven'tur·ous
ven'ue
Ve'nus
ve·ra'cious
truthful *(see:* voracious)
ve·rac'i·ty
ve·ran'da
ver'bal·i·za'tion
ver·ba'tim
ver·be'na
ver'bi·age
ver·bose'
ver·bos'i·ty
ver'dan·cy
ver'dant
ver'dict
ver'di·gris
ver'dure
verge
Ver'gil
(also: Virgil)
verg'ing
ver'i·fi'a·ble
ver'i·fi·ca'tion
ver'i·fied
ver'i·fy
ver'i·ly
ver'i·sim'i·lar
ver'i·si·mil'i·tude
ver'i·ta·ble
ver'mi·cel'li
ver'mi·cid'al
ver'mi·cide
ver·mic'u·lite
ver'mi·form
ver'mi·fuge
ver·mil'ion
ver'min
Ver·mont'
ver·mouth'
ver·nac'u·lar
ver'nal
ver'ni·er
ve·ron'i·ca
Ver·sailles'
ver'sa·tile
versed
ver'si·cle
ver'si·fied
ver'si·fy
ver'sion
ver'sus
ver'te·brae, *pl.*
ver'te·brate
ver'tex
ver'ti·cal
ver'ti·go
verve
ves'i·cant
ves'i·cate
ves'i·cle
ve·sic'u·lar
ves'per
ves'pers
ves'sel
ves'tal
ves'ti·bule
ves'tige
ves·tig'i·al
vest'ment
ves'try·man
ves'ture
Ve·su'vi·us
vetch
vet'er·an
vet'er·i·nar'i·an
vet'er·i·nar'y
ve'to
(plural: vetoes)
ve'to·ing
vex·a'tion
vex·a'tious
vex'ed·ly
vi'a·bil'i·ty
vi'a·ble
vi'a·duct
vi'al
vi'and
vi'bran·cy
vi'brant
vi'brate
vi'bra·tile
vi'brat·ing
vi·bra'tion
vi'bra·tor
vi·bur'num
vic'ar·age
vic'ar-gen'er·al
vi·car'i·ous
vice'-con'sul
vice'-pres'i·dent
vice'roy
vi'ce ver'sa
vi·cin'i·ty

vi′cious
vi·cis′si·tude
vic′tim·ize
vic′tor
Vic·to′ri·an
vic·to′ri·ous
vic′to·ry
vic·tro′la
vict′ual
vi·cu′na
vid′e·o
Vi·en′na
Vi′en·nese′
Vi·et′-Nam′
view′point′
vig′il
vig′i·lance
vig′i·lant
vig′i·lan′te
vi·gnette′
vig′or·ous
Vi′king
vile′ly
vil′i·fi·ca′tion
vil′i·fy
vil′i·fy·ing
vil′la
vil′lage
vil′lain
scoundrel
vil′lain·ous
vil′lain·y
vil′ein
peasant
vin′ai·grette′
vin′ci·bil′i·ty
vin′ci·ble
vin′di·cate
vin′di·ca′tion
vin·dic′tive
vin′e·gar
vine′yard
vin′tage
vint′ner
vi′nyl
vi′ol
vi·o′la
vi′o·la·ble
vi′o·late
vi′o·la′tion
vi′o·lence
vi′o·lent
vi′o·let
vi′o·lin′
vi′o·lon·cel′lo
(also: cello)
vi′per
vi·ra′go
vir′e·o
vi·res′cent
vir′gin
Vir·gin′ia
vir·gin′i·ty
vir′i·des′cent
vir′ile
vi·ril′i·ty
vir′tu·al
vir′tue
vir′tu·os′i·ty
vir′tu·o′so
vir′tu·ous
vir′u·lence
vir′u·lent
vi′rus
vi′sa
vis′age
vis′cer·a
vis′cid
vis′cose
vis·cos′i·ty
vis′count
vis′cous
vis′i·bil′i·ty
vis′i·ble
vi′sion·ar′y
vis′it·ant
vis′it·a′tion
vis′i·tor
vi′sor
vis′ta
vis′u·al
vis′u·al·i·za′tion
vis′u·al·ize
vis′u·al·ly
vi′tal
vi·tal′i·ty
vi′tal·i·za′tion
vi′tal·ize
vi′ta·min
vi′ti·ate
vi′ti·a′tion
vit′i·cul′ture
vit′re·ous
vit′ri·form
vit′ri·fi·ca′tion
vit′ri·fy
vit′ri·ol
vit′ri·ol′ic
vit′ri·os′i·ty

vi·tu′per·ate
vi·tu′per·a′tion
vi·tu′per·a′tive
vi′va
vi·va′cious
vi·vac′i·ty
viv′id·ly
viv′i·fied
viv′i·fy
vi·vip′a·rous
viv′i·sect
viv′i·sec′tion
vix′en
vi·zier′
vo′ca·ble
vo·cab′u·lar′y
vo′cal·ist
vo′cal·i·za′tion
vo′cal·ize
vo·ca′tion
voc′a·tive
vo·cif′er·ant
vo·cif′er·ate
vo·cif′er·a′tion
vo·cif′er·ous
vod′ka
vogue
voice′less
voic′ing
void′a·ble
voile
vo′lant
vol′a·tile
vol′a·til′i·ty
vol·can′ic
vol·ca′no
vo·li′tion
vol′ley·ball′
vol′plane′
volt′age
Vol·taire′
vol·tam′e·ter
vol′ta·met′ric
vol′u·bil′i·ty
vol′u·ble
vol′ume
vo·lu′mi·nous
vol′un·tar′y
vol′un·teer′
vo·lup′tu·ous
vo·lute′
vo·lu′tion
vom′it
voo′doo·ism
vo·ra′cious
greedy (*see:* veracious)
vo·rac′i·ty
vor′tex
vor′ti·cal·ly
vo′ta·ry
vot′er
vot′ing
vo′tive
vouch′er
vouch·safe′
vow′el
vox′ po′pu·li
voy′age
voy′ag·er
V-shaped
vul′can·ite
vul′can·i·za′tion
vul′can·ize
vul·gar′i·an
vul′gar·ism
vul·gar′i·ty
vul′gar·i·za′tion
vul′gar·ize
Vul′gate
vul′ner·a·bil′i·ty
vul′ner·a·ble
vul′pine
vul′ture
vul′va
vul′var
vy′ing

W

wab′ble
(also: wobble)

wack′y
wad′ded
wad′ding
wad′dle
wad′dling
wad′ing
wa′fer
waf′fle
wa′ger
wag′gish
wag′gle
wag′gling
wag′ing
wag′on
wag′on·load′
waif
Wai′ki·ki′
wail′ing
wain′scot
wain′wright′
waist′band′
waist′coat′
waist′line′
wait′er
wait′ing room
wait′ress
waive
waiv′er
give up *(see:* waver)

wake′ful
wak′en
walk′a·way′
walk′ie-talk′ie
walk′ing
walk′out′
walk′up′
wal′la·by
wall′board′
wal′let
wall′eyed′
wall′flow′er
wal′lop
wal′low
wall′pa′per
wal′nut
wal′rus
waltz
wam′pum
wan′der·ing
wan′der·lust′
wan′gle
wan′gling
wan′ing
wan′ly
want′ing
wan′ton
wap′i·ti
war′ble
war′bling
ward′en
ward′robe′
ward′room′
ware′house′
war′fare′
war′i·ly
war′like′
warm′-heart′ed
war′mon′ger
warmth
warn′ing
warp′ing
war′path′
war′rant
war′ran·tee′
war′rant·er
(also: -tor)

war′ran·ty
war′ren
war′ring
war′ri·or
War′saw
war′ship′
war′time′
war′y
wash′a·ble
wash′bowl′
wash′cloth′
washed′-out′
wash′er
wash′ing
Wash′ing·ton
wash′out′
wash′room′
wash′stand′
wash′tub′
wasp′ish
was′sail
Was′ser·mann
wast′age
waste′bas′ket
waste′ful

waste′pa′per
wast′ing
wast′rel
watch′dog′
watch′ful
watch′mak′er
watch′man
watch′tow′er
watch′word′
wa′ter·col′or
wa′ter·course′
wa′ter·fall′
wat′er lev′el
wa′ter-logged′
Wa′ter·loo
wa′ter·mark′
wa′ter·mel′on
wa′ter pow′er
wa′ter·proof′
wa′ter·shed′
wa′ter·spout′
wa′ter·tight′
wa′ter·way′
wa′ter·works′
wa′ter·y
watt′age
wat′tle
watt′me′ter
wave′let
wa′ver
hesitate (*see:* waiver)

wa′ver·ing·ly
wav′ing
wav′y
wax′en
wax′ing
wax pa′per
wax′works′
wax′y
way′bill′
way′far′er
way′laid′
way′side′
way′ward
weak′en
weak′ling
weak′-mind′ed
wealth′y
weap′on
wea′ri·ly
wear′ing
wea′ri·some
wea′ry
wea′sel
weath′er
atmospheric condition (*see:* wether; whether)

weath′er·beat′en
weath′er·man′
weath′er·proof′
weath′er·strip′
weave
weav′ing
web′bing
web′foot′ed
wed′ding
wedge′-shaped
wedg′ing
Wedg′wood
wed′lock
Wednes′day
weed′y
week′day
week′end′
wee′vil
weigh
weight
weight′y
weird′ly
wel′come
weld′er
wel′fare′
well
In general, place a hyphen between well and any other word when the combination is used as an adjective to modify a noun *(the well-balanced wheel).* After a noun, the hyphen is usually omitted *(the wheel is well balanced).*

well′-bal′anced
well′-be·haved′
well′-be′ing
well′-bred′
Wel′ling·ton
well-known′
well′-to-do′
Welsh′man
wel′ter
wel′ter·weight′
wend′ing
were′wolf′
Wes′ley·an

west′er·ly
west′ern
West′min′ster
west′ward
wet′back′
weth′er
sheep (*see:* weather; whether)
wet′ness
wet′ting
whack′ing
whale′back′
whale′boat′
whale′bone′
whal′er
whal′ing
wharf
(*plural:* wharves)
what·ev′er
what′not′
what′so·ev′er
wheal
wheat′en
whee′dle
wheel′bar′row
wheel′base′
wheel′wright′
wheeze
wheez′ing·ly
whelp
when·as′
whence
when·ev′er
when′so·ev′er
where′a·bouts′
where·as′
where·by′
where′fore
where·in′
where·of′
where′up·on′
wher·ev′er
where′with·al
wher′ry
wheth′er
if (*see:* weather; wether)
whet′stone′
whet′ting
which·ev′er
which′so·ev′er
whif′fet
whif′fle·tree′
whim′per
whim′per·ing
whim′si·cal
whim′si·cal′i·ty
whim′sy
whined
whin′ing
whin′ny
whip′cord′
whip′lash′
whip′per·snap′per
whip′pet
whip′ping
whip′poor·will′
whip′saw′
whirl′i·gig′
whirl′pool′
whirl′wind′
whirl′y·bird′
whir′ring
whisk′er
whis′key
whis′pered
whis′per·ing
whis′tle
whis′tling
white′bait′
white′cap′
white′fish′
white′-hot′
white′ly
whit′en
white′wash′
whith′er
whit′ing
whit′ish
whit′low
Whit′sun′day
whit′tle
whit′tling
who·dun′it, *Sl.*
who·ev′er
whole′heart′ed
whole′sale′
whole′some
whol′ly
whoop′ee
whoop′ing
whop′ping
whore
whorl
who′so·ev′er
wick′ed
wick′er·work′
wick′et
wide′-eyed′

wid′en
wide′spread′
widg′eon
wid′ow
wid′ow·er
width
wield′y
wie′ner
wie′ner·wurst′
wife
(*plural:* wives)

wife′ly
wig′gle
wig′gling
wig′wag′
wig′wam
wild′cat′
wil′de·beest′
wil′der·ness
wild′-eyed′
wild′fire′
wild′wood′
wil′ful
(*also:* willful)

wil′i·ness
will′ing
will′-o'-the-wisp′
wil′low
wil′low·y
wil′ly-nil′ly
Wil′ming·ton
wil′y
wim′ple
wince
winc′ing
wind′bag′
wind′break′er
wind′ed
wind′fall′
wind′ing
wind′jam′mer
wind′lass
wind′mill′
win′dow
win′dow·pane′
win′dow-shop′ping
wind′pipe′
wind′row′
wind′shield′
wind′storm′
wind′-up′
wind′ward
wind′y
win′er·y
Wine′sap′
wine′skin′
winged
wing′spread′
win′ner
win′ning
Win′ni·peg
win′now
win′some
win′ter
win′ter·green′
win′ter·time′
win′try
wip′er
wip′ing
wire′less
wire′pho′to
wir′ing
wir′y
wis′dom
wise′a′cre
wise′crack′
wise′ly
wis′est
wish′bone′
wish′ful
wish′y-wash′y
wis·te′ri·a
(*also:* wistaria)

wist′ful
witch′craft′
witch′er·y
with·al′
with·draw′
with·draw′al
with′er
with′er·ing
with′ers
with·hold′
with·in′
with·out′
with·stand′ing
wit′less
wit′ness
wit′ti·cism
wit′ty
wiz′ard
wiz′ard·ry
wiz′ened
wob′ble
(*also:* wabble)

woe′be·gone′
woe′ful
wolf
(*plural:* wolves)

wolf′hound′
wol′fram
wol′ver·ine′
(*also:* -ene)

wom′an
(*plural:* women)

wom′bat
won′al
won′der·ful
won′der·land′
won′drous
wont
(custom)

won't
(will not)

woo′er
wood
wood′chuck′
wood′cock′
wood′craft′
wood′cut′
wood′cut′ter
wood′en
wood′i·er
wood′land′
wood′peck′er
woods′y
wood′work′
wood′y
woof
wool′en
wool′gath′er·ing
wool′li·ness
wool′ly
(*also:* wooly)

Worces′ter
word′age
word′i·ly
word′ing
word′y
work′a·day′
work′book′
work′day′
work′ing
work′man·ship
work′out′
work′room′
work′shop′
world′li·ness
world′ling
world′ly
world′ly-wise′
world′-wide′
worm′-eat′en
worm′hole′
worm′wood′
worm′y
wor′ried
wor′ri·some
wor′ry
wor′ry·ing
wors′en
wor′ship
wor′ship·ing
wor′sted
wor′thi·ly
worth′while′
wor′thy
would
wound′ed
wo′ven
wrack

wraith
wran′gle
wran′gler
wran′gling
wrap′per
wrap′ping
wrath′ful
wreak
inflict *or* vent

wreath, *n.*
wreathe, *v.*
wreath′ing
wreck
destroy

wreck′age
wrench
wrest
wres′tle
wretch
unhappy person (*see:* retch)

wretch′ed
wrig′gle
wright
wring′er
wring′ing
wrin′kle
wrin′kling
wrin′kly
wrist′band′
write-off
writ′er
writhed
writh′ing
writ′ing

writ′ten
wrong′do′er
wrong′do′ing
wrong′ly
wroth
wrought
wry′ly

X

xan′tho·chroid′
xan′thous
Xa′vi·er
xe′non
xen′o·phobe′
xen′o·pho′bi·a
xe′ro·der′ma
xe·rog′ra·phy
xe′ro·phyte
Xer′ox
X′-ray′
xy-lem
xy′lo·graph′
xy′lo·phone
xy′lo·phon′ist

Y

yacht′ing
yachts′man
yak
Yang′tze′
Yan′kee
yap′ping
yard′age
yard′arm′
yard′stick′
yar′row
yawn′ing·ly
year′book′
year′ling
year′long′
year′ly
yearn′ing
yeast′y
yel′low·ish
Yel′low·stone
yelp′er
yeo′man
yes′ter·day
yes′ter·year′
Yid′dish
yield′a·ble
yield′ing
yipped
yip′ping
yo′del·er
yo′del·ing
yo′ga
Hindu philosopher
yo′gi
follower of yoga
yo′kel
Yo′ko·ha′ma
Yom Kip′pur
yon′der
Yon′kers
Yo·sem′i·te
young′ber′ry
young′ster
your·self′
(plural: -selves)
youth′ful·ly
Yo′yo
yt·ter′bi·um
Yu′ca·tan′
yuc′ca
Yu′go·slav′
(also: Jugo-)
Yu′go·sla′vi·a
Yu′kon
Yule′tide′

Z

zai·bat′su
Zam·be′zi
za′ny
Zan′zi·bar
zeal′ot
zeal′ous
ze′bra
ze′bu
ze′nith
zeph′yr
Zep′pe·lin
ze′ro
zest′ful·ly
ze′ta
Zeus
zig′zag′ging
zincked
(*also:* zinced)
zin′ni·a
Zi′on·ism
zip′per
zip′py
zir′con
zir·co′ni·um
zith′er
zo′di·ac
zom′bie
zon′al
zoned
zon′ing
zo′o·ge·og′ra·phy
zo·og′ra·pher
zo·og′ra·phy
zo′o·log′i·cal
zo·ol′o·gist
zo·ol′o·gy
zo′o·phyte
Zou·ave′
zuc·chet′to
Zu′lu
Zu′rich
zwie′back′
zy′gote
zy′mase
zy′mur·gy

GUIDE TO SPELLING

Since English is a mixture of words from many languages, there is no set of rules that will cover the spelling of all English words. However, the six basic rules given here, together with the general rules for plurals, possessives, verbs, adjectives, and adverbs, will be of great aid in learning and understanding the correct spelling of the majority of English words. Each rule is illustrated with examples, and exceptions (if any) are noted.

THE SIX BASIC RULES

Rule 1. Words ending with a silent e usually drop the e before a suffix beginning with a vowel.

Root Word		Suffix		Complete Word
survive	+	al	=	survival
divide	+	ing	=	dividing
fortune	+	ate	=	fortunate
abuse	+	ive	=	abusive

Exceptions to the rule:

a. Words containing the soft sounds of **g** or **c** retain the e before the suffixes **able** or **ous.** *Examples:* courageous, advantageous, peaceable, noticeable, changeable, manageable.

b. Retain the **e** in words that might be mistaken for another word if the rule were applied. *Examples:* singe, singeing; dye, dyeing; shoe, shoeing; canoe, canoeing.

c. Words ending in **ie** drop the **e** and change the **i** to **y** when the suffix **ing** is added. This is done to prevent two **i's** from coming together. *Examples:* die, dying; tie, tying; lie, lying.

d. In the words *mileage, acreage, lineage,* the **e** is not dropped before the suffix **age.**

Rule 2. Words ending with a silent **e** usually retain the **e** before a suffix beginning with a consonant.

Word		Suffix		Complete Word
arrange	+	ment	=	arrangement
forgive	+	ness	=	forgiveness
safe	+	ty	=	safety
shame	+	less	=	shameless

Exceptions to the rule: judge, judgment; acknowledge, acknowledgment; argue, argument; true, truly; nine, ninth; wise, wisdom; whole, wholly; awe, awful.

Rule 3. Words of *one* syllable, ending in a *single* consonant preceded by a *single* vowel, double the final consonant before a suffix beginning with a vowel.

run	+	ing	=	running
big	+	est	=	biggest
hot	+	er	=	hotter
bag	+	age	=	baggage

If the word ends with **two** or **more** consonants, or if the final consonant is preceded by **two** vowels instead of one, the rule does **not** apply.

		Two Consonants		
debt	+	or	=	debtor
yard	+	age	=	yardage
		Two Vowels		
frail	+	est	=	frailest
swear	+	ing	=	swearing

Rule 4. In words of *two* or *more* syllables that are accented on the final syllable and end in a single consonant preceded by a single vowel, double the final consonant before a suffix beginning with a vowel. If the accent is *not* on the last syllable, the final consonant is *not* doubled.

		Accent on Last Syllable		
refer	+	ing	=	referring
regret	+	able	=	regrettable

Accent Not on Last Syllable

benefit	+	ed	=	benefited
differ	+	ence	=	difference

Exception to the rule: transferable.

If the word ends in *two* consonants, if the final consonant is preceded by *two* vowels, or if the accent shifts to the *first* syllable when the suffix is added, the rule does *not* apply.

perform	+	ance	=	performance	(two consonants)
repeal	+	ing	=	repealing	(two vowels)
refer	+	ence	=	reference	(accent shifts)

Rule 5. Use of "ei" and "ie." Use **i** before **e** except when the two letters follow **c** and have a long **e** sound, or when the two vowels are pronounced long **a.**

Long e After c	Long a	Other letters
conceit	vein	shield
deceive	weight	believe
ceiling	veil	grieve
perceive	neighbor	mischievous

Exceptions to the rule:

weird	foreign	seize
either	forfeit	height
neither	sleight	surfeit
leisure	ancient	sovereign

Rule 6. Words ending in **y** preceded by a consonant usually change the **y** to **i** before any suffix except one beginning with an **i.**

beauty	+	ful	=	beautiful
lady	+	es	=	ladies
accompany	+	ment	=	accompaniment
accompany	+	ing	=	accompanying

Exceptions to the rule:

shyness	ladylike	plenteous
babyhood	beauteous	wryly

If the final **y** is preceded by a vowel, the rule does *not* apply.

journeys	obeying	essays
buys	repaying	attorneys

Note: This rule will be referred to later in the section on forming plurals.

FORMING PLURALS OF NOUNS

1. Plurals of most nouns are formed by adding **s** to the singular word.

Singular	**Plural**
bell	bells
college	colleges
pencil	pencils

2. When nouns end in **y** preceded by a consonant, the plural is formed by changing the **y** to **i** and adding **es**.

Final y preceded by a consonant	
baby	babies
century	centuries
Final y preceded by a vowel	
valley	valleys
donkey	donkeys

Note: See Rule 6 under Basic Spelling Rules.

3. When nouns end in **ch, sh, ss, s, x,** or **z,** add **es** to form the plural.

dress	dresses	church	churches
fox	foxes	dish	dishes

4. The plurals of nouns ending in **f**, **ff**, or **fe** are formed by adding **s** to the singular. However, some nouns with these endings change the **f** or **fe** to **v** and add **es**.

Add s for plural	**Change f to v and add es**
cliffs	wives
handkerchiefs	leaves
safes	selves

5. *(a)* The plurals of nouns ending in **o** preceded by a vowel usually are formed by adding **s** to the singular. Musical terms ending in **o** add **s** although the final **o** is not always preceded by a vowel.

studios	pianos
ratios	trios
portfolios	sopranos

(b) Nouns ending in **o** preceded by a consonant usually add **es** to form the plural.

mottoes	heroes
tomatoes	echoes
potatoes	Negroes

(c) Some nouns ending in **o** have two plural forms. In the following examples, the preferred plural form is given first:

mementos or mementoes
cargoes or cargos
zeros or zeroes

6. *(a)* Plurals of compound nouns are formed by adding **s** to the most important word or most essential part of the compound.

sisters-in-law	co-editors	editors-in-chief
passers-by	teaspoonfuls	cupfuls

(b) Sometimes both parts of a compound are made plural.

Example: manservant menservants

Compounds ending in **ful** form the plural by adding **s** to the end of the compound.

cupfuls spoonfuls handfuls

(c) If there is no important word in the compound, or if both words are equal in importance, make the last part of the compound plural.

scrubwomen clothesbrushes washcloths

7. Plurals of some nouns are formed either by a change in the vowel or by a change in spelling.

man	men	foot	feet
child	children	woman	women
mouse	mice	goose	geese
ox	oxen	tooth	teeth

8. Some nouns have the same form in both the singular and plural.

Examples: athletics, corps, deer, fish, moose, sheep.

9. Some nouns are plural in form but are almost always considered to be singular in usage.

Examples: economics, mathematics, news, politics.

10. Some nouns are rarely or never used in the singular.

Examples: cattle, scissors, trousers.

11. Some words derived from a foreign language retain their foreign plurals.

datum	data
alumnus	alumni (masculine)

alumna	alumnae (feminine)
analysis	analyses

12. The plurals of proper nouns are formed by adding **s** if the name does **not** end in **s**, or by adding **es** if the name ends in **s**.

The **Joneses** and the **Halls** are old college friends.

13. Titles are made plural as follows: the plural of *Miss* is *Misses;* the plural of *Mr.* is *Messrs.* (abbreviation of *Messieurs);* the word *Mrs.* has no plural. The plural of *Madam* is *Mesdames* and corresponds somewhat to a plural form for *Mrs. Miss* and *Misses* are not abbreviations and should not be followed by periods.

14. Plurals of letters, symbols, and numbers are formed by adding an apostrophe and **s** (**'s**).

Examples: A's x's 2's ?'s +'s if's

FORMING POSSESSIVES

1. If the *singular* form of the noun does not end in **s**, add the apostrophe and **s** (**'s**). If the singular ends in **s**, add the apostrophe (**'**).

Note: In the possessive singular of nouns that end in **s**, if you want the *sound* of an additional **s**, the apostrophe and **s** (**'s**) may be added.

Singular	**Possessive**
boy	boy's
child	child's
woman	woman's
Jones	Jones' (or Jones's)

2. If the *plural* does not end in **s**, add the apostrophe and **s** (**'s**). If the plural ends in **s**, add the apostrophe (**'**).

Helpful hint: Make the word plural first; then make it possessive.

Plural	**Possessive**
calves	calves'
boys	boys'
men	men's
Joneses	Joneses'

3. Possessive personal pronouns do *not* require an apostrophe.

my, mine	your, yours	he, his
it, its	we, ours	who, whose

Note: It's is a contraction of *it is* and not the possessive of *it.*

4. Possessives of indefinite pronouns are formed by adding an apostrophe and **s ('s).**

else's	someone's	everybody's

5. Possession of a compound word is shown at the *end* of the word, regardless of which part of the compound may be pluralized.

Singular	**Possessive**
mother-in-law	mother-in-law's
milkman	milkman's
Plural	**Possessive**
mothers-in-law	mothers-in-law's
milkmen	milkmen's

VERBS

1. To form the past or perfect tenses of most verbs, add **ed** to the present tense. Add **d** if the present tense ends in **e.** (For rule governing doubling of final consonant, see Basic Rule 4.)

walk—walked	love—loved
object—objected	dispose—disposed
laugh—laughed	defer—deferred

2. To form past or perfect tenses of verbs ending in **y,** change the **y** to **i** and add **ed.** (See Basic Rule 6.)

marry	married	fry	fried

3. Irregular verbs have entirely different forms in the past and perfect tenses.

fly; flew; flown — write; wrote; written
freeze; froze; frozen — take; took; taken

4. To form the participles of verbs that do not end in **e**, add **ing** to the present tense. If the present tense does end in **e**, drop the **e** and add **ing**. (See Basic Rules 1 and 2.)

talk—talking — make—making
worry—worrying — breathe—breathing
refer—referring — crave—craving

Note: An exception to this rule may be found in participial forms which can be mistaken for other verbs.

To avoid confusion, in such cases the final **e** is often retained. (See Basic Rule 1b.)

E.g.: dye—dyeing singe—singeing

5. When a verb ends in **ie**, its participle is formed by changing the **ie** to **y**, then adding **ing**. (See Basic Rule 1c.)

die—dying — belie—belying

6. Contractions are negative verbal combinations, usually formed by adding **n't** (not) to the verb.

isn't (is not) — didn't (did not)
couldn't (could not) — haven't (have not)

Some contractions are exceptions to this general rule.

can't (cannot) — won't (will not)

ADJECTIVES AND ADVERBS

1. The comparison of adjectives is usually made by adding **er** (comparative mood), or **est** (superlative mood) to the word. When an adjective ends in **y**, change to **ie**, then add the ending.

Adjective	Comparative	Superlative
large	larger	largest
quiet	quieter	quietest
heavy	heavier	heaviest

2. The use of the words *more* (comparative) and *most* (superlative) before the original adjective is never wholly incorrect, although the **er** and **est** suffixes are often preferred. In some cases, however, the use of *more* and *most* is the only permitted form.

Note: Never use both forms of comparison at the same time.

Adjective	Comparative	Superlative
beautiful	more beautiful	most beautiful
lively	more lively (or livelier)	most lively (or liveliest)

3. Some adjectives, like some verbs, are irregular.

E.g.: good—better—best bad—worse—worst.

4. Adverbs are usually formed by adding **ly** to the adjective or participle. When the adjective ends in **l,** therefore, the **l** is doubled in the adverb. When the adjective ends in **y,** change to **i,** then add **ly.**

light—lightly
laughing—laughingly
wonderful—wonderfully
merry—merrily

5. Adverbs are compared by use of *more* (comparative) and *most* (superlative) before the word itself.

Adverb	Comparative	Superlative
hugely	more hugely	most hugely
beautifully	more beautifully	most beautifully

GUIDE TO WORD DIVISION

1. Do not divide a word at the end of a line unless necessary. Good margins can usually be maintained without dividing many words. Avoid dividing at the end of the first line of writing. Do not divide the last word in a paragraph or the last word on a page.

2. When necessary to divide a word, divide it only between syllables. Even then, use the following rules.

3. A single letter syllable should not be separated from the rest of the word.

Right: abil-ity	Wrong: a-bility
Right: about (no division)	Wrong: a-bout

4. Do not divide a word before or after a two letter syllable.

Right: abil-ity	Wrong: abili-ty

5. If a final consonant is doubled before a suffix, the added consonant goes with the suffix. However, if the root word ends in a double letter, divide after the double letter.

Right: allot-ted	Wrong: allott-ed
Right: pass-ing	Wrong: pas-sing

6. Words of one syllable should never be divided.

Examples: where gnarled whoop

7. Do not divide words of five or fewer letters even if the word has more than one syllable.

Examples: idea odium uvula

PUNCTUATION MADE EASY

All punctuation marks are "signals" from the writer to the reader. A period shows that a sentence has been ended or that an abbreviation has been used. A comma may show a slight break in thought, separate the two parts of a compound sentence, or be used in one of several other ways.

Keep in mind that some sentences may be punctuated in more than one way and that, in some instances, a punctuation mark may or may not be used at the writer's discretion. The following rules and examples will help you to punctuate expertly.

USE OF THE APOSTROPHE

For rules on use of the apostrophe, see pages 257–258.

USE OF THE PERIOD

1. The period (.) is used after a declarative or an imperative sentence. (Also see Rule 5 under quotations.)

The order was shipped yesterday. (declarative)
Ship the order immediately. (imperative)

2. After courteous requests, use a period rather than a question mark.

Will you send me a copy of your latest bulletin.

3. The period is used after abbreviations and initials.

Dr. Mrs. A.M.

Note: When a sentence ends with an abbreviation, one period is sufficient for both the abbreviation and the sentence.

Mail the package to Conley and Green, Inc.

4. The period is used to indicate the omission of words in quoted passages.

(a) Repeat the period three times (. . .) to indicate the omission of words within a quoted passage.

"I pledge allegiance to the flag of the United States . . . one nation under God, indivisible, with liberty and justice for all."
—Francis Bellamy

(b) Repeat the period four times (. . . .) to indicate the omission of words at the end of a quoted passage.

"Fame is the spur. . . ."—John Milton

USE OF THE COMMA

1. The comma (,) is used after an adverbial dependent clause when the dependent clause precedes the main clause. When the dependent clause does not begin the sentence, the comma is usually unnecessary.

After the director had read the minutes of the meeting, he called for the financial report. (comma)
The director called for the financial report after he had read the minutes of the meeting. (no comma)

2. The comma is used after a participial phrase or an absolute phrase at the beginning of a sentence.

Seeing the foreman enter the plant, he quickly went to work.
The rain having stopped, we went to lunch.

3. The comma is used after an introductory infinitive phrase.

To be successful, you must read widely.

Note: When the subject of the sentence is an infinitive, do not separate the subject from the rest of the sentence.

To be successful was his goal.

4. The comma is used to set off parenthetical expressions, whether words, phrases, or clauses. (Also see Rule 1 under parentheses and Rule 1 under the dash.)

(a) Transitional words such as *however, therefore, moreover, besides, consequently* should be set off by commas.

Consequently, I did not receive an answer to his letter.

(b) Phrases such as *so to speak, in short, as a result, of course* should be set off by commas.

We found, in short, many errors in his work.
Of course, there are many ways to tackle the problem.

(c) Clauses such as *I think, we suppose, he says* should be set off by commas.

Someone, I suppose, should check the report.

(d) Explanatory expressions, such as *and I agree with him, so far as he is concerned,* etc., which break the logical sequence of words should be set off by commas.

The president disliked the policy, and I agreed with him, of letting all employees name their vacation time.

5. The comma is used after introductory expressions such as *yes, indeed, surely* (when it means *yes*), well.

Yes, I will attend to the matter.

6. The comma is used to set off a nonrestrictive clause. A nonrestrictive clause is set off because *it is not needed to complete the meaning of a sentence.* A nonrestrictive clause is similar to a parenthetical expression in that it gives added information about the word it modifies.

Restrictive clauses are never set off by commas. *A restrictive clause is a clause that is needed to complete the meaning of the sentence* because the clause identifies the word it modifies. A restrictive clause *cannot* be left out of a sentence, whereas a nonrestrictive clause can be.

The girl who lives next door came to work in our office. (The clause *who lives next door* is restrictive because it is needed to identify the word *girl.* The clause is not set off by commas.)

Mary Jones, who lives next door, came to work in our office. (The clause *who lives next door* is nonrestrictive because it is not needed to identify the name *Mary Jones.* The name *Mary Jones* clearly identifies the person being talked about, and the clause merely gives added information about the person *Mary Jones.*)

7. The comma is used to set off words in apposition. An appositive is a word or phrase that defines or identifies another word. An appositive means the same as the word it defines.

Jones, our office manager, is ill.
Robert Brown, our sales manager, is a capable man.

8. The comma is used to set off words used in direct address.

We regret, Mr. Thomas, that your order was unsatisfactorily filled.

9. The comma is used to separate a series of three or more words, phrases, or clauses.

She asked for paper, pencils, and a ruler.
He stalked off the stage, turned around, came back, and glared at the audience.
At the meeting it was decided to (1) give two weeks' vacation with pay, (2) give pensions at age sixty-five, (3) establish a profit-sharing plan.

10. The comma is used to separate coordinate adjectives which modify the same noun. Adjectives are coordinate if the word *and* can be used between them.

The efficient, business-like secretary received an increase in pay. (Comma—the efficient *and* business-like secretary. Both adjectives modify *secretary.*)
The five silver spoons were very expensive. (No comma. You would not say *five and silver spoons.*)

11. The comma is used in a compound sentence to separate independent clauses joined by one of the coordinate conjunctions *and, but, for, or, nor,* and *while* when it means the same as *but.*

I dictated the letter as you ordered, but she did not transcribe it correctly.
Minneapolis is a large industrial center, and it has many cultural attractions.

(a) If the clauses of a compound sentence are very short and closely connected, the comma may be omitted.

He looked but he did not see her.

(b) Do not use a comma between two independent clauses unless a coordinate conjunction is used. The use of a comma without a coordinate conjunction between two independent clauses is called the *comma fault.* The following sentence illustrates the comma fault:

The men in the shipping department will not follow instructions, they repeatedly make serious errors. (Incorrect—comma should not be used without a coordinate conjunction.)

Note 1: The comma fault may be eliminated by punctuating the sentence in one of the three following ways:
(a) Use a coordinate conjunction after the comma:

The men in the shipping department will not follow instructions, and they repeatedly make serious errors. (correct)

(b) Use a semicolon between the two independent clauses:

The men in the shipping department will not follow instructions; they repeatedly make serious errors. (Correct—see Rule 1 under semicolons.)

(c) Punctuate the two independent clauses as two simple sentences:

The men in the shipping department will not follow instructions. They repeatedly make serious errors. (correct)

Note 2: When the independent clauses of a compound sentence are very long or have *internal punctuation,* a semicolon is generally used before the coordinate conjunction. Internal punctuation means that there are commas within one or both of the independent clauses.

The men in the shipping department will not follow instructions; and, as a result, they repeatedly make serious errors.

12. The comma is used to set off words or phrases expressing contrast.

I asked you to file the contract, not destroy it.
You may be excused from the conference this time, but never again.

13. The comma is used to set off a definite place, month or year.

The president was born April 8, 1872, at 1224 Elm Street, Cleveland, Ohio.

14. The comma is used to set off a short direct quotation. (See Rule 4 under Quotations.)

The director asked, "How many of you are in favor of this change in policy?"

15. The comma is used to separate a declarative clause and an interrogative clause which immediately follows.

The plane will arrive on time, will it not?
Jack is to get a promotion, isn't he?

16. The comma is used to separate a phrase from the rest of the sentence when the phrase is inverted or out of its natural order.

Like you, I think the policy is a worthwhile one.
In spite of his promise, he was late to work again.

17. The comma is used to indicate the omission of a word.

Fishing forms a quiet man; hunting, an eager man; racing, a greedy man.

18. The comma is used to set off a proper name when followed by an academic degree or honorary title. The comma is used to separate two or more degrees or titles.

Philip F. Adams, A.B., M.A., Ph.D., lecturer in English.

19. The comma is used to point off the thousands in figures of four digits or more.

1,117   20,718   1,817,000

20. The comma is used to separate two sets of figures or two identical words.

As I told you, you should write immediately.
Send me 10, No. 1234 and 7, No. 138.
Since 1933, 12,000 new machines have been sold.

USE OF THE SEMICOLON

The semicolon (;) is used to show a stronger separation between the parts of a sentence than does a comma. In most writing, however, the use of the semicolon should be avoided because it is generally too stiff and formal. If you use a great many semicolons, the chances are that you are either using them incorrectly, or you are writing sentences that are too long. Semicolons produce rather involved sentence patterns. Use them sparingly.

1. The semicolon is used to separate independent coordinate clauses closely connected in meaning when no coordinate conjunction is used. (See Rule 11 under commas.)

The sales staff meets every other Tuesday; the production staff meets only once a month.

He would not approve the art layout as presented; he suggested several drastic changes.

2. The semicolon is used between coordinate clauses of a compound sentence when they are joined by transitional words and phrases.

The members of the board of directors approved the change in distribution; consequently, you should appeal to them.

Following is a list of the most commonly used transitional words:

accordingly	indeed	as a result
consequently	moreover	for example
finally	namely	for this reason
furthermore	nevertheless	in fact
however	therefore	that is
yet	thus	in addition

3. The semicolon is used before a coordinate conjunction (**and, but, for, or, nor**) between two independent clauses when either one or both have internal punctuation. (See Rule 11 under commas.)

The president, a well-read man, predicted a cost of living increase for the first of the year; but his prediction, which spread throughout the plant, proved to be wrong.

4. The semicolon is used before such words as *for example, for instance, that is,* and *namely* that introduce an example, enumeration, or a list in a sentence. A comma is placed after such words.

These special artist's pencils are available in three colors; namely, red, green, and blue.

5. The semicolon is used in lists where a comma is insufficient to separate the members clearly.

Guests at the convention were Mr. Leonard Key, the past president of the corporation; Mrs. F. K. Small, the wife of the founder; and Mr. Paul Wells, the speaker of the evening.

USE OF THE COLON

The colon (:) indicates the strongest possible break within a sentence.

1. The colon is used before a list of items or details.

Please send out the following items: No. 378, No. 315, No. 519, and No. 570.

His actions were as follows: He went to the drugstore, purchased a hypodermic needle, got into his car, and drove away.

Note 1: Capitalize the first letter of each item in a list when the list is in column form.

You should know how to use the following office machines:

1. Typewriter
2. Duplicator
3. Dictaphone

Note 2: Do not capitalize the first letter of each item in a list when the items are included in a sentence.

You should know how to use the following office machines: typewriter, duplicator, and dictaphone.

2. The colon is used before an appositive phrase or clause.

Our company has always had this policy: The customer is always right.

3. The colon is used after the salutation of a business letter.

Dear Mr. Roe: Gentlemen:

Note: Never use a semicolon after a salutation. A comma may be used after the salutation of a friendly or informal letter. Some modern writers do not use any punctuation after the salutation.

Dear Jane,   Dear Father,

4. The colon is used to divide the parts of references, titles, formulas, and numerals.

The meeting will be held at 9:15 P.M.
He quoted from Chapter XII: Section 19.

USE OF PARENTHESES

1. Parentheses ( ) are used to set off words, phrases, clauses, or sentences which are used by way of explanation, translation, or comment. (Also see Rule 4 under commas and Rule 1 under the dash.)

His appointment (which will be announced next week) will be a surprise to many.
The motto read as follows: *"De gustibus non disputandum est."* (In matters of taste there is no dispute.)

2. Parentheses are used to enclose a number, letter, or symbol when used as an appositive.

She ordered twelve (12) night stands for the hotel.

Note 1: When using parentheses with other punctuation marks, punctuate the main part of the sentence as if the parenthetical portion were not there. A punctuation mark comes after the second parenthesis if the punctuation mark applies to the whole sentence and not just to the parenthetical portion.

He analyzed and presented standards of evaluation (business and technical), but his analysis proved nothing.

Note 2: Place the punctuation mark inside the second parenthesis if the punctuation mark applies only to material within the parenthetical portion.

A simplified fire-fighting plan will help you.
(See the back cover of this brochure.)

USE OF THE DASH

The dash (—) is used to indicate an abrupt change of ideas, but should be used sparingly. At times, the dash may be used for visual effect or emphasis in place of commas or parentheses. (See Rule 4 under commas and Rule 1 under parentheses.)

1. The dash may be used to indicate a sudden change of thought in a sentence.

I am certain that the manager—indeed, all of the office force —expected John would receive the promotion.

2. The dash may be used to indicate a summarizing thought or an afterthought added to the end of the sentence.

I shall make an estimate, draw up a contract, send samples of material—in fact, give you every help I can.

3. The dash may be used to set off a word or phrase repeated for emphasis.

We invited them for one meeting—one meeting only—not for the entire convention!

USE OF THE QUESTION MARK

1. The question mark (?) is used after all interrogative sentences that ask direct questions.

Where are the current files?
Are you going to the next meeting of the club?

Note: After courteous requests, use a period instead of a question mark. (See Rule 2 under periods.)

2. The question mark may be used after each separate part of a sentence containing more than one question.

Can we be sure of his willingness? his capability? his honesty?

Note: If the question is not complete until the end of the sentence, place a question mark at the end only.

Will delivery be made today, tomorrow, or Friday?

3. The question mark is used in several ways when only part of the sentence is a question. In such sentences the question is generally introduced by a comma or colon; a semicolon or dash may also be used.

May I ask, what is his purpose?
This is our problem: What should be done to prevent further damage?

USE OF THE EXCLAMATION MARK

1. The exclamation mark (!) is used after all exclamatory sentences—sentences that express surprise, emotion, or deep feeling.

Your answer was hard to believe!

2. The exclamation mark is used after interjections or after statements which are commands or which imply need for immediate action.

Hurry! Send your order now!
Return the card today! Don't delay!

3. The exclamation point is used after an interrogative sentence that is exclamatory in form or intended to be exclamatory.

Oh, how could he say that!
But can he be trusted!

4. The exclamation point is sometimes used to add emphasis.

Realize what this means!
This offer absolutely expires April 6!

QUOTATIONS

1. Quotation marks (" ") are used to enclose a direct quotation. Each part of an interrupted quotation begins and ends with quotation marks.

The inspector said, "Well, your case is not hopeless."
"Where," he asked, "are you going to keep it?"
"What will we do?" he asked. "Where can we raise the money?"

Note: Capitalize the first word of a direct quotation. Do not capitalize the first word in the second part of an interrupted quotation unless the second part begins a new sentence. Do not use quotation marks or capital letters in an indirect quotation.

The inspector said that your case is not hopeless. (Many indirect quotations are introduced by the word *that.*)
He asked where we would keep it.

2. Quotation marks are used to enclose the titles of magazine articles, chapters of books, names of songs, titles of poems, and other titles. In typing or writing, underline the titles of books, magazines, operas, and any other works of art long enough to appear in book form. Underlining signifies italics for printing.

<u>The New Yorker</u> includes a section entitled "The Talk of the Town."
"Rabbi Ben Ezra" is one of my favorite poems.

3. Quotation marks are used to set off words, phrases, or sentences referred to within a sentence.

The word "hospitable" is frequently mispronounced.

4. If several paragraphs are quoted, use quotation marks at the beginning of each paragraph, but at the end of the last paragraph only. Long quotations are usually introduced by a colon instead of a comma. (See Rule 14 under commas.) Quotations of three or more lines are usually indented and set apart from the body of the text.

5. Use of quotation marks with other punctuation:

(a) The period and comma are always placed before ending quotation marks.

He said, "They are not here."
"They are not here," he said.

(b) The question mark and exclamation point are placed before quotation marks when they refer to the quoted material, or after when they refer to the entire sentence.

She asked, "When are you going to be promoted?"
Did she say, "You are to be promoted next month"?

(c) The semicolon and colon follow ending quotation marks unless they are part of the quoted matter.

She said, "You are to be promoted next month"; consequently, I expected to be promoted.

GUIDE TO CAPITALIZATION

GENERAL RULES FOR SENTENCES

1. **Sentence.** Capitalize the first word of a sentence or of an expression that stands for a sentence.

Our tests are now complete. Tomorrow we start production.
Withdraw our proposal? Never!

2. **Questions Within a Sentence.** Direct questions within a sentence may or may not be capitalized as desired by the writer, but usually are.

The question is, will they deliver on time?
The question is, Will they deliver on time?

3. **Words After a Semicolon.** Do not capitalize a word following a semicolon.

You promised prompt delivery; deliver the material now.

4. **Words After a Colon.** (a) Capitalize the first word after a colon when it introduces a complete sentence having independent meaning, such as in summaries or in quotations.

Finally, let me say: You will achieve your quota if . . .
His plan is: Write to the manager and then . . .
He replied: "We will never accept your terms."

(b) When the word does not begin a complete sentence, do not capitalize it. (Also see Rule 6, page 277.)

Each office unit will include the following: a desk, a chair, a typewriter, and two file cabinets.

5. **Quotations.** (a) Capitalize the first word of a direct quotation that is a complete sentence except when it is introduced indirectly.

The supervisor said, "You must increase production."
The supervisor said *that* "you must increase production."

(b) Do not capitalize a quotation resumed within a sentence or a quotation that is only a partial sentence.

"Speed," she replied, "is essential on this job."
Your co-operation is, as he said, "absolutely necessary."

6. **Listings or Enumerations.** (a) Capitalize the first word of each item in an enumeration that has been introduced in formal sentence style. Punctuate each item as a sentence.

He gave three reasons for the delay: (1) Bad weather held up delivery of raw materials. (2) Poor scheduling created confusion and slow-downs. (3) Lack of proper machine maintenance caused equipment failure.

(b) Do not capitalize if the introduction is indirect or not in sentence style. Use semicolons between items.

He stated *that* (1) bad weather held up delivery of raw materials; (2) poor scheduling created confusion and slow-downs; (3) lack of proper machine maintenance caused equipment failure.

(c) Do not capitalize brief items which do not make complete sentences. Use commas between items.

Three reasons for the delay were given: (1) bad weather, (2) poor scheduling, and (3) lack of machine maintenance.

(d) Capitalize items placed in list form.

The reasons for the delay are as follows:
(1) Bad weather
(2) Poor scheduling
(3) Lack of machine maintenance

RULES FOR PROPER NOUNS AND ADJECTIVES

1. Capitalize the proper name of persons, places, and their derivatives.

Mr. Smith	Great Britain	British
Helen Thomas	Chicago	Chicagoan

2. Capitalize *geographic names:* continents, countries, states, cities, rivers, mountains, lakes, falls, harbors, valleys, bays, etc.

Montana	Rocky Mountains	New York Harbor
The Hague	Victoria Falls	Gulf of Mexico

3. Capitalize names of *definite regions, localities,* and *political divisions.*

Wheeling Township	First Ward (of a city)
the Wheat Belt	the Dominion (Canada)
the Arctic Circle	the Republic (U.S.)
United Kingdom	French Republic

4. Capitalize names of *bridges, buildings, monuments, parks, ships, automobiles, hotels, forts, dams, railroads, streets,* etc.

Statue of Liberty	Fort Knox
Michigan Avenue	the White House
Fine Arts Building	Alton Railroad

5. Capitalize names of historic *events, periods,* and *documents.*

the Civil War	Fourteenth Amendment
World War II	Battle of Gettysburg
Atlantic Charter	Louisiana Purchase

6. Capitalize names of *government units.*

the Federal Government	United States Senate
the President's Cabinet	Eighty-third Congress
Bureau of Mines	Civil Service Commission

7. Capitalize names of *political parties, business* and *fraternal organizations, clubs* and *societies, companies,* and *institutions.*

Republicans	Democratic Party
Gold Star Mothers	Northwestern University
Ford Motor Company	a Shriner

8. Capitalize *titles of rank* when they are joined to a person's name.

President Johnson	Cardinal Spellman
His Honor Mayor Harris	Professor R. T. Clark

9. Capitalize *days of the week, months of the year, holidays,* and *days of special observance,* including *feast and fast days.*

Easter Sunday	Lincoln's Birthday
Veterans Day	Mother's Day
Ash Wednesday	Good Friday

10. Do not capitalize the *names of the seasons* unless they are personified. When something is personified it is represented or considered as if it were a person. Personification is often used in poetry.

spring	winter
Spring's warm touch	Winter's icy breath

11. The words *north, east, south,* and *west* are capitalized when they refer to *sections of the country.* These words are not capitalized when they refer to directions.

the Midwest	The sun rises in the east.
the Near East	The colonists moved westward.

12. Capitalize the proper names of *stars* and *planets.*

Milky Way	Scientists have discovered a new star.
Jupiter	A planet shines by reflected light.

13. Capitalize proper adjectives derived from proper nouns. If a word has acquired a special meaning, it is no longer considered a proper adjective and is not capitalized.

Capitalized	**Not Capitalized**
a Pullman car	navy blue
Manila hemp	chinaware
English tweeds	morocco leather

14. Capitalize the principal words in *titles* of books, magazines, pictures, songs, articles, etc. Prepositions, conjunctions, and the articles *a, an,* and *the* are not capitalized unless the title begins with one of these words.

The Last of the Mohicans (book)	Battle Hymn of the Republic (song)
The Angelus (picture)	The Saturday Evening Post (magazine)

15. Capitalize the definite article *the* only when it is the first word of a title. Many titles do not begin with *the.* The only way to be sure about the correct form of a title is to check the official form, or the form adopted by the company, publication, etc.

The Christian Science Monitor
The John C. Winston Company
the National Geographic Magazine
the Pinnacle Oil Company

16. Capitalize all words referring to the *Deity,* the *Bible, books of the Bible,* and other *sacred books.*

God, the Father	Talmud	Supreme Being
the Trinity	Bible	Book of Job

17. Capitalize the pronoun *I* and the interjection *O.* The word *oh* is capitalized only when it is the first word of a sentence.

"O say! Can you see, by the dawn's early light, . . ."
"Tis the Star-Spangled Banner, oh, long may it wave . . ."

18. Capitalize the names of *school subjects* only when they are names of languages. Subjects listed in school catalogs as names of specific courses are capitalized.

economics	Economics 101
mathematics	Advanced Chemistry II
English	Physics II

19. Capitalize words which show family relationships when they are used with a person's name. The words *father* and *mother* are not capitalized when they are preceded by a pronoun. When used without a pronoun and to refer to one's own parent, capitalization is optional.

Aunt Martha	Yesterday, my father arrived.
Sister Sue	Frank went with Mother (or mother).

20. Capitalize the first word in a *compound word* if it is a proper noun. If the second word is a proper noun, it also should be capitalized.

Eighty-third Congress	Forty-second Street
Army-Navy game	un-American activities

21. Capitalize both parts of *compound titles of distinction.*

Chief Justice Hughes	ex-President Hoover
The Honorable John Wills	Vice-President Nixon

22. The names of special departments of business firms may be written with small or capital letters. Titles, such as *President, Office Manager,* etc., also may be capitalized or not. Follow the form preferred by your company or organization.

claim department *or* Claim Department
The Company (or company) will reimburse you for your loss.
Our President (or president) will grant you an interview.

23. Capitalize trade names or registered trademarks.

Vaseline	Snow Crop
Xerox	Birdseye

RULES FOR ABBREVIATIONS

Rules for use of abbreviations that will apply to all situations cannot be given. However, the following general rules may be used as a guide.

1. **Use in Business Writing.** Abbreviations should generally be avoided, except for such abbreviations as *Mr., Mrs., Co., Inc., lbs., No., COD,* etc., which are customarily used and easily recognized.

2. **Titles.** (a) Titles, such as *Mr., Mrs., Dr.,* and *Prof.,* may be abbreviated when they appear with the full proper name following. However, a word such as *doctor* should not be abbreviated when it appears in a sentence without a proper name.

(b) Titles, such as *governor, senator, reverend, doctor, professor,* etc., normally should not be abbreviated when they appear with the last name alone, such as *Governor Jones.*

(c) Academic titles may be abbreviated after a proper name: *Robert E. Johnson, Ph.D.*

3. **Dates, Units of Measurement.** (a) In letterwriting, the names of months should be spelled in full. However, in informal writing (invoices, tables, etc.), the month may be abbreviated. In letterwriting, commonly used units of measurement that are accompanied by figures may be abbreviated, such as 36 *lbs.* In invoices, tables, and statistical work, such abbreviations would normally be used and usually without the period.

4. **Abbreviation of Addresses and Names.** In addresses, it is good practice not to abbreviate words such as *Street, Avenue,* or the name of the State. Some firms do permit such abbreviations. Abbreviations such as *Inc.* and *Co.* should be used only if the company being addressed abbreviates such words on its letterhead.

5. **Government Agencies and Departments.** (a) *United States* should not be abbreviated unless it precedes the word *Government* or the name of some Government department or agency.

(b) The abbreviations for Government agencies generally are written without periods: *FBI, FTC, HEW.*

6. **Plurals of Abbreviations.** (a) The plural in many abbreviations is formed by adding *s:* gallons—*gals.;* pounds—*lbs.*

(b) The plural of some abbreviations is formed by doubling the single form: *p.* (page)—*pp.* (pages).

(c) For units of measurement the abbreviation often is the same for both the singular and the plural: *mi.* (mile—miles); *oz.* (ounce —ounces).

(d) For some abbreviations the use of *'s* is preferred to the use of *s* alone: *CPA's COD's; B/L's.*

7. **Use of Periods.** In statistical tables, tabulations, catalogs, invoices, etc., periods usually are omitted, particularly for units of measurement. In letterwriting or other general writing, periods should be used for each part of an abbreviation that represents a single word except where a slash sign is used: b.l. or B/L.

On the following pages standard forms for the most common and important abbreviations are given. The forms given are widely accepted for common usage. However, in case of question, follow the form used in your field of work or in accordance with the custom of your company.

LIST OF ABBREVIATIONS

STATES AND TERRITORIES

	ZIP 2-Letter	Regular		ZIP 2-Letter	Regular
Alabama	AL	Ala.	Missouri	MO	Mo.
Alaska	AK	*Alas.	Montana	MT	Mont.
Arizona	AZ	Ariz.	Nebraska	NE	Nebr.
Arkansas	AR	Ark.	Nevada	NV	Nev.
California	CA	Calif.	New Hampshire	NH	N.H.
Canal Zone	CZ	C.Z.	New Jersey	NJ	N.J.
Colorado	CO	Colo.	New Mexico	NM	N. Mex.
Connecticut	CT	Conn.	New York	NY	N.Y.
Delaware	DE	Del.	North Carolina	NC	N.C.
District of Columbia	DC	D.C.	North Dakota	ND	N. Dak.
			Ohio	OH	*O.
Florida	FL	Fla.	Oklahoma	OK	Okla.
Georgia	GA	Ga.	Oregon	OR	Ore.
Guam	GU	**	Pennsylvania	PA	Penna.
Hawaii	HI	**	Puerto Rico	PR	P.R.
Idaho	ID	*Ida.	Rhode Island	RI	R.I.
Illinois	IL	Ill.	South Carolina	SC	S.C.
Indiana	IN	Ind.	South Dakota	SD	S. Dak.
Iowa	IA	*Ia.	Tennessee	TN	Tenn.
Kansas	KS	Kans.	Texas	TX	*Tex.
Kentucky	KY	Ky.	Utah	UT	**
Louisiana	LA	La.	Vermont	VT	Vt.
Maine	ME	*Me.	Virginia	VA	Va.
Maryland	MD	Md.	Virgin Islands	VI	V.I.
Massachusetts	MA	Mass.	Washington	WA	Wash.
Michigan	MI	Mich.	West Virginia	WV	W. Va.
Minnesota	MN	Minn.	Wisconsin	WI	Wis.
Mississippi	MS	Miss.	Wyoming	WY	Wyo.

* Avoid abbreviating   ** No regular abbreviation

Note: The 2-letter abbreviation without periods is authorized by the U.S. Post Office for use only with ZIP code.

CANADIAN PROVINCES

Alberta	AB	Nova Scotia	NS
British Columbia	BC	Ontario	ON
Labrador	LB	Prince Edward Island	PE
Manitoba	MB	Quebec	PQ
New Brunswick	NB	Saskatchewan	SK
Newfoundland	NF	Yukon Territory	YT
Northwest Territories	NT		

MONTHS OF THE YEAR

January	Jan.	July	*Jul. or Jy.
February	Feb.	August	Aug.
March	Mar.	September	Sep. or Sept.
April	Apr.	October	Oct.
May	*My.	November	Nov.
June	*Jun. or Je.	December	Dec.

*Avoid abbreviating

DAYS OF THE WEEK

Sunday	Sun. or S.	Thursday	Thurs. or Th.
Monday	Mon. or M.	Friday	Fri. or F.
Tuesday	Tues. or Tu.	Saturday	Sat. or Sa.
Wednesday	Wed. or W.		

Avoid use of the short abbreviation

U.S. MILITARY ABBREVIATIONS

AAF, Army airfield
Adj, adjutant
ADM, Admiral; Admiralty
AFB, air force base
AIC, airman, first class
AG, Adjutant General
AHQ, Army headquarters
AMG, Allied Military Government
ANC, Army Nurse Corps
APO, Army Post Office
AR, Army regulation
ASN, Army service number
AUS, Army of the United States
AWOL, absent without leave

BG, Brigadier General

CAPT, Captain, (Navy)
CDR, Commander, (Navy)
CG, Coast Guard; Commanding General
CH, Chaplain
CINC, Commander in Chief
CMC, Commandant of the Marine Corps
Cmdr, Commander, (Army)
CO, Commanding Officer
COL, Colonel
Comdt, Commandant
CPL, corporal
CPO, chief petty officer
CPT, Captain (Army)
CWO, Chief Warrant Officer
CW2, Chief Warrant Officer, W-2

DA, Department of the Army
DD, dishonorable discharge
DN, Department of the Navy
DOD, Department of Defense

ENS, Ensign

1LT, First Lieutenant
1Sg, first sergeant
FAdm, Fleet Admiral
FPO, Fleet Post Office

GA, General of the Army
GCM, general court martial
GEN, General
GFI, Government free issue
GHQ, general headquarters
GI, general issue; Government issue

HD, honorable discharge
HG, headquarters

IG, Inspector General
inf, infantry

JAG, Judge Advocate General

LCdr, Lieutenant Commander
LT, Lieutenant
LTC, Lieutenant Colonel
LTjg, Lieutenant (junior grade)

MAJ, Major
MG, Major General
mil, military
MOS, military occupational specialty
MP, military police
MSG, master sergeant

nav, naval; navigate
NCO, noncommissioned officer
NG, National Guard
NR, Navy regulation

OCS, officer candidate school
OD, officer of the day
OG, officer of the guard

OPNAV, Office of the Chief of Naval Operations
OSA, Office of the Secretary of the Army
OSD, Office of the Secretary of Defense

PFC, private, first class
PG, permanent grade
PM, Provost Marshal

PO, petty officer
POW, PW, prisoner of war
PSG, platoon sergeant
PVT, private
PX, post exchange

QM, quartermaster

RAdm, Rear Admiral
ROTC, Reserve Officers' Training Corps
RG, reserve grade

S1c, seaman, first class
2LT, Second Lieutenant
SECDEF, Secretary of Defense
SECNAV, Secretary of the Navy
SFC, sergeant, first class
SGT, sergeant
SL, squad leader
SN, service number
SP, shore patrol; shore police
Sp4, specialist 4
SPAR, Coast Guard Women's Reserve
SR, service record
SSG, staff sergeant
SSS, Selective Service System
SG, Surgeon General

UMTS, Universal Military Training Service (or System)
USA, U.S. Army
U.S.A., United States of America
USAF, U.S. Air Force
USCG, U.S. Coast Guard
USGLI, U.S. Government Life Insurance
USMC, U.S. Marine Corps
USN, U.S. Navy
USNR, U.S. Naval Reserve
U.S.S., United States Senate; United States ship

VAdm, Vice Admiral

WAC, Women's Army Corps; a Wac
WAF, Women in the Air Force; a Waf
WAVES, women accepted for volunteer emergency service; women in the U.S. Navy; a Wave
WO, warrant officer

GENERAL ABBREVIATIONS

a, acre; ampere; are (Metric System); arteria; artillery
A., Absolute (temperature); angstrom unit; acre
AA, antiaircraft; Alcoholics Anonymous; Associate in Arts
AAA, antiaircraft artillery; Automobile Association of America
AAAS, American Association for the Advancement of Science
AAS, Associate in Applied Science

A.B., B.A., Bachelor of Arts
ABA, American Bankers Association
abbr., abbrev., abbreviated; -tion
ABC, atomic, biological, and chemical; Audit Bureau of Circulation; American Broadcasting Company
abr., abridged; abridgment
abs., absolute; abstract
ABS, American Bible Society; American Bureau of Shipping
abst., abstr., abstract; -ed
AC, ac, alternating current; author's change
A/C, a/c, ac., acct., account
acad., academic; academy
acct., account
accts. pay., AP, accounts payable
accts. rec., AR, accounts receivable
ack., ackgt., acknowledgment
ACS, American Chemical Society
ACTH, adrenocorticotropic hormone
acpt., acceptance
a.d., after date
A.D. (anno Domini), in the year of our Lord; average deviation
ADA, American Dental Association
adj., adjective; adjourned; adjunct; adjustment
ad lib. (ad libitum), freely
ad loc. (ad locum), to, or at, the place
adm., administrative
adm., admr., adms., admstr., administrator
admix., admrx., admx., administratrix
adv., advtg., ad, advertising
adv., adverb; advice
ad val. (ad valorem), according to value
A.E., Agricultural Engineer
A-E, architect-engineer
AEC, Atomic Energy Commission
AESC, American Engineering Standards Committee
afft., affidavit
AF, af, audio frequency
AFL-CIO, A.F. of L.-CIO, American Federation of Labor and Congress of Industrial Organizations
A.G., Adjutant General; Accountant General; Attorney General; Agent General
agcy., agency
agr., agric., agricultural; -ture
agt., agent; agreement
a-h, amp-hr, ampere-hour
AIB, American Institute of Banking
AIChE, American Institute of Chemical Engineers
AID, Agency for International Development
AIEE, American Institute of Electrical Engineers
Al, alum., aluminum; aluminium
ALA, American Library Association
Ald., Alderman
ALR, American Law Reports
alt., alternate; alternating; alternations; altitude; alto
Am., am., ammeter
Am., Amer., America; American
AM, amplitude modulation
A.M. (anno mundi), in the year of the world
A.M., a.m. (ante meridiem), before noon
A.M., M.A., Master of Arts
AMA, American Medical Association; American Management Association
Amb., Ambassador

amdt., amendment
AMG, Allied Military Government
amp, amperage; ampere
amp-hr, a-h, ampere-hour
amt., amount
AMVETS, American Veterans of World War II
a.n., arrival notice
anal., analogous; analogy; analysis; analytic
analyt., analytical
anat., anatomy; -ical; -ist
antilog, antilogarithm
ann., annals; annual; annuity
annot., annotated; annotator
anon., anonymous
ans., answer; answered
ant., antiq., antiquarian; -quities
ant., antonym
anthrop., anthropol., anthropological; anthropology
AOA, American Osteopathic Assn.
AP, Associated Press
AP, A/P, ap, accounts payable
app., apps., appendix; appendixes
App. Div., Appellate Division
approx., approximate; -ly
appt., appoint; appointment
apt., apartment
AR, A/R, ar, accounts receivable
ARC, American Red Cross
arch., archit., architect; -tural
archeol., archeology
arith., arithmetic; arithmetical
ARPA, Advanced Research Projects Agency
arr., arranged; -ments; arrival
ASA, American Statistical Association; Acoustical Society of America; American Standards Association
ASAP, as soon as possible
ASCE, American Society of Civil Engineers
asgd., assigned
ASME, American Society of Mechanical Engineers
assn., ass'n, association
assoc., associate; association
asst., assistant
Atl., Atlantic
A.s.t., Atlantic standard time
ASTM, American Society for Testing Materials
astron., astronomer; astronomy
atm. press., atmosphere pressure
att., atty., attorney at law
attn., attention
at. no., atomic number
at. vol., atomic volume
at. wt., atomic weight
auth., author; authentic; authorized
auto., automatic; automotive
av., average; avoirdupois
Av., Ave., Avenue
advp., avoir., avoirdupois
avg., average

b, born
B, Bé, Baumé
B/B, bank balance
bal., balance
bbl, barrel
B.C., before Christ
BCG (bacillus Calmette-Guérin), antituberculosis vaccine
bd., band; board; bond; bound
bd ft, board foot
bdl., bundle
BDSA, Business and Defense Services Administration
BE, B/E, be, bill of exchange
BEC, Bureau of Employees' Compensation
BEV, bev, billion electron volts
bf, boldface

bg, bgs, bag; bags
bhp, brake horsepower
Bib., Bible; Biblical
bibliog., bibliography; -er; -ical
biog., biography; -er; -ical
biol., biology; -ical; -ist
BIS, Bank for International Settlements
bk., bank; block; book
bkg., banking
BL, B/L, bl, bill of lading
bldg., building
B.Litt., Littl.B., Bachelor of Literature
blk., black; block
BLS, Bureau of Labor Statistics
Blvd., Boulevard
bm, board measure
BO, B/O, bo, buyer's option
bot., botany; -ical; -ist
bp, boiling point
BP, B/P, bp, bills payable
bpd, barrels per day
BR, B/R, br, bills receivable
Bros., Brothers
B.S., B. Sc., Bachelor of Science
BS, B/S, bs, bill of sale
Btu, British thermal units
bu, bushel
bur., bureau
bull., bulletin
Bus. Mgr., Business Manager
bx, box

c, curie; cycle; circa
c., ct., cent
C., Celsius (centigrade)
C., Centigrade; hundred
©, copyright
ca. (circa), about; centare
CAA, Civil Aeronautics Administration
CAF, caf, cost and freight
cal., Calories
c and sc, capitals and small capitals (letters)
cap., capital
CAP, Civil Air Patrol
CARE, Cooperative for American Remittances to Europe
cat., catalog
cbd, cash before delivery
CBS, Columbia Broadcasting System
cc, cubic centimeter
CC, C/C, cc, carbon copy
CCA, Circuit Court of Appeals
CCC, Commodity Credit Corporation
C. Cls., Court of Claims
CCPA, Court of Customs and Patent Appeals
CCR, Commission on Civil Rights
CD, Civil Defense
cd-ft, cord-foot
CE, Civil Engineer; Chemical Engineer
CEA, Council of Economic Advisers
CED, Committee for Economic Development
cent., centigrade; century
cf., compare
CFI, cfi, cost, freight, and insurance
cfm, cubic feet per minute
CFR Supp., Code of Federal Regulations Supplement
cfs, cubic feet per second
cg, centigram; center of gravity
CGS, cgs, centimeter-gram-second
c-h, candle-hour
ch., chap., chapter
chem., chemical; chemist; chemistry
chg., change; charge
chgd., charged
chm., chmn., chairman
CIA, Central Intelligence Agency

CIC, Counterintelligence Corps
CIF, cif, cost, insurance, and freight
cit., citation; cited; citizen
C.J. (corpus juris), body of law; Chief Justice
ck., cask; check
cl, carload; centiliter
CLU, Chartered Life Underwriter
cm, centimeter; circular mil (wire measure)
cml., coml., commercial
C/O, c/o, care of; carried over
Co., Company
COD, cod, cash on delivery
col., column; colonel
com., comm., commentary; commerce; commission; committee; commonwealth
conelrad, control of electromagnetic radiation (civil defense)
cons., consolidated; consonant; consul
cont., cont'd, continued
contr., contract
co-op., co-operative
cop., ©, copyright
Corp., Corporation
cos, cosine
cosec, cosecant
cosh, hyperbolic cosine
cot, cotangent
coth, hyperbolic cotangent
cp, chemically pure; candlepower
CPA, Certified Public Accountant
CPI, Consumer Price Index
cpm, cycles per minute
cps, cycles per second
cr., credit; creditor
cs., case; cases
CSS, Commodity Stabilization Service
c.s.t., central standard time
ct., court, cent
c.t., central time
ctn., carton; cotangent
ctr., center
cu-ft, cubic foot (feet)
cu-in, cubic inch
cur., current; currency
CWO, cwo, cash with order
cwt, hundredweight
cyl., cylinder

d, daughter; died; dyne; pence
da., day; days
DA, district attorney
DAR, Daughters of the American Revolution
dB, db, decibel
dba, doing business as
dc, DC, direct current; Doctor of Chiropractic
D.D., Doctor of Divinity
DCN, design change notice
dd., delivered
D.D.S., Doctor of Dental Surgery
DDT, dichlorodiphenyltrichloroethane
deb., deben., debenture
dec., deceased
def., defendant; deferred; defined
Dem., Democrat; Democratic
dept., dep't, department
der., deriv., derived; -ation
dft., defendant; draft
dg, decigram
dia., diam., diameter
diag., diagram
dict., dictionary
dioc., diocese
disc., discount; discovered
dir., director
dist., distance; distinguish; district
Dist. Ct., District Court
div., divided; dividend; division; divorced
dkg, dekagram
dkl, dekaliter

dkm, dekameter
dl, deciliter
D.Litt., Doctor of Letters
dm, decimeter
do. (ditto), the same
D.O., Doctor of Osteopathy
doc., document
dol., dollar
dom., domestic; dominion
doz, dozen
D.P.H., Doctor of Public Health
D.P.Hy., Doctor of Public Hygiene
dr., debit; debtor; dram
Dr., Doctor; Drive (street)
d.s.t., daylight saving time
dup., duplicate
D.V.M., Doctor of Veterinary Medicine
DWT, deadweight tons

E, east
e, erg
ea., each
Ecosoc, Economic and Social Council
Ed.D., Doctor of Education
e.d.t., eastern daylight time
ee, errors excepted
e.g. (exempli gratia), for example
EHF, extremely high frequency
emf, electromotive force
enc., encl., enclosure
ency., encyclopedia
engr., engineer; engraved
eom, end of month
ERP, European recovery program
esp., especially
Esq., Esqr., Esquire
est., estate; established; estimated
e.s.t., eastern standard time
estab., established
esu, electrostatic unit
e.t., eastern time
et al. (et alii), and others
etc. (et cetera), and so forth
et seq. (et sequens), and the following
ex., example; exchange
exch., exchange
exec., executor; executive
ex lib. (ex libris), from the books of
exp., expenses; export; express

F, Fahr., Fahrenheit
f, farad; feminine; feet; foot
f., and following page; ff., pages
f., fol., folio; following
FAA, Federal Aviation Agency
fas, free alongside ship
FBI, Federal Bureau of Investigation
FCA, Farm Credit Administration
FCC, Federal Communications Commission
FDA, Food and Drug Administration
FDIC, Federal Deposit Insurance Corporation
Fed., Federal
fem., f., feminine
FHA, Federal Housing Administration; Farmers Home Administration
FHLBB, Federal Home Loan Bank Board
FICA, Federal Insurance Contributions Act
fig., figurative; figure
fl., flange; flash; fluid
FM, frequency modulation
FMB, Federal Maritime Board
FMCS, Federal Mediation and Conciliation Service
FNMA, Federal National Mortgage Association (Fannie Mae)
F.O., foreign office
FOB, fob, free on board

fol., folio; following
foll., following
FPC, Federal Power Commission
fpm, feet per minute
fps, feet per second; frames per second
Fr., Father; franc; France; French
FR, Federal Register; full rate
FRS, Federal Reserve System
FS, Forest Service
FSA, Federal Security Agency
FSLIC, Federal Savings & Loan Insurance Corporation
F. Supp., Federal Supplement
frt., freight
ft, feet; foot; fort
ft bm, fbm, feet board measure
ft-c, foot-candle
FTC, Federal Trade Commission
ft-l, foot-lambert
ft-lb, foot-pound
fut., future; futures
fwd., forward

G, g, gauge; gold; grain; gram; gravity
gal, gallon
GAO, General Accounting Office
GAR, Grand Army of the Republic
GAW, guaranteed annual wage
GCA, ground control approach
gcd, greatest common divisor
GCI, ground control intercept
Gct, Greenwich civil time
geog., geography; -er; -ical
geol., geology; -ist; -ical
geom., geometry; -ical
GFA, General Freight Agent
GI, general issue; Government issue
Gm, gm, gram
G.M., General Manager; Grand Master
G.m.t., Greenwich mean time
GNP, gross national product
GOP, Grand Old Party; Republican Party
Gov., Governor
Govt., Government
GPA, General Passenger Agent
gpm, gallons per minute
gps, gallons per second
gr, grade; grain; gram; grammar; gross
gr-wt, gross weight
GSA, General Services Administration
guar., guaranteed

h, henry
ha, hectare
H.C., House of Commons
hcf, highest common factor
hdkf., handkerchief
hdqrs., headquarters
hdwe., hardware
HE, high explosive; His Excellency; His Eminence
HEW, Department of Health, Education, and Welfare
hf, half
HF, high frequency
hg, hectogram; heliogram
HHFA, Housing and Home Finance Agency
hl, hectoliter
H.L., House of Lords
hm, hectometer
Hon., Honorable
hosp., hospital
hp, horsepower
hr, hour
H.R., House of Representatives
ht, hgt, height
hwy., highway
hyp., hypoth., hypothesis
Hz, Hertz (cycles per second)

I., Is., Island
IAEA, International Atomic Energy Commission
ibid. (ibidem), in the same place
ICC, Interstate Commerce Commission
id. (idem), the same
ID, inside diameter; inside dimensions; identification (card)
i.e. (id est), that is
IEEE, Institute of Electrical & Electronic Engineers
IF, if, intermediate frequency
in, inch
inc., incl., inclosure; including; inclusive
Inc., Incorporated
incog. (incognito), in secret, unknown
indef., indefinite
in-lb, inch-pound
ins., inches; inspector; insurance
INS, International News Service
insp., inspected; inspector
inst., institute; institution
int., interest; interior; internal
inv., inventor; invoice
invt., inventory
I/O, input/output
IQ, intelligence quotient
IRE, Institute of Radio Engineers
IRS, Internal Revenue Service
ital., italics

j, joule
J/A, joint account
jato, jet-assisted takeoff
J.D., Doctor of Laws
jour., journal
J.P., Justice of the Peace
Jr., Junior
J/T, joint tenants
junc., junction

k, kt, carat
K, Kelvin
kc, kilocycle
Kev, kilo electron volts
kg, keg; kilogram
kl, kiloliter
km, kilometer
kt, carat; kiloton
kv, kilovolt
kv-a, kilovolt-ampere
kw, kilowatt
kw-hr, kilowatt-hour

l, L, latitude; left; line; liter
L, pound sterling
lat., latitude
Lat., Latin
lb, pound
LC, L/C, letter of credit
lc, lowercase
LCD, least common denominator
LCL, lcl, less-than-carload lot
LCM, least common multiple
LD, lethal dose
Legis., Legislature
lf, lightface
LF, low frequency
lit., liter; literal; literature
Litt.D., Doctor of Letters
LL.B., Bachelor of Laws
LL.D., Doctor of Laws
loc. cit. (loco citato), in the place cited
log, logarithm
long., longitude
loran, long-range navigation
LOX, liquid oxygen
LPG, liquefied petroleum gas
L.S. (locus sigilli), place of the seal
l.s.t., local standard time
l.t., local time
Ltd., Limited
lwl, load waterline
lwm, low watermark

m, married; masculine; meter; mile; minute; moon; mother
M, thousand
M., monsieur; noon
ma, milliampere
MA, Maritime Administration
M.A., Master of Arts
mas., masc., m., masculine
M.A.T., Masters in the Art of Teaching
math., mathematics; -ical
max., maximum
mb, millibar
Mbm, Mfbm, thousand feet board measure
mc, megacycle
MC, Medical Corps; Master of Ceremonies
Mcf, thousand cubic feet
M.D., doctor of medicine
mdse., merchandise
mech., mechanic; -ical; -ism
med., median; medical; medicine; medieval; medium
M.Ed., Master of Education
mem., member
memo, memorandum
meq, milliequivalent
Messrs., MM., Messieurs
Mev, million electron volts
mf, millifarad
MF, machine finish; medium frequency; mill finish; motor freight
mfd, manufactured; microfarad
mfg., manufacturing
mfr., manufacture; manufacturer
mg, margin; milligram
mG, milligauss
MG, machine glazed; mill glazed
Mgr., Manager
mh, millihenry
mi, mile; minute
min., minimum; minute
misc., miscellaneous
ml, milliliter
MLD, minimum lethal dose
Mlle., Mademoiselle; Miss
mm, millimeter
Mm, mym, myriameter
Mme., Mmes., Madame; Mesdames
mmf, magnetomotive force
mmfd, micromicrofarad
mo., month
m.o., mail order; money order
mol-wt, molecular weight
mp, melting point
M.P., Member of Parliament; Military Police
mph, miles per hour
Mr., Mister
Mrs., Mistress; Madam
ms, megasecond
M.S., Master of Science
ms., mss., manuscript; -scripts
msec, millisecond
msgr., messenger; monsignor
msl, mean sea level
m.s.t., mountain standard time
mt, megaton
Mt., mount; mountain
m.t., mountain time
mtg., mtge., mortgage
mun., municipal
mus., museum; music; musical
Mus.D., Doctor of Music
M/V, motor vessel
mya, myriare
myg, myriagram
myl, myrialiter
mym, Mm, myriameter

N, north
n/30, net in 30 days
N.A., North America
NASA, National Aeronautics and Space Administration
nat., national; natural
natl., nat'l, national

NATO, North Atlantic Treaty Organization
naut., nautical
nav., naval; navigation
N.B. (nota bene), note carefully
NBC, National Broadcasting Company
NBS, National Bureau of Standards
n.d., no date
NE, northeast
NEA, National Education Association
neg., negative
N.F., National Formulary
NG, ng, no good; National Guard
NL, nightletter
NLRB, National Labor Relations Board
NLT, night letter cable
NM, night message
No., Nos., number; numbers
NOMA, National Office Management Association
n.o.s., not otherwise specified
non seq. (non sequitur), does not follow; not in order
NOS, not otherwise specified
NOVS, National Office of Vital Statistics
N.P., notary public; no protest
nr., near
NSA, National Shipping Authority; National Secretaries Association
NSC, National Security Council
NSF, not sufficient funds; National Science Foundation
N.T., New Testament
NW, northwest

O, oxygen
OASI, old-age and survivors insurance
ob., obit., died
obs., obsolete; observatory
OCD, Office of Civil Defense
OD, outside diameter; outside dimensions
OEM, original equipment manufacturer
OK, OK'd, correct; approved
OP, O/P, op, out of print
op. cit. (opere citato), in the work cited
opp., opposite; opposed; opponent
O.R., o.r., owner's risk
org., organized; organic
OS, O/S, o/s, out of stock
OSD, Office of the Secretary of Defense
O.T., Old Testament
oz, ounce

p., page; pp., pages
p.a., (per annum), by the year
PA, public address system; passenger agent
Pac., Pacif., Pacific
par., paragraph; parallel
Pat. Off., Patent Office
pat. pend., patent pending
payt., pmt., pymt., payment
pc., piece; price; percent; postcard
P.C., Peace Corps; petty cash
PCM, punched card machines; pulse code modulation
pct, percent
pd., paid; pound
P.D. (per diem), by the day
P.E., p.e., printer's error
pf., pfd., preferred; picofard
pF, water energy (p, logarithm; F, frequency)
pH, hydrogen-ion concentration
PHA, Public Housing Administration
Phar.D., Doctor of Pharmacy
Ph.B., B.Ph., Bachelor of Philosophy

Ph.D., D.Ph., Doctor of Philosophy
Ph.G., Graduate in Pharmacy
PHS, Public Health Service
pk., pack; park; peck
pkg., package
pl., plate; plural
Pl., Place (street)
PL, P/L, P&L, profit and loss
plf., plff., plaintiff
P.M., p.m. (post meridiem), afternoon
P.M., paymaster; postmaster; postmortem; Prime Minister
pmkd., postmarked
P/N, p.n., promissory note
P.O., p.o., postal order; post office; purchase order
poc, port of call
POD, pay on delivery; Post Office Department
POR, pay on return
pos., possession; position; positive
poss., possession; possessive
pot., potential
pp., pages
P.P., p.p., parcel post
PP, pellagra preventive (factor)
ppd., prepaid
ppm, parts per million
P.P.S., post postscript
pr., pair; price
pref., preface
prep., preposition
Pres., President
prim., primary
prin., princ., principal; principle
prob., problem
Proc., Proceedings
prod., produce; produced; product
Prof., Professor
pron., pronoun; pronounced; pronunciation
prop., property; proposition; proprietary; proprietor
pro tem (pro tempore), for the time being
prox. (proximo), in the next month
P.S., postscript
psf, pounds per square foot
psi, pounds per square inch
psia, pounds per square inch absolute
P.s.t., Pacific standard time
P.t., Pacific time
pt., part; pint; point; port
PTA, Parent-Teacher Association
ptg., printing
pto, please turn over
pub., public; -ations; publish; -er
pvt., private
pwt, pennyweight

q., qq., question; questions
q, qt, quart
qr, quarter; quire
qt, quart; quantity
qtr, quart., quarter; quarterly
quot., quotation
q.v. (quo vide), which see

r, radium dosage; right
R., Réaumur; River
racon, radar beacon
radar, radio detection and ranging
R&D, RD, research and development
rato, rocket-assisted takeoff
Rd., Road
re, with regard to
REA, Rural Electrification Administration
rec., receipt; receiver; recommended; record
recd., received
ref., referee; reference; referred; refinery; refund
refd., referred; reformed
reg., registered; regular; regulation

rep, roentgen equivalent physical
Rep., Republican; Representative; Republic
req., requisition
retd., returned
rev., revelation; reverend; revised; reverse; revolution
Rev. Stat., Revised Statutes
RF, rf., radio frequency
RFD, rural free delivery
Rh, Rhesus (blood factor)
Riv., River
rm, ream; room
rms, root mean square
ROP, run of paper
rpm, revolutions per minute
rps, revolutions per second
RR, Railroad
RRB, Railroad Retirement Board
RSVP, please answer
Rt. Rev., Right Reverend
Ry., Railway

s, second; shilling; son
S, south
S.A., South America
SAE, Society of Automotive Engineers
S.B., Bachelor of Science
SBA, Small Business Administration
s and sc, sized and supercalendered
sc, sized and calendered
sc, sm. caps, small capital letters
SC, sc (scilicet), namely (see SS)
Sc.D., Doctor of Science
s.d. (sine die), without date
SE, southeast
SEATO, Southeast Asia Treaty Organization
sec, secant; second
sec., sect., section
sec., secy., secretary
SEC, Securities and Exchange Commission
sec-ft, second-foot
sech, hyperbolic secant
2d, 3d; 2nd, 3rd, second, third
Sen., Senate; Senator
seq., the following
ser., series
Sf, Svedberg flotation
sgd., signed
sh., share
SHF, superhigh frequency
shoran, short range (radio)
shp., shaft horsepower
shpt., shpmt., shipment
shtg., shortage
sic, thus; exactly as shown
sin, sine
sing., singular
sinh, hyperbolic sine
S.M., Master of Science
SO, S/O, so, seller's option
soc., society
sociol., sociology; sociologist
sofar, sound fixing and ranging
sonar, sound, navigation and ranging
SOP, standard operating procedure
S O S, wireless distress signal
s.p. (sine prole), without issue
Sp., Spaniard; Spanish
sp. gr., specific gravity
Sq., Square (street)
sq-in, or in^2, square inch
Sr., Senior; Señor
SRO, standing room only
SS, steamship
SS, ss (scilicet), namely (see SC)
SSA, Social Security Administration
SSF, standard Saybolt furol
SSU, standard Saybolt universal
St., Street

St., Ste., SS., Saint; Sainte (f.); Saints
sta., station; stationary; stator
stat., statuary; statue; statute
std., standard; steward
std-cf, standard cubic foot (feet)
stk., stock
sub., substitute; suburb
subch., subchapter
subj., subject
subpar., subparagraph
subsec., subsection
SUNFED, Special United Nations Fund for Economic Development
sup., superior; supply
supp., suppl., supplement
supt., superintendent; support
supv., supervise
supvr., supervisor
surg., surgeon; -ery; -ical
SUS, Saybolt universal second
SW, southwest
syn., synonym

t., tp., twp., township
T, ton (s)
tan, tangent
tanh, hyperbolic tangent
TB, tuberculosis
TB, T/B, tb, trial balance
tbsp, tablespoonful
tech., technical; technician
tel., telegram; -graph; -phone
Ter., Terrace (street)
tm, true mean
TM, transverse mercator
T/M, telemetry
TNT, trinitrotoluol
tr., transfer; translate; transpose; treasurer; trustee
trans., transaction(s)
transp., transportation
treas., treasurer; treasury
tsp, teaspoonful
TV, television
TVA, Tennessee Valley Authority
twp., t., tp., township
TWS, timed wire service (telegraph)

u&lc, upper and lowercase
uc, uppercase
UGT, urgent
UHF, ultrahigh frequency
utl. (ultimo), in the last month; ultimately
U.N., United Nations
UNESCO, United Nations Educational, Scientific, and Cultural Organization
UNICEF, United Nations Children's Fund
univ., universal; university
UP, United Press
URA, Urban Renewal Administration
USA, U.S. Army
U.S.A., United States of America; Union of South Africa
U.S.C. Supp., United States Code Supplement
USES, U.S. Employment Service
USIA, U.S. Information Agency
U.S.P., United States Pharmacopoeia
U.S.S., United States Senate; United States ship
U.S.S.R., Union of Soviet Socialist Republics
u.t., universal time

v, valve; vapor; verse; volt
v., vs. (versus), against
VA, Veterans' Administration
var., variable; variation; variegated; variety; variometer; various
VAR, visual-aural range; volt-ampere reactive

VD, vd, vapor density; various dates; venereal disease
VHF, very high frequency
VIP, very important person
vid. (vide), see
viz. (videlicet), namely
VLF, very low frequency
V.M.D., Doctor of Veterinary Medicine
vol, volume
vv, verses; vice versa; volumes

w, watt; with
W, west
WB, W/B, wb, way bill
wf, wrong font
WG, wire gauge
WHO, World Health Organization
w-hr, watt-hour
whsle., wholesale
w.i., when issued
wk, week; work
wl, wavelength
w/o, without
w.o.c., without compensation
wt, warrant; weight

x, unknown quantity
XD, xd, x-div., ex-div., ex-dividend
Xmas, Christmas

yd, yard
YMCA, Young Men's Christian Association
YPO, Young Presidents' Organization
yr, year; younger; your
YWCA, Young Women's Christian Association

Z, zo., zone
zool., zoology; -ical; -ist

DATA PROCESSING ABBREVIATIONS

ADP, automatic data processing
ALGOL, algorithmic oriented language
ALU, arithmetic and logical unit
ASA Code, ASCH, ASCII, American standard code for information interchange
ASR, automatic send-receive set
BCD, binary coded decimal
BIT, a binary digit
BYTE, a sequence of adjacent binary digits
CDC, call direction code
COBOL, common business oriented language
CPU, central processing unit
DDA, digital differential analyzer
EAM, electrical accounting machine
EDP, electronic data processing
EOF, end of file
EOR, end of reel
FORTRAN, formula translation
FOSDIC, film optical sensing device for input to computers
GIGO, garbage in—garbage out
HSP, high-speed printer
HSR, high-speed reader
IAL, international algebraic language
IDP, integrated data processing
I/O, input/output
IOCS, input/output control system

LPM, lines per minute
MICR, magnetic ink character recognition
MIT, master instruction tape
MLP, multiple line printing
OCR, optical character recognition
OR, operations research
PCM, punched card machines, pulse code modulation
PERT, program evaluation and review technique
PRT, production run tape
PTT, program test tape
RAM, random access memory
RAMAC, random access methods of accounting and control
RWC, read-write channel
SDA, source data automation
SODA, source oriented data acquisition
SPT, symbolic program tape
SPS, symbolic programming system
TABSIM, tabulator simulator
TIPTOP, tape input—tape output

GUIDE FOR COMPOUNDING WORDS

A compound is two or more words joined either with a hyphen *(right-of-way)* or without a hyphen *(cupboard).* The purpose of a compound is to express a thought or idea more clearly and precisely than might be expressed if the words were not joined. Some words are joined simply because they have been so commonly and regularly used in succession that through custom or usage they have become one word *(racehorse)* even though the compound word is not necessarily any clearer in meaning than when the two words are written separately.

The hyphen, when used in a compound word, is a mark of punctuation. Its purpose is to join the parts of the compound but also to separate the parts for better readability, clearer understanding, and correct pronunciation. In general, the hyphen should be omitted unless it fulfills one of these purposes.

Several hundred compound words are included in the 25,000 words contained in this dictionary. If the word is not given, use the following rules as a guide. Rules for the hyphenation of prefixes and suffixes also are given.

1. **General Rule.** In general, avoid joining two or more words unless the compounding aids understanding or readability. If the words appear in regular order and if the first word serves principally as an adjective to describe the second word, the words usually are not joined.

book value	day laborer	printing press
brick house	fellow citizen	real estate

2. **Nouns.** Many nouns are formed by two other nouns (including gerunds) and are written as one word either by custom or repeated usage or because by being written as one word they better express a single thought or unit idea than by not being connected.

bathroom	footnote	southwest
bookstore	laughingstock	workingman
dressmaker	locksmith	workman

3. **Improvised Compounds.** Many words such as a verb and an adverb are joined to express either a literal or a nonliteral (figura-

tive) thought. Use a hyphen for most three-word combinations or in a compound where meaning might be confused. Otherwise write solid.

afterglow	holdup	*but:* cut-in
bloodthirsty	loudspeaker	father-in-law
blowout	overestimate	right-of-way
gentleman	showdown	up-to-date
giveaway	windfall	well-to-do

4. **Double or Triple Letters.** Use a hyphen to avoid doubling vowels or tripling consonants.

brass-smith	ill-looking	fire-escape
cross-stitch	shell-like	sea-air

5. **Any, every, no, some.** Write as one word *any, every, no,* and *some* when combined with *body, thing,* and *where.* When *one* is the second element, and the meaning is a single or particular person or thing, write as two words. *No one* is always two words.

anybody	everything	no one
anywhere	nobody	someone
everyone	nothing	somewhere

Everyone is going. *but:* Every one of the teachers is going.

6. **Compound Personal Pronouns.** Write as one word.

herself	oneself	myself
himself	ourselves	yourself
itself	themselves	yourselves

7. **Compound Modifiers (Adjectives).** Words, or abbreviations and words, combined to form a unit modifier should be hyphenated when they precede the word modified, particularly if one element is a present or past participle. However, see additional rules that follow.

fire-tested material
4-page letter
six-mile run
Chicago-New York train
short-term loan
well-known person
bluish-green fabric
part-time job

(a) Certain types of unit modifiers preceding a noun are not hyphenated when the meaning is clear and readability is not aided by the hyphen. A clear-cut rule cannot be given, but the following list may be used as a guide for nonhyphenated compounds.

atomic energy plant
civil rights law
high school student
income tax return
life insurance policy
real estate tax
social security law
special delivery mail

(b) Omit the hyphen in a unit modifier when it follows the word modified.

The area was disease ridden. *but:* The disease-ridden area was aided.
He is well known. *but:* He is a well-known author.

(c) Omit the hyphen in a unit modifier if the first word is a comparative or superlative.

higher priced house — *but:* high-priced house
best liked book — well-liked book
lowest income group — low-income group

(d) Omit the hyphen in a unit modifier in which the first element is an adverb ending in *-ly.*

eagerly awaited day
happily married couple
unusually long period
regularly scheduled work

(e) When a series of two or more compounds has a common basic word and this word is omitted in all except the last term, retain all hyphens.

long- and short-term rates
three-, four-, and five-foot lengths
2-, 3-, and 4-inch squares

(f) Omit the hyphen in a foreign phrase unit modifier.

bona fide sale
per diem allowance
ex officio member
prima facie evidence

8. **Civil and Military Titles.** Most titles denoting a single office are not hyphenated. However, some persons prefer to hyphenate certain titles such as *vice-president* and *ambassador-at-large.* Use a hyphen to join a double title such as *secretary-treasurer.*

9. **Numbers.** Use a hyphen to join numbers from twenty-one to ninety-nine.

twenty-one
twenty-first
eighty-seven
one hundred eighty-seven

10. **Numbers and Letters.** Use a hyphen to join numbers or letters combined with words to form a unit modifier or a unit idea.

20-minute delay
.22-caliber cartridge
five-to-one ratio *(or:* 5-to-1)
X-ray
T-shape
U-turn

11. **Number and Possessive.** Omit the hyphen when a modifier consists of a possessive preceded by a numeral.

1 week's trial
3 hours' pay

12. **Fractions.** Use a hyphen to join fractions used as adjectives. Omit the hyphen between the numerator and denominator when the hyphen appears in either or both.

two-thousandths
one-fourth
three two-thousandths
two twenty-fifths

13. **Units of Measurement.** Use a hyphen.

candle-hour	kilowatt-hour
light-year	passenger-mile

14. **Prefixes, Suffixes, and Combining Forms** are written solid, as one word, except as indicated here.

(a) Use a hyphen to avoid doubling a vowel except after the short prefixes *co, de, pre, pro,* and *re,* which are usually printed solid.

cooperate	*or*	co-operate	anti-inflation
deenergize	*or*	de-energize	micro-organism
preeminent	*or*	pre-eminent	semi-independent

(b) Use a hyphen to avoid ambiguity, to avoid tripling a consonant, or to avoid any other confusing combination of letters.

shell-like	ball-less	re-treat (treat again)
co-author	un-ionized	re-sort (sort again)
intra-urban	un-united	cell-less

(c) Use a hyphen with the prefixes *ex, self,* and *quasi.*

ex-president	self-educated	quasi-deposit
ex-soldier	self-governing	quasi-official

(d) Use a hyphen when the main word is capitalized unless usage demands otherwise.

non-Communist	Pan-American *but:* Pan American Union
un-American	mid-Atlantic *but:* transatlantic

FORMS FOR ADDRESSING LETTERS

The correct use of titles and forms of address is a matter of courtesy. Following are the preferred forms.

Business Names and Titles

1. All titles in a business address should be capitalized. The "Zip" code (for the United States) should be placed two spaces after the state name without separating punctuation. Do not abbreviate "Company" or "Incorporated" unless the firm does so on its official letterhead.

<table><tr><td>Mr. Roy Thompson, President
Arco Products, Inc.
Gary, Indiana 46402</td><td>Mr. Peter Brown
Chairman of the Board
Loomis Textile Company
Richmond, Virginia 23214</td></tr></table>

2. A position title may be placed on the same line as the name or on a separate line, depending on length and convenience.

<table><tr><td>Mr. John Doe, Superintendent
Longdale Public Schools
Longdale, New York</td><td>Mr. John Doe
Superintendent of Schools
Longdale, New York</td></tr></table>

3. A personal title or degree may be used with a business or educational title for the same person.

<table><tr><td>Dr. Ray Evans
Director of Research
Ace Electronics, Inc.</td><td>Thomas Harmon, Ph.D.
Professor of English
Yale University</td></tr></table>

4. Use the salutation *Gentlemen* if the letter is not addressed to a specific individual within the company, even though the letter is marked for the attention of an individual.

Raven Brake Company
Peoria, Illinois
Attention: Mr. William Anderson
Gentlemen:

Titles for Addressing Men

1. When addressing letters to a man, the title *Mr.* precedes the name, if he has no professional title.

Mr. James Cain *or* Mr. James Cain, Manager
Salutation: Dear Sir: *or* Dear Mr. Cain:

2. For two or more men who have no other title, *Mr.* should precede each name.

Mr. Leo Moore and Mr. Thomas Jones
Salutation: Dear Sirs: *or* Gentlemen:

3. *Master* is the proper title for a boy under age 12. From ages 12 to 18 usually no title is used. At age 18, *Mr.* becomes the correct title.

Master Larry Smith
Masters Larry and Tom Smith
Salutation: Dear Larry and Tom:

4. Designations such as *Sr., Jr., III,* etc., should be capitalized and preferably are separated from the name by commas.

Mr. T. R. Roberts, Sr.
Peter Grady, Jr., Ph.D.
Dr. Tito Janis, III
Mr. Arno Griffith, Sr., President

Titles for Professional Men and Women

1. The title *Messrs. (Messieurs)* may precede the names of two or more professional men (such as lawyers or accountants) jointly engaged in practice.

Messrs. Robert Arnold and Harry Black
Attorneys at Law

2. The title *Doctor* is used for persons who have that degree conferred on them.

Gerald Thorne, Ph.D.	*or*	Dr. Gerald Thorne
Helen Brown, M.D.	*or*	Dr. Helen Brown

Salutation: Dear Dr. Brown:

3. *Dr.* and *Mr.* should not be used with the same name.

Gerald Thorne, Ph.D.	*not*	Mr. Gerald Thorne, Ph.D.

4. Use *Professor* or *Prof.* only for college or university teachers who hold professorial rank.

Professor Arnold Buick	*not*	Professor Mr. Buick
Prof. Ronald Harr	*not*	Prof. Harr

5. Address a professional man and his wife as:

Dr. and Mrs. Robert Henderson
Professor and Mrs. Donald Jones

Titles for Addressing Women

1.(a) Use the title *Miss* when addressing an unmarried woman, or when you do not know whether or not she is married. **Note:** Some authorities recommend use of the title *Ms.* for a woman whose marital status is unknown.

Miss Joan Pederson	Ms. Ann Weber, Office Manager
Secretary to the President	Waddell Supply Company

(b) *Misses* is used when addressing two or more unmarried women.

The Misses Lawrence and Henderson
The Misses Edith and Susan Andrews

2.(a) Use *Mrs.* to address a married woman. In business correspondence, the woman's personal first name is usually used. In social correspondence, her husband's name should be used.

Mrs. Julia Thompson (business) | Mrs. Robert T. Thompson (social)

(b) *Mesdames* is used for two or more married women (or if one is married and one is single).

Mesdames Julia Thompson and Ruth Brown
Salutation: Dear Ladies: *or* Mesdames: *or* Ladies:

3. The wife of a professional man, such as a doctor or professor, should not be addressed as Mrs. Dr. Jamison Olander or Mrs. Prof. T. A. Smith. The correct form is *Mrs. T. A. Smith.*

4. A widow is addressed with her husband's name (Mrs. James Hill) for social correspondence. In business letters either her first name or her husband's name may be used, usually determined by what the widow prefers.

5. A divorced woman may use either her maiden name or her married name, and may use either *Miss* or *Mrs.* The usage preferred by the divorcee should be followed.

Military Titles

1. Military personnel should be addressed with the grade or rank held. If the military title contains a prefix such as *Brigadier,* the prefix is omitted in the salutation. *(Dear Sir:* also may be used for all military personnel.)

Brigadier General Robert Brown, U.S.A.
Address
Dear General Brown: *or* Dear Sir:

2. Naval personnel below the rank of *Commander* are addressed as *Mr.* in the salutation.

Lieutenant Fred Harris, U.S.N.
Address
Dear Mr. Harris:

THE COMPLIMENTARY CLOSE

1. There are several acceptable complimentary closes for business correspondence. The close used is largely determined by the preference of the writer and the degree of friendliness with the person being written to. The first word of the close should be capitalized.

Sincerely,
Sincerely yours,
Very sincerely yours,
Yours truly,
Very truly yours,
Respectfully,
Yours very truly,
Cordially,
Respectfully yours,

2. For government officials use any of the following:

Very truly yours,
Yours very truly,
Respectfully yours,
Yours respectfully,
Respectfully,
Sincerely yours,

3. For church dignitaries, any of the following may be used:

Respectfully yours,
Respectfully,
Sincerely yours in Christ,
Yours in Christ,
Sincerely yours,
Faithfully yours,

Table of Addresses and Salutations for Government, Church, and School Dignitaries

Title	Address	Salutation
Ambassador, American	The Honorable ___ The American Ambassador Address	Sir: Dear Mr. Ambassador:
Ambassador, Foreign	His Excellency ___ The Ambassador of France Address	Sir: Excellency: Dear Mr. Ambassador:
Archbishop (Catholic)	The Most Reverend ___ Archbishop of New York Address	Your Excellency: Your Grace: Most Reverend Sir:
Bishop (Catholic)	The Most Reverend ___ Bishop of St. Paul Address	Your Excellency: Most Reverend Sir:
Bishop (Episcopal)	The Right Reverend ___ Bishop of Chicago Address	Your Excellency: Right Reverend Sir: Dear Bishop __:
Bishop (Methodist)	The Reverend Bishop ___ Bishop of Detroit Address	Dear Sir: Dear Bishop __:
Brother	Brother ___,* Loyola University Address *Add abbreviation of order.	Dear Brother: Dear Brother __:
Cabinet Officer (Federal or State)	The Honorable ___ Secretary of __ (State, etc.) Address	Sir: Dear Sir: Dear Mr. Secretary:
Cardinal	His Eminence Francis, Cardinal __ Address	Your Eminence:

Title	Address	Salutation
Chaplain	Chaplain — — Captain, U.S. Army Address	Dear Chaplain: Dear Chaplain —:
City Council	The City Council City of — Address	Honorable Sirs: Honorable Gentlemen:
Congressman or State Representative	The Honorable — — The House of Representaties Address	Sir: Dear Mr. —: Dear Congressman —: (United States only)
Consul, American	The American Consul *(or:* — —, Esquire) American Consul Address	Sir: Dear Sir: Dear Mr. Consul:
Consul, Foreign	The French Consul Address	Sir: Dear Sir: Dear Mr. Consul:
Dean (church)	The Very Reverend — — St. John's Church Address	Very Reverend Sir: Dear Dean —:
Dean (college)	Dean — —,* Name of University or College Address *Add abbreviation of degree.	Dear Sir: Dear Dean —:
Governor	The Honorable — — Governor, State of — Address	Dear Sir: Dear Governor —:
Judge	The Honorable — — Judge of the Circuit Court Address	Dear Sir: Dear Judge —:

Title	Address	Salutation
Mayor	The Honorable ___ ___ Mayor, City of ___ Address	Sir: Dear Mr. Mayor: Dear Mayor ___:
Minister (Protestant)	The Reverend ___ ___ Third Methodist Church Address	Dear Sir: Dear Doctor: (if D.D.) Dear Mr. ___:
Monsignor	The Right Reverend Monsignor ___ ___ Name of Church Address	Right Reverend Sir: Dear Monsignor: Right Reverend and Dear Monsignor:
The Pope	His Holiness, Pope ___ ___ The Vatican Vatican City, Italy	Your Holiness: Most Holy Father:
President (college or university)	John Smith,* President, ___ University Address *Add abbreviation of highest degree.	Dear Sir: Dear President ___:
President of the United States	The President The White House Washington, D.C.	Sir: Dear Mr. President:
Priest	The Reverend ___ ___,* University of ___ Address *Add abbreviation of order.	Reverend Father: Dear Reverend Father: Dear Father ___:
Rabbi	Rabbi ___ ___ (*or:* The Reverend ___ ___) Sinai Congregation Address	Reverend Sir: My Dear Sir: Dear Rabbi ___:
Rector	The Very Reverend ___ ___ Name of Church Address	Dear Father ___: Very Reverend Sir: Dear Reverend ___:

Title	Address	Salutation
Senator (U. S. or State)	The Honorable ___ United States Senate *(or:* The State Capitol) Address	Sir: Dear Senator: Dear Senator __:
Sister	Sister ___,* St. Mary's Convent Address *Add abbreviation of order.	Dear Sister: Dear Sister __:
Superior of Sister Order	Mother ___,* Mother General Address *Add abbreviation of order.	Reverend Mother: Dear Mother General: Dear Sister Superior:
Vice-President	The Honorable ___ The Vice-President of the United States Washington, D.C. 20025	Sir: Mr. Vice-President Dear Mr. Vice-President:

PROOFREADER'S MARKS

Use the following symbols and abbreviations when preparing copy to be sent to the printer or to correct copy that has been set in type.

Delete

Delete and close up

Reverse

Close up

Insert space

/# Close up and insert space

¶ Paragraph

□ Indent 1 em

Move to left

Move to right

Lower

Raise

∧ Insert marginal addition

V∧ Space evenly

X Broken letter—used in margin

Push down space

= Straighten line

|| Align type

Insert comma

Insert apostrophe

Insert quotation mark

=/ Insert hyphen

em/ Insert em dash

en/ Insert en dash

Insert semicolon

Insert colon and en quad

Insert period and en quad

?/ Insert interrogation point

Query to author—in margin

Use ligature

Sp Spell out

tr Transpose

wf Wrong font

bf Set in boldface type

rom Set in roman type

ital Set in *italic* type

caps Set in CAPITALS

sc Set in SMALL CAPITALS

lc Set in lower case

Lower-case letter

stet Let it stand; restore words crossed out

no ¶ Run in same paragraph

ld in Insert lead between lines

hr # Hair space between letters